Environment Act 1995

CHAPTER 25

ARRANGEMENT OF SECTIONS

PART I

THE ENVIRONMENT AGENCY AND THE SCOTTISH ENVIRONMENT PROTECTION AGENCY

CHAPTER I

THE ENVIRONMENT AGENCY

Establishment of the Agency

Chapter II

The Scottish Environment Protection Agency

Establishment of SEPA

Chapter III

Miscellaneous, General and Supplemental Provisions Relating to the New Agencies

Additional general powers and duties

Environment Act 1995

1995 CHAPTER 25

An Act to provide for the establishment of a body corporate to be known as the Environment Agency and a body corporate to be known as the Scottish Environment Protection Agency; to provide for the transfer of functions, property, rights and liabilities to those bodies and for the conferring of other functions on them; to make provision with respect to contaminated land and abandoned mines; to make further provision in relation to National Parks; to make further provision for the control of pollution, the conservation of natural resources and the conservation or enhancement of the environment; to make provision for imposing obligations on certain persons in respect of certain products or materials; to make provision in relation to fisheries; to make provision for certain enactments to bind the Crown; to make provision with respect to the application of certain enactments in relation to the Isles of Scilly; and for connected purposes.   [19th July 1995]

B E IT ENACTED by the Queen's most Excellent Majesty, by and with the advice and consent of the Lords Spiritual and Temporal, and Commons, in this present Parliament assembled, and by the authority of the same, as follows:—

PART I

THE ENVIRONMENT AGENCY AND THE SCOTTISH ENVIRONMENT PROTECTION AGENCY

CHAPTER I

THE ENVIRONMENT AGENCY

Establishment of the Agency

The Environment Agency. **1.**—(1) There shall be a body corporate to be known as the Environment Agency or, in Welsh, Asiantaeth yr Amgylchedd (in this Act referred to as "the Agency"), for the purpose of carrying out the functions transferred or assigned to it by or under this Act.

(2) The Agency shall consist of not less than eight nor more than fifteen members of whom—

(a) three shall be appointed by the Minister; and

(b) the others shall be appointed by the Secretary of State.

(3) The Secretary of State shall designate—

(a) one of the members as the chairman of the Agency, and

(b) another of them as the deputy chairman of the Agency.

(4) In appointing a person to be a member of the Agency, the Secretary of State or, as the case may be, the Minister shall have regard to the desirability of appointing a person who has experience of, and has shown capacity in, some matter relevant to the functions of the Agency.

(5) Subject to the provisions of section 38 below, the Agency shall not be regarded—

(a) as the servant or agent of the Crown, or as enjoying any status, immunity or privilege of the Crown; or

(b) by virtue of any connection with the Crown, as exempt from any tax, duty, rate, levy or other charge whatsoever, whether general or local;

and the Agency's property shall not be regarded as property of, or property held on behalf of, the Crown.

(6) The provisions of Schedule 1 to this Act shall have effect with respect to the Agency.

Transfer of functions, property etc. to the Agency

Transfer of functions to the Agency. **2.**—(1) On the transfer date there shall by virtue of this section be transferred to the Agency—

(a) the functions of the National Rivers Authority, that is to say—

1991 c. 57. (i) its functions under or by virtue of Part II (water resources management) of the Water Resources Act 1991 (in this Part referred to as "the 1991 Act");

(ii) its functions under or by virtue of Part III of that Act (control of pollution of water resources);

1991 c. 59. (iii) its functions under or by virtue of Part IV of that Act (flood defence) and the Land Drainage Act 1991 and the functions transferred to the Authority by virtue of section

136(8) of the Water Act 1989 and paragraph 1(3) of Schedule 15 to that Act (transfer of land drainage functions under local statutory provisions and subordinate legislation);

 (iv) its functions under or by virtue of Part VII of the 1991 Act (land and works powers);

 (v) its functions under or by virtue of the Diseases of Fish Act 1937, the Sea Fisheries Regulation Act 1966, the Salmon and Freshwater Fisheries Act 1975, Part V of the 1991 Act or any other enactment relating to fisheries;

 (vi) the functions as a navigation authority, harbour authority or conservancy authority which were transferred to the Authority by virtue of Chapter V of Part III of the Water Act 1989 or paragraph 23(3) of Schedule 13 to that Act or which have been transferred to the Authority by any order or agreement under Schedule 2 to the 1991 Act;

 (vii) its functions under Schedule 2 to the 1991 Act;

 (viii) the functions assigned to the Authority by or under any other enactment, apart from this Act;

(b) the functions of waste regulation authorities, that is to say, the functions conferred or imposed on them by or under—

 (i) the Control of Pollution (Amendment) Act 1989, or

 (ii) Part II of the Environmental Protection Act 1990 (in this Part referred to as "the 1990 Act"),

or assigned to them by or under any other enactment, apart from this Act;

(c) the functions of disposal authorities under or by virtue of the waste regulation provisions of the Control of Pollution Act 1974;

(d) the functions of the chief inspector for England and Wales constituted under section 16(3) of the 1990 Act, that is to say, the functions conferred or imposed on him by or under Part I of that Act or assigned to him by or under any other enactment, apart from this Act;

(e) the functions of the chief inspector for England and Wales appointed under section 4(2)(a) of the Radioactive Substances Act 1993, that is to say, the functions conferred or imposed on him by or under that Act or assigned to him by or under any other enactment, apart from this Act;

(f) the functions conferred or imposed by or under the Alkali, &c, Works Regulation Act 1906 (in this section referred to as "the 1906 Act") on the chief, or any other, inspector (within the meaning of that Act), so far as exercisable in relation to England and Wales;

(g) so far as exercisable in relation to England and Wales, the functions in relation to improvement notices and prohibition notices under Part I of the Health and Safety at Work etc. Act 1974 (in this section referred to as "the 1974 Act") of inspectors appointed under section 19 of that Act by the Secretary of State in his capacity as the enforcing authority responsible in relation to England and Wales for the enforcement of the 1906 Act and section 5 of the 1974 Act; and

1989 c. 15.

1937 c. 33.
1966 c. 38.
1975 c. 51.

1989 c. 14.

1990 c. 43.

1974 c. 40.

1993 c. 12.

1906 c. 14.

1974 c. 37.

(h) the functions of the Secretary of State specified in subsection (2) below.

(2) The functions of the Secretary of State mentioned in subsection (1)(h) above are the following, that is to say—

1993 c. 12.

(a) so far as exercisable in relation to England and Wales, his functions under section 30(1) of the Radioactive Substances Act 1993 (power to dispose of radioactive waste);

1991 c. 56.

(b) his functions under Chapter III of Part IV of the Water Industry Act 1991 in relation to special category effluent, within the meaning of that Chapter, other than any function of making regulations or of making orders under section 139 of that Act;

(c) so far as exercisable in relation to England and Wales, the functions conferred or imposed on him by virtue of his being, for the purposes of Part I of the 1974 Act, the authority which is by any of the relevant statutory provisions made responsible for the enforcement of the 1906 Act and section 5 of the 1974 Act;

(d) so far as exercisable in relation to England and Wales, his functions under, or under regulations made by virtue of, section 9 of the 1906 Act (registration of works), other than any functions of his as an appellate authority or any function of making regulations;

S.I. 1989/1263.

(e) so far as exercisable in relation to England and Wales, his functions under regulations 7(1) and 8(2) of, and paragraph 2(2)(c) of Schedule 2 to, the Sludge (Use in Agriculture) Regulations 1989 (which relate to the provision of information and the testing of soil).

(3) The National Rivers Authority and the London Waste Regulation Authority are hereby abolished.

Transfer of property, rights and liabilities to the Agency.

3.—(1) On the transfer date—

(a) the property, rights and liabilities—

(i) of the National Rivers Authority, and

(ii) of the London Waste Regulation Authority,

shall, by virtue of this paragraph, be transferred to and vested in the Agency;

(b) any property, rights or liabilities which are the subject of—

(i) a scheme made under the following provisions of this section by the Secretary of State, or

(ii) a scheme made under those provisions by a body which is a waste regulation authority and approved (with or without modifications) under those provisions by the Secretary of State,

shall be transferred to and vested in the Agency by and in accordance with the scheme.

(2) The Secretary of State may, before the transfer date, make a scheme for the transfer to the Agency of such of—

(a) his property, rights and liabilities, or

(b) the property, rights and liabilities of any of the inspectors or chief inspectors mentioned in subsection (1) of section 2 above,

as appear to the Secretary of State appropriate to be so transferred in consequence of the transfer of any functions to the Agency by virtue of any of paragraphs (d) to (h) of that subsection.

(3) It shall be the duty of every body which is a waste regulation authority, other than the London Waste Regulation Authority—

(a) to make a scheme, after consultation with the Agency, for the transfer to the Agency of such of the body's property, rights and liabilities as appear to the body appropriate to be so transferred in consequence of the transfer of any functions to the Agency by virtue of section 2(1)(b) or (c) above; and

(b) to submit that scheme to the Secretary of State for his approval before such date as he may direct.

(4) Any body preparing a scheme in pursuance of subsection (3) above shall take into account any guidance given by the Secretary of State as to the provisions which he regards as appropriate for inclusion in the scheme.

(5) Where a scheme under subsection (3) above is submitted to the Secretary of State, he may—

(a) approve the scheme;

(b) approve the scheme subject to such modifications as he considers appropriate; or

(c) reject the scheme;

but the power conferred on the Secretary of State by paragraph (b) above shall only be exercisable after consultation with the body which submitted the scheme to him and with the Agency.

(6) The Secretary of State may, in the case of any body which is required to make a scheme under subsection (3) above, himself make a scheme for the transfer to the Agency of such of the body's property, rights or liabilities as appear to him appropriate to be so transferred in consequence of the transfer of any functions to the Agency by virtue of section 2(1)(b) or (c) above, if—

(a) the body fails to submit a scheme under subsection (3) above to him for approval before the due date; or

(b) the Secretary of State rejects a scheme under that subsection submitted to him by that body;

but nothing in this subsection shall prevent the Secretary of State from approving any scheme which may be submitted to him after the due date.

(7) The Secretary of State may, at any time before the transfer date, modify any scheme made or approved by him under this section but only after consultation with the Agency and, in the case of a scheme which was approved by him (with or without modifications), after consultation with the body which submitted the scheme to him for approval.

(8) Schedule 2 to this Act shall have effect in relation to transfers by or under this section.

4.—(1) It shall be the principal aim of the Agency (subject to and in accordance with the provisions of this Act or any other enactment and

Principal aim and objectives of the Agency.

taking into account any likely costs) in discharging its functions so to protect or enhance the environment, taken as a whole, as to make the contribution towards attaining the objective of achieving sustainable development mentioned in subsection (3) below.

(2) The Ministers shall from time to time give guidance to the Agency with respect to objectives which they consider it appropriate for the Agency to pursue in the discharge of its functions.

(3) The guidance given under subsection (2) above must include guidance with respect to the contribution which, having regard to the Agency's responsibilities and resources, the Ministers consider it appropriate for the Agency to make, by the discharge of its functions, towards attaining the objective of achieving sustainable development.

(4) In discharging its functions, the Agency shall have regard to guidance given under this section.

(5) The power to give guidance to the Agency under this section shall only be exercisable after consultation with the Agency and such other bodies or persons as the Ministers consider it appropriate to consult in relation to the guidance in question.

(6) A draft of any guidance proposed to be given under this section shall be laid before each House of Parliament and the guidance shall not be given until after the period of 40 days beginning with the day on which the draft was so laid or, if the draft is laid on different days, the later of the two days.

(7) If, within the period mentioned in subsection (6) above, either House resolves that the guidance, the draft of which was laid before it, should not be given, the Ministers shall not give that guidance.

(8) In reckoning any period of 40 days for the purposes of subsection (6) or (7) above, no account shall be taken of any time during which Parliament is dissolved or prorogued or during which both Houses are adjourned for more than four days.

(9) The Ministers shall arrange for any guidance given under this section to be published in such manner as they consider appropriate.

General functions with respect to pollution control.

5.—(1) The Agency's pollution control powers shall be exercisable for the purpose of preventing or minimising, or remedying or mitigating the effects of, pollution of the environment.

(2) The Agency shall, for the purpose—

    (a) of facilitating the carrying out of its pollution control functions, or

    (b) of enabling it to form an opinion of the general state of pollution of the environment,

compile information relating to such pollution (whether the information is acquired by the Agency carrying out observations or is obtained in any other way).

(3) If required by either of the Ministers to do so, the Agency shall—

(a) carry out assessments (whether generally or for such particular purpose as may be specified in the requirement) of the effect, or likely effect, on the environment of existing or potential levels of pollution of the environment and report its findings to that Minister; or

(b) prepare and send to that Minister a report identifying—

(i) the options which the Agency considers to be available for preventing or minimising, or remedying or mitigating the effects of, pollution of the environment, whether generally or in cases or circumstances specified in the requirement; and

(ii) the costs and benefits of such options as are identified by the Agency pursuant to sub-paragraph (i) above.

(4) The Agency shall follow developments in technology and techniques for preventing or minimising, or remedying or mitigating the effects of, pollution of the environment.

(5) In this section, "pollution control powers" and "pollution control functions", in relation to the Agency, mean respectively its powers or its functions under or by virtue of the following enactments, that is to say—

(a) the Alkali, &c, Works Regulation Act 1906; 1906 c. 14.

(b) Part I of the Health and Safety at Work etc. Act 1974; 1974 c. 37.

(c) Part I of the Control of Pollution Act 1974; 1974 c. 40.

(d) the Control of Pollution (Amendment) Act 1989; 1989 c. 14.

(e) Parts I, II and IIA of the 1990 Act (integrated pollution control etc, waste on land and contaminated land);

(f) Chapter III of Part IV of the Water Industry Act 1991 (special 1991 c. 56. category effluent);

(g) Part III and sections 161 to 161D of the 1991 Act (control of pollution of water resources);

(h) the Radioactive Substances Act 1993; 1993 c. 12.

(j) regulations made by virtue of section 2(2) of the European 1972 c. 68. Communities Act 1972, to the extent that the regulations relate to pollution.

6.—(1) It shall be the duty of the Agency, to such extent as it considers desirable, generally to promote—

General provisions with respect to water.

(a) the conservation and enhancement of the natural beauty and amenity of inland and coastal waters and of land associated with such waters;

(b) the conservation of flora and fauna which are dependent on an aquatic environment; and

(c) the use of such waters and land for recreational purposes;

and it shall be the duty of the Agency, in determining what steps to take in performance of the duty imposed by virtue of paragraph (c) above, to take into account the needs of persons who are chronically sick or disabled.

This subsection is without prejudice to the duties of the Agency under section 7 below.

(2) It shall be the duty of the Agency to take all such action as it may from time to time consider, in accordance with any directions given under section 40 below, to be necessary or expedient for the purpose—

    (a) of conserving, redistributing or otherwise augmenting water resources in England and Wales; and

    (b) of securing the proper use of water resources in England and Wales;

but nothing in this subsection shall be construed as relieving any water undertaker of the obligation to develop water resources for the purpose of performing any duty imposed on it by virtue of section 37 of the Water Industry Act 1991 (general duty to maintain water supply system).

1991 c. 56.

(3) The provisions of the 1991 Act relating to the functions of the Agency under Chapter II of Part II of that Act and the related water resources provisions so far as they relate to other functions of the Agency shall not apply to so much of any inland waters as—

    (a) are part of the River Tweed;

    (b) are part of the River Esk or River Sark at a point where either of the banks of the river is in Scotland; or

    (c) are part of any tributary stream of the River Esk or the River Sark at a point where either of the banks of the tributary stream is in Scotland.

(4) Subject to section 106 of the 1991 Act (obligation to carry out flood defence functions through committees), the Agency shall in relation to England and Wales exercise a general supervision over all matters relating to flood defence.

(5) The Agency's flood defence functions shall extend to the territorial sea adjacent to England and Wales in so far as—

    (a) the area of any regional flood defence committee includes any area of that territorial sea; or

    (b) section 165(2) or (3) of the 1991 Act (drainage works for the purpose of defence against sea water or tidal water, and works etc to secure an adequate outfall for a main river) provides for the exercise of any power in the territorial sea.

(6) It shall be the duty of the Agency to maintain, improve and develop salmon fisheries, trout fisheries, freshwater fisheries and eel fisheries.

(7) The area in respect of which the Agency shall carry out its functions relating to fisheries shall be the whole of England and Wales, together with—

    (a) such part of the territorial sea adjacent to England and Wales as extends for six miles from the baselines from which the breadth of that sea is measured,

    (b) in the case of—

1937 c. 33.

1975 c. 51.

        (i) the Diseases of Fish Act 1937,

        (ii) the Salmon and Freshwater Fisheries Act 1975,

        (iii) Part V of the 1991 Act (general control of fisheries), and

        (iv) subsection (6) above,

    so much of the River Esk, with its banks and tributary streams up to their source, as is situated in Scotland, and

(c) in the case of sections 31 to 34 and 36(2) of the Salmon and 1975 c. 51.
Freshwater Fisheries Act 1975 as applied by section 39(1B) of
that Act, so much of the catchment area of the River Esk as is
situated in Scotland,

but, in the case of the enactments specified in paragraph (b) above,
excluding the River Tweed.

(8) In this section—

"miles" means international nautical miles of 1,852 metres;

"the related water resources provisions" has the same meaning as it
has in the 1991 Act;

"the River Tweed" means "the river" within the meaning of the
Tweed Fisheries Amendment Act 1859 as amended by byelaws.   1859 c. lxx.

7.—(1) It shall be the duty of each of the Ministers and of the Agency,   General
in formulating or considering—   environmental
   and recreational
   (a) any proposals relating to any functions of the Agency other than   duties.
   its pollution control functions, so far as may be consistent—

      (i) with the purposes of any enactment relating to the
      functions of the Agency,

      (ii) in the case of each of the Ministers, with the objective
      of achieving sustainable development,

      (iii) in the case of the Agency, with any guidance under
      section 4 above,

      (iv) in the case of the Secretary of State, with his duties   1991 c. 56.
      under section 2 of the Water Industry Act 1991,

   so to exercise any power conferred on him or it with respect to
   the proposals as to further the conservation and enhancement
   of natural beauty and the conservation of flora, fauna and
   geological or physiographical features of special interest;

   (b) any proposals relating to pollution control functions of the
   Agency, to have regard to the desirability of conserving and
   enhancing natural beauty and of conserving flora, fauna and
   geological or physiographical features of special interest;

   (c) any proposal relating to any functions of the Agency—

      (i) to have regard to the desirability of protecting and
      conserving buildings, sites and objects of archaeological,
      architectural, engineering or historic interest;

      (ii) to take into account any effect which the proposals
      would have on the beauty or amenity of any rural or urban
      area or on any such flora, fauna, features, buildings, sites or
      objects; and

      (iii) to have regard to any effect which the proposals would
      have on the economic and social well-being of local
      communities in rural areas.

(2) Subject to subsection (1) above, it shall be the duty of each of the
Ministers and of the Agency, in formulating or considering any proposals
relating to any functions of the Agency—

(a) to have regard to the desirability of preserving for the public any freedom of access to areas of woodland, mountains, moor, heath, down, cliff or foreshore and other places of natural beauty;

(b) to have regard to the desirability of maintaining the availability to the public of any facility for visiting or inspecting any building, site or object of archaeological, architectural, engineering or historic interest; and

(c) to take into account any effect which the proposals would have on any such freedom of access or on the availability of any such facility.

(3) Subsections (1) and (2) above shall apply so as to impose duties on the Agency in relation to—

(a) any proposals relating to the functions of a water undertaker or sewerage undertaker,

(b) any proposals relating to the management, by the company holding an appointment as such an undertaker, of any land for the time being held by that company for any purpose whatever (whether or not connected with the carrying out of the functions of a water undertaker or sewerage undertaker), and

1991 c. 56.

(c) any proposal which by virtue of section 156(7) of the Water Industry Act 1991 (disposals of protected land) falls to be treated for the purposes of section 3 of that Act as a proposal relating to the functions of a water undertaker or sewerage undertaker,

as they apply in relation to proposals relating to the Agency's own functions, other than its pollution control functions.

(4) Subject to obtaining the consent of any navigation authority, harbour authority or conservancy authority before doing anything which causes obstruction of, or other interference with, navigation which is subject to the control of that authority, it shall be the duty of the Agency to take such steps as are—

(a) reasonably practicable, and

(b) consistent with the purposes of the enactments relating to the functions of the Agency,

for securing, so long as the Agency has rights to the use of water or land associated with water, that those rights are exercised so as to ensure that the water or land is made available for recreational purposes and is so made available in the best manner.

(5) It shall be the duty of the Agency, in determining what steps to take in performance of any duty imposed by virtue of subsection (4) above, to take into account the needs of persons who are chronically sick or disabled.

(6) Nothing in this section, the following provisions of this Act or the 1991 Act shall require recreational facilities made available by the Agency to be made available free of charge.

(7) In this section—

"building" includes structure;

"pollution control functions", in relation to the Agency, has the same meaning as in section 5 above.

8.—(1) Where the Nature Conservancy Council for England or the Countryside Council for Wales is of the opinion that any area of land in England or, as the case may be, in Wales—

   (a) is of special interest by reason of its flora, fauna or geological or physiographical features, and

   (b) may at any time be affected by schemes, works, operations or activities of the Agency or by an authorisation given by the Agency,

that Council shall notify the fact that the land is of special interest for that reason to the Agency.

Environmental duties with respect to sites of special interest.

   (2) Where a National Park authority or the Broads Authority is of the opinion that any area of land in a National Park or in the Broads—

   (a) is land in relation to which the matters for the purposes of which sections 6(1) and 7 above (other than section 7(1)(c)(iii) above) have effect are of particular importance, and

   (b) may at any time be affected by schemes, works, operations or activities of the Agency or by an authorisation given by the Agency,

the National Park authority or Broads Authority shall notify the Agency of the fact that the land is such land, and of the reasons why those matters are of particular importance in relation to the land.

   (3) Where the Agency has received a notification under subsection (1) or (2) above with respect to any land, it shall consult the notifying body before carrying out or authorising any works, operations or activities which appear to the Agency to be likely—

   (a) to destroy or damage any of the flora, fauna, or geological or physiographical features by reason of which the land is of special interest; or

   (b) significantly to prejudice anything the importance of which is one of the reasons why the matters mentioned in subsection (2) above are of particular importance in relation to that land.

   (4) Subsection (3) above shall not apply in relation to anything done in an emergency where particulars of what is done and of the emergency are notified to the Nature Conservancy Council for England, the Countryside Council for Wales, the National Park authority in question or, as the case may be, the Broads Authority as soon as practicable after that thing is done.

   (5) In this section—

   "authorisation" includes any consent or licence;

   "the Broads" has the same meaning as in the Norfolk and Suffolk Broads Act 1988; and

1988 c. 4.

   "National Park authority", subject to subsection (6) below, means a National Park authority established under section 63 below which has become the local planning authority for the National Park in question.

   (6) As respects any period before a National Park authority established under section 63 below in relation to a National Park becomes the local planning authority for that National Park, any reference in

subsections (1) to (4) above to a National Park authority shall be taken as a reference to the National Park Committee or joint or special planning board for that National Park.

Codes of practice with respect to environmental and recreational duties.

9.—(1) Each of the Ministers shall have power by order to approve any code of practice issued (whether by him or by another person) for the purpose of—

(a) giving practical guidance to the Agency with respect to any of the matters for the purposes of which sections 6(1), 7 and 8 above have effect, and

(b) promoting what appear to him to be desirable practices by the Agency with respect to those matters,

and may at any time by such an order approve a modification of such a code or withdraw his approval of such a code or modification.

(2) In discharging its duties under section 6(1), 7 or 8 above, the Agency shall have regard to any code of practice, and any modifications of a code of practice, for the time being approved under this section.

(3) Neither of the Ministers shall make an order under this section unless he has first consulted—

(a) the Agency;

(b) the Countryside Commission, the Nature Conservancy Council for England and the Countryside Council for Wales;

(c) the Historic Buildings and Monuments Commission for England;

(d) the Sports Council and the Sports Council for Wales; and

(e) such other persons as he considers it appropriate to consult.

(4) The power of each of the Ministers to make an order under this section shall be exercisable by statutory instrument; and any statutory instrument containing such an order shall be subject to annulment in pursuance of a resolution of either House of Parliament.

Incidental functions of the Agency.

10.—(1) This section has effect—

(a) for the purposes of section 37(1) below, as it applies in relation to the Agency; and

(b) for the construction of any other enactment which, by reference to the functions of the Agency, confers any power on or in relation to the Agency;

and any reference in this section to "the relevant purposes" is a reference to the purposes described in paragraphs (a) and (b) above.

(2) For the relevant purposes, the functions of the Agency shall be taken to include the protection against pollution of—

(a) any waters, whether on the surface or underground, which belong to the Agency or any water undertaker or from which the Agency or any water undertaker is authorised to take water;

(b) without prejudice to paragraph (a) above, any reservoir which belongs to or is operated by the Agency or any water undertaker or which the Agency or any water undertaker is proposing to acquire or construct for the purpose of being so operated; and

(c) any underground strata from which the Agency or any water undertaker is for the time being authorised to abstract water in pursuance of a licence under Chapter II of Part II of the 1991 Act (abstraction and impounding).

(3) For the relevant purposes, the functions of the Agency shall be taken to include joining with or acting on behalf of one or more relevant undertakers for the purpose of carrying out any works or acquiring any land which at least one of the undertakers with which it joins, or on whose behalf it acts, is authorised to carry out or acquire for the purposes of—

(a) any function of that undertaker under any enactment; or

(b) any function which is taken to be a function of that undertaker for the purposes to which section 217 of the Water Industry Act 1991 applies.

1991 c. 56.

(4) For the relevant purposes, the functions of the Agency shall be taken to include the provision of supplies of water in bulk, whether or not such supplies are provided for the purposes of, or in connection with, the carrying out of any other function of the Agency.

(5) For the relevant purposes, the functions of the Agency shall be taken to include the provision of houses and other buildings for the use of persons employed by the Agency and the provision of recreation grounds for persons so employed.

(6) In this section—

"relevant undertaker" means a water undertaker or sewerage undertaker; and

"supply of water in bulk" means a supply of water for distribution by a water undertaker taking the supply.

Advisory committees

11.—(1) The Secretary of State shall establish and maintain a committee for advising him with respect to matters affecting, or otherwise connected with, the carrying out in Wales of the Agency's functions.

Advisory committee for Wales.

(2) The committee shall consist of such persons as may from time to time be appointed by the Secretary of State.

(3) The committee shall meet at least once a year.

(4) The Secretary of State may pay to the members of the committee such sums by way of reimbursement (whether in whole or in part) for loss of remuneration, for travelling expenses and for other out-of-pocket expenses as he may determine.

12.—(1) It shall be the duty of the Agency—

Environment protection advisory committees.

(a) to establish and maintain advisory committees, to be known as Environment Protection Advisory Committees, for the different regions of England and Wales;

(b) to consult the advisory committee for any region as to any proposals of the Agency relating generally to the manner in which the Agency carries out its functions in that region; and

(c) to consider any representations made to it by the advisory committee for any region (whether in response to consultation under paragraph (b) above or otherwise) as to the manner in which the Agency carries out its functions in that region.

(2) The advisory committee for any region shall consist of—

(a) a chairman appointed by the Secretary of State; and

(b) such other members as the Agency may appoint in accordance with the provisions of the approved membership scheme for that region.

(3) In appointing the chairman of any advisory committee, the Secretary of State shall have regard to the desirability of appointing a person who has experience of, and has shown capacity in, some matter relevant to the functions of the committee.

(4) The members of advisory committees appointed by virtue of subsection (2)(b) above—

(a) must not be members of the Agency; but

(b) must be persons who appear to the Agency to have a significant interest in matters likely to be affected by the manner in which the Agency carries out any of its functions in the region of the advisory committee in question.

(5) The duty imposed by subsection (1)(a) above to establish and maintain advisory committees is a duty to establish and maintain an advisory committee for each area which the Agency considers it appropriate for the time being to regard as a region of England and Wales for the purposes of this section.

(6) It shall be the duty of the Agency, in determining the regions for which advisory committees are established and maintained under this section, to ensure that one of those regions consists wholly or mainly of, or of most of, Wales.

(7) For the purposes of this section, functions of the Agency which are carried out in any area of Scotland, or of the territorial sea, which is adjacent to any region for which an advisory committee is maintained, shall be regarded as carried out in that region.

(8) Schedule 3 to this Act shall have effect with respect to advisory committees.

(9) In this section—

"advisory committee" means an advisory committee under this section;

"approved membership scheme" means a scheme, as in force for the time being, prepared by the Agency and approved (with or without modification) by the Secretary of State under Schedule 3 to this Act which makes provision with respect to the membership of the advisory committee for a region.

Regional and local fisheries advisory committees.

13.—(1) It shall be the duty of the Agency—

(a) to establish and maintain advisory committees of persons who are not members of the Agency but appear to it to be interested in salmon fisheries, trout fisheries, freshwater fisheries or eel fisheries in the different parts of the controlled area; and

(b) to consult those committees as to the manner in which the Agency is to perform its duty under section 6(6) above.

(2) If the Agency, with the consent of the Ministers, so determines, it shall also be under a duty to consult those committees, or such of them as may be specified or described in the determination, as to—

   (a) the manner in which it is to perform its duties under or by virtue of such of the enactments relating to recreation, conservation or navigation as may be the subject of the determination, or

   (b) such matters relating to recreation, conservation or navigation as may be the subject of the determination.

(3) Where, by virtue of subsection (2) above, the Agency is under a duty to consult those committees or any of them, there may be included among the members of the committees in question persons who are not members of the Agency but who appear to it to be interested in matters—

   (a) likely to be affected by the manner in which it performs the duties to which the determination in question relates, or

   (b) which are the subject of the determination,

if the Ministers consent to the inclusion of persons of that description.

(4) The duty to establish and maintain advisory committees imposed by subsection (1) above is a duty to establish and maintain—

   (a) a regional advisory committee for each such region of the controlled area as the Agency considers it appropriate for the time being to regard as a region of that area for the purposes of this section; and

   (b) such local advisory committees as the Agency considers necessary to represent—

      (i) the interests referred to in subsection (1)(a) above, and

      (ii) where persons may be appointed members of those committees by virtue of subsection (3) above by reference to any such interests as are mentioned in that subsection, the interests in question,

   in the different parts of each such region.

(5) It shall be the duty of the Agency in determining the regions for which regional advisory committees are established and maintained under this section to ensure that one of those regions consists (apart from territorial waters) wholly or mainly of, or of most of, Wales.

(6) In addition to any members appointed under the foregoing provisions of this section, there shall, in the case of each regional advisory committee established and maintained under this section, also be a chairman appointed—

   (a) by the Secretary of State, in the case of the committee established and maintained for the region described in subsection (5) above; or

   (b) by the Minister, in any other case.

(7) There shall be paid by the Agency—

   (a) to the chairman of any regional or local advisory committee established and maintained under this section such remuneration and such travelling and other allowances; and

(b) to any other members of that committee such sums by way of reimbursement (whether in whole or in part) for loss of remuneration, for travelling expenses or for any other out-of-pocket expenses,

as may be determined by one of the Ministers.

(8) In this section "the controlled area" means the area specified in section 6(7) above in respect of which the Agency carries out functions under section 6(6) above and Part V of the 1991 Act.

Flood defence committees

Regional flood defence committees.

14.—(1) There shall be committees, known as regional flood defence committees, for the purpose of carrying out the functions which fall to be carried out by such committees by virtue of this Act and the 1991 Act.

(2) Subject to Schedule 4 to this Act (which makes provision for the alteration of the boundaries of and the amalgamation of the areas of regional flood defence committees)—

(a) there shall be a regional flood defence committee for each of the areas for which there was an old committee immediately before the transfer date; but

(b) where under section 165(2) or (3) of the 1991 Act any function of the Agency falls to be carried out at a place beyond the seaward boundaries of the area of any regional flood defence committee, that place shall be assumed for the purposes of this Act and the 1991 Act to be within the area of the regional flood defence committee to whose area the area of sea where that place is situated is adjacent.

(3) The Agency shall maintain a principal office for the area of each regional flood defence committee.

(4) In this section "old committee" means a regional flood defence committee for the purposes of section 9 of the 1991 Act.

Composition of regional flood defence committees.

15.—(1) Subject to subsection (2) below, a regional flood defence committee shall consist of the following, none of whom shall be a member of the Agency, that is to say—

(a) a chairman and a number of other members appointed by the relevant Minister;

(b) two members appointed by the Agency;

(c) a number of members appointed by or on behalf of the constituent councils.

(2) Any person who immediately before the transfer date is, by virtue of his appointment—

(a) by a Minister of the Crown,

(b) by or on behalf of any council, or

(c) by the National Rivers Authority,

the chairman or a member of an old committee which, by virtue of section 14 above, is replaced by a new committee shall be treated, on and after that date, for the remainder of the period for which he would, under the terms of his appointment, have held office in relation to the old committee, as if he had been appointed as the chairman or, as the case may be, a member of the new committee, and on the same terms, by that Minister or, as the case may be, by or on behalf of that council or, in the case of a person appointed by the National Rivers Authority, by the Agency.

(3) Subject to section 16 below and to any order under Schedule 4 to this Act amalgamating the areas of any two or more regional flood defence committees—

    (a) the total number of members of a new committee for any area shall be the same as the total number of members of the old committee for that area immediately before the transfer date;

    (b) the number of members to be appointed to a new committee for any area by or on behalf of each of the constituent councils or, as the case may be, jointly by or on behalf of more than one of them shall be the same as the number of members of the old committee for that area which fell to be so appointed immediately before the transfer date.

(4) In any case where—

    (a) the appointment of one or more members of a regional flood defence committee is (by virtue of subsection (3) above or an order under section 16(5) below), to be made jointly by more than one constituent council, and

    (b) the councils by whom that appointment is to be made are unable to agree on an appointment,

the member or members in question shall be appointed by the relevant Minister on behalf of those councils.

(5) In appointing a person to be the chairman or a member of a regional flood defence committee under subsection (1)(a) or (c) or (4) above the relevant Minister or, as the case may be, a constituent council shall have regard to the desirability of appointing a person who has experience of, and has shown capacity in, some matter relevant to the functions of the committee.

(6) The councils of every county, county borough, metropolitan district or London borough any part of which is in the area of a regional flood defence committee shall be the constituent councils for the regional flood defence committee for that area, and the Common Council of the City of London shall be a constituent council for the regional flood defence committee for any area which comprises any part of the City.

(7) In this section—

    "old committee" has the same meaning as in section 14 above;

    "new committee" means a regional flood defence committee established under section 14 above;

    "the relevant Minister"—

        (a) in relation to the regional flood defence committee for an area the whole or the greater part of which is in Wales, means the Secretary of State; and

        (b) in relation to any other regional flood defence committee, means the Minister.

Change of
composition of
regional flood
defence
committee.

16.—(1) The Agency may, in accordance with the following provisions of this section, from time to time make a determination varying the total number of members of a regional flood defence committee.

(2) The Agency shall submit any determination under subsection (1) above to the relevant Minister.

(3) For the purposes of this section—

(a) the total number of members of a regional flood defence committee shall not be less than eleven; and

(b) any determination by the Agency under subsection (1) above that a regional flood defence committee should consist of more than seventeen members shall be provisional and shall take effect only if the relevant Minister makes an order under subsection (4) below.

(4) If the Agency submits a provisional determination to the relevant Minister with respect to any regional flood defence committee and he considers that the committee should consist of more than seventeen members, he may by order made by statutory instrument—

(a) confirm it; or

(b) substitute for the number of members determined by the Agency some other number not less than seventeen.

(5) Subject to the following provisions of this section, whenever—

(a) the total number of members of a regional flood defence committee is varied under this section, or

(b) the relevant Minister considers it necessary or expedient to make an order under this subsection,

the relevant Minister shall by order made by statutory instrument specify the number of members to be appointed to the committee by each of the constituent councils.

(6) An order under subsection (5) above shall relate—

(a) where paragraph (a) of that subsection applies, to times after the coming into force of the variation; and

(b) where paragraph (b) of that subsection applies, to such times as are specified in the order.

(7) An order under subsection (5) above shall be so framed that the total number of members appointed under section 15(1)(a) and (b) above is one less than the number of those appointed by or on behalf of constituent councils.

(8) For the purpose of determining for the purposes of subsection (5) above the number of persons to be appointed to a regional flood defence committee by or on behalf of each constituent council, the relevant Minister—

(a) if he considers it to be inappropriate that that council should appoint a member of the committee, or

(b) if he considers that one or more members should be appointed jointly by that council and one or more other constituent councils,

may include provision to that effect in the order.

(9) In this section—

"member", in relation to a regional flood defence committee, includes the chairman of the committee;

"the relevant Minister" has the same meaning as in section 15 above.

17.—(1) A scheme, known as a local flood defence scheme, may be made by the Agency, in accordance with the following provisions of this section—

(a) for the creation in the area of a regional flood defence committee of one or more districts, to be known as local flood defence districts; and

(b) for the constitution, membership, functions and procedure of a committee for each such district, to be known as the local flood defence committee for that district.

Local flood defence schemes and local flood defence committees.

(2) Any local flood defence scheme which was made under the 1991 Act or continued in force by virtue of paragraph 14(1) of Schedule 2 to the Water Consolidation (Consequential Provisions) Act 1991 and which, immediately before the transfer date, is in force in relation to the area of a regional flood defence committee, shall on and after that date have effect, and may be amended or revoked, as if it were a local flood defence scheme made under this section in relation to that area; and, accordingly, subject to any such amendment or revocation—

1991 c. 60.

(a) any local flood defence district created by that scheme and in being immediately before that date shall be treated, on and after that date, as a local flood defence district created by a scheme under this section in relation to the area of that regional flood defence committee; and

(b) any local flood defence committee created by that scheme for any such district and in being immediately before that date shall be treated, on and after that date, as the local flood defence committee for that district.

(3) A regional flood defence committee may at any time submit to the Agency—

(a) a local flood defence scheme for any part of their area for which there is then no such scheme in force; or

(b) a scheme varying a local flood defence scheme or revoking such a scheme and, if the committee think fit, replacing it with another such scheme;

and references in the following provisions of this section and in section 18 below to local flood defence schemes are references to schemes under either of paragraphs (a) and (b) above.

(4) Before submitting a scheme to the Agency under subsection (3) above, a regional flood defence committee shall consult—

(a) every local authority any part of whose area will fall within the area to which the scheme is proposed to relate; and

(b) such organisations representative of persons interested in flood defence (within the meaning of Part IV of the 1991 Act) or agriculture as the regional flood defence committee consider to be appropriate.

(5) It shall be the duty of the Agency to send any scheme submitted to it under subsection (3) above to one of the Ministers.

(6) A local flood defence scheme may define a local flood defence district—

(a) by reference to the districts which were local land drainage districts immediately before 1st September 1989;

(b) by reference to the area of the regional flood defence committee in which that district is situated;

(c) by reference to a map;

or partly by one of those means and partly by another or others.

(7) A local flood defence scheme may contain incidental, consequential and supplementary provisions.

(8) Either of the Ministers may approve a local flood defence scheme with or without modifications; and any scheme approved under this subsection shall come into force on a date fixed by the Minister approving it.

Composition of
local flood defence
committees.

18.—(1) Subject to subsections (2) and (3) below, a local flood defence scheme shall provide that any local flood defence committee to which it relates shall consist of not less than eleven and not more than fifteen members.

(2) A regional flood defence committee may include in a local flood defence scheme which they submit to the Agency a recommendation that a committee to which the scheme relates should consist of a number of members greater than fifteen; and a scheme so submitted shall be taken to provide for the number of members of a committee if it contains a recommendation under this subsection relating to that committee.

(3) The power conferred on each of the Ministers by section 17(8) above shall include power to direct that a committee to which a recommendation under subsection (2) above relates shall consist either of the recommended number of members or of some other number of members greater than fifteen.

(4) A local flood defence committee shall consist of—

(a) a chairman appointed from among their own members by the regional flood defence committee;

(b) other members appointed by that committee; and

(c) members appointed, in accordance with and subject to the terms of the local flood defence scheme, by or on behalf of constituent councils.

(5) The number of members appointed to a local flood defence committee by or on behalf of constituent councils shall be one more than the total number of members appointed by the regional flood defence committee.

(6) In appointing a person to be a member of a local flood defence committee, the regional flood defence committee shall have regard to the desirability of appointing a person who has experience of, and has shown capacity in, some matter relevant to the functions of the committee to which he is appointed.

(7) Any person who, immediately before the transfer date is, by virtue of an appointment by an old regional committee or by or on behalf of any council, the chairman or a member of a local flood defence committee

which is continued in force by virtue of section 17(2) above shall be treated, on and after that date, for the remainder of the period for which he would, under the terms of his appointment, have held office in relation to the local flood defence committee—

(a) as if he had been appointed as such under this section by the regional flood defence committee or, as the case may be, by or on behalf of that council; and

(b) in the case of the chairman, as if he were a member of the regional flood defence committee.

(8) The councils of every county, county borough, metropolitan district or London borough any part of which is in a local flood defence district shall be the constituent councils for the local flood defence committee for that district, and the Common Council of the City of London shall be a constituent council for the local flood defence committee of any local flood defence district which comprises any part of the City.

(9) In this section "old regional committee" means a regional flood defence committee for the purposes of section 9 of the 1991 Act.

19. Schedule 5 to this Act shall have effect in relation to regional flood defence committees and local flood defence committees.

Membership and proceedings of flood defence committees.

CHAPTER II

THE SCOTTISH ENVIRONMENT PROTECTION AGENCY

Establishment of SEPA

20.—(1) There shall be a body to be known as the Scottish Environment Protection Agency (in this Act referred to as "SEPA"), for the purpose of carrying out the functions transferred or assigned to it by or under this Act.

The Scottish Environment Protection Agency.

(2) Schedule 6 to this Act shall have effect with respect to SEPA.

Transfer of functions, property etc. to SEPA

21.—(1) On the transfer date there shall by virtue of this section be transferred to SEPA—

Transfer of functions to SEPA.

(a) the functions of river purification authorities, that is to say—

(i) their functions with respect to water resources under or by virtue of Part III of the Rivers (Prevention of Pollution) (Scotland) Act 1951 (in this Part referred to as "the 1951 Act") and Part II of the Natural Heritage (Scotland) Act 1991;

1951 c. 66.
1991 c. 28.

(ii) their functions with respect to water pollution under or by virtue of Part III of the 1951 Act, the Rivers (Prevention of Pollution) (Scotland) Act 1965 and Part II of the Control of Pollution Act 1974;

1965 c. 13.
1974 c. 40.

(iii) their functions as enforcing authority, in relation to releases of substances into the environment, under or by virtue of Part I of the 1990 Act;

(iv) their functions with respect to flood warning systems under or by virtue of Part VI of the Agriculture Act 1970; and

1970 c. 40.

(v) the functions assigned to them by or under any other enactment apart from this Act;

(b) the functions of waste regulation authorities, that is to say, the functions conferred or imposed on them by or under—

1989 c. 14.

(i) the Control of Pollution (Amendment) Act 1989; or

(ii) Part II of the 1990 Act,

or assigned to them by or under any other enactment apart from this Act;

(c) the functions of disposal authorities under or by virtue of

1974 c. 40.

sections 3 to 10, 16, 17(1)(a) and 17(2)(b) to (d) of the Control of Pollution Act 1974;

(d) the functions of the chief inspector for Scotland constituted under section 16(3) of the 1990 Act, that is to say, the functions conferred or imposed on him by or under Part I of that Act or assigned to him by or under any other enactment apart from this Act;

(e) the functions of the chief inspector for Scotland appointed under

1993 c. 12.

section 4(2)(b) of the Radioactive Substances Act 1993, that is to say, the functions conferred or imposed on him by or under that Act or assigned to him by or under any other enactment apart from this Act;

1906 c. 14.

(f) the functions conferred or imposed by or under the Alkali, &c, Works Regulation Act 1906 (in this section referred to as "the 1906 Act") on the chief, or any other, inspector (within the meaning of that Act), so far as exercisable in relation to Scotland;

(g) so far as exercisable in relation to Scotland, the functions in relation to improvement notices and prohibition notices under

1974 c. 37.

Part I of the Health and Safety at Work etc. Act 1974 (in this section referred to as "the 1974 Act") of inspectors appointed under section 19 of that Act by the Secretary of State in his capacity as enforcing authority responsible in relation to Scotland for the enforcement of the 1906 Act and section 5 of the 1974 Act;

(h) the functions of local authorities as enforcing authority, in relation to releases of substances into the air, under or by virtue of Part I of the 1990 Act; and

(i) the functions of the Secretary of State specified in subsection (2) below.

(2) The functions of the Secretary of State mentioned in subsection (1)(i) above are, so far as exercisable in relation to Scotland—

(a) the functions conferred or imposed on him by virtue of his being, for the purposes of Part I of the 1974 Act, the authority which is by any of the relevant statutory provisions made responsible for the enforcement of the 1906 Act and section 5 of the 1974 Act;

(b) his functions under, or under regulations made by virtue of, section 9 of the 1906 Act (registration of works), other than any functions of his as an appellate authority or any function of making regulations;

(c) his functions under section 19 of the Clean Air Act 1993 with respect to the creation of smoke control areas by local authorities; and

(d) his functions under section 30(1) of the Radioactive Substances Act 1993 (power to dispose of radioactive waste).

(3) River purification boards shall be dissolved on the transfer date.

22.—(1) On the transfer date—

(a) the property, rights and liabilities of every river purification board shall, by virtue of this paragraph, be transferred to and vested in SEPA;

(b) any property, rights and liabilities which are the subject of a scheme under this section—

    (i) made by the Secretary of State; or

    (ii) made by a local authority and approved by the Secretary of State,

shall be transferred to and vested in SEPA by and in accordance with the scheme.

(2) The Secretary of State may, before the transfer date, make a scheme for the transfer to SEPA of such of—

(a) his property, rights and liabilities; or

(b) the property, rights and liabilities of any of the inspectors or chief inspectors mentioned in subsection (1) of section 21 above,

as appear to the Secretary of State appropriate to be so transferred in consequence of the transfer of any functions to SEPA by virtue of that subsection.

(3) It shall be the duty of every local authority to make a scheme, after consultation with SEPA, for the transfer to SEPA of—

(a) such of the authority's property and rights as are held by it for the purposes of its functions as—

    (i) a waste regulation authority;

    (ii) a disposal authority under or by virtue of the provisions mentioned in section 21(1)(c) above;

    (iii) enforcing authority, in relation to releases of substances into the air, by virtue of Part I of the 1990 Act; and

    (iv) in the case of an islands council, a river purification authority; and

(b) such of its liabilities as are liabilities to which it is subject by virtue of its being an authority mentioned in paragraph (a)(i) to (iv) above,

and to submit that scheme to the Secretary of State for his approval before such date as he may direct.

(4) Any local authority preparing a scheme in pursuance of subsection (3) above shall take into account any guidance given by the Secretary of State as to the provisions which he regards as appropriate for inclusion in the scheme.

(5) Where a scheme under subsection (3) above is submitted to the Secretary of State, he may—

(a) approve the scheme;

(b) approve the scheme subject to such modifications as he considers appropriate; or

(c) reject the scheme;

but the power conferred on the Secretary of State by paragraph (b) above shall be exercisable only after consultation with the local authority which submitted the scheme to him and with SEPA.

(6) The Secretary of State may, in the case of any local authority which is required to make a scheme under subsection (3) above, himself make a scheme for the transfer to SEPA of such of the body's property, rights or liabilities as are mentioned in paragraph (a) or (b) of that subsection, if—

(a) the authority fails to submit a scheme under that subsection to him for his approval before the due date; or

(b) the Secretary of State rejects a scheme under that subsection submitted to him by the authority;

but nothing in this subsection shall prevent the Secretary of State from approving any scheme which may be submitted to him after the due date.

(7) Where the Secretary of State makes a transfer scheme under subsection (6) above, he may recover his reasonable expenses in doing so, or such proportion of those expenses as he thinks fit, from the local authority in question by such means as appear to him to be appropriate including, without prejudice to that generality, setting off the expenses payable by the local authority against revenue support grant or non-domestic rate income payable by the Secretary of State to the local authority under paragraph 3 of Schedule 12 to the Local Government Finance Act 1992.

1992 c. 14.

(8) The Secretary of State may, at any time before the transfer date, modify any scheme made or approved by him under this section but only after consultation with SEPA and, in the case of a scheme which was approved by him (with or without modifications), after consultation with the local authority which submitted the scheme to him for approval.

(9) Schedule 2 to this Act shall have effect in relation to transfers by or under this section.

Functions of staff commission.
1994 c. 39.

23. The functions of the staff commission established under section 12 of the Local Government etc. (Scotland) Act 1994 shall include—

(a) considering and keeping under review the arrangements for the transfer to SEPA, in consequence of this Act or of any scheme made under it, of staff employed by local authorities;

(b) considering such staffing problems arising out of, consequential on or connected with any provision of, or scheme made under, this Act as may be referred to them by the Secretary of State or by any local authority;

(c) advising the Secretary of State as to the steps necessary to safeguard the interests of the staff referred to in paragraph (a) above.

Other functions etc. of SEPA

24.—(1) Subject to subsection (2) below, any person proposing to carry out drainage works shall—

    (a) before commencing such works, consult SEPA as to precautions to be taken to prevent pollution to controlled waters as a result of the works; and

    (b) in carrying out such works, take account of SEPA's views.

(2) The Secretary of State may, by regulations made by statutory instrument subject to annulment in pursuance of a resolution of either House of Parliament, prescribe types of drainage works in relation to which subsection (1) above shall not apply.

(3) In this section, "drainage works" has the same meaning as in the Land Drainage (Scotland) Act 1958 and "controlled waters" has the same meaning as in the Control of Pollution Act 1974.

25.—(1) Without prejudice to section 92 of the Agriculture Act 1970 (provision of flood warning systems), SEPA shall have the function of assessing, as far as it considers it appropriate, the risk of flooding in any area of Scotland.

(2) If requested by a planning authority to do so, SEPA shall, on the basis of such information as it holds with respect to the risk of flooding in any part of the authority's area, provide the authority with advice as to such risk.

26.—(1) The Secretary of State may authorise SEPA, for the purpose of any of its functions, to purchase land compulsorily.

(2) The Acquisition of Land (Authorisation Procedure) (Scotland) Act 1947 shall apply in relation to the compulsory purchase of land under this section as if this section had been in force immediately before the commencement of that Act and, in relation to such purchase of land, SEPA shall be treated as if it were a local authority within the meaning of that Act.

27.—(1) Where, with a view to performing a function conferred on it by any enactment, SEPA considers that it ought to have information connected with any land, it may serve on one or more of the persons mentioned in subsection (2) below a notice—

    (a) specifying the land, the function and the enactment; and

    (b) requiring the recipient of the notice to furnish to SEPA, within such period of not less than 14 days from the date of service of the notice as is specified in the notice—

        (i) the nature of his interest in the land; and

        (ii) the name and address of each person whom he believes is, as respects the land, a person mentioned in subsection (2) below.

(2) The persons referred to in subsection (1) above are—

    (a) the occupier of the land;

    (b) any person—

        (i) who has an interest in the land as owner, creditor in a heritable security or lessee; or

Consultation with respect to drainage works.

1958 c. 24.
1974 c. 40.

Assessing flood risk.
1970 c. 40.

Power of SEPA to purchase land compulsorily.
1947 c. 42.

Power of SEPA to obtain information about land.

(ii) who directly or indirectly receives rent for the land; and

(c) any person who, in pursuance of an agreement between himself and a person interested in the land, is authorised to manage the land or to arrange for the letting of it.

(3) A person who—

(a) fails to comply with the requirements of a notice served on him in pursuance of subsection (1) above; or

(b) in furnishing any information in compliance with such a notice makes a statement which he knows to be false in a material particular or recklessly makes a statement which is false in a material particular,

shall be guilty of an offence and liable on summary conviction to a fine not exceeding level 5 on the standard scale.

Power of SEPA to promote or oppose private legislation.
1936 c. 52.

28.—(1) SEPA may, where it is satisfied that it is expedient to do so—

(a) with the consent of the Secretary of State, petition for the issue of a provisional order under the Private Legislation Procedure (Scotland) Act 1936; or

(b) oppose any private legislation in Parliament.

(2) An application for the consent mentioned in paragraph (a) of subsection (1) above shall be accompanied by a concise summary of the purposes of the order petitioned for.

(3) In paragraph (b) of subsection (1) above, "private legislation in Parliament" includes—

(a) a provisional order and a Confirmation Bill relating to such an order; and

(b) any local or personal Bill.

Procedure relating to making of byelaws.
1973 c. 65.

29. The following provisions of the Local Government (Scotland) Act 1973—

(a) section 202 (procedure etc. for byelaws);

(b) section 202C (revocation of byelaws);

(c) section 204 (evidence of byelaws),

shall apply in relation to SEPA as they apply in relation to a local authority, provided that in the application of the said section 202 to SEPA for subsection (13) there shall be substituted—

"(13) The Scottish Environment Protection Agency shall send a copy of any byelaws made by it to the proper officer of the local authority for any area to the whole or any part of which the byelaws will apply.".

Records held by SEPA.

30.—(1) Subject to subsection (3) below—

(a) this section applies to all records (in whatever form or medium)—

(i) transferred to and vested in SEPA by or under section 22 above;

(ii) created or acquired by it in the exercise of any of its functions; or

(iii) otherwise in its keeping;

(b) SEPA shall ensure that the records, other than such as are mentioned in paragraph (c) below, are preserved and managed in accordance with such arrangements as it, after consulting the Keeper of the Records of Scotland, shall put into effect;

(c) records which in SEPA's opinion are not worthy of preservation may be disposed of by it;

(d) SEPA may from time to time revise the arrangements mentioned in paragraph (b) above but before making any material change to those arrangements shall consult the Keeper; and

(e) SEPA—

(i) shall secure that the Keeper has, at all reasonable hours, unrestricted access to the records preserved by it;

(ii) may afford members of the public, free of charge or on payment of reasonable charges, facilities for inspecting and for obtaining copies or extracts from those records.

(2) Nothing in subsection (1)(e)(ii) above permits infringement of copyright or contravention of conditions subject to which records are in SEPA's keeping.

(3) Insofar as any provision of any enactment, being a provision which relates to records of a specific kind, is (but for this subsection) inconsistent with subsection (1) above, that subsection is subject to the provision in question.

General powers and duties

31.—(1) The Secretary of State shall from time to time give guidance to SEPA with respect to aims and objectives which he considers it appropriate for SEPA to pursue in the performance of its functions.

Guidance on sustainable development and other aims and objectives.

(2) The guidance given under subsection (1) above must include guidance with respect to the contribution which, having regard to SEPA's responsibilities and resources, the Secretary of State considers it appropriate for SEPA to make, by the performance of its functions, towards attaining the objective of achieving sustainable development.

(3) In performing its functions, SEPA shall have regard to guidance given under this section.

(4) The power to give guidance to SEPA under this section shall be exercisable only after consultation with SEPA and such other bodies or persons as the Secretary of State considers it appropriate to consult in relation to the guidance in question.

(5) A draft of any guidance proposed to be given under this section shall be laid before each House of Parliament and the guidance shall not be given until after the period of 40 days beginning with the day on which the draft was so laid or, if the draft is laid on different days, the later of the two days.

(6) If, within the period mentioned in subsection (5) above, either House resolves that the guidance, the draft of which was laid before it, should not be given, the Secretary of State shall not give that guidance.

(7) In reckoning any period of 40 days for the purposes of subsection (5) or (6) above, no account shall be taken of any time during which Parliament is dissolved or prorogued or during which both Houses are adjourned for more than four days.

(8) The Secretary of State shall arrange for any guidance given under this section to be published in such manner as he considers appropriate.

General environmental and recreational duties.

32.—(1) It shall be the duty of the Secretary of State and of SEPA, in formulating or considering any proposals relating to any functions of SEPA—

    (a) to have regard to the desirability of conserving and enhancing the natural heritage of Scotland;

    (b) to have regard to the desirability of protecting and conserving buildings, sites and objects of archaeological, architectural, engineering or historic interest;

    (c) to take into account any effect which the proposals would have on the natural heritage of Scotland or on any such buildings, sites or objects; and

    (d) to have regard to the social and economic needs of any area or description of area of Scotland and, in particular, to such needs of rural areas.

(2) Subject to subsection (1) above, it shall be the duty of the Secretary of State and of SEPA, in formulating or considering any proposals relating to any functions of SEPA—

    (a) to have regard to the desirability of preserving for the public any freedom of access (including access for recreational purposes) to areas of forest, woodland, mountains, moor, bog, cliff, foreshore, loch or reservoir and other places of natural beauty;

    (b) to have regard to the desirability of maintaining the availability to the public of any facility for visiting or inspecting any building, site or object of archaeological, architectural, engineering or historic interest; and

    (c) to take into account any effect which the proposals would have on any such freedom of access or on the availability of any such facility.

(3) In this section—

"building" includes structure; and

1991 c. 28.

"the natural heritage of Scotland" has the same meaning as in section 1(3) of the Natural Heritage (Scotland) Act 1991.

General duties with respect to pollution control.

33.—(1) SEPA's pollution control powers shall be exercisable for the purpose of preventing or minimising, or remedying or mitigating the effects of, pollution of the environment.

(2) SEPA shall, for the purpose—

    (a) of facilitating the carrying out of its pollution control functions; or

(b) of enabling it to form an opinion of the general state of pollution of the environment,

compile information relating to such pollution (whether the information is acquired by SEPA carrying out observations or is obtained in any other way).

(3) If required by the Secretary of State to do so, SEPA shall—

(a) carry out assessments (whether generally or for such particular purpose as may be specified in the requirement) of the effect, or likely effect, on the environment of existing or potential levels of pollution of the environment and report its findings to the Secretary of State; or

(b) prepare and send to the Secretary of State a report identifying—

(i) the options which SEPA considers to be available for preventing or minimising, or remedying or mitigating the effects of, pollution of the environment, whether generally or in cases or circumstances specified in the requirement; and

(ii) the costs and benefits of such options as are identified by SEPA pursuant to sub-paragraph (i) above.

(4) SEPA shall follow developments in technology and techniques for preventing or minimising, or remedying or mitigating the effects of, pollution of the environment.

(5) In this section, "pollution control powers" and "pollution control functions" in relation to SEPA, mean respectively its powers or its functions under or by virtue of—

(a) the Alkali, &c. Works Regulation Act 1906;   1906 c. 14.

(b) Part III of the 1951 Act, the Rivers (Prevention of Pollution) (Scotland) Act 1965 and Parts I, IA and II of the Control of Pollution Act 1974;   1965 c. 13.
1974 c. 40.

(c) Part I of the Health and Safety at Work etc. Act 1974;   1974 c. 37.

(d) the Control of Pollution (Amendment) Act 1989;   1989 c. 14.

(e) Parts I, II and IIA of the 1990 Act;

(f) section 19 of the Clean Air Act 1993;   1993 c. 11.

(g) the Radioactive Substances Act 1993; and   1993 c. 12.

(h) regulations made by virtue of section 2(2) of the European Communities Act 1972, to the extent that the regulations relate to pollution.   1972 c. 68.

34.—(1) It shall be the duty of SEPA—   General duties with respect to water.

(a) to promote the cleanliness of—

(i) rivers, other inland waters and ground waters in Scotland; and

(ii) the tidal waters of Scotland; and

(b) to conserve so far as practicable the water resources of Scotland.

(2) Without prejudice to section 32 above, it shall be the duty of SEPA, to such extent as it considers desirable, generally to promote—

(a) the conservation and enhancement of the natural beauty and amenity of inland and coastal waters and of land associated with such waters; and

(b) the conservation of flora and fauna which are dependent on an aquatic environment.

1980 c. 45.

(3) Subsection (1) above is without prejudice to section 1 of the Water (Scotland) Act 1980 (general duties of Secretary of State and water authorities as respects water resources and supplies).

(4) In subsection (1) above, "tidal waters" means any part of the sea or the tidal part of any river, watercourse or inland water (whether natural or artificial) and includes the waters of any enclosed dock which adjoins tidal waters.

Environmental duties as respects Natural Heritage Areas and sites of special interest.

1991 c. 28.

35.—(1) Where an area of land—

(a) has been designated, under section 6(2) of the Natural Heritage (Scotland) Act 1991 (in this section referred to as "the 1991 Act") as a Natural Heritage Area; or

(b) is, in the opinion of Scottish Natural Heritage (in this section referred to as "SNH"), of special interest by reason of its flora, fauna or geological or physiographical features,

and SNH consider that it may at any time be affected by schemes, works, operations or activities of SEPA or by an authorisation given by SEPA, SNH shall give notice to SEPA in accordance with subsection (2) below.

(2) A notice under subsection (1) above shall specify—

(a) in the case of an area of land mentioned in paragraph (a) of that subsection, SNH's reasons for considering that the area is of outstanding value to the natural heritage of Scotland; and

(b) in the case of an area of land mentioned in paragraph (b) of that subsection, SNH's reasons for holding the opinion there mentioned.

(3) Where SNH has given notice under subsection (1) above in respect of an area of land and—

(a) in the case of an area of land mentioned in paragraph (a) of that subsection, the designation is cancelled or varied under section 6(7) of the 1991 Act; or

(b) in the case of an area of land mentioned in paragraph (b) of that subsection, SNH ceases to be of the opinion there mentioned,

SNH shall forthwith notify SEPA of that fact.

(4) Where SEPA has received notice under subsection (1) above with respect to any area of land, it shall (unless SNH has given notice under subsection (3) above with respect to the land) consult SNH before carrying out or authorising any schemes, works, operations or activities which appear to SEPA to be likely—

(a) in the case of an area of land mentioned in subsection (1)(a), significantly to prejudice the value of the land, or any part of it, as a Natural Heritage Area; and

(b) in the case of an area of land mentioned in subsection (1)(b), to destroy or damage any of the flora or fauna or features by reason of which SNH formed the opinion there mentioned.

(5) Subsection (4) above shall not apply in relation to anything done in an emergency if particulars of what is done and of the emergency are notified by SEPA to SNH as soon as practicable after the thing is done.

(6) In this section, "authorisation" includes any consent, licence or permission.

(7) Any expression used in this section and in Part I of the 1991 Act and not defined in this Act shall be construed in accordance with that Part.

36.—(1) The Secretary of State shall have power by order to approve any code of practice issued (whether by him or by another person) for the purpose of—

Codes of practice with respect to environmental and recreational duties.

(a) giving practical guidance to SEPA with respect to any of the matters for the purposes of which sections 32, 34(2) and 35 above have effect; and

(b) promoting what appear to him to be desirable practices by SEPA with respect to those matters,

and may at any time by such an order approve a modification of such a code or withdraw his approval of such a code or modification.

(2) In discharging its duties under section 32, 34(2) or 35 above, SEPA shall have regard to any code of practice, and any modifications of a code of practice, for the time being approved under this section.

(3) The Secretary of State shall not make an order under this section unless he has first consulted—

(a) SEPA;

(b) Scottish Natural Heritage;

(c) Scottish Enterprise;

(d) Highlands and Islands Enterprise;

(e) the East of Scotland Water Authority;

(f) the West of Scotland Water Authority;

(g) the North of Scotland Water Authority; and

(h) such other persons as he considers it appropriate to consult.

(4) The power of the Secretary of State to make an order under this section shall be exercisable by statutory instrument; and any statutory instrument containing such an order shall be subject to annulment in pursuance of a resolution of either House of Parliament.

CHAPTER III

MISCELLANEOUS, GENERAL AND SUPPLEMENTAL PROVISIONS RELATING TO THE NEW AGENCIES

Additional general powers and duties

37.—(1) Each new Agency (that is to say, in this Part, the Agency or SEPA)—

Incidental general functions.

(a) may do anything which, in its opinion, is calculated to facilitate, or is conducive or incidental to, the carrying out of its functions; and

(b) without prejudice to the generality of that power, may, for the purposes of, or in connection with, the carrying out of those functions, acquire and dispose of land and other property and carry out such engineering or building operations as it considers appropriate;

and the Agency may institute criminal proceedings in England and Wales.

(2) It shall be the duty of each new Agency to provide the Secretary of State or the Minister with such advice and assistance as he may request.

(3) Subject to subsection (4) below, each new Agency may provide for any person, whether in or outside the United Kingdom, advice or assistance, including training facilities, as respects any matter in which that new Agency has skill or experience.

(4) Without prejudice to any power of either new Agency apart from subsection (3) above to provide advice or assistance of the kind mentioned in that subsection, the power conferred by that subsection shall not be exercised in a case where the person for whom the advice or assistance is provided is outside the United Kingdom, except with the consent in writing of the appropriate Minister which consent may be given subject to such conditions as the Minister giving it thinks fit.

(5) Each new Agency—

(a) shall make arrangements for the carrying out of research and related activities (whether by itself or by others) in respect of matters to which its functions relate; and

(b) may make the results of any such research or related activities available to any person in return for payment of such fee as it considers appropriate.

(6) Subsection (5) above shall not be taken as preventing a new Agency from making the results of any research available to the public free of charge whenever it considers it appropriate to do so.

(7) Each new Agency may by agreement with any person charge that person a fee in respect of work done, or services or facilities provided, as a result of a request made by him for advice or assistance, whether of a general or specific character, in connection with any matter involving or relating to environmental licences.

(8) Subsection (7) above—

(a) is without prejudice to the generality of the powers of either new Agency to make charges; but

(b) is subject to any such express provision with respect to charging by the new Agency in question as is contained in the other provisions of this Part or in any other enactment.

(9) In this section "engineering or building operations", without prejudice to the generality of that expression, includes—

(a) the construction, alteration, improvement, maintenance or demolition of any building or structure or of any reservoir, watercourse, dam, weir, well, borehole or other works; and

(b) the installation, modification or removal of any machinery or apparatus.

Delegation of functions by Ministers etc. to the new Agencies.

38.—(1) Agreements may be made between—

(a) any Minister of the Crown, and

(b) a new Agency,

authorising the new Agency (or any of its employees) to exercise on behalf of that Minister, with or without payment, any eligible function of his.

(2) An agreement under subsection (1) above shall not authorise the new Agency (or any of its employees) to exercise on behalf of a Minister of the Crown any function which consists of a power to make regulations or other instruments of a legislative character or a power to fix fees or charges.

(3) An agreement under this section may provide for any eligible function to which it relates to be exercisable by the new Agency in question (or any of its employees)—

(a) either wholly or to such extent as may be specified in the agreement;

(b) either generally or in such cases or areas as may be so specified; or

(c) either unconditionally or subject to the fulfilment of such conditions as may be so specified.

(4) Subsection (5) below applies where, by virtue of an agreement under this section, a new Agency (or any of its employees) is authorised to exercise any function of a Minister of the Crown.

(5) Subject to subsection (6) below, anything done or omitted to be done by the new Agency (or an employee of the new Agency) in, or in connection with, the exercise or purported exercise of the function shall be treated for all purposes as done or omitted to be done by that Minister in his capacity as such.

(6) Subsection (5) above shall not apply—

(a) for the purposes of so much of any agreement made between that Minister and the new Agency as relates to the exercise of the function; or

(b) for the purposes of any criminal proceedings brought in respect of anything done or omitted to be done as mentioned in that subsection.

(7) An agreement under this section shall not prevent a Minister of the Crown exercising any function to which the agreement relates.

(8) Where a Minister of the Crown has power to include, in any arrangements which he makes in relation to the performance by him of an eligible function, provision for the making of payments to him—

(a) by other parties to the arrangements, or

(b) by persons who use any facilities or services provided by him pursuant to the arrangements or in relation to whom the function is otherwise exercisable,

he may include in any such arrangements provision for the making of such payments to him or a new Agency in cases where the new Agency (or any of its employees) acts on his behalf by virtue of an agreement under this section.

(9) The power conferred on a Minister of the Crown by subsection (1) above is in addition to any other power by virtue of which functions of his may be exercised by other persons on his behalf.

(10) In this section—

"eligible function" means any function of a Minister of the Crown which the Secretary of State, having regard to the functions conferred or imposed upon the new Agency in question under or by virtue of this Act or any other enactment, considers can appropriately be exercised by that new Agency (or any of its employees) on behalf of that Minister;

"Minister of the Crown" has the same meaning as in the Ministers of the Crown Act 1975.

1975 c. 26.

General duty of the new Agencies to have regard to costs and benefits in exercising powers.

39.—(1) Each new Agency—

(a) in considering whether or not to exercise any power conferred upon it by or under any enactment, or

(b) in deciding the manner in which to exercise any such power,

shall, unless and to the extent that it is unreasonable for it to do so in view of the nature or purpose of the power or in the circumstances of the particular case, take into account the likely costs and benefits of the exercise or non-exercise of the power or its exercise in the manner in question.

(2) The duty imposed upon a new Agency by subsection (1) above does not affect its obligation, nevertheless, to discharge any duties, comply with any requirements, or pursue any objectives, imposed upon or given to it otherwise than under this section.

Ministerial directions to the new Agencies.

40.—(1) The appropriate Minister may give a new Agency directions of a general or specific character with respect to the carrying out of any of its functions.

(2) The appropriate Minister may give a new Agency such directions of a general or specific character as he considers appropriate for the implementation of—

(a) any obligations of the United Kingdom under the Community Treaties, or

(b) any international agreement to which the United Kingdom is for the time being a party.

(3) Any direction under subsection (2) above shall be published in such manner as the Minister giving it considers appropriate for the purpose of bringing the matters to which it relates to the attention of persons likely to be affected by them; and—

(a) copies of the direction shall be made available to the public; and

(b) notice shall be given—

(i) in the case of a direction given to the Agency, in the London Gazette, or

(ii) in the case of a direction given to SEPA, in the Edinburgh Gazette,

of the giving of the direction and of where a copy of the direction may be obtained.

(4) The provisions of subsection (3) above shall have effect in relation to any direction given to a new Agency under an enactment other than subsection (2) above for the implementation of—

(a) any obligations of the United Kingdom under the Community Treaties, or

(b) any international agreement to which the United Kingdom is for the time being a party,

as those provisions have effect in relation to a direction given under subsection (2) above.

(5) In determining—

(a) any appeal against, or reference or review of, a decision of a new Agency, or

(b) any application transmitted from a new Agency,

the body or person making the determination shall be bound by any direction given under this section or any other enactment by a Minister of the Crown to the new Agency to the same extent as the new Agency.

(6) Any power to give a direction under this section shall be exercisable, except in an emergency, only after consultation with the new Agency concerned.

(7) Any power of the appropriate Minister to give directions to a new Agency otherwise than by virtue of this section shall be without prejudice to any power to give directions conferred by this section.

(8) It is the duty of a new Agency to comply with any direction which is given to that new Agency by a Minister of the Crown under this section or any other enactment.

Charging schemes

41.—(1) Subject to the following provisions of this section and section 42 below—

Power to make schemes imposing charges.

(a) in the case of any particular licence under Chapter II of Part II of the 1991 Act (abstraction and impounding), the Agency may require the payment to it of such charges as may from time to time be prescribed;

(b) in relation to other environmental licences, there shall be charged by and paid to a new Agency such charges as may from time to time be prescribed; and

(c) as a means of recovering costs incurred by it in performing functions conferred by regulations under section 62 of the 1990 Act (dangerous or intractable waste) each of the new Agencies may require the payment to it of such charges as may from time to time be prescribed;

and in this section "prescribed" means specified in, or determined under, a scheme (in this section referred to as a "charging scheme") made under this section by the new Agency in question.

(2) As respects environmental licences, charges may be prescribed in respect of—

(a) the grant or variation of an environmental licence, or any application for, or for a variation of, such a licence;

(b) the subsistence of an environmental licence;

(c) the transfer (where permitted) of an environmental licence to another person, or any application for such a transfer;

(d) the renewal (where permitted) of an environmental licence, or any application for such a renewal;

(e) the surrender (where permitted) of an environmental licence, or any application for such a surrender; or

(f) any application for the revocation (where permitted) of an environmental licence.

(3) A charging scheme may, for the purposes of subsection (2)(b) above, impose—

(a) a single charge in respect of the whole of any relevant licensed period;

(b) separate charges in respect of different parts of any such period; or

(c) both such a single charge and such separate charges;

and in this subsection "relevant licensed period" means the period during which an environmental licence is in force or such part of that period as may be prescribed.

(4) Without prejudice to subsection (7)(a) below, a charging scheme may, as respects environmental licences, provide for different charges to be payable according to—

(a) the description of environmental licence in question;

(b) the description of authorised activity in question;

(c) the scale on which the authorised activity in question is carried on;

(d) the description or amount of the substance to which the authorised activity in question relates;

(e) the number of different authorised activities carried on by the same person.

(5) A charging scheme—

(a) shall specify, in relation to any charge prescribed by the scheme, the description of person who is liable to pay the charge; and

(b) may provide that it shall be a condition of an environmental licence of any particular description that any charge prescribed by a charging scheme in relation to an environmental licence of that description is paid in accordance with the scheme.

(6) Without prejudice to subsection (5)(b) above, if it appears to a new Agency that any charges due and payable to it in respect of the subsistence of an environmental licence have not been paid, it may, in accordance with the appropriate procedure, suspend or revoke the environmental licence to the extent that it authorises the carrying on of an authorised activity.

(7) A charging scheme may—

(a) make different provision for different cases, including different provision in relation to different persons, circumstances or localities;

(b) provide for the times at which, and the manner in which, the charges prescribed by the scheme are to be paid;

(c) revoke or amend any previous charging scheme;

(d) contain supplemental, incidental, consequential or transitional provision for the purposes of the scheme.

(8) If and to the extent that a charging scheme relates to licences under Chapter II of Part II of the 1991 Act (abstraction and impounding), the scheme shall have effect subject to any provision made by or under sections 125 to 130 of that Act (exemption from charges, imposition of special charges for spray irrigation, and charges in respect of abstraction from waters of the British Waterways Board).

(9) A new Agency shall not make a charging scheme unless the provisions of the scheme have been approved by the Secretary of State under section 42 below.

(10) In this section—

"the appropriate procedure" means such procedure as may be specified or described in regulations made for the purpose by the Secretary of State;

"authorised activity" means any activity to which an environmental licence relates.

(11) Any power to make regulations under this section shall be exercisable by statutory instrument; and a statutory instrument containing any such regulations shall be subject to annulment pursuant to a resolution of either House of Parliament.

42.—(1) Before submitting a proposed charging scheme to the Secretary of State for his approval, a new Agency shall, in such manner as it considers appropriate for bringing it to the attention of persons likely to be affected by the scheme, publish a notice—

Approval of charging schemes.

(a) setting out its proposals; and

(b) specifying the period within which representations or objections with respect to the proposals may be made to the Secretary of State.

(2) Where any proposed charging scheme has been submitted to the Secretary of State for his approval, he shall, in determining whether or not to approve the scheme or to approve it subject to modifications,—

(a) consider any representations or objections duly made to him and not withdrawn; and

(b) have regard to the matter specified in subsection (3) below.

(3) The matter mentioned in subsection (2)(b) above is the desirability of ensuring that, in the case of each of the descriptions of environmental licence specified in the paragraphs of the definition of that expression in section 56 below, the amounts recovered by the new Agency in question by way of charges prescribed by charging schemes are the amounts which, taking one year with another, need to be recovered by that new Agency to meet such of the costs and expenses (whether of a revenue or capital nature)—

(a) which it incurs in carrying out its functions,

(b) in the case of environmental licences which are authorisations under section 13(1) of the Radioactive Substances Act 1993—   1993 c. 12.

(i) which the Minister incurs in carrying out his functions under or in consequence of that Act, and

(ii) which the Secretary of State incurs under that Act in carrying out in relation to Scotland or Wales such of his functions under or in consequence of that Act as are exercised by the Minister in relation to England,

as the Secretary of State may consider it appropriate to attribute to the carrying out of those functions in relation to activities to which environmental licences of the description in question relate.

(4) Without prejudice to the generality of the expression "costs and expenses", in determining for the purposes of subsection (3) above the amounts of the costs and expenses which the Secretary of State considers it appropriate to attribute to the carrying out of a new Agency's or the Minister's or the Secretary of State's functions in relation to the activities to which environmental licences of any particular description relate, the Secretary of State—

(a) shall take into account any determination of the new Agency's financial duties under section 44 below; and

(b) may include amounts in respect of the depreciation of, and the provision of a return on, such assets as are held by the new Agency, the Minister or the Secretary of State, as the case may be, for purposes connected with the carrying out of the functions in question.

(5) If and to the extent that a charging scheme relates to any licence under Chapter II of Part II of the 1991 Act (abstraction and impounding), the Secretary of State may consider it appropriate to attribute to the carrying out of the Agency's functions in relation to activities to which such a licence relates any costs and expenses incurred by the Agency in carrying out any of its functions under Part II of that Act or under section 6(2) above.

(6) Subsection (5) above is without prejudice to what costs and expenses the Secretary of State may consider it appropriate to attribute to the carrying out of any functions of a new Agency, the Minister or the Secretary of State in relation to activities to which environmental licences of any particular description relate.

(7) The consent of the Treasury shall be required for the giving of approval to a charging scheme and, if and to the extent that the scheme relates to authorisations by the Agency under section 13 of the Radioactive Substances Act 1993 (disposal of radioactive waste), the consent of the Minister shall also be required.

1993 c. 12.

(8) It shall be the duty of a new Agency to take such steps as it considers appropriate for bringing the provisions of any charging scheme made by it which is for the time being in force to the attention of persons likely to be affected by them.

(9) If and to the extent that any sums recovered by a new Agency by way of charges prescribed by charging schemes may fairly be regarded as so recovered for the purpose of recovering the amount required to meet (whether in whole or in part)—

(a) such of the costs and expenses incurred by the Secretary of State as fall within subsection (3) above, or

(b) such of the costs and expenses incurred by the Minister as fall within that subsection,

those sums shall be paid by that new Agency to the Secretary of State or, as the case may be, to the Minister.

(10) For the purposes of subsection (9) above, any question as to the extent to which any sums may fairly be regarded as recovered for the purpose of recovering the amount required to meet the costs and expenses falling within paragraph (a) or paragraph (b) of that subsection shall be determined—

(a) in the case of costs and expenses falling within paragraph (a) of that subsection, by the Secretary of State; and

(b) in the case of costs and expenses falling within paragraph (b) of that subsection, by the Secretary of State and the Minister.

(11) In this section "charging scheme" has the same meaning as in section 41 above.

Incidental power to impose charges

43. Without prejudice to the generality of its powers by virtue of section 37(1)(a) above and subject to any such express provision with respect to charging by a new Agency as is contained in the preceding provisions of this Chapter or any other enactment, each new Agency shall have power to fix and recover charges for services and facilities provided in the course of carrying out its functions.

Incidental power of the new Agencies to impose charges.

General financial provisions

44.—(1) The appropriate Ministers may—

General financial duties.

(a) after consultation with a new Agency, and

(b) with the approval of the Treasury,

determine the financial duties of that new Agency; and different determinations may be made for different functions and activities of the new Agency.

(2) The appropriate Ministers shall give a new Agency notice of every determination of its financial duties under this section, and such a determination may—

(a) relate to a period beginning before, on, or after, the date on which it is made;

(b)· contain supplemental provisions; and

(c) be varied by a subsequent determination.

(3) The appropriate Minister may, after consultation with the Treasury and a new Agency, give a direction to that new Agency requiring it to pay to him an amount equal to the whole or such part as may be specified in the direction of any sum, or any sum of a description, so specified which is or has been received by that new Agency.

(4) Where it appears to the appropriate Minister that a new Agency has a surplus, whether on capital or revenue account, he may, after consultation with the Treasury and the new Agency, direct the new Agency to pay to him such amount not exceeding the amount of that surplus as may be specified in the direction.

(5) In the case of the Agency—

(a) subsection (1) above is subject to section 118 of the 1991 Act (special duties with respect to flood defence revenue);

(b) subsection (3) above is subject to sections 118(1)(a) and 119(1) of the 1991 Act (special duties with respect to flood defence revenue and funds raised for fishery purposes under local enactments); and

(c) subsection (4) above is subject to sections 118(1)(b) and 119(2) of the 1991 Act (which provide for flood defence revenue and certain funds raised under local enactments to be disregarded in determining whether there is a surplus).

Accounts and records.

45.—(1) Each new Agency shall—

(a) keep proper accounts and proper accounting records; and

(b) prepare in respect of each accounting year a statement of accounts giving a true and fair view of the state of affairs and the income and expenditure of the new Agency.

(2) Every statement of accounts prepared by a new Agency in accordance with this section shall comply with any requirement which the appropriate Ministers have, with the consent of the Treasury, notified in writing to the new Agency and which relates to any of the following matters, namely—

(a) the information to be contained in the statement;

(b) the manner in which that information is to be presented;

(c) the methods and principles according to which the statement is to be prepared.

(3) In this section—

"accounting records", in the case of a new Agency, includes all books, papers and other records of the new Agency relating to, or to matters dealt with in, the accounts required to be kept by virtue of this section;

"accounting year", subject to subsection (4) below, means, in relation to a new Agency, a financial year.

(4) If the Secretary of State so directs in relation to any accounting year of either new Agency, that accounting year shall end with such date other than the next 31st March as may be specified in the direction; and, where the Secretary of State has given such a direction, the following accounting year shall begin with the day after the date so specified and, subject to any further direction under this subsection, shall end with the next 31st March.

Audit.

46.—(1) The accounts of each new Agency shall be audited by an auditor appointed for each accounting year by the Secretary of State.

(2) A person shall not be qualified for appointment under subsection (1) above unless—

1989 c. 40.

(a) he is eligible for appointment as a company auditor under Part II of the Companies Act 1989; and

(b) he would not be ineligible for appointment as company auditor of the new Agency in question by virtue of section 27 of that Act (ineligibility on ground of lack of independence), if that new Agency were a body to which section 384 of the Companies Act 1985 (duty to appoint auditor) applies.

1985 c. 6.

(3) A copy of—

(a) any accounts of a new Agency which are audited under subsection (1) above, and

(b) the report made on those accounts by the auditor,

shall be sent to each of the appropriate Ministers as soon as reasonably practicable after the report is received by the new Agency; and the Secretary of State shall lay before each House of Parliament a copy of those accounts and that report.

(4) The Comptroller and Auditor General—

(a) shall be entitled to inspect the contents of all accounts and accounting records of a new Agency; and

(b) may report to the House of Commons the results of any inspection carried out by him under paragraph (a) above;

and section 6 of the National Audit Act 1983 (examinations of economy, efficiency and effectiveness) accordingly applies to each new Agency.

1983 c. 44.

(5) In this section—

"accounting records" has the same meaning as in section 45 above;

"accounting year" has the same meaning as in section 45 above;

"accounts", in relation to the Agency, includes any statement under section 45 above.

47. The appropriate Minister may, with the approval of the Treasury, make to a new Agency grants of such amounts, and on such terms, as he thinks fit.

Grants to the new Agencies.

48.—(1) Each new Agency shall be entitled to borrow in accordance with the following provisions of this section, but not otherwise.

Borrowing powers.

(2) Subject to subsection (5) below, each new Agency may—

(a) with the consent of the appropriate Minister, and

(b) with the approval of the Treasury,

borrow temporarily in sterling, by way of overdraft or otherwise, from persons other than the appropriate Ministers, such sums as it may require for meeting its obligations and carrying out its functions.

(3) Subject to subsection (5) below, each new Agency may borrow from the appropriate Minister, by way of temporary loan or otherwise, such sums in sterling as it may require for meeting its obligations and carrying out its functions.

(4) Any consent under subsection (2)(a) above may be granted subject to conditions.

(5) The aggregate amount outstanding in respect of the principal of sums borrowed under this section by a new Agency shall not at any time exceed—

(a) in the case of the Agency, £100 million or such greater sum, not exceeding £160 million, as the Ministers may by order specify; or

(b) in the case of SEPA, £5 million or such greater sum, not exceeding £10 million, as the Secretary of State may by order specify.

(6) The power to make an order under subsection (5) above shall be exercisable by statutory instrument; but no order shall be made under that subsection unless a draft of the order has been laid before, and approved by a resolution of, the House of Commons.

Government loans to the new Agencies.

49.—(1) The appropriate Minister may, with the approval of the Treasury, lend to a new Agency any sums which it has power to borrow under section 48(3) above.

(2) Any loan made under this section by one of the appropriate Ministers shall be repaid to him at such times and by such methods, and interest on the loan shall be paid to him at such rates and at such times, as that Minister may with the approval of the Treasury from time to time determine.

(3) If in any financial year any of the appropriate Ministers lends any sums to a new Agency under this section, he shall—

(a) prepare in respect of that financial year an account of the sums so lent by him; and

(b) send that account to the Comptroller and Auditor General before the end of September in the following financial year;

and the form of the account and the manner of preparing it shall be such as the Treasury may direct.

(4) The Comptroller and Auditor General shall examine, certify and report on each account sent to him under this section and shall lay copies of it and of his report before each House of Parliament.

(5) The Treasury may issue to any of the appropriate Ministers—

(a) out of the National Loans Fund, or

(b) out of money provided by Parliament,

such sums as are necessary to enable him to make loans to a new Agency under this section; and any sums received by a Minister of the Crown in pursuance of subsection (2) above shall be paid into the National Loans Fund or, as the case may be, the Consolidated Fund.

Government guarantees of a new Agency's borrowing.

50.—(1) The appropriate Minister may, with the consent of the Treasury, guarantee, in such manner and on such conditions as he may think fit, the repayment of the principal of, the payment of interest on, and the discharge of any other financial obligation in connection with, any sum which a new Agency borrows from any person.

(2) A Minister who gives a guarantee under this section shall forthwith lay a statement of the guarantee before each House of Parliament.

(3) Where any sum is paid out for fulfilling a guarantee under this section, the Minister who gave the guarantee shall, as soon as reasonably practicable after the end of each financial year (beginning with that in which the sum is paid out and ending with that in which all liability in

respect of the principal of the sum and in respect of interest on it is finally discharged), lay before each House of Parliament a statement relating to that sum.

(4) If any sums are paid out in fulfilment of a guarantee under this section, the new Agency which borrowed the sum by reference to which the guarantee was given shall make to the Minister who gave the guarantee, at such times and in such manner as he may from time to time direct,—

    (a) payments of such amounts as he may so direct in or towards repayment of the sums so paid out; and

    (b) payments of interest, at such rate as he may so direct, on what is outstanding for the time being in respect of sums so paid out;

and the consent of the Treasury shall be required for the giving of a direction under this subsection.

Information

51.—(1) A new Agency shall furnish the appropriate Minister with all such information as he may reasonably require relating to—

    (a) the new Agency's property;

    (b) the carrying out and proposed carrying out of its functions; and

    (c) its responsibilities generally.

Provision of information by the new Agencies.

(2) Information required under this section shall be furnished in such form and manner, and be accompanied or supplemented by such explanations, as the appropriate Minister may reasonably require.

(3) The information which a new Agency may be required to furnish to the appropriate Minister under this section shall include information which, although it is not in the possession of the new Agency or would not otherwise come into the possession of the new Agency, is information which it is reasonable to require the new Agency to obtain.

(4) A requirement for the purposes of this section shall be contained in a direction which—

    (a) may describe the information to be furnished in such manner as the Minister giving the direction considers appropriate; and

    (b) may require the information to be furnished on a particular occasion, in particular circumstances or from time to time.

(5) For the purposes of this section a new Agency shall—

    (a) permit any person authorised for the purpose by the appropriate Minister to inspect and make copies of the contents of any accounts or other records of the new Agency; and

    (b) give such explanation of them as that person or the appropriate Minister may reasonably require.

52.—(1) As soon as reasonably practicable after the end of each financial year, each new Agency shall prepare a report on its activities during that year and shall send a copy of that report to each of the appropriate Ministers.

Annual report.

(2) Every such report shall set out any directions under section 40 above which have been given to the new Agency in question during the year to which the report relates, other than directions given under

subsection (1) of that section which are identified to that new Agency in writing by the appropriate Minister as being directions the disclosure of which would, in his opinion, be contrary to the interests of national security.

(3) The Secretary of State shall lay a copy of every such report before each House of Parliament and shall arrange for copies of every such report to be published in such manner as he considers appropriate.

(4) A new Agency's annual report shall be in such form and contain such information as may be specified in any direction given to the new Agency by the appropriate Ministers.

Supplemental provisions

Inquiries and other hearings.

53.—(1) Without prejudice to any other provision of this Act or any other enactment by virtue of which an inquiry or other hearing is authorised or required to be held, the appropriate Minister may cause an inquiry or other hearing to be held if it appears to him expedient to do so—

(a) in connection with any of the functions of a new Agency; or

(b) in connection with any of his functions in relation to a new Agency.

1972 c. 70.

(2) Subsections (2) to (5) of section 250 of the Local Government Act 1972 (which contain supplementary provisions with respect to local inquiries held in pursuance of that section) shall apply to inquiries or other hearings under this section or any other enactment—

(a) in connection with any of the functions of the Agency, or

(b) in connection with any functions of the Secretary of State or the Minister in relation to the Agency,

as they apply to inquiries under that section, but taking the reference in subsection (4) of that section to a local authority as including a reference to the Agency.

1973 c. 65.

(3) The provisions of subsections (2) to (8) of section 210 of the Local Government (Scotland) Act 1973 (which relate to the holding of local inquiries) shall apply to inquiries or other hearings held under this section or any other enactment—

(a) in connection with any of the functions of SEPA, or

(b) in connection with any functions of the Secretary of State in relation to SEPA,

as they apply to inquiries held under that section.

Appearance in legal proceedings.

54. In England and Wales, a person who is authorised by the Agency to prosecute on its behalf in proceedings before a magistrates' court shall be entitled to prosecute in any such proceedings although not of counsel or a solicitor.

Continuity of exercise of functions: the new Agencies.

55.—(1) The abolition of—

(a) the National Rivers Authority,

(b) the London Waste Regulation Authority, or

(c) a river purification board,

shall not affect the validity of anything done by that Authority or board before the transfer date.

(2) Anything which, at the transfer date, is in the process of being done by or in relation to a transferor in the exercise of, or in connection with, any of the transferred functions may be continued by or in relation to the transferee.

(3) Anything done by or in relation to a transferor before the transfer date in the exercise of, or otherwise in connection with, any of the transferred functions, shall, so far as is required for continuing its effect on and after that date, have effect as if done by or in relation to the transferee.

(4) Subsection (3) above applies in particular to—

(a) any decision, determination, declaration, designation, agreement or instrument made by a transferor;

(b) any regulations or byelaws made by a transferor;

(c) any licence, permission, consent, approval, authorisation, exemption, dispensation or relaxation granted by or to a transferor;

(d) any notice, direction or certificate given by or to a transferor;

(e) any application, request, proposal or objection made by or to a transferor;

(f) any condition or requirement imposed by or on a transferor;

(g) any fee or charge paid by or to a transferor;

(h) any appeal allowed by or in favour of or against a transferor;

(j) any proceedings instituted by or against a transferor.

(5) Any reference in the foregoing provisions of this section to anything done by or in relation to a transferor includes a reference to anything which, by virtue of any enactment, is treated as having been done by or in relation to that transferor.

(6) Any reference to a transferor in any document constituting or relating to anything to which the foregoing provisions of this section apply shall, so far as is required for giving effect to those provisions, be construed as a reference to the transferee.

(7) The foregoing provisions of this section—

(a) are without prejudice to any provision made by this Act in relation to any particular functions; and

(b) shall not be construed as continuing in force any contract of employment made by a transferor;

and the Secretary of State may, in relation to any particular functions, by order exclude, modify or supplement any of the foregoing provisions of this section or make such other transitional provisions as he thinks necessary or expedient.

(8) Where, by virtue of any provision of Schedule 15 to this Act, the Minister is the transferor in the case of any functions, he shall have the same powers under subsection (7) above in relation to those functions as the Secretary of State.

(9) The power to make an order under subsection (7) above shall be exercisable by statutory instrument; and any statutory instrument containing such an order shall be subject to annulment pursuant to a resolution of either House of Parliament.

(10) In this section—

"the transferee", in the case of any transferred functions, means the new Agency whose functions they become by virtue of any provision made by or under this Act;

"transferred functions" means any functions which, by virtue of any provision made by or under this Act, become functions of a new Agency; and

"transferor" means any body or person any or all of whose functions become, by virtue of any provision made by or under this Act, functions of a new Agency.

Interpretation of
Part I.

56.—(1) In this Part of this Act, except where the context otherwise requires—

1951 c. 66.

"the 1951 Act" means the Rivers (Prevention of Pollution) (Scotland) Act 1951;

1990 c. 43.

"the 1990 Act" means the Environmental Protection Act 1990;

1991 c. 57.

"the 1991 Act" means the Water Resources Act 1991;

"the appropriate Minister"—

(a) in the case of the Agency, means the Secretary of State or the Minister; and

(b) in the case of SEPA, means the Secretary of State;

"the appropriate Ministers"—

(a) in the case of the Agency, means the Secretary of State and the Minister; and

(b) in the case of SEPA, means the Secretary of State;

"conservancy authority" has the meaning given by section 221(1) of the 1991 Act;

"costs" includes—

(a) costs to any person; and

(b) costs to the environment;

"disposal authority"—

1974 c. 40.

(a) in the application of this Part in relation to the Agency, has the same meaning as it has in Part I of the Control of Pollution Act 1974 by virtue of section 30(1) of that Act; and

(b) in the application of this Part in relation to SEPA, has the meaning assigned to it by section 30(2) of that Act;

"the environment" has the same meaning as in Part I of the 1990 Act;

"environmental licence", in the application of this Part in relation to the Agency, means any of the following—

1989 c. 14.

(a) registration of a person as a carrier of controlled waste under section 2 of the Control of Pollution (Amendment) Act 1989,

(b) an authorisation under Part I of the 1990 Act, other than any such authorisation granted by a local enforcing authority,

(c) a waste management licence under Part II of that Act,

(d) a licence under Chapter II of Part II of the 1991 Act,

(e) a consent for the purposes of section 88(1)(a), 89(4)(a) or 90 of that Act,

(f) registration under the Radioactive Substances Act 1993,   1993 c. 12.

(g) an authorisation under that Act,

(h) registration of a person as a broker of controlled waste under the Waste Management Licensing Regulations 1994,   S.I. 1994/1056.

(j) registration in respect of an activity falling within paragraph 45(1) or (2) of Schedule 3 to those Regulations,

so far as having effect in relation to England and Wales;

"environmental licence", in the application of this Part in relation to SEPA, means any of the following—

(a) a consent under Part II of the Control of Pollution Act 1974,   1974 c. 40.

(b) registration of a person as a carrier of controlled waste under section 2 of the Control of Pollution (Amendment) Act 1989,   1989 c. 14.

(c) an authorisation under Part I of the 1990 Act,

(d) a waste management licence under Part II of that Act,

(e) a licence under section 17 of the Natural Heritage (Scotland) Act 1991,   1991 c. 28.

(f) registration under the Radioactive Substances Act 1993,

(g) an authorisation under that Act,

(h) registration of a person as a broker of controlled waste under the Waste Management Licensing Regulations 1994,

(j) registration in respect of an activity falling within paragraph 45(1) or (2) of Schedule 3 to those Regulations,

so far as having effect in relation to Scotland;

"flood defence functions", in relation to the Agency, has the same meaning as in the 1991 Act;

"harbour authority" has the meaning given by section 221(1) of the 1991 Act;

"local authority", in the application of this Part in relation to SEPA, means a district or islands council in Scotland;

"the Minister" means the Minister of Agriculture, Fisheries and Food;

"the Ministers" means the Secretary of State and the Minister;

"navigation authority" has the meaning given by section 221(1) of the 1991 Act;

"new Agency" means the Agency or SEPA;

"river purification authority" means a river purification authority within the meaning of the 1951 Act;

1973 c. 65.

"river purification board" means a river purification board established by virtue of section 135 of the Local Government (Scotland) Act 1973;

"the transfer date" means such date as the Secretary of State may by order made by statutory instrument appoint as the transfer date for the purposes of this Part; and different dates may be appointed for the purposes of this Part—

(i) as it applies for or in connection with transfers under or by virtue of Chapter I above, and

(ii) as it applies for or in connection with transfers under or by virtue of Chapter II above;

"waste regulation authority"—

(a) in the application of this Part in relation to the Agency, means any authority in England or Wales which, by virtue of section 30(1) of the 1990 Act, is a waste regulation authority for the purposes of Part II of that Act; and

(b) in the application of this Part in relation to SEPA, means any council which, by virtue of section 30(1)(g) of the 1990 Act, is a waste regulation authority for the purposes of Part II of that Act.

(2) In relation to any time on or after 1st April 1996—

(a) subsection (1) above shall have effect as if, in the definition of "local authority", for the words "district or islands council in Scotland" there were substituted the words "council constituted under section 2 of the Local Government etc. (Scotland) Act 1994"; and

1994 c. 39.

(b) in section 22(3)(a)(iv) above the reference to an islands council shall be construed as a reference to a council mentioned in section 3(1) of the Local Government etc. (Scotland) Act 1994.

(3) Where by virtue of any provision of this Part any function of a Minister of the Crown is exercisable concurrently by different Ministers, that function shall also be exercisable jointly by any two or more of those Ministers.

PART II

CONTAMINATED LAND AND ABANDONED MINES

Contaminated land.
1990 c. 43.

57. After section 78 of the Environmental Protection Act 1990 there shall be inserted—

"PART IIA

CONTAMINATED LAND

Preliminary.

78A.—(1) The following provisions have effect for the interpretation of this Part.

(2) "Contaminated land" is any land which appears to the local authority in whose area it is situated to be in such a condition, by reason of substances in, on or under the land, that—

(a) significant harm is being caused or there is a significant possibility of such harm being caused; or

(b) pollution of controlled waters is being, or is likely to be, caused;

and, in determining whether any land appears to be such land, a local authority shall, subject to subsection (5) below, act in accordance with guidance issued by the Secretary of State in accordance with section 78YA below with respect to the manner in which that determination is to be made.

(3) A "special site" is any contaminated land—

(a) which has been designated as such a site by virtue of section 78C(7) or 78D(6) below; and

(b) whose designation as such has not been terminated by the appropriate Agency under section 78Q(4) below.

(4) "Harm" means harm to the health of living organisms or other interference with the ecological systems of which they form part and, in the case of man, includes harm to his property.

(5) The questions—

(a) what harm is to be regarded as "significant",

(b) whether the possibility of significant harm being caused is "significant",

(c) whether pollution of controlled waters is being, or is likely to be caused,

shall be determined in accordance with guidance issued for the purpose by the Secretary of State in accordance with section 78YA below.

(6) Without prejudice to the guidance that may be issued under subsection (5) above, guidance under paragraph (a) of that subsection may make provision for different degrees of importance to be assigned to, or for the disregard of,—

(a) different descriptions of living organisms or ecological systems;

(b) different descriptions of places; or

(c) different descriptions of harm to health or property, or other interference;

and guidance under paragraph (b) of that subsection may make provision for different degrees of possibility to be regarded as "significant" (or as not being "significant") in relation to different descriptions of significant harm.

(7) "Remediation" means—

(a) the doing of anything for the purpose of assessing the condition of—

(i) the contaminated land in question;

(ii) any controlled waters affected by that land; or

(iii) any land adjoining or adjacent to that land;

(b) the doing of any works, the carrying out of any operations or the taking of any steps in relation to any such land or waters for the purpose—

(i) of preventing or minimising, or remedying or mitigating the effects of, any significant harm, or any pollution of controlled waters, by reason of which the contaminated land is such land; or

(ii) of restoring the land or waters to their former state; or

(c) the making of subsequent inspections from time to time for the purpose of keeping under review the condition of the land or waters;

and cognate expressions shall be construed accordingly.

(8) Controlled waters are "affected by" contaminated land if (and only if) it appears to the enforcing authority that the contaminated land in question is, for the purposes of subsection (2) above, in such a condition, by reason of substances in, on or under the land, that pollution of those waters is being, or is likely to be caused.

(9) The following expressions have the meaning respectively assigned to them—

"the appropriate Agency" means—

(a) in relation to England and Wales, the Environment Agency;

(b) in relation to Scotland, the Scottish Environment Protection Agency;

"appropriate person" means any person who is an appropriate person, determined in accordance with section 78F below, to bear responsibility for any thing which is to be done by way of remediation in any particular case;

"charging notice" has the meaning given by section 78P(3)(b) below;

"controlled waters"—

1991 c. 57.

(a) in relation to England and Wales, has the same meaning as in Part III of the Water Resources Act 1991; and

1974 c. 40.

(b) in relation to Scotland, has the same meaning as in section 30A of the Control of Pollution Act 1974;

1970 c. 35.

"creditor" has the same meaning as in the Conveyancing and Feudal Reform (Scotland) Act 1970;

"enforcing authority" means—

(a) in relation to a special site, the appropriate Agency;

(b) in relation to contaminated land other than a special site, the local authority in whose area the land is situated;

"heritable security" has the same meaning as in the Conveyancing and Feudal Reform (Scotland) Act 1970;

1970 c. 35.

"local authority" in relation to England and Wales means—

> (a) any unitary authority;

> (b) any district council, so far as it is not a unitary authority;

> (c) the Common Council of the City of London and, as respects the Temples, the Sub-Treasurer of the Inner Temple and the Under-Treasurer of the Middle Temple respectively;

and in relation to Scotland means a council for an area constituted under section 2 of the Local Government etc. (Scotland) Act 1994;

1994 c. 39.

"notice" means notice in writing;

"notification" means notification in writing;

"owner", in relation to any land in England and Wales, means a person (other than a mortgagee not in possession) who, whether in his own right or as trustee for any other person, is entitled to receive the rack rent of the land, or, where the land is not let at a rack rent, would be so entitled if it were so let;

"owner", in relation to any land in Scotland, means a person (other than a creditor in a heritable security not in possession of the security subjects) for the time being entitled to receive or who would, if the land were let, be entitled to receive, the rents of the land in connection with which the word is used and includes a trustee, factor, guardian or curator and in the case of public or municipal land includes the persons to whom the management of the land is entrusted;

"pollution of controlled waters" means the entry into controlled waters of any poisonous, noxious or polluting matter or any solid waste matter;

"prescribed" means prescribed by regulations;

"regulations" means regulations made by the Secretary of State;

"remediation declaration" has the meaning given by section 78H(6) below;

"remediation notice" has the meaning given by section 78E(1) below;

"remediation statement" has the meaning given by section 78H(7) below;

"required to be designated as a special site" shall be construed in accordance with section 78C(8) below;

"substance" means any natural or artificial substance, whether in solid or liquid form or in the form of a gas or vapour;

"unitary authority" means—

(a) the council of a county, so far as it is the council of an area for which there are no district councils;

(b) the council of any district comprised in an area for which there is no county council;

(c) the council of a London borough;

(d) the council of a county borough in Wales.

Identification of contaminated land.

78B.—(1) Every local authority shall cause its area to be inspected from time to time for the purpose—

(a) of identifying contaminated land; and

(b) of enabling the authority to decide whether any such land is land which is required to be designated as a special site.

(2) In performing its functions under subsection (1) above a local authority shall act in accordance with any guidance issued for the purpose by the Secretary of State in accordance with section 78YA below.

(3) If a local authority identifies any contaminated land in its area, it shall give notice of that fact to—

(a) the appropriate Agency;

(b) the owner of the land;

(c) any person who appears to the authority to be in occupation of the whole or any part of the land; and

(d) each person who appears to the authority to be an appropriate person;

and any notice given under this subsection shall state by virtue of which of paragraphs (a) to (d) above it is given.

(4) If, at any time after a local authority has given any person a notice pursuant to subsection (3)(d) above in respect of any land, it appears to the enforcing authority that another person is an appropriate person, the enforcing authority shall give notice to that other person—

(a) of the fact that the local authority has identified the land in question as contaminated land; and

(b) that he appears to the enforcing authority to be an appropriate person.

Identification and designation of special sites.

78C.—(1) If at any time it appears to a local authority that any contaminated land in its area might be land which is required to be designated as a special site, the authority—

(a) shall decide whether or not the land is land which is required to be so designated; and

(b) if the authority decides that the land is land which is required to be so designated, shall give notice of that decision to the relevant persons.

(2) For the purposes of this section, "the relevant persons" at any time in the case of any land are the persons who at that time fall within paragraphs (a) to (d) below, that is to say—

(a) the appropriate Agency;

(b) the owner of the land;

(c) any person who appears to the local authority concerned to be in occupation of the whole or any part of the land; and

(d) each person who appears to that authority to be an appropriate person.

(3) Before making a decision under paragraph (a) of subsection (1) above in any particular case, a local authority shall request the advice of the appropriate Agency, and in making its decision shall have regard to any advice given by that Agency in response to the request.

(4) If at any time the appropriate Agency considers that any contaminated land is land which is required to be designated as a special site, that Agency may give notice of that fact to the local authority in whose area the land is situated.

(5) Where notice under subsection (4) above is given to a local authority, the authority shall decide whether the land in question—

(a) is land which is required to be designated as a special site, or

(b) is not land which is required to be so designated,

and shall give notice of that decision to the relevant persons.

(6) Where a local authority makes a decision falling within subsection (1)(b) or (5)(a) above, the decision shall, subject to section 78D below, take effect on the day after whichever of the following events first occurs, that is to say—

. (a) the expiration of the period of twenty-one days beginning with the day on which the notice required by virtue of subsection (1)(b) or, as the case may be, (5)(a) above is given to the appropriate Agency; or

(b) if the appropriate Agency gives notification to the local authority in question that it agrees with the decision, the giving of that notification;

and where a decision takes effect by virtue of this subsection, the local authority shall give notice of that fact to the relevant persons.

(7) Where a decision that any land is land which is required to be designated as a special site takes effect in accordance with subsection (6) above, the notice given under subsection (1)(b) or, as the case may be, (5)(a) above shall have effect, as from the time when the decision takes effect, as the designation of that land as such a site.

(8) For the purposes of this Part, land is required to be designated as a special site if, and only if, it is land of a description prescribed for the purposes of this subsection.

(9) Regulations under subsection (8) above may make different provision for different cases or circumstances or different areas or localities and may, in particular, describe land by reference to the area or locality in which it is situated.

(10) Without prejudice to the generality of his power to prescribe any description of land for the purposes of subsection (8) above, the Secretary of State, in deciding whether to prescribe a particular description of contaminated land for those purposes, may, in particular, have regard to—

(a) whether land of the description in question appears to him to be land which is likely to be in such a condition, by reason of substances in, on or under the land that—

(i) serious harm would or might be caused, or

(ii) serious pollution of controlled waters would be, or would be likely to be, caused; or

(b) whether the appropriate Agency is likely to have expertise in dealing with the kind of significant harm, or pollution of controlled waters, by reason of which land of the description in question is contaminated land.

Referral of special site decisions to the Secretary of State.

78D.—(1) In any case where—

(a) a local authority gives notice of a decision to the appropriate Agency pursuant to subsection (1)(b) or (5)(b) of section 78C above, but

(b) before the expiration of the period of twenty-one days beginning with the day on which that notice is so given, that Agency gives the local authority notice that it disagrees with the decision, together with a statement of its reasons for disagreeing,

the authority shall refer the decision to the Secretary of State and shall send to him a statement of its reasons for reaching the decision.

(2) Where the appropriate Agency gives notice to a local authority under paragraph (b) of subsection (1) above, it shall also send to the Secretary of State a copy of the notice and of the statement given under that paragraph.

(3) Where a local authority refers a decision to the Secretary of State under subsection (1) above, it shall give notice of that fact to the relevant persons.

(4) Where a decision of a local authority is referred to the Secretary of State under subsection (1) above, he—

(a) may confirm or reverse the decision with respect to the whole or any part of the land to which it relates; and

(b) shall give notice of his decision on the referral—

(i) to the relevant persons; and

(ii) to the local authority.

(5) Where a decision of a local authority is referred to the Secretary of State under subsection (1) above, the decision shall not take effect until the day after that on which the Secretary of State gives the notice required by subsection (4) above to the persons there mentioned and shall then take effect as confirmed or reversed by him.

(6) Where a decision which takes effect in accordance with subsection (5) above is to the effect that at least some land is land which is required to be designated as a special site, the notice given under subsection (4)(b) above shall have effect, as from the time when the decision takes effect, as the designation of that land as such a site.

(7) In this section "the relevant persons" has the same meaning as in section 78C above.

Duty of enforcing authority to require remediation of contaminated land etc.

78E.—(1) In any case where—

(a) any land has been designated as a special site by virtue of section 78C(7) or 78D(6) above, or

(b) a local authority has identified any contaminated land (other than a special site) in its area,

the enforcing authority shall, in accordance with such procedure as may be prescribed and subject to the following provisions of this Part, serve on each person who is an appropriate person a notice (in this Part referred to as a "remediation notice") specifying what that person is to do by way of remediation and the periods within which he is required to do each of the things so specified.

(2) Different remediation notices requiring the doing of different things by way of remediation may be served on different persons in consequence of the presence of different substances in, on or under any land or waters.

(3) Where two or more persons are appropriate persons in relation to any particular thing which is to be done by way of remediation, the remediation notice served on each of them shall state the proportion, determined under section 78F(7) below, of the cost of doing that thing which each of them respectively is liable to bear.

(4) The only things by way of remediation which the enforcing authority may do, or require to be done, under or by virtue of this Part are things which it considers reasonable, having regard to—

(a) the cost which is likely to be involved; and

(b) the seriousness of the harm, or pollution of controlled waters, in question.

(5) In determining for any purpose of this Part—

(a) what is to be done (whether by an appropriate person, the enforcing authority or any other person) by way of remediation in any particular case,

(b) the standard to which any land is, or waters are, to be remediated pursuant to the notice, or

(c) what is, or is not, to be regarded as reasonable for the purposes of subsection (4) above,

the enforcing authority shall have regard to any guidance issued for the purpose by the Secretary of State.

(6) Regulations may make provision for or in connection with—

(a) the form or content of remediation notices; or

(b) any steps of a procedural nature which are to be taken in connection with, or in consequence of, the service of a remediation notice.

Determination of the appropriate person to bear responsibility for remediation.

78F.—(1) This section has effect for the purpose of determining who is the appropriate person to bear responsibility for any particular thing which the enforcing authority determines is to be done by way of remediation in any particular case.

(2) Subject to the following provisions of this section, any person, or any of the persons, who caused or knowingly permitted the substances, or any of the substances, by reason of which the contaminated land in question is such land to be in, on or under that land is an appropriate person.

(3) A person shall only be an appropriate person by virtue of subsection (2) above in relation to things which are to be done by way of remediation which are to any extent referable to substances which he caused or knowingly permitted to be present in, on or under the contaminated land in question.

(4) If no person has, after reasonable inquiry, been found who is by virtue of subsection (2) above an appropriate person to bear responsibility for the things which are to be done by way of remediation, the owner or occupier for the time being of the contaminated land in question is an appropriate person.

(5) If, in consequence of subsection (3) above, there are things which are to be done by way of remediation in relation to which no person has, after reasonable inquiry,

been found who is an appropriate person by virtue of subsection (2) above, the owner or occupier for the time being of the contaminated land in question is an appropriate person in relation to those things.

(6) Where two or more persons would, apart from this subsection, be appropriate persons in relation to any particular thing which is to be done by way of remediation, the enforcing authority shall determine in accordance with guidance issued for the purpose by the Secretary of State whether any, and if so which, of them is to be treated as not being an appropriate person in relation to that thing.

(7) Where two or more persons are appropriate persons in relation to any particular thing which is to be done by way of remediation, they shall be liable to bear the cost of doing that thing in proportions determined by the enforcing authority in accordance with guidance issued for the purpose by the Secretary of State.

(8) Any guidance issued for the purposes of subsection (6) or (7) above shall be issued in accordance with section 78YA below.

(9) A person who has caused or knowingly permitted any substance ("substance A") to be in, on or under any land shall also be taken for the purposes of this section to have caused or knowingly permitted there to be in, on or under that land any substance which is there as a result of a chemical reaction or biological process affecting substance A.

(10) A thing which is to be done by way of remediation may be regarded for the purposes of this Part as referable to the presence of any substance notwithstanding that the thing in question would not have to be done—

    (a) in consequence only of the presence of that substance in any quantity; or

    (b) in consequence only of the quantity of that substance which any particular person caused or knowingly permitted to be present.

Grant of, and compensation for, rights of entry etc.

78G.—(1) A remediation notice may require an appropriate person to do things by way of remediation, notwithstanding that he is not entitled to do those things.

(2) Any person whose consent is required before any thing required by a remediation notice may be done shall grant, or join in granting, such rights in relation to any of the relevant land or waters as will enable the appropriate person to comply with any requirements imposed by the remediation notice.

(3) Before serving a remediation notice, the enforcing authority shall reasonably endeavour to consult every person who appears to the authority—

    (a) to be the owner or occupier of any of the relevant land or waters, and

(b) to be a person who might be required by subsection (2) above to grant, or join in granting, any rights,

concerning the rights which that person may be so required to grant.

(4) Subsection (3) above shall not preclude the service of a remediation notice in any case where it appears to the enforcing authority that the contaminated land in question is in such a condition, by reason of substances in, on or under the land, that there is imminent danger of serious harm, or serious pollution of controlled waters, being caused.

(5) A person who grants, or joins in granting, any rights pursuant to subsection (2) above shall be entitled, on making an application within such period as may be prescribed and in such manner as may be prescribed to such person as may be prescribed, to be paid by the appropriate person compensation of such amount as may be determined in such manner as may be prescribed.

(6) Without prejudice to the generality of the regulations that may be made by virtue of subsection (5) above, regulations by virtue of that subsection may make such provision in relation to compensation under this section as may be made by regulations by virtue of subsection (4) of section 35A above in relation to compensation under that section.

(7) In this section, "relevant land or waters" means—

(a) the contaminated land in question;

(b) any controlled waters affected by that land; or

(c) any land adjoining or adjacent to that land or those waters.

Restrictions and prohibitions on serving remediation notices.

78H.—(1) Before serving a remediation notice, the enforcing authority shall reasonably endeavour to consult—

(a) the person on whom the notice is to be served,

(b) the owner of any land to which the notice relates,

(c) any person who appears to that authority to be in occupation of the whole or any part of the land, and

(d) any person of such other description as may be prescribed,

concerning what is to be done by way of remediation.

(2) Regulations may make provision for, or in connection with, steps to be taken for the purposes of subsection (1) above.

(3) No remediation notice shall be served on any person by reference to any contaminated land during any of the following periods, that is to say—

(a) the period—

(i) beginning with the identification of the contaminated land in question pursuant to section 78B(1) above, and

(ii) ending with the expiration of the period of three months beginning with the day on which the notice required by subsection (3)(d) or, as the case may be, (4) of section 78B above is given to that person in respect of that land;

(b) if a decision falling within paragraph (b) of section 78C(1) above is made in relation to the contaminated land in question, the period beginning with the making of the decision and ending with the expiration of the period of three months beginning with—

(i) in a case where the decision is not referred to the Secretary of State under section 78D above, the day on which the notice required by section 78C(6) above is given, or

(ii) in a case where the decision is referred to the Secretary of State under section 78D above, the day on which he gives the notice required by subsection (4)(b) of that section;

(c) if the appropriate Agency gives a notice under subsection (4) of section 78C above to a local authority in relation to the contaminated land in question, the period beginning with the day on which that notice is given and ending with the expiration of the period of three months beginning with—

(i) in a case where notice is given under subsection (6) of that section, the day on which that notice is given;

(ii) in a case where the authority makes a decision falling within subsection (5)(b) of that section and the appropriate Agency fails to give notice under paragraph (b) of section 78D(1) above, the day following the expiration of the period of twenty-one days mentioned in that paragraph; or

(iii) in a case where the authority makes a decision falling within section 78C(5)(b) above which is referred to the Secretary of State under section 78D above, the day on which the Secretary of State gives the notice required by subsection (4)(b) of that section.

(4) Neither subsection (1) nor subsection (3) above shall preclude the service of a remediation notice in any case where it appears to the enforcing authority that the land in question is in such a condition, by reason of substances in, on or under the land, that there is imminent danger of serious harm, or serious pollution of controlled waters, being caused.

(5) The enforcing authority shall not serve a remediation notice on a person if and so long as any one or more of the following conditions is for the time being satisfied in the particular case, that is to say—

(a) the authority is satisfied, in consequence of section 78E(4) and (5) above, that there is nothing by way of remediation which could be specified in a remediation notice served on that person;

(b) the authority is satisfied that appropriate things are being, or will be, done by way of remediation without the service of a remediation notice on that person;

(c) it appears to the authority that the person on whom the notice would be served is the authority itself; or

(d) the authority is satisfied that the powers conferred on it by section 78N below to do what is appropriate by way of remediation are exercisable.

(6) Where the enforcing authority is precluded by virtue of section 78E(4) or (5) above from specifying in a remediation notice any particular thing by way of remediation which it would otherwise have specified in such a notice, the authority shall prepare and publish a document (in this Part referred to as a "remediation declaration") which shall record—

(a) the reasons why the authority would have specified that thing; and

(b) the grounds on which the authority is satisfied that it is precluded from specifying that thing in such a notice.

(7) In any case where the enforcing authority is precluded, by virtue of paragraph (b), (c) or (d) of subsection (5) above, from serving a remediation notice, the responsible person shall prepare and publish a document (in this Part referred to as a "remediation statement") which shall record—

(a) the things which are being, have been, or are expected to be, done by way of remediation in the particular case;

(b) the name and address of the person who is doing, has done, or is expected to do, each of those things; and

(c) the periods within which each of those things is being, or is expected to be, done.

(8) For the purposes of subsection (7) above, the "responsible person" is—

(a) in a case where the condition in paragraph (b) of subsection (5) above is satisfied, the person who is doing or has done, or who the enforcing authority is satisfied will do, the things there mentioned; or

(b) in a case where the condition in paragraph (c) or (d) of that subsection is satisfied, the enforcing authority.

(9) If a person who is required by virtue of subsection (8)(a) above to prepare and publish a remediation statement fails to do so within a reasonable time after the date on which a remediation notice specifying the things there mentioned could, apart from subsection (5) above, have been served, the enforcing authority may itself prepare and publish the statement and may recover its reasonable costs of doing so from that person.

(10) Where the enforcing authority has been precluded by virtue only of subsection (5) above from serving a remediation notice on an appropriate person but—

(a) none of the conditions in that subsection is for the time being satisfied in the particular case, and

(b) the authority is not precluded by any other provision of this Part from serving a remediation notice on that appropriate person,

the authority shall serve a remediation notice on that person; and any such notice may be so served without any further endeavours by the authority to consult persons pursuant to subsection (1) above, if and to the extent that that person has been consulted pursuant to that subsection concerning the things which will be specified in the notice.

Restrictions on liability relating to the pollution of controlled waters.

78J.—(1) This section applies where any land is contaminated land by virtue of paragraph (b) of subsection (2) of section 78A above (whether or not the land is also contaminated land by virtue of paragraph (a) of that subsection).

(2) Where this section applies, no remediation notice given in consequence of the land in question being contaminated land shall require a person who is an appropriate person by virtue of section 78F(4) or (5) above to do anything by way of remediation to that or any other land, or any waters, which he could not have been required to do by such a notice had paragraph (b) of section 78A(2) above (and all other references to pollution of controlled waters) been omitted from this Part.

(3) If, in a case where this section applies, a person permits, has permitted, or might permit, water from an abandoned mine or part of a mine—

(a) to enter any controlled waters, or

(b) to reach a place from which it is or, as the case may be, was likely, in the opinion of the enforcing authority, to enter such waters,

no remediation notice shall require him in consequence to do anything by way of remediation (whether to the contaminated land in question or to any other land or waters) which he could not have been required to do by such a notice had paragraph (b) of section 78A(2) above (and all other references to pollution of controlled waters) been omitted from this Part.

(4) Subsection (3) above shall not apply to the owner or former operator of any mine or part of a mine if the mine or part in question became abandoned after 31st December 1999.

(5) In determining for the purposes of subsection (4) above whether a mine or part of a mine became abandoned before, on or after 31st December 1999 in a case where the mine or part has become abandoned on two or more occasions, of which—

(a) at least one falls on or before that date, and

(b) at least one falls after that date,

the mine or part shall be regarded as becoming abandoned after that date (but without prejudice to the operation of subsection (3) above in relation to that mine or part at, or in relation to, any time before the first of those occasions which falls after that date).

(6) Where, immediately before a part of a mine becomes abandoned, that part is the only part of the mine not falling to be regarded as abandoned for the time being, the abandonment of that part shall not be regarded for the purposes of subsection (4) or (5) above as constituting the abandonment of the mine, but only of that part of it.

(7) Nothing in subsection (2) or (3) above prevents the enforcing authority from doing anything by way of remediation under section 78N below which it could have done apart from that subsection, but the authority shall not be entitled under section 78P below to recover from any person any part of the cost incurred by the authority in doing by way of remediation anything which it is precluded by subsection (2) or (3) above from requiring that person to do.

(8) In this section "mine" has the same meaning as in the Mines and Quarries Act 1954.

1954 c. 70.

Liability in respect of contaminating substances which escape to other land.

78K.—(1) A person who has caused or knowingly permitted any substances to be in, on or under any land shall also be taken for the purposes of this Part to have caused or, as the case may be, knowingly permitted those substances to be in, on or under any other land to which they appear to have escaped.

(2) Subsections (3) and (4) below apply in any case

where it appears that any substances are or have been in, on or under any land (in this section referred to as "land A") as a result of their escape, whether directly or indirectly, from other land in, on or under which a person caused or knowingly permitted them to be.

(3) Where this subsection applies, no remediation notice shall require a person—

(a) who is the owner or occupier of land A, and

(b) who has not caused or knowingly permitted the substances in question to be in, on or under that land,

to do anything by way of remediation to any land or waters (other than land or waters of which he is the owner or occupier) in consequence of land A appearing to be in such a condition, by reason of the presence of those substances in, on or under it, that significant harm is being caused, or there is a significant possibility of such harm being caused, or that pollution of controlled waters is being, or is likely to be caused.

(4) Where this subsection applies, no remediation notice shall require a person—

(a) who is the owner or occupier of land A, and

(b) who has not caused or knowingly permitted the substances in question to be in, on or under that land,

to do anything by way of remediation in consequence of any further land in, on or under which those substances or any of them appear to be or to have been present as a result of their escape from land A ("land B") appearing to be in such a condition, by reason of the presence of those substances in, on or under it, that significant harm is being caused, or there is a significant possibility of such harm being caused, or that pollution of controlled waters is being, or is likely to be caused, unless he is also the owner or occupier of land B.

(5) In any case where—

(a) a person ("person A") has caused or knowingly permitted any substances to be in, on, or under any land,

(b) another person ("person B") who has not caused or knowingly permitted those substances to be in, on or under that land becomes the owner or occupier of that land, and

(c) the substances, or any of the substances, mentioned in paragraph (a) above appear to have escaped to other land,

no remediation notice shall require person B to do anything by way of remediation to that other land in consequence of the apparent acts or omissions of person A, except to the extent that person B caused or knowingly permitted the escape.

(6) Nothing in subsection (3), (4) or (5) above prevents the enforcing authority from doing anything by way of remediation under section 78N below which it could have done apart from that subsection, but the authority shall not be entitled under section 78P below to recover from any person any part of the cost incurred by the authority in doing by way of remediation anything which it is precluded by subsection (3), (4) or (5) above from requiring that person to do.

(7) In this section, "appear" means appear to the enforcing authority, and cognate expressions shall be construed accordingly.

Appeals against remediation notices.

78L.—(1) A person on whom a remediation notice is served may, within the period of twenty-one days beginning with the day on which the notice is served, appeal against the notice—

(a) if it was served by a local authority, to a magistrates' court or, in Scotland, to the sheriff by way of summary application; or

(b) if it was served by the appropriate Agency, to the Secretary of State;

and in the following provisions of this section "the appellate authority" means the magistrates' court, the sheriff or the Secretary of State, as the case may be.

(2) On any appeal under subsection (1) above the appellate authority—

(a) shall quash the notice, if it is satisfied that there is a material defect in the notice; but

(b) subject to that, may confirm the remediation notice, with or without modification, or quash it.

(3) Where an appellate authority confirms a remediation notice, with or without modification, it may extend the period specified in the notice for doing what the notice requires to be done.

(4) Regulations may make provision with respect to—

(a) the grounds on which appeals under subsection (1) above may be made;

(b) the cases in which, grounds on which, court or tribunal to which, or person at whose instance, an appeal against a decision of a magistrates' court or sheriff court in pursuance of an appeal under subsection (1) above shall lie; or

(c) the procedure on an appeal under subsection (1) above or on an appeal by virtue of paragraph (b) above.

(5) Regulations under subsection (4) above may (among other things)—

(a) include provisions comparable to those in section 290 of the Public Health Act 1936 (appeals against notices requiring the execution of works);   1936 c. 49.

(b) prescribe the cases in which a remediation notice is, or is not, to be suspended until the appeal is decided, or until some other stage in the proceedings;

(c) prescribe the cases in which the decision on an appeal may in some respects be less favourable to the appellant than the remediation notice against which he is appealing;

(d) prescribe the cases in which the appellant may claim that a remediation notice should have been served on some other person and prescribe the procedure to be followed in those cases;

(e) make provision as respects—

    (i) the particulars to be included in the notice of appeal;

    (ii) the persons on whom notice of appeal is to be served and the particulars, if any, which are to accompany the notice; and

    (iii) the abandonment of an appeal;

(f) make different provision for different cases or classes of case.

(6) This section, so far as relating to appeals to the Secretary of State, is subject to section 114 of the Environment Act 1995 (delegation or reference of appeals etc).   1995 c. 25.

Offences of not complying with a remediation notice.   78M.—(1) If a person on whom an enforcing authority serves a remediation notice fails, without reasonable excuse, to comply with any of the requirements of the notice, he shall be guilty of an offence.

(2) Where the remediation notice in question is one which was required by section 78E(3) above to state, in relation to the requirement which has not been complied with, the proportion of the cost involved which the person charged with the offence is liable to bear, it shall be a defence for that person to prove that the only reason why he has not complied with the requirement is that one or more of the other persons who are liable to bear a proportion of that cost refused, or was not able, to comply with the requirement.

(3) Except in a case falling within subsection (4) below, a person who commits an offence under subsection (1) above shall be liable, on summary conviction, to a fine not exceeding level 5 on the standard scale and to a further fine of an amount equal to one-tenth of level 5 on the standard scale for each day on which the failure continues after conviction of the offence and before the enforcing authority has begun to exercise its powers by virtue of section 78N(3)(c) below.

(4) A person who commits an offence under subsection (1) above in a case where the contaminated land to which the remediation notice relates is industrial, trade or business premises shall be liable on summary conviction to a fine not exceeding £20,000 or such greater sum as the Secretary of State may from time to time by order substitute and to a further fine of an amount equal to one-tenth of that sum for each day on which the failure continues after conviction of the offence and before the enforcing authority has begun to exercise its powers by virtue of section 78N(3)(c) below.

(5) If the enforcing authority is of the opinion that proceedings for an offence under this section would afford an ineffectual remedy against a person who has failed to comply with any of the requirements of a remediation notice which that authority has served on him, that authority may take proceedings in the High Court or, in Scotland, in any court of competent jurisdiction, for the purpose of securing compliance with the remediation notice.

(6) In this section, "industrial, trade or business premises" means premises used for any industrial, trade or business purposes or premises not so used on which matter is burnt in connection with any industrial, trade or business process, and premises are used for industrial purposes where they are used for the purposes of any treatment or process as well as where they are used for the purpose of manufacturing.

(7) No order shall be made under subsection (4) above unless a draft of the order has been laid before, and approved by a resolution of, each House of Parliament.

Powers of the enforcing authority to carry out remediation.

78N.—(1) Where this section applies, the enforcing authority shall itself have power, in a case falling within paragraph (a) or (b) of section 78E(1) above, to do what is appropriate by way of remediation to the relevant land or waters.

(2) Subsection (1) above shall not confer power on the enforcing authority to do anything by way of remediation if the authority would, in the particular case, be precluded by section 78YB below from serving a remediation notice requiring that thing to be done.

(3) This section applies in each of the following cases, that is to say—

(a) where the enforcing authority considers it necessary to do anything itself by way of remediation for the purpose of preventing the occurrence of any serious harm, or serious pollution of controlled waters, of which there is imminent danger;

(b) where an appropriate person has entered into a written agreement with the enforcing authority for that authority to do, at the cost of that person, that which he would otherwise be required to do under this Part by way of remediation;

(c) where a person on whom the enforcing authority serves a remediation notice fails to comply with any of the requirements of the notice;

(d) where the enforcing authority is precluded by section 78J or 78K above from including something by way of remediation in a remediation notice;

(e) where the enforcing authority considers that, were it to do some particular thing by way of remediation, it would decide, by virtue of subsection (2) of section 78P below or any guidance issued under that subsection,—

(i) not to seek to recover under subsection (1) of that section any of the reasonable cost incurred by it in doing that thing; or

(ii) to seek so to recover only a portion of that cost;

(f) where no person has, after reasonable inquiry, been found who is an appropriate person in relation to any particular thing.

(4) Subject to section 78E(4) and (5) above, for the purposes of this section, the things which it is appropriate for the enforcing authority to do by way of remediation are—

(a) in a case falling within paragraph (a) of subsection (3) above, anything by way of remediation which the enforcing authority considers necessary for the purpose mentioned in that paragraph;

(b) in a case falling within paragraph (b) of that subsection, anything specified in, or determined under, the agreement mentioned in that paragraph;

(c) in a case falling within paragraph (c) of that subsection, anything which the person mentioned in that paragraph was required to do by virtue of the remediation notice;

(d) in a case falling within paragraph (d) of that subsection, anything by way of remediation which the enforcing authority is precluded by section 78J or 78K above from including in a remediation notice;

(e) in a case falling within paragraph (e) or (f) of that subsection, the particular thing mentioned in the paragraph in question.

(5) In this section "the relevant land or waters" means—

(a) the contaminated land in question;

(b) any controlled waters affected by that land; or

(c) any land adjoining or adjacent to that land or those waters.

Recovery of, and security for, the cost of remediation by the enforcing authority.

78P.—(1) Where, by virtue of section 78N(3)(a), (c), (e) or (f) above, the enforcing authority does any particular thing by way of remediation, it shall be entitled, subject to sections 78J(7) and 78K(6) above, to recover the reasonable cost incurred in doing it from the appropriate person or, if there are two or more appropriate persons in relation to the thing in question, from those persons in proportions determined pursuant to section 78F(7) above.

(2) In deciding whether to recover the cost, and, if so, how much of the cost, which it is entitled to recover under subsection (1) above, the enforcing authority shall have regard—

(a) to any hardship which the recovery may cause to the person from whom the cost is recoverable; and

(b) to any guidance issued by the Secretary of State for the purposes of this subsection.

(3) Subsection (4) below shall apply in any case where—

(a) any cost is recoverable under subsection (1) above from a person—

(i) who is the owner of any premises which consist of or include the contaminated land in question; and

(ii) who caused or knowingly permitted the substances, or any of the substances, by reason of which the land is contaminated land to be in, on or under the land; and

(b) the enforcing authority serves a notice under this subsection (in this Part referred to as a "charging notice") on that person.

(4) Where this subsection applies—

(a) the cost shall carry interest, at such reasonable rate as the enforcing authority may determine, from the date of service of the notice until the whole amount is paid; and

(b) subject to the following provisions of this section, the cost and accrued interest shall be a charge on the premises mentioned in subsection (3)(a)(i) above.

(5) A charging notice shall—

(a) specify the amount of the cost which the enforcing authority claims is recoverable;

(b) state the effect of subsection (4) above and the rate of interest determined by the authority under that subsection; and

(c) state the effect of subsections (7) and (8) below.

(6) On the date on which an enforcing authority serves a charging notice on a person, the authority shall also serve a copy of the notice on every other person who, to the knowledge of the authority, has an interest in the premises capable of being affected by the charge.

(7) Subject to any order under subsection (9)(b) or (c) below, the amount of any cost specified in a charging notice and the accrued interest shall be a charge on the premises—

    (a) as from the end of the period of twenty-one days beginning with the service of the charging notice, or

    (b) where an appeal is brought under subsection (8) below, as from the final determination or (as the case may be) the withdrawal, of the appeal,

until the cost and interest are recovered.

(8) A person served with a charging notice or a copy of a charging notice may appeal against the notice to a county court within the period of twenty-one days beginning with the date of service.

(9) On an appeal under subsection (8) above, the court may—

    (a) confirm the notice without modification;

    (b) order that the notice is to have effect with the substitution of a different amount for the amount originally specified in it; or

    (c) order that the notice is to be of no effect.

(10) Regulations may make provision with respect to—

    (a) the grounds on which appeals under this section may be made; or

    (b) the procedure on any such appeal.

(11) An enforcing authority shall, for the purpose of enforcing a charge under this section, have all the same powers and remedies under the Law of Property Act 1925, and otherwise, as if it were a mortgagee by deed having powers of sale and lease, of accepting surrenders of leases and of appointing a receiver.   1925 c. 20.

(12) Where any cost is a charge on premises under this section, the enforcing authority may by order declare the cost to be payable with interest by instalments within the specified period until the whole amount is paid.

(13) In subsection (12) above—

"interest" means interest at the rate determined by the enforcing authority under subsection (4) above; and "the specified period" means such period of thirty years or less from the date of service of the charging notice as is specified in the order.

(14) Subsections (3) to (13) above do not extend to Scotland.

Special sites.

78Q.—(1) If, in a case where a local authority has served a remediation notice, the contaminated land in question becomes a special site, the appropriate Agency may adopt the remediation notice and, if it does so,—

(a) it shall give notice of its decision to adopt the remediation notice to the appropriate person and to the local authority;

(b) the remediation notice shall have effect, as from the time at which the appropriate Agency decides to adopt it, as a remediation notice given by that Agency; and

(c) the validity of the remediation notice shall not be affected by—

(i) the contaminated land having become a special site;

(ii) the adoption of the remediation notice by the appropriate Agency; or

(iii) anything in paragraph (b) above.

(2) Where a local authority has, by virtue of section 78N above, begun to do any thing, or any series of things, by way of remediation—

(a) the authority may continue doing that thing, or that series of things, by virtue of that section, notwithstanding that the contaminated land in question becomes a special site; and

(b) section 78P above shall apply in relation to the reasonable cost incurred by the authority in doing that thing or those things as if that authority were the enforcing authority.

(3) If and so long as any land is a special site, the appropriate Agency may from time to time inspect that land for the purpose of keeping its condition under review.

(4) If it appears to the appropriate Agency that a special site is no longer land which is required to be designated as such a site, the appropriate Agency may give notice—

(a) to the Secretary of State, and

(b) to the local authority in whose area the site is situated,

terminating the designation of the land in question as a special site as from such date as may be specified in the notice.

(5) A notice under subsection (4) above shall not prevent the land, or any of the land, to which the notice relates being designated as a special site on a subsequent occasion.

(6) In exercising its functions under subsection (3) or (4) above, the appropriate Agency shall act in accordance with any guidance given for the purpose by the Secretary of State.

Registers.

78R.—(1) Every enforcing authority shall maintain a register containing prescribed particulars of or relating to—

(a) remediation notices served by that authority;

(b) appeals against any such remediation notices;

(c) remediation statements or remediation declarations prepared and published under section 78H above;

(d) in relation to an enforcing authority in England and Wales, appeals against charging notices served by that authority;

(e) notices under subsection (1)(b) or (5)(a) of section 78C above which have effect by virtue of subsection (7) of that section as the designation of any land as a special site;

(f) notices under subsection (4)(b) of section 78D above which have effect by virtue of subsection (6) of that section as the designation of any land as a special site;

(g) notices given by or to the enforcing authority under section 78Q(4) above terminating the designation of any land as a special site;

(h) notifications given to that authority by persons—

(i) on whom a remediation notice has been served, or

(ii) who are or were required by virtue of section 78H(8)(a) above to prepare and publish a remediation statement,

of what they claim has been done by them by way of remediation;

(j) notifications given to that authority by owners or occupiers of land—

(i) in respect of which a remediation notice has been served, or

(ii) in respect of which a remediation statement has been prepared and published,

of what they claim has been done on the land in question by way of remediation;

(k) convictions for such offences under section 78M above as may be prescribed;

(l) such other matters relating to contaminated land as may be prescribed;

but that duty is subject to sections 78S and 78T below.

(2) The form of, and the descriptions of information to be contained in, notifications for the purposes of subsection (1)(h) or (j) above may be prescribed by the Secretary of State.

(3) No entry made in a register by virtue of subsection (1)(h) or (j) above constitutes a representation by the body maintaining the register or, in a case where the entry is made by virtue of subsection (6) below, the authority which sent the copy of the particulars in question pursuant to subsection (4) or (5) below—

(a) that what is stated in the entry to have been done has in fact been done; or

(b) as to the manner in which it has been done.

(4) Where any particulars are entered on a register maintained under this section by the appropriate Agency, the appropriate Agency shall send a copy of those particulars to the local authority in whose area is situated the land to which the particulars relate.

(5) In any case where—

(a) any land is treated by virtue of section 78X(2) below as situated in the area of a local authority other than the local authority in whose area it is in fact situated, and

(b) any particulars relating to that land are entered on the register maintained under this section by the local authority in whose area the land is so treated as situated,

that authority shall send a copy of those particulars to the local authority in whose area the land is in fact situated.

(6) Where a local authority receives a copy of any particulars sent to it pursuant to subsection (4) or (5) above, it shall enter those particulars on the register maintained by it under this section.

(7) Where information of any description is excluded by virtue of section 78T below from any register maintained under this section, a statement shall be entered in the register indicating the existence of information of that description.

(8) It shall be the duty of each enforcing authority—

(a) to secure that the registers maintained by it under this section are available, at all reasonable times, for inspection by the public free of charge; and

> (b) to afford to members of the public facilities for obtaining copies of entries, on payment of reasonable charges;

and, for the purposes of this subsection, places may be prescribed by the Secretary of State at which any such registers or facilities as are mentioned in paragraph (a) or (b) above are to be available or afforded to the public in pursuance of the paragraph in question.

(9) Registers under this section may be kept in any form.

Exclusion from registers of information affecting national security.

78S.—(1) No information shall be included in a register maintained under section 78R above if and so long as, in the opinion of the Secretary of State, the inclusion in the register of that information, or information of that description, would be contrary to the interests of national security.

(2) The Secretary of State may, for the purpose of securing the exclusion from registers of information to which subsection (1) above applies, give to enforcing authorities directions—

> (a) specifying information, or descriptions of information, to be excluded from their registers; or

> (b) specifying descriptions of information to be referred to the Secretary of State for his determination;

and no information referred to the Secretary of State in pursuance of paragraph (b) above shall be included in any such register until the Secretary of State determines that it should be so included.

(3) The enforcing authority shall notify the Secretary of State of any information which it excludes from the register in pursuance of directions under subsection (2) above.

(4) A person may, as respects any information which appears to him to be information to which subsection (1) above may apply, give a notice to the Secretary of State specifying the information and indicating its apparent nature; and, if he does so—

> (a) he shall notify the enforcing authority that he has done so; and

> (b) no information so notified to the Secretary of State shall be included in any such register until the Secretary of State has determined that it should be so included.

Exclusion from registers of certain confidential information.

78T.—(1) No information relating to the affairs of any individual or business shall be included in a register maintained under section 78R above, without the consent of that individual or the person for the time being carrying on that business, if and so long as the information—

(a) is, in relation to him, commercially confidential; and

(b) is not required to be included in the register in pursuance of directions under subsection (7) below;

but information is not commercially confidential for the purposes of this section unless it is determined under this section to be so by the enforcing authority or, on appeal, by the Secretary of State.

(2) Where it appears to an enforcing authority that any information which has been obtained by the authority under or by virtue of any provision of this Part might be commercially confidential, the authority shall—

(a) give to the person to whom or whose business it relates notice that that information is required to be included in the register unless excluded under this section; and

(b) give him a reasonable opportunity—

(i) of objecting to the inclusion of the information on the ground that it is commercially confidential; and

(ii) of making representations to the authority for the purpose of justifying any such objection;

and, if any representations are made, the enforcing authority shall, having taken the representations into account, determine whether the information is or is not commercially confidential.

(3) Where, under subsection (2) above, an authority determines that information is not commercially confidential—

(a) the information shall not be entered in the register until the end of the period of twenty-one days beginning with the date on which the determination is notified to the person concerned;

(b) that person may appeal to the Secretary of State against the decision;

and, where an appeal is brought in respect of any information, the information shall not be entered in the register until the end of the period of seven days following the day on which the appeal is finally determined or withdrawn.

(4) An appeal under subsection (3) above shall, if either party to the appeal so requests or the Secretary of State so decides, take or continue in the form of a hearing (which must be held in private).

(5) Subsection (10) of section 15 above shall apply in relation to an appeal under subsection (3) above as it applies in relation to an appeal under that section.

(6) Subsection (3) above is subject to section 114 of the Environment Act 1995 (delegation or reference of appeals etc).

(7) The Secretary of State may give to the enforcing authorities directions as to specified information, or descriptions of information, which the public interest requires to be included in registers maintained under section 78R above notwithstanding that the information may be commercially confidential.

(8) Information excluded from a register shall be treated as ceasing to be commercially confidential for the purposes of this section at the expiry of the period of four years beginning with the date of the determination by virtue of which it was excluded; but the person who furnished it may apply to the authority for the information to remain excluded from the register on the ground that it is still commercially confidential and the authority shall determine whether or not that is the case.

(9) Subsections (3) to (6) above shall apply in relation to a determination under subsection (8) above as they apply in relation to a determination under subsection (2) above.

(10) Information is, for the purposes of any determination under this section, commercially confidential, in relation to any individual or person, if its being contained in the register would prejudice to an unreasonable degree the commercial interests of that individual or person.

(11) For the purposes of subsection (10) above, there shall be disregarded any prejudice to the commercial interests of any individual or person so far as relating only to the value of the contaminated land in question or otherwise to the ownership or occupation of that land.

Reports by the appropriate Agency on the state of contaminated land.

78U.—(1) The appropriate Agency shall—

(a) from time to time, or

(b) if the Secretary of State at any time so requests,

prepare and publish a report on the state of contaminated land in England and Wales or in Scotland, as the case may be.

(2) A local authority shall, at the written request of the appropriate Agency, furnish the appropriate Agency with such information to which this subsection applies as the appropriate Agency may require for the purpose of enabling it to perform its functions under subsection (1) above.

(3) The information to which subsection (2) above applies is such information as the local authority may have, or may reasonably be expected to obtain, with respect to the condition of contaminated land in its area, being information which the authority has acquired or may acquire in the exercise of its functions under this Part.

Site-specific guidance by the appropriate Agency concerning contaminated land.

78V.—(1) The appropriate Agency may issue guidance to any local authority with respect to the exercise or performance of the authority's powers or duties under this Part in relation to any particular contaminated land; and in exercising or performing those powers or duties in relation to that land the authority shall have regard to any such guidance so issued.

(2) If and to the extent that any guidance issued under subsection (1) above to a local authority is inconsistent with any guidance issued under this Part by the Secretary of State, the local authority shall disregard the guidance under that subsection.

(3) A local authority shall, at the written request of the appropriate Agency, furnish the appropriate Agency with such information to which this subsection applies as the appropriate Agency may require for the purpose of enabling it to issue guidance for the purposes of subsection (1) above.

(4) The information to which subsection (3) above applies is such information as the local authority may have, or may reasonably be expected to obtain, with respect to any contaminated land in its area, being information which the authority has acquired, or may acquire, in the exercise of its functions under this Part.

The appropriate Agency to have regard to guidance given by the Secretary of State.

78W.—(1) The Secretary of State may issue guidance to the appropriate Agency with respect to the exercise or performance of that Agency's powers or duties under this Part; and in exercising or performing those powers or duties the appropriate Agency shall have regard to any such guidance so issued.

(2) The duty imposed on the appropriate Agency by subsection (1) above is without prejudice to any duty imposed by any other provision of this Part on that Agency to act in accordance with guidance issued by the Secretary of State.

Supplementary provisions.

78X.—(1) Where it appears to a local authority that two or more different sites, when considered together, are in such a condition, by reason of substances in, on or under the land, that—

(a) significant harm is being caused or there is a significant possibility of such harm being caused, or

(b) pollution of controlled waters is being, or is likely to be, caused,

this Part shall apply in relation to each of those sites, whether or not the condition of the land at any of them, when considered alone, appears to the authority to be such that significant harm is being caused, or there is a significant possibility of such harm being caused, or that pollution of controlled waters is being or is likely to be caused.

(2) Where it appears to a local authority that any land outside, but adjoining or adjacent to, its area is in such a condition, by reason of substances in, on or under the land, that significant harm is being caused, or there is a significant possibility of such harm being caused, or that pollution of controlled waters is being, or is likely to be, caused within its area—

(a) the authority may, in exercising its functions under this Part, treat that land as if it were land situated within its area; and

(b) except in this subsection, any reference—

(i) to land within the area of a local authority, or

(ii) to the local authority in whose area any land is situated,

shall be construed accordingly;

but this subsection is without prejudice to the functions of the local authority in whose area the land is in fact situated.

(3) A person acting in a relevant capacity—

(a) shall not thereby be personally liable, under this Part, to bear the whole or any part of the cost of doing any thing by way of remediation, unless that thing is to any extent referable to substances whose presence in, on or under the contaminated land in question is a result of any act done or omission made by him which it was unreasonable for a person acting in that capacity to do or make; and

(b) shall not thereby be guilty of an offence under or by virtue of section 78M above unless the requirement which has not been complied with is a requirement to do some particular thing for which he is personally liable to bear the whole or any part of the cost.

(4) In subsection (3) above, "person acting in a relevant capacity" means—

(a) a person acting as an insolvency practitioner, within the meaning of section 388 of the Insolvency Act 1986 (including that section as it applies in relation to an insolvent partnership by virtue of any order made under section 421 of that Act); 1986 c. 45.

(b) the official receiver acting in a capacity in which he would be regarded as acting as an insolvency practitioner within the meaning of section 388 of the Insolvency Act 1986 if subsection (5) of that section were disregarded;

(c) the official receiver acting as receiver or manager;

(d) a person acting as a special manager under section 177 or 370 of the Insolvency Act 1986;

(e) the Accountant in Bankruptcy acting as permanent or interim trustee in a sequestration (within the meaning of the Bankruptcy (Scotland) Act 1985);

(f) a person acting as a receiver or receiver and manager—

(i) under or by virtue of any enactment; or

(ii) by virtue of his appointment as such by an order of a court or by any other instrument.

(5) Regulations may make different provision for different cases or circumstances.

Application to the Isles of Scilly.

78Y.—(1) Subject to the provisions of any order under this section, this Part shall not apply in relation to the Isles of Scilly.

(2) The Secretary of State may, after consultation with the Council of the Isles of Scilly, by order provide for the application of any provisions of this Part to the Isles of Scilly; and any such order may provide for the application of those provisions to those Isles with such modifications as may be specified in the order.

(3) An order under this section may—

(a) make different provision for different cases, including different provision in relation to different persons, circumstances or localities; and

(b) contain such supplemental, consequential and transitional provision as the Secretary of State considers appropriate, including provision saving provision repealed by or under any enactment.

Supplementary provisions with respect to guidance by the Secretary of State.

78YA.—(1) Any power of the Secretary of State to issue guidance under this Part shall only be exercisable after consultation with the appropriate Agency and such other bodies or persons as he may consider it appropriate to consult in relation to the guidance in question.

(2) A draft of any guidance proposed to be issued under section 78A(2) or (5), 78B(2) or 78F(6) or (7) above shall be laid before each House of Parliament and the guidance shall not be issued until after the period of 40 days beginning with the day on which the draft was so laid or, if the draft is laid on different days, the later of the two days.

(3) If, within the period mentioned in subsection (2) above, either House resolves that the guidance, the draft of which was laid before it, should not be issued, the Secretary of State shall not issue that guidance.

(4) In reckoning any period of 40 days for the purposes of subsection (2) or (3) above, no account shall be taken

of any time during which Parliament is dissolved or prorogued or during which both Houses are adjourned for more than four days.

(5) The Secretary of State shall arrange for any guidance issued by him under this Part to be published in such manner as he considers appropriate.

Interaction of this Part with other enactments.

78YB.—(1) A remediation notice shall not be served if and to the extent that it appears to the enforcing authority that the powers of the appropriate Agency under section 27 above may be exercised in relation to—

(a) the significant harm (if any), and

(b) the pollution of controlled waters (if any),

by reason of which the contaminated land in question is such land.

(2) Nothing in this Part shall apply in relation to any land in respect of which there is for the time being in force a site licence under Part II above, except to the extent that any significant harm, or pollution of controlled waters, by reason of which that land would otherwise fall to be regarded as contaminated land is attributable to causes other than—

(a) breach of the conditions of the licence; or

(b) the carrying on, in accordance with the conditions of the licence, of any activity authorised by the licence.

(3) If, in a case falling within subsection (1) or (7) of section 59 above, the land in question is contaminated land, or becomes such land by reason of the deposit of the controlled waste in question, a remediation notice shall not be served in respect of that land by reason of that waste or any consequences of its deposit, if and to the extent that it appears to the enforcing authority that the powers of a waste regulation authority or waste collection authority under that section may be exercised in relation to that waste or the consequences of its deposit.

(4) No remediation notice shall require a person to do anything the effect of which would be to impede or prevent the making of a discharge in pursuance of a consent given under Chapter II of Part III of the Water Resources Act 1991 (pollution offences) or, in relation to Scotland, in pursuance of a consent given under Part II of the Control of Pollution Act 1974.

1991 c. 57.

1974 c. 40.

This Part and radioactivity.

78YC. Except as provided by regulations, nothing in this Part applies in relation to harm, or pollution of controlled waters, so far as attributable to any radioactivity possessed by any substance; but regulations may—

(a) provide for prescribed provisions of this Part to have effect with such modifications as the Secretary of State considers appropriate for the

PART II

1993 c. 12.

Abandoned
mines: England
and Wales.

1986 c. 45.

1985 c. 66.

1954 c. 70.

purpose of dealing with harm, or pollution of controlled waters, so far as attributable to any radioactivity possessed by any substances; or

(b) make such modifications of the Radioactive Substances Act 1993 or any other Act as the Secretary of State considers appropriate."

58. After Chapter II of Part III of the Water Resources Act 1991 (pollution offences) there shall be inserted—

"CHAPTER IIA

ABANDONED MINES

Introductory.

91A.—(1) For the purposes of this Chapter, "abandonment", in relation to a mine,—

(a) subject to paragraph (b) below, includes—

(i) the discontinuance of any or all of the operations for the removal of water from the mine;

(ii) the cessation of working of any relevant seam, vein or vein-system;

(iii) the cessation of use of any shaft or outlet of the mine;

(iv) in the case of a mine in which activities other than mining activities are carried on (whether or not mining activities are also carried on in the mine)—

(A) the discontinuance of some or all of those other activities in the mine; and

(B) any substantial change in the operations for the removal of water from the mine; but

(b) does not include—

(i) any disclaimer under section 178 or 315 of the Insolvency Act 1986 (power of liquidator, or trustee of a bankrupt's estate, to disclaim onerous property) by the official receiver acting in a compulsory capacity; or

(ii) the abandonment of any rights, interests or liabilities by the Accountant in Bankruptcy acting as permanent or interim trustee in a sequestration (within the meaning of the Bankruptcy (Scotland) Act 1985);

and cognate expressions shall be construed accordingly.

(2) In this Chapter, except where the context otherwise requires—

"the 1954 Act" means the Mines and Quarries Act 1954;

"acting in a compulsory capacity", in the case of the official receiver, means acting as—

(a) liquidator of a company;

    (b) receiver or manager of a bankrupt's estate, pursuant to section 287 of the Insolvency Act 1986;

    (c) trustee of a bankrupt's estate;

    (d) liquidator of an insolvent partnership;

    (e) trustee of an insolvent partnership;

    (f) trustee, or receiver or manager, of the insolvent estate of a deceased person;

"mine" has the same meaning as in the 1954 Act;

"the official receiver" has the same meaning as it has in the Insolvency Act 1986 by virtue of section 399(1) of that Act;

"prescribed" means prescribed in regulations;

    "regulations" means regulations made by the Secretary of State;

relevant seam, vein or vein-system", in the case of any mine, means any seam, vein or vein-system for the purpose of, or in connection with, whose working any excavation constituting or comprised in the mine was made.

Mine operators to give the Agency six months' notice of any proposed abandonment.

91B.—(1) If, in the case of any mine, there is to be an abandonment at any time after the expiration of the initial period, it shall be the duty of the operator of the mine to give notice of the proposed abandonment to the Agency at least six months before the abandonment takes effect.

(2) A notice under subsection (1) above shall contain such information (if any) as is prescribed for the purpose, which may include information about the operator's opinion as to any consequences of the abandonment.

(3) A person who fails to give the notice required by subsection (1) above shall be guilty of an offence and liable—

    (a) on summary conviction, to a fine not exceeding the statutory maximum;

    (b) on conviction on indictment, to a fine.

(4) A person shall not be guilty of an offence under subsection (3) above if—

    (a) the abandonment happens in an emergency in order to avoid danger to life or health; and

    (b) notice of the abandonment, containing such information as may be prescribed, is given as soon as reasonably practicable after the abandonment has happened.

(5) Where the operator of a mine is—

    (a) the official receiver acting in a compulsory capacity, or

1985 c. 66.

(b) the Accountant in Bankruptcy acting as permanent or interim trustee in a sequestration (within the meaning of the Bankruptcy (Scotland) Act 1985),

he shall not be guilty of an offence under subsection (3) above by reason of any failure to give the notice required by subsection (1) above if, as soon as reasonably practicable (whether before or after the abandonment), he gives to the Agency notice of the abandonment or proposed abandonment, containing such information as may be prescribed.

(6) Where a person gives notice under subsection (1), (4)(b) or (5) above, he shall publish prescribed particulars of, or relating to, the notice in one or more local newspapers circulating in the locality where the mine is situated.

(7) Where the Agency—

(a) receives notice under this section or otherwise learns of an abandonment or proposed abandonment in the case of any mine, and

(b) considers that, in consequence of the abandonment or proposed abandonment taking effect, any land has or is likely to become contaminated land, within the meaning of Part IIA of the Environmental Protection Act 1990,

1990 c. 43.

it shall be the duty of the Agency to inform the local authority in whose area that land is situated of the abandonment or proposed abandonment.

(8) In this section—

"the initial period" means the period of six months beginning with the day on which subsection (1) above comes into force;

"local authority" means—

(a) any unitary authority;

(b) any district council, so far as it is not a unitary authority;

(c) the Common Council of the City of London and, as respects the Temples, the Sub-Treasurer of the Inner Temple and the Under-Treasurer of the Middle Temple respectively;

"unitary authority" means—

(a) the council of a county, so far as it is the council of an area for which there are no district councils;

(b) the council of any district comprised in an area for which there is no county council;

(c) the council of a London borough;

(d) the council of a county borough in Wales."

59. After Part I of the Control of Pollution Act 1974 (waste on land) there shall be inserted—

"PART IA

ABANDONED MINES

Introductory.

30Y.—(1) For the purposes of this Part, "abandonment", in relation to a mine,—

(a) subject to paragraph (b) below, includes—

(i) the discontinuance of any or all of the operations for the removal of water from the mine;

(ii) the cessation of working of any relevant seam, vein or vein-system;

(iii) the cessation of use of any shaft or outlet of the mine;

(iv) in the case of a mine in which activities other than mining activities are carried on (whether or not mining activities are also carried on in the mine)—

(A) the discontinuance of some or all of those other activities in the mine; and

(B) any substantial change in the operations for the removal of water from the mine; but

(b) does not include—

(i) the abandonment of any rights, interests or liabilities by the Accountant in Bankruptcy acting as permanent or interim trustee in a sequestration (within the meaning of the Bankruptcy (Scotland) Act 1985); or

1985 c. 66.

(ii) any disclaimer under section 178 or 315 of the Insolvency Act 1986 (power of liquidator, or trustee of bankrupt's estate, to disclaim onerous property) by the official receiver acting in a compulsory capacity;

1986 c. 45.

and cognate expressions shall be construed accordingly.

(2) In this Part, except where the context otherwise requires—

"acting in a compulsory capacity", in the case of the official receiver, means acting as—

(a) liquidator of a company;

(b) receiver or manager of a bankrupt's estate, pursuant to section 287 of the Insolvency Act 1986;

(c) trustee of a bankrupt's estate;

(d) liquidator of an insolvent partnership;

(e) trustee of an insolvent partnership;

(f) trustee, or receiver or manager, of the insolvent estate of a deceased person;

1986 c. 45.

"the official receiver" has the same meaning as it has in the Insolvency Act 1986 by virtue of section 399(1) of that Act;

"relevant seam, vein or vein-system", in the case of any mine, means any seam, vein or vein-system for the purpose of, or in connection with, whose working any excavation constituting or comprised in the mine was made.

(3) This Part extends only to Scotland.

Mine operators to give SEPA six months' notice of any proposed abandonment.

30Z.—(1) If, in the case of any mine, there is to be an abandonment at any time after the expiration of the initial period, it shall be the duty of the operator of the mine to give notice of the proposed abandonment to SEPA at least six months before the abandonment takes effect.

(2) A notice under subsection (1) above shall contain such information (if any) as is prescribed for the purpose, which may include information about the operator's opinion as to any consequences of the abandonment.

(3) A person who fails to give the notice required by subsection (1) above shall be guilty of an offence and liable—

(a) on summary conviction, to a fine not exceeding the statutory maximum;

(b) on conviction on indictment, to a fine.

(4) A person shall not be guilty of an offence under subsection (3) above if—

(a) the abandonment happens in an emergency in order to avoid danger to life or health; and

(b) notice of the abandonment, containing such information as may be prescribed, is given as soon as reasonably practicable after the abandonment has happened.

(5) Where the operator of a mine is—

(a) the Accountant in Bankruptcy acting as permanent or interim trustee in a sequestration (within the meaning of the Bankruptcy (Scotland) Act 1985); or

1985 c. 66.

(b) the official receiver acting in a compulsory capacity,

he shall not be guilty of an offence under subsection (3) above by reason of any failure to give the notice required by subsection (1) above if, as soon as is reasonably practicable (whether before or after the abandonment), he gives to SEPA notice of the abandonment or proposed abandonment, containing such information as may be prescribed.

(6) Where a person gives notice under subsection (1), (4)(b) or (5) above, he shall publish prescribed particulars

of, or relating to, the notice in one or more local newspapers circulating in the locality where the mine is situated.

(7) Where SEPA—

(a) receives notice under this section or otherwise learns of an abandonment or proposed abandonment in the case of any mine, and

(b) considers that, in consequence of the abandonment or proposed abandonment taking effect, any land has or is likely to become contaminated land, within the meaning of Part IIA of the Environmental Protection Act 1990,

1990 c.43.

it shall be the duty of SEPA to inform the local authority in whose area that land is situated of the abandonment or proposed abandonment.

(8) In this section—

"the initial period" means the period of six months beginning with the day on which subsection (1) above comes into force;

"local authority" means a council constituted under section 2 of the Local Government etc. (Scotland) Act 1994."

1994 c. 39.

60.—(1) In section 89 of the Water Resources Act 1991 (defences) in subsection (3) (person not to be guilty of an offence under section 85 by reason only of permitting water from an abandoned mine to enter controlled waters) after the words "an abandoned mine" there shall be inserted the words "or an abandoned part of a mine".

Amendments to sections 89 and 161 of the Water Resources Act 1991.

1991 c. 57.

(2) After that subsection there shall be inserted—

"(3A) Subsection (3) above shall not apply to the owner or former operator of any mine or part of a mine if the mine or part in question became abandoned after 31st December 1999.

(3B) In determining for the purposes of subsection (3A) above whether a mine or part of a mine became abandoned before, on or after 31st December 1999 in a case where the mine or part has become abandoned on two or more occasions, of which—

(a) at least one falls on or before that date, and

(b) at least one falls after that date,

the mine or part shall be regarded as becoming abandoned after that date (but without prejudice to the operation of subsection (3) above in relation to that mine or part at, or in relation to, any time before the first of those occasions which falls after that date).

(3C) Where, immediately before a part of a mine becomes abandoned, that part is the only part of the mine not falling to be regarded as abandoned for the time being, the abandonment of that part shall not be regarded for the purposes of subsection (3A) or (3B) above as constituting the abandonment of the mine, but only of that part of it."

(3) In section 161 of that Act (anti-pollution works and operations) in subsection (1), after paragraph (b) there shall be inserted the words—

"and, in either case, the Agency shall be entitled to carry out investigations for the purpose of establishing the source of the matter and the identity of the person who has caused or knowingly permitted it to be present in controlled waters or at a place from which it was likely, in the opinion of the Agency, to enter controlled waters."

(4) In subsection (3) of that section (Agency entitled to recover expenses of works or operations from the person responsible for the pollution) for the words "or operations" there shall be substituted the words "operations or investigations".

(5) In subsection (4) of that section (exception for expenses of works or operations in respect of water from an abandoned mine)—

(a) for the words "or operations" there shall be substituted the words "operations or investigations"; and

(b) after the words "an abandoned mine" there shall be inserted the words "or an abandoned part of a mine".

(6) After that subsection there shall be inserted—

"(4A) Subsection (4) above shall not apply to the owner or former operator of any mine or part of a mine if the mine or part in question became abandoned after 31st December 1999.

(4B) Subsections (3B) and (3C) of section 89 above shall apply in relation to subsections (4) and (4A) above as they apply in relation to subsections (3) and (3A) of that section."

(7) In subsection (6) of that section (definitions), after the definition of "controlled waters" there shall be inserted—

""expenses" includes costs;".

PART III

NATIONAL PARKS

Purposes of National Parks

Purposes of National Parks. 1949 c. 97.

61.—(1) In section 5 of the National Parks and Access to the Countryside Act 1949 (National Parks) for subsection (1) (which provides that Part II of that Act has effect for the purpose of preserving and enhancing the natural beauty of the areas specified in subsection (2) of that section and for the purpose of promoting their enjoyment by the public) there shall be substituted—

"(1) The provisions of this Part of this Act shall have effect for the purpose—

(a) of conserving and enhancing the natural beauty, wildlife and cultural heritage of the areas specified in the next following subsection; and

(b) of promoting opportunities for the understanding and enjoyment of the special qualities of those areas by the public."

(2) The amendment made by subsection (1) above is without prejudice to the continuing validity of any designation of an area as a National Park under subsection (3) of that section.

(3) The following enactments (which refer to the purposes specified in section 5(1) of the National Parks and Access to the Countryside Act 1949), that is to say—

1949 c. 97.

(a) sections 6(3) and (4)(g), 11 and 101(3) of that Act, and

(b) sections 2(5)(b) and 13(4) of the Countryside Act 1968,

1968 c. 41.

shall have effect in accordance with subsection (4) below.

(4) In the application of any provision specified in subsection (3) above, any reference to the purposes specified in subsection (1) of section 5 of the National Parks and Access to the Countryside Act 1949—

(a) in relation to any particular National Park, shall be construed as a reference to the substituted purposes as from the time when a National Park authority becomes the local planning authority for that Park; and

(b) in relation to National Parks generally, shall be construed as a reference—

(i) to the original purposes, so far as relating to National Parks in the case of which the National Park authority has not become the local planning authority since the coming into force of this section, and

(ii) to the substituted purposes, so far as relating to National Parks in the case of which the National Park authority has become the local planning authority since the coming into force of this section.

(5) In subsection (4) above—

"original purposes" means the purposes specified in subsection (1) of section 5 of that Act, as originally enacted;

"substituted purposes" means the purposes specified in that subsection as substituted by subsection (1) above.

62.—(1) After section 11 of the National Parks and Access to the Countryside Act 1949 (general powers of local planning authorities in relation to National Parks) there shall be inserted—

Duty of certain bodies and persons to have regard to the purposes for which National Parks are designated.

"Duty of certain bodies and persons to have regard to the purposes for which National Parks are designated.

11A.—(1) A National Park authority, in pursuing in relation to the National Park the purposes specified in subsection (1) of section five of this Act, shall seek to foster the economic and social well-being of local communities within the National Park, but without incurring significant expenditure in doing so, and shall for that purpose co-operate with local authorities and public bodies whose functions include the promotion of economic or social development within the area of the National Park.

(2) In exercising or performing any functions in relation to, or so as to affect, land in a National Park, any relevant authority shall have regard to the purposes specified in subsection (1) of section five of this Act and, if it appears that there is a conflict between those

purposes, shall attach greater weight to the purpose of conserving and enhancing the natural beauty, wildlife and cultural heritage of the area comprised in the National Park.

(3) For the purposes of this section "relevant authority" means—

  (a) any Minister of the Crown,

  (b) any public body,

  (c) any statutory undertaker, or

  (d) any person holding public office.

(4) In subsection (3) of this section—

  "public body" includes—

    (a) any local authority, joint board or joint committee;

    (b) any National Park authority;

  "public office" means—

    (a) an office under Her Majesty;

    (b) an office created or continued in existence by a public general Act of Parliament; or

    (c) an office the remuneration in respect of which is paid out of money provided by Parliament.

(5) In subsection (4) of this section, "joint board" and "joint committee" mean—

  (a) a joint or special planning board for a National Park reconstituted by order under paragraph 1 or 3 of Schedule 17 to the Local Government Act 1972, or a joint planning board within the meaning of section 2 of the Town and Country Planning Act 1990;

  (b) a joint committee appointed under section 102(1)(b) of the Local Government Act 1972.

1972 c. 70.

1990 c. 8.

(6) In this section, "local authority"—

  (a) in relation to England, means a county council, district council or parish council;

  (b) in relation to Wales, means a county council, county borough council, district council or community council."

(2) The duty imposed by subsection (1) of the section 11A inserted by subsection (1) above shall take effect, in the case of any particular National Park, as from the time when a National Park authority becomes the local planning authority for that Park.

Establishment of National Park authorities

63.—(1) The Secretary of State may—

(a) in the case of any National Park for which there is an existing authority, or

(b) in connection with the designation of any area as a new such Park,

by order establish an authority (to be known as "a National Park authority") to carry out in relation to that Park the functions conferred on such an authority by or under this Part.

Establishment of National Park authorities.

(2) An order under this section may provide, in relation to any National Park for which there is an existing authority—

(a) for the existing authority to cease to have any functions in relation to that Park as from the time when a National Park authority becomes the local planning authority for that Park;

(b) for such (if any) of the functions of the existing authority as, by virtue of this Part, are not as from that time to be functions of the National Park authority for that Park to become functions of the person on whom they would be conferred if the area in question were not in a National Park; and

(c) for the winding up of the existing authority and for that authority to cease to exist, or to be dissolved, as from such time as may be specified in the order.

(3) Subject to any order under subsection (4) below, where there is a variation of the area of a National Park for which there is or is to be a National Park authority, the Park for which that authority is or is to be the authority shall be deemed, as from the time when the variation takes effect, to be that area as varied.

(4) Where provision is made for the variation of the area of a National Park for which there is or is to be a National Park authority, the Secretary of State may by order make such transitional provision as he thinks fit with respect to—

(a) any functions which, in relation to any area that becomes part of the National Park, are by virtue of the variation to become functions of that authority; and

(b) any functions which, in relation to any area that ceases to be part of the National Park, are by virtue of the variation to become functions of a person other than that authority.

(5) Schedule 7 to this Act shall have effect with respect to National Park authorities.

64.—(1) Where a National Park planning board has been constituted for the area of any particular existing National Park in Wales, the Secretary of State may exercise his power under section 63 above to establish a National Park authority in relation to that National Park by making an order under that section designating for the body corporate constituted as that board a date earlier than 31st March 1997 on which that body—

National Park authorities in Wales.

(a) shall cease to be a National Park planning board, and

(b) shall be constituted the National Park authority in relation to that National Park,

without affecting its corporate status (and an order made under or by virtue of that section may make provision re-naming that body accordingly).

(2) Any order under—

(a) paragraph 3A of Schedule 17 to the 1972 Act (special planning boards), or

1990 c. 8.
(b) section 2(1B) of the Town and Country Planning Act 1990 (joint planning boards),

relating to the body corporate constituted as the National Park planning board in question shall have effect on and after the designated date for that body as an order under section 63 above relating to that body in its capacity as the National Park authority in relation to the National Park in question.

(3) For the purposes of any order establishing a National Park authority under section 63 above by virtue of subsection (1) above, or any order which, by virtue of subsection (2) above, has effect as an order under that section—

(a) the requirements of paragraph 2(3) of Schedule 7 to this Act with respect to consultation with councils for principal areas shall, by virtue of the establishment of the National Park planning board, be deemed to have been complied with as respects any provision of the order;

(b) in the case of any member of the National Park planning board immediately before the designated date who was holding that office by virtue of his appointment as such by the Secretary of State under and in accordance with paragraph 11 of Schedule 17 to the 1972 Act (which requires prior consultation), the appointment shall, on and after the designated date, have effect for the remainder of the period for which it was made as an appointment as a member of the National Park authority made by the Secretary of State in accordance with paragraph 4(1) of Schedule 7 to this Act;

(c) in the case of any other member of the National Park planning board immediately before the designated date who is on that date a member of a principal council for an area which includes the whole or any part of the National Park in question, his appointment as a member of that board shall, on and after the designated date, have effect for the remainder of the period for which it was made as an appointment as a local authority member of the National Park authority made in accordance with paragraph 2 of that Schedule; and

(d) any other requirement, whether statutory or otherwise, which must be complied with in connection with the establishment of a National Park authority shall be deemed to have been complied with by virtue of the establishment of the National Park planning board;

and, except as provided by paragraphs (b) and (c) above, no person who is a member of the National Park planning board immediately before the designated date shall, by virtue of the order, become a member of the National Park authority.

(4) The functions of a National Park planning board shall include the duty to take such steps as it considers necessary to enable it (that is to say, the body corporate constituted as that board) on being constituted the National Park authority in relation to the National Park in question by an order made by virtue of subsection (1) above, to perform its functions as a National Park authority on and after the designated date; and the functions conferred on such a board by this subsection—

(a) shall be exercisable before (as well as on or after) 1st April 1996; and

(b) are in addition to any other functions which are exercisable by such a board before that date by virtue of paragraph 13 of Schedule 17 to the Local Government (Wales) Act 1994.

1994 c. 19.

(5) The functions of a principal council for an area which includes the whole or any part of the area of a National Park planning board shall include the duty to take such steps as it considers necessary to enable the body corporate constituted as that board, on being constituted the National Park authority in relation to the National Park in question by an order made by virtue of subsection (1) above, to perform those functions which would, apart from the order, be exercisable by a principal council but which will become functions of that body, as the National Park authority, on the designated date.

(6) Where the Secretary of State—

(a) has taken any steps with a view to, or otherwise in connection with, the establishment of a National Park planning board for the area of an existing National Park in Wales ("the proposed board"), but

(b) decides not to proceed with the establishment of the proposed board and to establish instead a National Park authority in relation to that National Park ("the proposed authority"), and

(c) the proposed authority is, or is to be, established before 31st March 1997,

the doing of anything by or in relation to the Secretary of State (other than the making by the Secretary of State of an instrument of a legislative character) with a view to, or otherwise in connection with, establishing the proposed board shall be treated, as respects the proposed authority, as the doing of any corresponding or reasonably similar thing falling to be done for the purposes of, or otherwise in connection with, the establishment of that authority.

(7) Without prejudice to the generality of subsection (6) above, in any case falling within paragraphs (a) to (c) of that subsection—

(a) any consultation with a principal council after 15th December 1994 by the Secretary of State as respects the proposed board (whether or not required by or under any enactment) shall be deemed, as respects the proposed authority, to have been carried out for the purposes of the consultation with councils for principal areas required by paragraph 2(3) of Schedule 7 to this Act;

(b) anything done by or in relation to the Secretary of State for the purposes of the consultation required by paragraph 11 of Schedule 17 to the 1972 Act (appointment of members by Secretary of State) preparatory to the appointment of a person as a member of the proposed board shall be deemed, as respects the proposed authority, to have been done for the purposes of the consultation required by paragraph 4(1) of Schedule 7 to this Act preparatory to the appointment of that person as a member of that authority;

(c) anything done by or in relation to the Secretary of State (other than the making by the Secretary of State of an instrument of a legislative character) for the purposes of, or otherwise in connection with, any other requirement, whether statutory or otherwise, of a consultative or procedural nature—

(i) which relates to a National Park planning board, and

(ii) for which there is a corresponding or reasonably similar requirement which relates to a National Park authority,

shall be treated, as respects the proposed authority, as done for the purposes of, or otherwise in connection with, that other corresponding or reasonably similar requirement.

1994 c. 19.

(8) Section 54 of the Local Government (Wales) Act 1994 (powers to make incidental, consequential, transitional or supplemental provision) shall have effect as if this Part were contained in that Act, except that subsection (2)(e) of that section shall have effect as if this Part were contained in an Act passed in the same Session as that Act.

(9) In this section—

"the designated date", in the case of any body corporate constituted as a National Park planning board which becomes, or is to become, a National Park authority by virtue of this section, means the date designated by virtue of subsection (1) above in the order relating to that body;

1949 c. 97.

"existing National Park" means a National Park in respect of which there was in force on 15th December 1994 an order under section 5 of the National Parks and Access to the Countryside Act 1949 (designation of areas as National Parks);

"National Park planning board" means—

(a) a special planning board constituted by order under paragraph 3A of Schedule 17 to the 1972 Act to discharge, as respects the area of a National Park in Wales, the functions to which Part I of that Schedule applies, or

1990 c. 8.

(b) a joint planning board constituted by order under subsection (1B) of section 2 of the Town and Country Planning Act 1990 for a united district comprising the area of a National Park in Wales.

Functions of National Park authorities

General purposes and powers.

65.—(1) This Part so far as it relates to the establishment and functions of National Park authorities shall have effect for the purposes specified in section 5(1) of the National Parks and Access to the Countryside Act 1949 (purposes of conserving and enhancing the natural beauty, wildlife and cultural heritage of National Parks and of promoting opportunities for the understanding and enjoyment of the special qualities of those Parks by the public).

(2) Sections 37 and 38 of the Countryside Act 1968 (general duties as to the protection of interests of the countryside and the avoidance of pollution) shall apply to National Park authorities as they apply to local authorities.

(3) The functions of a National Park authority in the period (if any) between the time when it is established and the time when it becomes the local planning authority for the relevant Park shall be confined to the taking of such steps as the authority, after consultation with the Secretary of State and any existing authority for that Park, considers appropriate for securing that it is able properly to carry out its functions after that time.

(4) In the application of subsection (3) above in the case of a National Park authority established in relation to a National Park in Wales, the reference to any existing authority for that Park shall have effect as respects consultation carried out during so much of that period as falls before 1st April 1996 as including a reference to any principal council whose area is wholly or partly comprised in that Park.

(5) The powers of a National Park authority shall include power to do anything which, in the opinion of that authority, is calculated to facilitate, or is conducive or incidental to—

    (a) the accomplishment of the purposes mentioned in subsection (1) above; or

    (b) the carrying out of any functions conferred on it by virtue of any other enactment.

(6) The powers conferred on a National Park authority by subsection (5) above shall not include either—

    (a) power to do anything in contravention of any restriction imposed by virtue of this Part in relation to any express power of the authority; or

    (b) a power to raise money (whether by borrowing or otherwise) in a manner which is not authorised apart from that subsection;

but the things that may be done in exercise of those powers shall not be treated as excluding anything by reason only that it involves the expenditure, borrowing or lending of money or the acquisition or disposal of any property or rights.

(7) Schedule 8 to this Act shall have effect with respect to the supplemental and incidental powers of a National Park authority.

66.—(1) Subject to subsection (2) below, every National Park authority shall, within three years after its operational date, prepare and publish a plan, to be known as a National Park Management Plan, which formulates its policy for the management of the relevant Park and for the carrying out of its functions in relation to that Park.

National Park Management Plans.

(2) A National Park authority for a Park wholly or mainly comprising any area which, immediately before the authority's operational date, was or was included in an area for which there was a National Park Plan prepared and published under paragraph 18 of Schedule 17 to the 1972 Act (National Park plans) shall not be required to prepare a Management Plan under subsection (1) above if, within six months of that date, it adopts the existing National Park Plan as its Management Plan and publishes notice that it has done so.

(3) Where a National Park authority is proposing to adopt a plan under subsection (2) above, it may review the plan before adopting it and shall do so if the plan would have fallen to be reviewed under paragraph 18 of Schedule 17 to the 1972 Act in the period of twelve months beginning with the authority's operational date.

(4) A National Park authority shall review its National Park Management Plan within the period of five years of its operational date and, after the first review, at intervals of not more than five years.

(5) Where a National Park authority has adopted a plan under subsection (2) above as its National Park Management Plan and has not reviewed that Plan before adopting it, the first review of that Plan under subsection (4) above shall take place no later than the time when the adopted plan would otherwise have fallen to be reviewed under paragraph 18 of Schedule 17 to the 1972 Act.

(6) Where a National Park authority reviews any plan under this section, it shall—

(a) determine on that review whether it would be expedient to amend the plan and what (if any) amendments would be appropriate;

(b) make any amendments that it considers appropriate; and

(c) publish a report on the review specifying any amendments made.

(7) A National Park authority which is proposing to publish, adopt or review any plan under this section shall—

(a) give notice of the proposal to every principal council whose area is wholly or partly comprised in the relevant Park and, according to whether that Park is in England or in Wales, to the Countryside Commission and the Nature Conservancy Council for England or to the Countryside Council for Wales;

(b) send a copy of the plan, together (where appropriate) with any proposed amendments of the plan, to every body to which notice of the proposal is required to be given by paragraph (a) above; and

(c) take into consideration any observations made by any such body.

(8) A National Park authority shall send to the Secretary of State a copy of every plan, notice or report which it is required to publish under this section.

(9) In this section "operational date", in relation to a National Park authority, means the date on which the authority becomes the local planning authority for the relevant Park.

National Park authority to be local planning authority.
1990 c. 8.

67.—(1) After section 4 of the Town and Country Planning Act 1990 (National Parks) there shall be inserted—

"National Parks with National Park authorities.

4A.—(1) Where a National Park authority has been established for any area, this section, instead of section 4(1) to (4), shall apply, as from such time as may be specified for the purposes of this section in the order establishing that authority, in relation to the Park for which it is the authority.

(2) Subject to subsections (4) and (5) below, the

National Park authority for the Park shall be the sole local planning authority for the area of the Park and, accordingly—

   (a) functions conferred by or under the planning Acts on a planning authority of any description (including the functions of a mineral planning authority under those Acts and under the Planning and Compensation Act 1991) shall, in relation to the Park, be functions of the National Park authority, and not of any other authority; and

1991 c. 34.

   (b) so much of the area of any other authority as is included in the Park shall be treated as excluded from any area for which that other authority is a planning authority of any description.

(3) For the purposes of subsection (2) above functions under the planning Acts which (apart from this section) are conferred—

   (a) in relation to some areas on the county or district planning authorities for those areas, and

   (b) in relation to other areas on the councils for those areas,

shall be treated, in relation to those other areas, as conferred on each of those councils as the local planning authority for their area.

(4) The functions of a local planning authority by virtue of sections 198 to 201, 206 to 209 and 211 to 215, so far as they are functions of a National Park authority by virtue of this section, shall be exercisable as respects any area which is or is included in an area for which there is a district council, concurrently with the National Park authority, by that council.

(5) For the purposes of any enactment relating to the functions of a district planning authority, the functions of a district council by virtue of subsection (4) above shall be deemed to be conferred on them as a district planning authority and as if the district were the area for which they are such an authority."

(2) The Secretary of State may by order make provision—

   (a) for applying Chapter I of Part II of that Act of 1990 (unitary development plans), instead of provisions of Chapter II of that Part (structure and local plans), in relation to the area of any National Park; or

   (b) for applying Chapter II of that Part in relation to the area of such a Park—

      (i) as if functions under that Chapter of a planning authority of any description were functions of such public authority as may be specified in the order (and not of the National Park authority); and

          (ii) as if that Part had effect with such other modifications as may be so specified in relation to the carrying out of those functions by an authority so specified.

(3) Without prejudice to any power conferred by virtue of section 75 below, the Secretary of State shall have power by order, for the purposes of any provision made by virtue of this section, to modify the provisions of Part II of that Act of 1990 (development plans) in relation to any such area of a local planning authority as, but for any exclusion by virtue of section 4A of that Act, would include the whole or any part of a National Park.

(4) References in this section to provisions of Part II of that Act of 1990 include references to any provisions for modifying those provisions which are contained in any enactment passed after this Act.

(5) Before section 148 of that Act of 1990 (interpretation of provisions relating to purchase notices) there shall be inserted—

"Application of Chapter I to National Parks.

147A. This Chapter shall have effect as if—

    (a) the bodies on whom a purchase notice may be served under section 137 included any National Park authority which is the local planning authority for the area in which the land is situated; and

    (b) a National Park authority were a local authority for the purposes of this Act and the National Park for which it is the local planning authority were its area;

and the references in this Chapter and in section 288(10)(a) to a council and to a local authority shall be construed accordingly."

Planning authority functions under National Parks legislation etc.

68.—(1) Where a National Park authority is the local planning authority for any National Park, section 184 of the 1972 Act and paragraph 37 of Schedule 17 to that Act (functions under certain legislation relating to the National Parks and the countryside) shall not apply as respects that Park in relation to any of the functions conferred by or under—

1949 c. 97.

    (a) the National Parks and Access to the Countryside Act 1949 ("the 1949 Act"), or

1968 c. 41.

    (b) the Countryside Act 1968 ("the 1968 Act"),

on a planning authority of any description.

(2) In consequence of subsection (1) above, but subject to subsections (3) to (7) below—

    (a) functions which are conferred on a local planning authority by or under the 1949 Act or the 1968 Act, and the functions conferred on a county planning authority (or, in relation to Wales, a local planning authority) by section 69 of the 1949 Act (suspension of access to avoid risk of fire), shall, as respects the whole or any part of a National Park for which a National Park authority is the local planning authority, be functions of that authority and not of any other authority;

(b) references in those Acts to a local planning authority whose area consists of or includes the whole or any part of a National Park shall be construed, in relation to any National Park for which a National Park authority is the local planning authority, as references to the National Park authority; and

(c) other references in those Acts to a local planning authority and the references to a local authority in section 103 of the 1949 Act and sections 10 and 43 to 45 of the 1968 Act (which contain provision applying in relation to local authorities in their capacity as local planning authorities) shall have effect accordingly.

(3) Section 11 of the 1949 Act (which makes provision in relation to a local planning authority that corresponds to provision made by section 65 above in relation to a National Park authority) shall not apply in relation to any National Park authority.

(4) The functions conferred by or under section 12 of the 1949 Act or section 12 of the 1968 Act (facilities for National Parks) which are exercisable by virtue of this section by a National Park authority in a National Park—

(a) shall be exercisable by that authority outside the relevant Park on any land in the neighbourhood of that Park; but

(b) shall be so exercisable only under arrangements made with the local planning authority for the area where they are exercised.

(5) Sections 61 to 63 of the 1949 Act (survey of access requirements and action in response to the survey) shall have effect in accordance with subsection (2) above as respects the area of any National Park for which a National Park authority has become the local planning authority—

(a) in the case of a Park designated after the commencement of this section, as if section 61(1) applied with the substitution for the reference to the commencement of that Act of a reference to the time when that authority became the local planning authority for that Park;

(b) as if no area were required by virtue of subsection (3) of section 61 of that Act, or of any previous review under that section, to be excluded from any area to be reviewed by virtue of paragraph (a) above; and

(c) in the case of a Park designated before the commencement of this section, as if—

(i) the power (if any) to make a resolution for the purposes of the proviso to that subsection (3) as respects any part of the area of the Park which has not previously been reviewed under that section, and

(ii) the functions which, where such a resolution has been so made, are conferred on the authority which made it or on any authority which has conducted a review in pursuance of the resolution,

were a power or, as the case may be, functions of the National Park authority, and not of any other authority.

(6) The following functions, so far as exercisable by a National Park authority in relation to land or countryside in a National Park in England for which that authority is the local planning authority, that is to say—

(a) those conferred by or under section 89 of the 1949 Act (planting of trees and treatment of derelict land), and

(b) those conferred by section 10 of the 1968 Act (camping and picnic sites),

shall be exercisable in relation to so much of that Park as is comprised in a district for which there is a district council, concurrently with the National Park authority, by that district council.

(7) For the purposes of any enactment relating to the functions of a district planning authority, the functions of a district council by virtue of subsection (6) above shall be deemed to be conferred on them as a district planning authority and as if the district were the area for which they are such an authority.

(8) The following powers, that is to say—

(a) those conferred on a local authority by or under section 92 of the 1949 Act (wardens), and

(b) those conferred on a local authority by or under section 41 of the 1968 Act (byelaws),

so far as they are conferred in relation to any of the functions which by virtue of this section are functions of a National Park authority as respects the relevant Park, shall be exercisable by that authority and also, in the case of those conferred by or under section 41 of the 1968 Act, by a district council in relation to that council's functions by virtue of subsection (6)(b) above, but not by any other authority.

(9) Section 104 of the 1949 Act (general provisions as to appropriation and disposal of land), except subsection (11), shall have effect as if references in that section to a local authority included references to a National Park authority.

(10) For the purposes of any functions conferred on a National Park authority by virtue of this section references in any enactment to the area of the authority shall be construed as references to the relevant Park.

Planning
authority
functions under
the Wildlife and
Countryside Act
1981.

1981 c. 69.

69.—(1) A National Park authority which is the local planning authority for any National Park, and not any other authority, shall have all the functions under the Wildlife and Countryside Act 1981 which are conferred as respects that Park on a planning authority of any description.

(2) Accordingly—

(a) a National Park authority shall be the relevant authority for the purposes of sections 39, 41 and 50 of that Act (management agreements and duties of agriculture Ministers in relation to the countryside) as respects any land in any National Park for which that authority is the local planning authority; and

(b) section 52(2) of that Act (construction of references to a local planning authority) shall not apply as respects any National Park for which a National Park authority is the local planning authority.

(3) Section 43 of that Act (maps of National Parks) shall have effect in accordance with the preceding provisions of this section—

(a) in the case of a National Park designated after the commencement of this section, as if the relevant date for the purposes of that section were the date on which a National Park authority becomes the local planning authority for the Park; and

(b) in any other case, as if the function of reviewing and revising any map of a part of the Park in question included a power, in pursuance of the review and revisions, to consolidate that map with other maps prepared under that section as respects other parts of that Park.

(4) In section 44 of that Act (grants and loans for purposes of National Parks), after subsection (1) there shall be inserted the following subsection—

"(1A) Subsection (1) above shall not apply in relation to any National Park for which a National Park authority is the local planning authority; but the National Park authority for such a Park may give financial assistance by way of grant or loan, or partly in one way and partly in the other, to any person in respect of expenditure incurred by him in doing anything which, in the opinion of the authority, is conducive to the attainment in the Park in question of any of the purposes mentioned in section 5(1) of the 1949 Act (purposes of conserving and enhancing the natural beauty, wildlife and cultural heritage of National Parks and of promoting opportunities for the understanding and enjoyment of the special qualities of those Parks by the public)."

70. In addition to its functions under the enactments mentioned in sections 67 to 69 above and to such of its functions under any other enactment as are conferred by virtue of its being a local planning authority within the meaning of the Town and Country Planning Act 1990, a National Park authority shall have the further miscellaneous functions conferred on it by virtue of Schedule 9 to this Act.

Other statutory functions.

1990 c. 8.

Finances of National Park authorities

71.—(1) A National Park authority shall have power in respect of every financial year beginning after the establishment of that authority to issue levies to the councils by whom the local authority members of that authority fall to be appointed.

National Park authorities to be levying bodies.

(2) Subject to the following provisions of this section, a levy issued by virtue of this section shall be issued in accordance with regulations under section 74 of the Local Government Finance Act 1988 (power to make regulations authorising a levying body to issue a levy); and, accordingly, a National Park authority shall be deemed to be a levying body within the meaning of that section.

1988 c. 41.

(3) Subject to any maximum specified in or determined in accordance with any regulations under that section 74, the amount of the levies issued by a National Park authority in respect of any financial year shall be equal to the sum by which the aggregate of the amounts specified in subsection (4) below is exceeded by the aggregate of the sums which it estimates it will require in respect of that year for the following purposes, that is to say—

(a) meeting the expenditure of the authority which will fall to be charged for that year to any revenue account;

(b) making such provision as may be appropriate for meeting contingencies the expenditure on which would fall to be so charged;

(c) securing the availability to the authority of adequate working balances on its revenue accounts; and

(d) providing the authority with the funds required for covering any deficit carried forward from a previous financial year in any revenue account.

(4) The amounts mentioned in subsection (3) above in relation to any financial year are—

(a) any amounts to be received by the authority in respect of that year by way of grant under section 72 below;

(b) the authority's estimate of the amounts which are likely for that year to be credited to any revenue account in respect of sums payable to the authority for things done in the course of, or in connection with, the carrying out of its functions; and

(c) the authority's estimate of the amounts not falling within paragraph (a) or (b) above which apart from this section are, or are likely to be, available to it for that year for the purposes mentioned in subsection (3) above.

(5) Where agreement as to the apportionment of the amount to be raised by a National Park authority in respect of any financial year by way of levies is entered into, before 1st December in the immediately preceding financial year, by all the authorities to whom the levies in respect of that year may be issued by that authority, that amount shall be apportioned between those authorities in accordance with the agreement, instead of in accordance with any provision made by virtue of that section 74.

(6) Regulations under that section 74 may include provision for requiring an authority to anticipate a levy by virtue of this section when making any calculations which fall, for the financial year following that in which any National Park authority is established, to be made (whether originally or by way of substitute) under section 32 or 43 of the Local Government Finance Act 1992 (calculation of budget requirement).

1992 c. 14.

(7) A National Park authority shall not by virtue of this section be a local authority within the meaning of the Town and Country Planning Act 1990.

1990 c. 8.

National Park grant.

72.—(1) The Secretary of State may make grants to a National Park authority for such purposes, of such amounts and on such terms and conditions as he thinks fit.

(2) Before determining the amount of any grant which he proposes to make to a National Park authority under this section, or the purpose for which it is to be made, the Secretary of State shall consult, according to whether the relevant Park is in England or in Wales, either the Countryside Commission or the Countryside Council for Wales.

(3) The consent of the Treasury shall be required for the making of a grant under this section.

Part III

73. In section 39(1) of the Local Government and Housing Act 1989 (which specifies the authorities to which the provisions of Part IV of that Act relating to capital accounts and borrowing powers apply), after paragraph (i) there shall be inserted—

Capital finances and borrowing.
1989 c. 42.

"(ia) a National Park authority;".

74.—(1) No payment made for any year beginning on or after 1st April 1990 and ending on or before 31st March 1996 by the Secretary of State by way of grant to the council of a county or a metropolitan district in respect of the council's expenditure or estimated expenditure in connection with National Parks shall be regarded as made otherwise than under and in accordance with the relevant enactments by reason only of—

Validation of certain grants paid to local authorities in respect of expenditure relating to National Parks.

(a) the aggregate amount of such grants for the year to such councils not having been duly prescribed;

(b) the method of determining the proportion of such aggregate amount payable to that council not having been duly prescribed; or

(c) payment of the grant being, or having been, made—

(i) otherwise than in accordance with an approved Rate Support Grant Report or such a Report as varied by an approved supplementary report for the year; or

(ii) without there being an approved Rate Support Grant Report for the year.

(2) Any reference in this section to a payment by way of grant made under and in accordance with the relevant enactments is a reference to a payment of grant made under section 7 of the Local Government Act 1974 (supplementary grants towards expenditure with respect to National Parks) in accordance with the provisions of that section and those of section 60 or 61 of the Local Government, Planning and Land Act 1980 (rate support grant reports and supplementary reports) as they apply in relation to grants under the said section 7.

1974 c. 7.

1980 c. 65.

(3) In this section—

"approved Rate Support Grant Report" means a Rate Support Grant Report which has been laid before and approved by a resolution of the House of Commons;

"approved supplementary report" means a supplementary report which has been laid before and approved by a resolution of the House of Commons;

"duly prescribed" means prescribed by a Rate Support Grant Report or a supplementary report;

"Rate Support Grant Report" means a Rate Support Grant Report made under section 60 of the Local Government, Planning and Land Act 1980;

"supplementary report" means a supplementary report made under section 61 of that Act; and

"year" means a period of 12 months beginning with 1st April.

Supplemental provisions

Powers to make
orders.

75.—(1) This section applies to every power of the Secretary of State under the preceding provisions of this Part to make an order.

(2) The powers to which this section applies shall, in each case, be exercisable by statutory instrument; and, except in the case of a statutory instrument made by virtue of section 64 above which only—

    (a) designates a date,

1990 c. 8.

    (b) specifies a time for the purposes of section 4A of the Town and Country Planning Act 1990,

    (c) renames a body,

    (d) makes provision under paragraph 2 of Schedule 7 to this Act—

        (i) for excluding a council from the councils by whom the local authority members of a National Park authority are to be appointed, or

        (ii) for so increasing the number of local authority members of a National Park authority to be appointed by any council as to secure that the number of local authority members of that authority remains unchanged notwithstanding any such exclusion of a council, or

    (e) makes provision under section 63(2) above,

any such statutory instrument shall be subject to annulment in pursuance of a resolution of either House of Parliament.

(3) The powers to which this section applies shall, in each case, include power to make such incidental, supplemental, consequential and transitional provision as the Secretary of State thinks necessary or expedient.

(4) A power of the Secretary of State by an order under this Part to make incidental, supplemental, consequential or transitional provision shall include power for any incidental, supplemental, consequential or, as the case may be, transitional purpose—

    (a) to apply with or without modifications,

    (b) to extend, exclude or modify, or

    (c) to repeal or revoke with or without savings,

any enactment or any instrument made under any enactment.

(5) The provision that may be made for incidental, supplemental, consequential or transitional purposes in the case of any order under this Part which—

    (a) establishes a National Park authority or winds up the existing authority for any National Park, or

    (b) otherwise has the effect of transferring functions from one person to another or of providing for functions to become exercisable concurrently by two or more persons or to cease to be so exercisable,

shall include provision for the transfer of property, rights and liabilities from one person to another.

(6) A power of the Secretary of State under this Part to provide by order for the transfer of any property, rights or liabilities, or to make

transitional provision in connection with any such transfer or with any order by which functions become or cease to be exercisable by any authority, shall include power to provide, in particular—

(a) for the management and custody of any transferred property (whether real or personal);

(b) for any liabilities transferred to include liabilities under any enactment;

(c) for legal proceedings commenced by or against any person to be continued by or against a person to whom property, rights or liabilities are transferred or, as the case may be, any authority by whom any functions are to become exercisable;

(d) for the transfer of staff, compensation for loss of office, pensions and other staffing matters; and

(e) for treating any person to whom a transfer of property, rights or liabilities is made or, as the case may be, by whom any functions are to become exercisable as, for some or all purposes, the same person in law as the person from whom the transfer is made or the authority by whom the functions have previously been exercisable.

(7) The powers to which this section applies shall, in each case, include power to make different provision for different cases, including different provision for different areas or localities and for different authorities.

(8) The powers to which this section applies shall be without prejudice to any powers conferred by Part II of the Local Government Act 1992 or any other enactment.

1992 c. 19.

(9) In this section "enactment" includes an enactment contained in an Act passed after this Act.

76.—(1) Any public authorities affected by an order under this Part may from time to time make agreements with respect to—

Agreements as to incidental matters.

(a) any property, income, rights, liabilities or expenses (so far as affected by the order) of the parties to the agreement; or

(b) any financial relations between those parties.

(2) Such an agreement may provide—

(a) for the transfer or retention of any property, rights and liabilities, with or without conditions, and for the joint use of any property;

(b) for the making of payments by any party to the agreement in respect of—

(i) property, rights and liabilities transferred or retained,

(ii) the joint use of any property, or

(iii) remuneration or compensation payable to any person;

and

(c) for the making of any such payment either by way of a capital sum or of a terminable annuity.

(3) In default of agreement as to any disputed matter, the matter shall be referred to the arbitration of a single arbitrator agreed on by the parties

or, in default of agreement, appointed by the Secretary of State; and the award of the arbitrator may make any provision that might be contained in an agreement under this section.

(4) In subsection (3) above "disputed matter" means any matter which—

(a) might be the subject of provision contained in an agreement under this section; and

(b) is the subject of such a dispute between two or more public authorities as is not resolved by or under provision contained in any order under this Part.

Isles of Scilly.

77.—(1) This Part shall have effect in relation to the Isles of Scilly subject to any such modifications as may be provided for by the Secretary of State by order made by statutory instrument.

(2) Before making an order under this section the Secretary of State shall consult with the Council of the Isles of Scilly.

(3) The power to make an order under this section shall include power to make such incidental, supplemental, consequential or transitional provision as the Secretary of State thinks necessary or expedient.

Minor and consequential amendments relating to National Parks.

78. The enactments mentioned in Schedule 10 to this Act shall have effect subject to the amendments contained in that Schedule (being minor amendments and consequential amendments in connection with the provisions of this Part).

Interpretation of Part III.
1972 c. 70.

79.—(1) In this Part, except in so far as the context otherwise requires—

"the 1972 Act" means the Local Government Act 1972;

"existing authority", in relation to a National Park, means—

(a) any such joint or special planning board for that Park or for any area wholly or partly comprised in that Park as was reconstituted by an order under paragraph 1 or 3 of Schedule 17 to the 1972 Act or constituted by an order under paragraph 3A of that Schedule or section 2(1B) of the Town and Country Planning Act 1990; or

1990 c. 8.

(b) any National Park Committee for that Park or for any such area;

"liability", in relation to the transfer of liabilities from one person to another, does not include any criminal liability;

"principal council" and "principal area" have the same meanings as in the 1972 Act;

"public authority" means any local authority within the meaning of the 1972 Act (including any such authority in their capacity as a local planning authority), any National Park authority, any existing authority for a National Park, any joint authority or residuary body established under Part II of the Local Government Act 1992, any joint authority established under section 34 of the Local Government (Wales) Act 1994 or the Residuary Body for Wales established by section 39 of that Act;

1992 c. 19.

1994 c. 19.

"the relevant Park", in relation to a National Park authority, means the area for which that authority is or is to be the National Park authority.

(2) Where—

    (a) any enactment that is applied by virtue of this Part in relation to National Park authorities refers, or falls to be construed as referring, to any other enactment, and

    (b) that other enactment is also one which is so applied,

the reference shall be construed (so far as it would not be so construed apart from this subsection) as including a reference to the other enactment as it is applied in relation to National Park authorities.

PART IV

AIR QUALITY

80.—(1) The Secretary of State shall as soon as possible prepare and publish a statement (in this Part referred to as "the strategy") containing policies with respect to the assessment or management of the quality of air.

National air quality strategy.

(2) The strategy may also contain policies for implementing—

    (a) obligations of the United Kingdom under the Community Treaties, or

    (b) international agreements to which the United Kingdom is for the time being a party,

so far as relating to the quality of air.

(3) The strategy shall consist of or include—

    (a) a statement which relates to the whole of Great Britain; or

    (b) two or more statements which between them relate to every part of Great Britain.

(4) The Secretary of State—

    (a) shall keep under review his policies with respect to the quality of air; and

    (b) may from time to time modify the strategy.

(5) Without prejudice to the generality of what may be included in the strategy, the strategy must include statements with respect to—

    (a) standards relating to the quality of air;

    (b) objectives for the restriction of the levels at which particular substances are present in the air; and

    (c) measures which are to be taken by local authorities and other persons for the purpose of achieving those objectives.

(6) In preparing the strategy or any modification of it, the Secretary of State shall consult—

    (a) the appropriate new Agency;

    (b) such bodies or persons appearing to him to be representative of the interests of local government as he may consider appropriate;

    (c) such bodies or persons appearing to him to be representative of the interests of industry as he may consider appropriate; and

    (d) such other bodies or persons as he may consider appropriate.

(7) Before publishing the strategy or any modification of it, the Secretary of State—

(a) shall publish a draft of the proposed strategy or modification, together with notice of a date before which, and an address at which, representations may be made to him concerning the draft so published; and

(b) shall take into account any such representations which are duly made and not withdrawn.

Functions of the new Agencies.

81.—(1) In discharging its pollution control functions, each new Agency shall have regard to the strategy.

(2) In this section "pollution control functions", in relation to a new Agency, means—

(a) in the case of the Agency, the functions conferred on it by or under the enactments specified in section 5(5) above; or

(b) in the case of SEPA, the functions conferred on it by or under the enactments specified in section 33(5) above.

Local authority reviews.

82.—(1) Every local authority shall from time to time cause a review to be conducted of the quality for the time being, and the likely future quality within the relevant period, of air within the authority's area.

(2) Where a local authority causes a review under subsection (1) above to be conducted, it shall also cause an assessment to be made of whether air quality standards and objectives are being achieved, or are likely to be achieved within the relevant period, within the authority's area.

(3) If, on an assessment under subsection (2) above, it appears that any air quality standards or objectives are not being achieved, or are not likely within the relevant period to be achieved, within the local authority's area, the local authority shall identify any parts of its area in which it appears that those standards or objectives are not likely to be achieved within the relevant period.

Designation of air quality management areas.

83.—(1) Where, as a result of an air quality review, it appears that any air quality standards or objectives are not being achieved, or are not likely within the relevant period to be achieved, within the area of a local authority, the local authority shall by order designate as an air quality management area (in this Part referred to as a "designated area") any part of its area in which it appears that those standards or objectives are not being achieved, or are not likely to be achieved within the relevant period.

(2) An order under this section may, as a result of a subsequent air quality review,—

(a) be varied by a subsequent order; or

(b) be revoked by such an order, if it appears on that subsequent air quality review that the air quality standards and objectives are being achieved, and are likely throughout the relevant period to be achieved, within the designated area.

Duties of local authorities in relation to designated areas.

84.—(1) Where an order under section 83 above comes into operation, the local authority which made the order shall, for the purpose of supplementing such information as it has in relation to the designated area in question, cause an assessment to be made of—

(a) the quality for the time being, and the likely future quality within the relevant period, of air within the designated area to which the order relates; and

(b) the respects (if any) in which it appears that air quality standards or objectives are not being achieved, or are not likely within the relevant period to be achieved, within that designated area.

(2) A local authority which is required by subsection (1) above to cause an assessment to be made shall also be under a duty—

    (a) to prepare, before the expiration of the period of twelve months beginning with the coming into operation of the order mentioned in that subsection, a report of the results of that assessment; and

    (b) to prepare, in accordance with the following provisions of this Part, a written plan (in this Part referred to as an "action plan") for the exercise by the authority, in pursuit of the achievement of air quality standards and objectives in the designated area, of any powers exercisable by the authority.

(3) An action plan shall include a statement of the time or times by or within which the local authority in question proposes to implement each of the proposed measures comprised in the plan.

(4) A local authority may from time to time revise an action plan.

(5) This subsection applies in any case where the local authority preparing an action plan or a revision of an action plan is the council of a district in England which is comprised in an area for which there is a county council; and if, in a case where this subsection applies, the county council disagrees with the authority about the contents of the proposed action plan or revision of the action plan—

    (a) either of them may refer the matter to the Secretary of State;

    (b) on any such reference the Secretary of State may confirm the authority's proposed action plan or revision of the action plan, with or without modifications (whether or not proposed by the county council) or reject it and, if he rejects it, he may also exercise any powers of his under section 85 below; and

    (c) the authority shall not finally determine the content of the action plan, or the revision of the action plan, except in accordance with his decision on the reference or in pursuance of directions under section 85 below.

85.—(1) In this section, "the appropriate authority" means—

Reserve powers of the Secretary of State or SEPA.

    (a) in relation to England and Wales, the Secretary of State; and

    (b) in relation to Scotland, SEPA acting with the approval of the Secretary of State.

(2) The appropriate authority may conduct or make, or cause to be conducted or made,—

    (a) a review of the quality for the time being, and the likely future quality within the relevant period, of air within the area of any local authority;

    (b) an assessment of whether air quality standards and objectives are being achieved, or are likely to be achieved within the relevant period, within the area of a local authority;

    (c) an identification of any parts of the area of a local authority in which it appears that those standards or objectives are not likely to be achieved within the relevant period; or

(d) an assessment of the respects (if any) in which it appears that air quality standards or objectives are not being achieved, or are not likely within the relevant period to be achieved, within the area of a local authority or within a designated area.

(3) If it appears to the appropriate authority—

(a) that air quality standards or objectives are not being achieved, or are not likely within the relevant period to be achieved, within the area of a local authority,

(b) that a local authority has failed to discharge any duty imposed on it under or by virtue of this Part,

(c) that the actions, or proposed actions, of a local authority in purported compliance with the provisions of this Part are inappropriate in all the circumstances of the case, or

(d) that developments in science or technology, or material changes in circumstances, have rendered inappropriate the actions or proposed actions of a local authority in pursuance of this Part,

the appropriate authority may give directions to the local authority requiring it to take such steps as may be specified in the directions.

(4) Without prejudice to the generality of subsection (3) above, directions under that subsection may, in particular, require a local authority—

(a) to cause an air quality review to be conducted under section 82 above in accordance with the directions;

(b) to cause an air quality review under section 82 above to be conducted afresh, whether in whole or in part, or to be so conducted with such differences as may be specified or described in the directions;

(c) to make an order under section 83 above designating as an air quality management area an area specified in, or determined in accordance with, the directions;

(d) to revoke, or modify in accordance with the directions, any order under that section;

(e) to prepare in accordance with the directions an action plan for a designated area;

(f) to modify, in accordance with the directions, any action plan prepared by the authority; or

(g) to implement, in accordance with the directions, any measures in an action plan.

(5) The Secretary of State shall also have power to give directions to local authorities requiring them to take such steps specified in the directions as he considers appropriate for the implementation of—

(a) any obligations of the United Kingdom under the Community Treaties, or

(b) any international agreement to which the United Kingdom is for the time being a party,

so far as relating to the quality of air.

(6) Any direction given under this section shall be published in such manner as the body or person giving it considers appropriate for the purpose of bringing the matters to which it relates to the attention of persons likely to be affected by them; and—

(a) copies of the direction shall be made available to the public; and

(b) notice shall be given—

(i) in the case of a direction given to a local authority in England and Wales, in the London Gazette, or

(ii) in the case of a direction given to a local authority in Scotland, in the Edinburgh Gazette,

of the giving of the direction and of where a copy of the direction may be obtained.

(7) It is the duty of a local authority to comply with any direction given to it under or by virtue of this Part.

86.—(1) This section applies in any case where a district in England for which there is a district council is comprised in an area for which there is a county council; and in this paragraph—

Functions of county councils for areas for which there are district councils.

(a) any reference to the county council is a reference to the council of that area; and

(b) any reference to a district council is a reference to the council of a district comprised in that area.

(2) The county council may make recommendations to a district council with respect to the carrying out of—

(a) any particular air quality review,

(b) any particular assessment under section 82 or 84 above, or

(c) the preparation of any particular action plan or revision of an action plan,

and the district council shall take into account any such recommendations.

(3) Where a district council is preparing an action plan, the county council shall, within the relevant period, submit to the district council proposals for the exercise (so far as relating to the designated area) by the county council, in pursuit of the achievement of air quality standards and objectives, of any powers exercisable by the county council.

(4) Where the county council submits proposals to a district council in pursuance of subsection (3) above, it shall also submit a statement of the time or times by or within which it proposes to implement each of the proposals.

(5) An action plan shall include a statement of—

(a) any proposals submitted pursuant to subsection (3) above; and

(b) any time or times set out in the statement submitted pursuant to subsection (4) above.

(6) If it appears to the Secretary of State—

(a) that air quality standards or objectives are not being achieved, or are not likely within the relevant period to be achieved, within the area of a district council,

(b) that the county council has failed to discharge any duty imposed on it under or by virtue of this Part,

(c) that the actions, or proposed actions, of the county council in purported compliance with the provisions of this Part are inappropriate in all the circumstances of the case, or

(d) that developments in science or technology, or material changes in circumstances, have rendered inappropriate the actions or proposed actions of the county council in pursuance of this Part,

the Secretary of State may give directions to the county council requiring it to take such steps as may be specified in the directions.

(7) Without prejudice to the generality of subsection (6) above, directions under that subsection may, in particular, require the county council—

(a) to submit, in accordance with the directions, proposals pursuant to subsection (3) above or a statement pursuant to subsection (4) above;

(b) to modify, in accordance with the directions, any proposals or statement submitted by the county council pursuant to subsection (3) or (4) above;

(c) to submit any proposals or statement so modified to the district council in question pursuant to subsection (3) or (4) above; or

(d) to implement, in accordance with the directions, any measures included in an action plan.

(8) The Secretary of State shall also have power to give directions to county councils for areas for which there are district councils requiring them to take such steps specified in the directions as he considers appropriate for the implementation of—

(a) any obligations of the United Kingdom under the Community Treaties, or

(b) any international agreement to which the United Kingdom is for the time being a party,

so far as relating to the quality of air.

(9) Any direction given under this section shall be published in such manner as the Secretary of State considers appropriate for the purpose of bringing the matters to which it relates to the attention of persons likely to be affected by them; and—

(a) copies of the direction shall be made available to the public; and

(b) notice of the giving of the direction, and of where a copy of the direction may be obtained, shall be given in the London Gazette.

(10) It is the duty of a county council for an area for which there are district councils to comply with any direction given to it under or by virtue of this Part.

Regulations for the purposes of Part IV.

87.—(1) Regulations may make provision—

(a) for, or in connection with, implementing the strategy;

(b) for, or in connection with, implementing—

(i) obligations of the United Kingdom under the Community Treaties, or

(ii) international agreements to which the United Kingdom is for the time being a party,

so far as relating to the quality of air; or

(c) otherwise with respect to the assessment or management of the quality of air.

(2) Without prejudice to the generality of subsection (1) above, regulations under that subsection may make provision—

(a) prescribing standards relating to the quality of air;

(b) prescribing objectives for the restriction of the levels at which particular substances are present in the air;

(c) conferring powers or imposing duties on local authorities;

(d) for or in connection with—

(i) authorising local authorities (whether by agreements or otherwise) to exercise any functions of a Minister of the Crown on his behalf;

(ii) directing that functions of a Minister of the Crown shall be exercisable concurrently with local authorities; or

(iii) transferring functions of a Minister of the Crown to local authorities;

(e) prohibiting or restricting, or for or in connection with prohibiting or restricting,—

(i) the carrying on of prescribed activities, or

(ii) the access of prescribed vehicles or mobile equipment to prescribed areas,

whether generally or in prescribed circumstances;

(f) for or in connection with the designation of air quality management areas by orders made by local authorities in such cases or circumstances not falling within section 83 above as may be prescribed;

(g) for the application, with or without modifications, of any provisions of this Part in relation to areas designated by virtue of paragraph (f) above or in relation to orders made by virtue of that paragraph;

(h) with respect to—

(i) air quality reviews;

(ii) assessments under this Part;

(iii) orders designating air quality management areas; or

(iv) action plans;

(j) prescribing measures which are to be adopted by local authorities (whether in action plans or otherwise) or other persons in pursuance of the achievement of air quality standards or objectives;

(k) for or in connection with the communication to the public of information relating to quality for the time being, or likely future quality, of the air;

(l) for or in connection with the obtaining by local authorities from any person of information which is reasonably necessary for the discharge of functions conferred or imposed on them under or by virtue of this Part;

(m) for or in connection with the recovery by a local authority from prescribed persons in prescribed circumstances, and in such manner as may be prescribed, of costs incurred by the authority in discharging functions conferred or imposed on the authority under or by virtue of this Part;

(n) for a person who contravenes, or fails to comply with, any prescribed provision of the regulations to be guilty of an offence and liable on summary conviction to a fine not exceeding level 5 on the standard scale or such lower level on that scale as may be prescribed in relation to the offence;

(o) for or in connection with arrangements under which a person may discharge any liability to conviction for a prescribed offence by payment of a penalty of a prescribed amount;

(p) for or in connection with appeals against determinations or decisions made, notices given or served, or other things done under or by virtue of the regulations.

(3) Without prejudice to the generality of paragraph (h) of subsection (2) above, the provision that may be made by virtue of that paragraph includes provision for or in connection with any of the following, that is to say—

(a) the scope or form of a review or assessment;

(b) the scope, content or form of an action plan;

(c) the time at which, period within which, or manner in which a review or assessment is to be carried out or an action plan is to be prepared;

(d) the methods to be employed—

(i) in carrying out reviews or assessments; or

(ii) in monitoring the effectiveness of action plans;

(e) the factors to be taken into account in preparing action plans;

(f) the actions which must be taken by local authorities or other persons in consequence of reviews, assessments or action plans;

(g) requirements for consultation;

(h) the treatment of representations or objections duly made;

(j) the publication of, or the making available to the public of, or of copies of,—

(i) the results, or reports of the results, of reviews or assessments; or

(ii) orders or action plans;

(k) requirements for—

(i) copies of any such reports, orders or action plans, or

(ii) prescribed information, in such form as may be prescribed, relating to reviews or assessments,

to be sent to the Secretary of State or to the appropriate new Agency.

(4) In determining—

(a) any appeal against, or reference or review of, a decision of a local authority under or by virtue of regulations under this Part, or

(b) any application transmitted from a local authority under or by virtue of any such regulations,

the body or person making the determination shall be bound by any direction given by a Minister of the Crown or SEPA to the local authority to the same extent as the local authority.

(5) The provisions of any regulations under this Part may include—

(a) provision for anything that may be prescribed by the regulations to be determined under the regulations and for anything falling to be so determined to be determined by such persons, in accordance with such procedure and by reference to such matters, and to the opinion of such persons, as may be prescribed;

(b) different provision for different cases, including different provision in relation to different persons, circumstances, areas or localities; and

(c) such supplemental, consequential, incidental or transitional provision (including provision amending any enactment or any instrument made under any enactment) as the Secretary of State considers appropriate.

(6) Nothing in regulations under this Part shall authorise any person other than a constable in uniform to stop a vehicle on any road.

(7) Before making any regulations under this Part, the Secretary of State shall consult—

(a) the appropriate new Agency;

(b) such bodies or persons appearing to him to be representative of the interests of local government as he may consider appropriate;

(c) such bodies or persons appearing to him to be representative of the interests of industry as he may consider appropriate; and

(d) such other bodies or persons as he may consider appropriate.

(8) Any power conferred by this Part to make regulations shall be exercisable by statutory instrument; and no statutory instrument containing regulations under this Part shall be made unless a draft of the instrument has been laid before, and approved by a resolution of, each House of Parliament.

(9) If, apart from this subsection, the draft of an instrument containing regulations under this Part would be treated for the purposes of the Standing Orders of either House of Parliament as a hybrid instrument, it shall proceed in that House as if it were not such an instrument.

88.—(1) The Secretary of State may issue guidance to local authorities with respect to, or in connection with, the exercise of any of the powers conferred, or the discharge of any of the duties imposed, on those authorities by or under this Part.

Guidance for the purposes of Part IV.

(2) A local authority, in carrying out any of its functions under or by virtue of this Part, shall have regard to any guidance issued by the Secretary of State under this Part.

(3) This section shall apply in relation to county councils for areas for which there are district councils as it applies in relation to local authorities.

89.—(1) Subject to the provisions of any order under this section, this Part, other than section 80, shall not apply in relation to the Isles of Scilly.

(2) The Secretary of State may, after consultation with the Council of the Isles of Scilly, by order provide for the application of any provisions of this Part (other than section 80) to the Isles of Scilly; and any such order may provide for the application of those provisions to those Isles with such modifications as may be specified in the order.

(3) An order under this section may—

(a) make different provision for different cases, including different provision in relation to different persons, circumstances or localities; and

(b) contain such supplemental, consequential and transitional provision as the Secretary of State considers appropriate, including provision saving provision repealed by or under any enactment.

(4) The power of the Secretary of State to make an order under this section shall be exercisable by statutory instrument; and a statutory instrument containing such an order shall be subject to annulment in pursuance of a resolution of either House of Parliament.

Supplemental
provisions.

90.   Schedule 11 to this Act shall have effect.

Interpretation of
Part IV.

91.—(1) In this Part—

"action plan" shall be construed in accordance with section 84(2)(b) above;

"air quality objectives" means objectives prescribed by virtue of section 87(2)(b) above;

"air quality review" means a review under section 82 or 85 above;

"air quality standards" means standards prescribed by virtue of section 87(2)(a) above;

"the appropriate new Agency" means—

(a) in relation to England and Wales, the Agency;

(b) in relation to Scotland, SEPA;

"designated area" has the meaning given by section 83(1) above;

"local authority", in relation to England and Wales, means—

(a) any unitary authority,

(b) any district council, so far as it is not a unitary authority,

(c) the Common Council of the City of London and, as respects the Temples, the Sub-Treasurer of the Inner Temple and the Under-Treasurer of the Middle Temple respectively,

1994 c. 39.

and, in relation to Scotland, means a council for an area constituted under section 2 of the Local Government etc. (Scotland) Act 1994;

"new Agency" means the Agency or SEPA;

"prescribed" means prescribed, or of a description prescribed, by or under regulations;

"regulations" means regulations made by the Secretary of State;

"the relevant period", in the case of any provision of this Part, means such period as may be prescribed for the purposes of that provision;

"the strategy" has the meaning given by section 80(1) above;

"unitary authority" means—

    (a) the council of a county, so far as it is the council of an area for which there are no district councils;

    (b) the council of any district comprised in an area for which there is no county council;

    (c) the council of a London borough;

    (d) the council of a county borough in Wales.

(2) Any reference in this Part to it appearing that any air quality standards or objectives are not likely within the relevant period to be achieved includes a reference to it appearing that those standards or objectives are likely within that period not to be achieved.

PART V

MISCELLANEOUS, GENERAL AND SUPPLEMENTAL PROVISIONS

Waste

92.—(1) Before section 45 of the Environmental Protection Act 1990 there shall be inserted—

National waste strategy.
1990 c. 43.

"National waste strategy: England and Wales.

    44A.—(1) The Secretary of State shall as soon as possible prepare a statement ("the strategy") containing his policies in relation to the recovery and disposal of waste in England and Wales.

    (2) The strategy shall consist of or include—

        (a) a statement which relates to the whole of England and Wales; or

        (b) two or more statements which between them relate to the whole of England and Wales.

    (3) The Secretary of State may from time to time modify the strategy.

    (4) Without prejudice to the generality of what may be included in the strategy, the strategy must include—

        (a) a statement of the Secretary of State's policies for attaining the objectives specified in Schedule 2A to this Act;

        (b) provisions relating to each of the following, that is to say—

            (i) the type, quantity and origin of waste to be recovered or disposed of;

            (ii) general technical requirements; and

            (iii) any special requirements for particular wastes.

    (5) In preparing the strategy or any modification of it, the Secretary of State—

        (a) shall consult the Environment Agency,

(b) shall consult—

>   (i) such bodies or persons appearing to him to be representative of the interests of local government, and

>   (ii) such bodies or persons appearing to him to be representative of the interests of industry,

as he may consider appropriate, and

(c) may consult such other bodies or persons as he considers appropriate.

(6) Without prejudice to any power to give directions conferred by section 40 of the Environment Act 1995, the Secretary of State may give directions to the Environment Agency requiring it—

(a) to advise him on the policies which are to be included in the strategy;

(b) to carry out a survey of or investigation into—

>   (i) the kinds or quantities of waste which it appears to that Agency is likely to be situated in England and Wales,

>   (ii) the facilities which are or appear to that Agency likely to be available or needed in England and Wales for recovering or disposing of any such waste,

>   (iii) any other matter upon which the Secretary of State wishes to be informed in connection with his preparation of the strategy or any modification of it,

and to report its findings to him.

(7) A direction under subsection (6)(b) above—

(a) shall specify or describe the matters or the areas which are to be the subject of the survey or investigation; and

(b) may make provision in relation to the manner in which—

>   (i) the survey or investigation is to be carried out, or

>   (ii) the findings are to be reported or made available to other persons.

(8) Where a direction is given under subsection (6)(b) above, the Environment Agency shall, in accordance with any requirement of the direction,—

(a) before carrying out the survey or investigation, consult—

>   (i) such bodies or persons appearing to it to be representative of local planning authorities, and

> (ii) such bodies or persons appearing to it to be representative of the interests of industry,
>
> as it may consider appropriate; and

(b) make its findings available to those authorities.

(9) In this section—

"local planning authority" has the same meaning as in the Town and Country Planning Act 1990;   1990 c. 8.

"strategy" includes the strategy as modified from time to time and "statement" shall be construed accordingly.

(10) This section makes provision for the purpose of implementing Article 7 of the directive of the Council of   75/442/EEC. the European Communities, dated 15th July 1975, on waste, as amended by—

(a) the directive of that Council, dated 18th March   91/156/EEC. 1991, amending directive 75/442/EEC on waste; and

(b) the directive of that Council, dated 23rd   91/692/EEC. December 1991, standardising and rationalising reports on the implementation of certain Directives relating to the environment.

National waste strategy: Scotland.

44B.—(1) SEPA shall as soon as possible prepare a statement ("the strategy") containing its policies in relation to the recovery and disposal of waste in Scotland.

(2) SEPA may from time to time modify the strategy.

(3) Without prejudice to the generality of what may be included in the strategy, the strategy must include—

(a) a statement of SEPA's policies for attaining the objectives specified in Schedule 2A to this Act;

(b) provisions relating to each of the following, that is to say—

> (i) the type, quantity and origin of waste to be recovered or disposed of;
>
> (ii) general technical requirements; and
>
> (iii) any special requirements for particular wastes.

(4) In preparing the strategy or any modification of it SEPA shall consult—

(a) such bodies or persons appearing to it to be representative of the interests of industry as it may consider appropriate;

(b) such local authorities as appear to it to be likely to be affected by the strategy or modification,

and may consult such other bodies or persons as it considers appropriate.

(5) Without prejudice to any power to give directions conferred by section 40 of the Environment Act 1995, the Secretary of State may give directions to SEPA—

  (a) as to the policies which are to be included in the strategy;

  (b) requiring it to carry out a survey or investigation into—

      (i) the kinds or quantities of waste which it appears to it is likely to be situated in Scotland,

      (ii) the facilities which are or appear to it likely to be available or needed in Scotland for recovering or disposing of any such waste,

      (iii) any other matter which the Secretary of State considers appropriate in connection with its preparation of the strategy or any modifications of it.

(6) A direction under subsection (5)(b) above—

  (a) shall specify or describe the matters or the areas which are to be the subject of the survey or investigation; and

  (b) may make provision in relation to the manner in which—

      (i) the survey or investigation is to be carried out, or

      (ii) the findings are to be reported or made available to other persons.

(7) Where a direction is given under subsection (5)(b) above SEPA shall, in accordance with any requirement of the direction—

  (a) before carrying out the survey or investigation, consult—

      (i) such bodies or persons appearing to it to be representative of planning authorities, and

      (ii) such bodies or persons appearing to it to be representative of the interests of industry,

  as it may consider appropriate; and

  (b) make its findings available to those authorities.

(8) In this section—

1973 c. 65.

"planning authority" means an authority within the meaning of section 172 of the Local Government (Scotland) Act 1973;

"strategy" includes the strategy as modified from time to time and "statement" shall be construed accordingly.

(9) This section makes provision for the purpose of implementing Article 7 of the directive of the Council of the European Communities dated 15th July 1975 on waste, as amended by— 75/442/EEC.

> (a) the directive of that Council dated 18th March 1991 amending directive 75/442/EEC on waste; and 91/156/EEC.

> (b) the directive of that Council dated 23rd December 1991 standardising and rationalising reports on the implementation of certain Directives relating to the environment." 91/692/EEC.

(2) After Schedule 2 to that Act there shall be inserted the Schedule set out in Schedule 12 to this Act.

93.—(1) For the purpose of promoting or securing an increase in the re-use, recovery or recycling of products or materials, the Secretary of State may by regulations make provision for imposing producer responsibility obligations on such persons, and in respect of such products or materials, as may be prescribed.

Producer responsibility: general.

(2) The power of the Secretary of State to make regulations shall be exercisable only after consultation with bodies or persons appearing to him to be representative of bodies or persons whose interests are, or are likely to be, substantially affected by the regulations which he proposes to make.

(3) Except in the case of regulations for the implementation of—

> (a) any obligations of the United Kingdom under the Community Treaties, or

> (b) any international agreement to which the United Kingdom is for the time being a party,

the power to make regulations shall be exercisable only where the Secretary of State, after such consultation as is required by subsection (2) above, is satisfied as to the matters specified in subsection (6) below.

(4) The powers conferred by subsection (1) above shall also be exercisable, in a case falling within paragraph (a) or (b) of subsection (3) above, for the purpose of sustaining at least a minimum level of (rather than promoting or securing an increase in) re-use, recovery or recycling of products or materials.

(5) In making regulations by virtue of paragraph (a) or (b) of subsection (3) above, the Secretary of State shall have regard to the matters specified in subsection (6) below; and in its application in relation to the power conferred by virtue of subsection (4) above, subsection (6) below shall have effect as if—

> (a) any reference to an increase in the re-use, recovery or recycling of products or materials were a reference to the sustaining of at least a minimum level of re-use, recovery or recycling of the products or materials in question, and

   (b) any reference to the production of environmental or economic benefits included a reference to the sustaining of at least a minimum level of any such existing benefits,

and any reference in this section or section 94 below to securing or achieving any such benefits shall accordingly include a reference to sustaining at least a minimum level of any such existing benefits.

   (6) The matters mentioned in subsections (3) and (5) above are—

   (a) that the proposed exercise of the power would be likely to result in an increase in the re-use, recovery or recycling of the products or materials in question;

   (b) that any such increase would produce environmental or economic benefits;

   (c) that those benefits are significant as against the likely costs resulting from the imposition of the proposed producer responsibility obligation;

   (d) that the burdens imposed on businesses by the regulations are the minimum necessary to secure those benefits; and

   (e) that those burdens are imposed on persons most able to make a contribution to the achievement of the relevant targets—

      (i) having regard to the desirability of acting fairly between persons who manufacture, process, distribute or supply products or materials; and

      (ii) taking account of the need to ensure that the proposed producer responsibility obligation is so framed as to be effective in achieving the purposes for which it is to be imposed;

but nothing in sub-paragraph (i) of paragraph (e) above shall be taken to prevent regulations imposing a producer responsibility obligation on any class or description of person to the exclusion of any others.

   (7) The Secretary of State shall have a duty to exercise the power to make regulations in the manner which he considers best calculated to secure that the exercise does not have the effect of restricting, distorting or preventing competition or, if it is likely to have any such effect, that the effect is no greater than is necessary for achieving the environmental or economic benefits mentioned in subsection (6) above.

   (8) In this section—

   "prescribed" means prescribed in regulations;

   "product" and "material" include a reference to any product or material (as the case may be) at a time when it becomes, or has become, waste;

   "producer responsibility obligation" means the steps which are required to be taken by relevant persons of the classes or descriptions to which the regulations in question apply in order to secure attainment of the targets specified or described in the regulations;

   "recovery", in relation to products or materials, includes—

      (a) composting, or any other form of transformation by biological processes, of products or materials; or

      (b) the obtaining, by any means, of energy from products or materials;

"regulations" means regulations under this section;

"relevant persons", in the case of any regulations or any producer responsibility obligation, means persons of the class or description to which the producer responsibility obligation imposed by the regulations applies;

"relevant targets" means the targets specified or described in the regulations imposing the producer responsibility obligation in question;

and regulations may prescribe, in relation to prescribed products or materials, activities, or the activities, which are to be regarded for the purposes of this section and sections 94 and 95 below or any regulations as re-use, recovery or recycling of those products or materials.

(9) The power to make regulations shall be exercisable by statutory instrument.

(10) Subject to the following provisions of this section, a statutory instrument containing regulations shall not be made unless a draft of the instrument has been laid before and approved by a resolution of each House of Parliament.

(11) Subsection (10) above shall not apply to a statutory instrument by reason only that it contains regulations varying any relevant targets.

(12) A statutory instrument which, by virtue of subsection (11) above, is not subject to any requirement that a draft of the instrument be laid before and approved by a resolution of each House of Parliament shall be subject to annulment in pursuance of a resolution of either House of Parliament.

94.—(1) Without prejudice to the generality of section 93 above, regulations may, in particular, make provision for or with respect to—

Producer responsibility: supplementary provisions.

(a) the classes or descriptions of person to whom the producer responsibility obligation imposed by the regulations applies;

(b) the classes or descriptions of products or materials in respect of which the obligation applies;

(c) the targets which are to be achieved with respect to the proportion (whether by weight, volume or otherwise) of the products or materials in question which are to be re-used, recovered or recycled, whether generally or in any prescribed way;

(d) particulars of the obligation imposed by the regulations;

(e) the registration of persons who are subject to a producer responsibility obligation and who are not members of registered exemption schemes, the imposition of requirements in connection with such registration, the variation of such requirements, the making of applications for such registration, the period for which any such registration is to remain in force and the cancellation of any such registration;

(f) the approval, or withdrawal of approval, of exemption schemes by the Secretary of State;

(g) the imposition of requirements on persons who are not members of registered exemption schemes to furnish certificates of compliance to the appropriate Agency;

(h) the approval of persons by the appropriate Agency for the purpose of issuing certificates of compliance;

(j) the registration of exemption schemes, the imposition of conditions in connection with such registration, the variation of such conditions, the making of applications for such registration and the period for which any such registration is to remain in force;

(k) the requirements which must be fulfilled, and the criteria which must be met, before an exemption scheme may be registered;

(l) the powers of the appropriate Agency in relation to applications received by it for registration of exemption schemes;

(m) the cancellation of the registration of an exemption scheme;

(n) competition scrutiny of registered exemption schemes or of exemption schemes in whose case applications for registration have been received by the appropriate Agency;

1976 c. 34 &
1977 c. 19.

(o) the exclusion or modification of any provision of the Restrictive Trade Practices Acts 1976 and 1977 in relation to exemption schemes or in relation to agreements where at least one of the parties is an operator of an exemption scheme;

(p) the fees, or the method of determining the fees, which are to be paid to the appropriate Agency—

(i) in respect of the approval of persons for the purpose of issuing certificates of compliance;

(ii) on the making of an application for registration of an exemption scheme;

(iii) in respect of the subsistence of the registration of that scheme;

(iv) on submission to the appropriate Agency of a certificate of compliance;

(v) on the making of an application for, or for the renewal of, registration of a person required to register under the regulations;

(vi) in respect of the renewal of the registration of that person;

(q) appeals against the refusal of registration, the imposition of conditions in connection with registration, or the cancellation of the registration, of any exemption scheme;

(r) the procedure on any such appeal;

(s) cases, or classes of case,—

(i) in which an exemption scheme is, or is not, to be treated as registered, or

(ii) in which a person is, or is not, to be treated as a member of a registered exemption scheme,

pending the determination or withdrawal of an appeal, and otherwise with respect to the position of persons and exemption schemes pending such determination or withdrawal;

(t) the imposition on the appropriate Agency of a duty to monitor compliance with any of the obligations imposed by the regulations;

(u) the imposition on prescribed persons of duties to maintain records, and furnish to the Secretary of State or to the appropriate Agency returns, in such form as may be prescribed of such information as may be prescribed for any purposes of, or for any purposes connected with, or related to, sections 93 to 95 of this Act or any regulations;

(w) the imposition on the appropriate Agency of a duty to maintain, and make available for inspection by the public, a register containing prescribed information relating to registered exemption schemes or persons required to register under the regulations;

(y) the powers of entry and inspection which are exercisable by a new Agency for the purposes of its functions under the regulations;

(ya) the conferring on prescribed persons of power to require, for the purposes of or otherwise in connection with competition scrutiny, the provision by any person of any information which he has, or which he may at any future time acquire, relating to any exemption scheme or to any acts or omissions of an operator of such a scheme or of any person dealing with such an operator.

(2) If it appears to the Secretary of State—

(a) that any action proposed to be taken by the operator of a registered exemption scheme would be incompatible with—

(i) any obligations of the United Kingdom under the Community Treaties, or

(ii) any international agreement to which the United Kingdom is for the time being a party, or

(b) that any action which the operator of such a scheme has power to take is required for the purpose of implementing any such obligations or agreement,

he may direct that operator not to take or, as the case may be, to take the action in question.

(3) Regulations may make provision as to which of the new Agencies is the appropriate Agency for the purposes of any function conferred or imposed by or under this section or section 93 above, or for the purposes of the exercise of that function in relation to the whole or a prescribed part of Great Britain, and may make provision for things done or omitted to be done by either new Agency in relation to any part of Great Britain to be treated for prescribed purposes as done or omitted to be done by the other of them in relation to some other part of Great Britain.

(4) Persons issuing certificates of compliance shall act in accordance with guidance issued for the purpose by the appropriate Agency, which may include guidance as to matters which are, or are not, to be treated as evidence of compliance or as evidence of non-compliance.

(5) In making any provision in relation to fees, regard shall be had to the desirability of securing that the fees received by each new Agency under the regulations are sufficient to meet the costs and expenses incurred by that Agency in the performance of its functions under the regulations.

(6) In this section—

"the appropriate Agency", subject to regulations made by virtue of subsection (3) above, means—

    (a) in relation to England and Wales, the Agency;

    (b) in relation to Scotland, SEPA;

"certificate of compliance" means a certificate issued by a person approved for the purpose by the appropriate Agency to the effect that that person is satisfied that the person in respect of whom the certificate is issued is complying with any producer responsibility obligation to which he is subject;

"competition scrutiny", in the case of any scheme, means scrutiny of the scheme for the purpose of enabling the Secretary of State to satisfy himself—

    (i) whether or not the scheme has or is likely to have the effect of restricting, distorting or preventing competition or, if it appears to him that the scheme has or is likely to have any such effect, that the effect is or is likely to be no greater than is necessary for achieving the environmental or economic benefits mentioned in section 93(6) above; or

    (ii) whether or not the scheme leads or is likely to lead to an abuse of market power;

"exemption scheme" means a scheme which is (or, if it were to be registered in accordance with the regulations, would be) a scheme whose members for the time being are, by virtue of the regulations and their membership of that scheme, exempt from the requirement to comply with the producer responsibility obligation imposed by the regulations;

"new Agency" means the Agency or SEPA;

"operator", in relation to an exemption scheme, includes any person responsible for establishing, maintaining or managing the scheme;

"registered exemption scheme" means an exemption scheme which is registered pursuant to regulations;

and expressions used in this section and in section 93 above have the same meaning in this section as they have in that section.

(7) Regulations—

    (a) may make different provision for different cases;

    (b) without prejudice to the generality of paragraph (a) above, may impose different producer responsibility obligations in respect of different classes or descriptions of products or materials and for different classes or descriptions of person or exemption scheme;

    (c) may include incidental, consequential, supplemental or transitional provision.

(8) Any direction under this section—

    (a) may include such incidental, consequential, supplemental or transitional provision as the Secretary of State considers necessary or expedient; and

(b) shall, on the application of the Secretary of State, be enforceable by injunction or, in Scotland, by interdict or by an order for specific performance under section 45 of the Court of Session Act 1988.

1988 c. 36.

95.—(1) Regulations may make provision for a person who contravenes a prescribed requirement of the regulations to be guilty of an offence and liable—

Producer responsibility: offences.

(a) on summary conviction, to a fine not exceeding the statutory maximum;

(b) on conviction on indictment, to a fine.

(2) Where an offence under any provision of the regulations committed by a body corporate is proved to have been committed with the consent or connivance of, or to have been attributable to any neglect on the part of, any director, manager, secretary or other similar officer of the body corporate or a person who was purporting to act in any such capacity, he as well as the body corporate shall be guilty of that offence and shall be liable to be proceeded against and punished accordingly.

(3) Where the affairs of a body corporate are managed by its members, subsection (2) above shall apply in relation to the acts or defaults of a member in connection with his functions of management as if he were a director of the body corporate.

(4) Where the commission by any person of an offence under the regulations is due to the act or default of some other person, that other person may be charged with and convicted of the offence by virtue of this section whether or not proceedings for the offence are taken against the first-mentioned person.

(5) Expressions used in this section and in section 93 or 94 above have the same meaning in this section as they have in that section.

Mineral planning permissions

96.—(1) Schedules 13 and 14 to this Act shall have effect.

Mineral planning permissions.

(2) This section, those Schedules as they apply to England and Wales, and the 1990 Act shall have effect as if this section and those Schedules (as so applying) were included in Part III of that Act.

(3) This section, those Schedules as they apply to Scotland, and the 1972 Act shall have effect as if this section and those Schedules (as so applying) were included in Part III of that Act.

(4) Section 105 of the 1990 Act and section 251A of the 1972 Act shall cease to have effect.

(5) Without prejudice to the generality of sections 59 to 61 of the 1990 Act or, as the case may be, section 21 of the 1972 Act, a development order may make, in relation to any planning permission which is granted by a development order for minerals development, provision similar to any provision made by Schedule 13 or 14 to this Act.

(6) In this section and those Schedules—

"the 1972 Act" means the Town and Country Planning (Scotland) Act 1972;

1972 c. 52.

"the 1990 Act" means the Town and Country Planning Act 1990;

1990 c. 8.

"the 1991 Act" means the Planning and Compensation Act 1991; and

"minerals development" means development consisting of the winning and working of minerals, or involving the depositing of mineral waste.

Hedgerows etc.

Hedgerows.

97.—(1) The appropriate Ministers may by regulations make provision for, or in connection with, the protection of important hedgerows in England or Wales.

(2) The question whether a hedgerow is or is not "important" for the purposes of this section shall be determined in accordance with prescribed criteria.

(3) For the purpose of facilitating the protection of important hedgerows, regulations under subsection (1) above may also make provision in relation to other hedgerows in England or Wales.

(4) Without prejudice to the generality of subsections (1) to (3) above, regulations under subsection (1) above may provide for the application (with or without modifications) of, or include provision comparable to, any provision contained in the planning Acts and may, in particular, make provision—

(a) prohibiting, or for prohibiting, the removal of, or the carrying out of prescribed acts in relation to, a hedgerow except in prescribed cases;

(b) for or with respect to appeals against determinations or decisions made, or notices given or served, under or by virtue of the regulations, including provision authorising or requiring any body or person to whom an appeal lies to consult prescribed persons with respect to the appeal in prescribed cases;

(c) for a person who contravenes, or fails to comply with, any prescribed provision of the regulations to be guilty of an offence;

(d) for a person guilty of an offence by virtue of paragraph (c) above which consists of the removal, in contravention of the regulations, of a hedgerow of a description prescribed for the purposes of this paragraph to be liable—

(i) on summary conviction, to a fine not exceeding the statutory maximum, or

(ii) on conviction on indictment, to a fine;

(e) for a person guilty of any other offence by virtue of paragraph (c) above to be liable on summary conviction to a fine not exceeding such level on the standard scale as may be prescribed.

(5) Regulations under this section may make different provision for different cases, including different provision in relation to different descriptions of hedgerow, different descriptions of person, different areas or localities or different circumstances.

(6) Before making any regulations under this section the appropriate Ministers shall consult—

(a) such bodies appearing to them to be representative of persons whose business interests are likely to be affected by the proposed regulations,

    (b) such bodies appearing to them to be representative of the interests of owners or occupiers of land,

    (c) such bodies appearing to them to be representative of the interests of local authorities,

    (d) such bodies whose statutory functions include the provision to Ministers of the Crown of advice concerning matters relating to environmental conservation, and

    (e) such bodies not falling within paragraphs (a) to (d) above,

as the appropriate Ministers may consider appropriate.

(7) No statutory instrument containing regulations under this section shall be made unless a draft of the instrument has been laid before, and approved by a resolution of, each House of Parliament.

(8) In this section—

"the appropriate Ministers" means—

        (a) as respects England, the Secretary of State and the Minister of Agriculture, Fisheries and Food;

        (b) as respects Wales, the Secretary of State;

"environmental conservation" means conservation—

        (a) of the natural beauty or amenity, or flora or fauna, of England or Wales; or

        (b) of features of archaeological or historic interest in England or Wales;

"hedgerow" includes any stretch of hedgerow;

"local authority" means—

        (a) the council of a county, county borough, district, London borough, parish or community;

        (b) the Common Council of the City of London;

        (c) the Council of the Isles of Scilly;

"the planning Acts" has the same meaning as it has in the Town and Country Planning Act 1990 by virtue of section 336(1) of that Act;   1990 c. 8.

"prescribed" means specified, or of a description specified, in regulations;

"regulations" means regulations made by statutory instrument;

"remove", in relation to a hedgerow, means uproot or otherwise destroy, and cognate expressions shall be construed accordingly;

"statutory functions" means functions conferred or imposed by or under any enactment.

(9) Any reference in this section to removing, or carrying out an act in relation to, a hedgerow includes a reference to causing or permitting another to remove, or (as the case may be) carry out an act in relation to, a hedgerow.

98.—(1) The appropriate Minister, with the consent of the Treasury, may by regulations make provision for and in connection with the making of grants to persons who do, or who undertake to that Minister that they will do, anything which in the opinion of that Minister is conducive to—   Grants for purposes conducive to conservation.

   (a) the conservation or enhancement of the natural beauty or amenity of the countryside (including its flora and fauna and geological and physiographical features) or of any features of archaeological interest there; or

   (b) the promotion of the enjoyment of the countryside by the public.

(2) Regulations under this section may—

   (a) make different provision for different cases or classes of case or for different areas;

   (b) provide for grants to be made subject to conditions;

   (c) confer power on the appropriate Minister to modify, in any particular case, the conditions to which a grant would otherwise be subject, if he is satisfied that the making of that grant, subject to the conditions as so modified, is consistent with the purposes for which the regulations are made;

   (d) make provision for or in connection with the recovery of any sums paid by way of grant, or the withholding of any further payments of grant, in cases where the applicant for the grant—

      (i) in making the application, or in furnishing any information in connection with the application, has made a statement which was false or misleading in a material respect;

      (ii) has failed to do something which he undertook to do if the grant was made; or

      (iii) is in breach of any condition subject to which the grant was made.

(3) The power to make regulations under this section shall be exercisable by statutory instrument; and a statutory instrument containing any such regulations shall be subject to annulment pursuant to a resolution of either House of Parliament.

(4) The powers conferred by this section are in addition to any other powers of the Secretary of State or the Minister of Agriculture, Fisheries and Food.

(5) In this section "the appropriate Minister" means—

   (a) as respects England, the Minister of Agriculture, Fisheries and Food;

   (b) as respects Wales, the Secretary of State;

   (c) as respects Scotland, the Secretary of State.

Consultation before making or modifying certain subordinate legislation for England.

99.—(1) The Minister shall consult the bodies and persons specified in subsection (2) below before—

   (a) making any legislation to which this section applies (other than a modification of any such legislation);

   (b) modifying any such legislation in a way which changes the purpose of the legislation in question; or

   (c) modifying any such legislation in a way which modifies, in a respect which he considers material, any conditions subject to which grants or other payments are payable under that legislation.

(2) The bodies and persons mentioned in subsection (1) above are—

(a) the Secretary of State;

(b) the Countryside Commission;

(c) the Nature Conservancy Council for England;

(d) the Historic Buildings and Monuments Commission for England.

(3) The legislation to which this section applies is—

(a) any order under section 18 of the Agriculture Act 1986 (orders establishing environmentally sensitive areas); 1986 c. 49.

(b) any regulations under section 98 above;

(c) any statutory instrument specified in subsection (4) below;

(d) any other statutory instrument which concerns the management of land and whose primary purpose is the promotion of—

(i) the conservation or enhancement of the natural beauty or amenity of the countryside (including its flora and fauna and geological and physiographical features) or of any features of archaeological interest there; or

(ii) the enjoyment of the countryside by the public.

(4) The statutory instruments mentioned in subsection (3)(c) above are—

(a) the Farm Woodlands Premium Scheme 1992; S.I. 1992/905.

(b) the Habitat (Water Fringe) Regulations 1994; S.I. 1994/1291.

(c) the Habitat (Former Set-Aside Land) Regulations 1994; S.I. 1994/1292.

(d) the Habitat (Salt Marsh) Regulations 1994; S.I. 1994/1293.

(e) the Organic Farming (Aid) Regulations 1994; S.I. 1994/1721.

(f) the Nitrate Sensitive Areas Regulations 1994; S.I. 1994/1729.

(g) the Countryside Access Regulations 1994; S.I. 1994/2349.

(h) the Moorland (Livestock Extensification) Regulations 1995. S.I. 1995/904.

(5) In this section, "the Minister" means the Minister of Agriculture, Fisheries and Food.

(6) This section applies in relation to any legislation only so far as relating to land in England.

Drainage

100.—(1) In the definition of "drainage" in section 113(1) of the Water Resources Act 1991, after paragraph (c) there shall be added the words "and

Meaning of "drainage" in certain enactments. 1991 c. 57.

(d) the carrying on, for any purpose, of any other practice which involves management of the level of water in a watercourse;".

(2) For the definition of "drainage" in section 72(1) of the Land Drainage Act 1991 there shall be substituted— 1991 c. 59.

""drainage" includes—

(a) defence against water (including sea water);

(b) irrigation, other than spray irrigation;

(c) warping; and

(d) the carrying on, for any purpose, of any other practice which involves management of the level of water in a watercourse;".

Grants in
connection with
drainage works.
1991 c. 57.

101.—(1) In section 147 of the Water Resources Act 1991 (grants for drainage works) in subsection (4), after the words "expenditure properly incurred by it with a view to" there shall be inserted "(a)" and at the end of that subsection there shall be added—

"(b) enabling it to determine in any particular case whether drainage works, or drainage works of any particular description, should or should not be carried out;

(c) obtaining or organising information, including information about natural processes affecting the coastline, to enable it to formulate or develop its plans with respect to the defence against sea water of any part of the coastline; or

(d) obtaining, at any time after the carrying out of drainage works, information with respect to—

(i) the quality or effectiveness, or the effect on the environment, of those works; or

(ii) any matter of a financial nature relating to those works.

(4A) Paragraphs (b) to (d) of subsection (4) above are without prejudice to any power—

(a) to make any grant under subsection (1) or (4)(a) above, or

(b) to impose any condition under subsection (2) above,

which could be made or imposed apart from those paragraphs."

1991 c. 59.

(2) In section 59 of the Land Drainage Act 1991 (grants to drainage bodies) in subsection (4), after the words "expenditure properly incurred by them with a view to" there shall be inserted "(a)" and at the end of that subsection there shall be added—

"(b) enabling them to determine in any particular case whether drainage works, or drainage works of any particular description, should or should not be carried out;

(c) obtaining or organising information, including information about natural processes affecting the coastline, to enable them to formulate or develop their plans with respect to the defence against sea water of any part of the coastline; or

(d) obtaining, at any time after the carrying out of drainage works, information with respect to—

(i) the quality or effectiveness, or the effect on the environment, of those works; or

(ii) any matter of a financial nature relating to those works.

(4A) Paragraphs (b) to (d) of subsection (4) above are without prejudice to any power—

(a) to make any grant under subsection (1) or (4)(a) above, or

(b) to impose any condition under subsection (2) above,

which could be made or imposed apart from those paragraphs."

Fisheries

102.—(1) The Sea Fisheries Regulation Act 1966 shall be amended in accordance with the following provisions of this section.

Sea fisheries.
1966 c. 38.

(2) In section 2 (constitution of local fisheries committees) in subsection (2) (which includes provision for the members appointed by the Minister to be persons acquainted with the needs and opinions of the fishing interests of that district) after the words "of that district" there shall be added the words "or as being persons having knowledge of, or expertise in, marine environmental matters".

(3) After that subsection there shall be inserted—

"(2A) In addition to the members appointed as mentioned in subsection (1) above, a local fisheries committee may appoint such number of persons with knowledge of or expertise in marine environmental matters as it thinks fit as further members of the committee for those occasions on which it is considering any proposed byelaw under section 5 below by virtue of section 5A below, or any proposed amendment or revocation of such a byelaw."

(4) At the end of that section there shall be added—

"(7) In this section "marine environmental matters" means—

(a) the conservation or enhancement of the natural beauty or amenity of marine or coastal areas (including their geological or physiographical features) or of any features of archaeological or historic interest in such areas; or

(b) the conservation of flora or fauna which are dependent on, or associated with, a marine or coastal environment."

(5) After section 5 (byelaws for regulation etc of sea fisheries) there shall be inserted—

"Byelaws under section 5 for marine environmental purposes.

5A.—(1) Any power to make byelaws conferred by section 5 above may be exercised for marine environmental purposes.

(2) The power to make byelaws under section 5 above by virtue of this section is in addition to, and not in derogation from, the power to make byelaws under that section otherwise than by virtue of this section.

(3) Byelaws under section 5 above by virtue of this section shall be submitted for confirmation under section 7 below—

(a) in the case of a byelaw which is to have effect in England, only after consultation with the Nature Conservancy Council for England;

(b) in the case of a byelaw which is to have effect in Wales, only after consultation with the Countryside Council for Wales.

(4) In this section "marine environmental purposes" means the purposes—

    (a) of conserving or enhancing the natural beauty or amenity of marine or coastal areas (including their geological or physiographical features) or of any features of archaeological or historic interest in such areas; or

    (b) of conserving flora or fauna which are dependent on, or associated with, a marine or coastal environment."

(6) In section 8 (power of Minister to revoke byelaws if it appears necessary or desirable for the maintenance or improvement of fisheries) after the words "maintenance or improvement of fisheries" there shall be inserted the words "or for marine environmental purposes, within the meaning of section 5A above,".

Other marine or aquatic environmental conservation powers.
1967 c. 84.

103.—(1) After section 5 of the Sea Fish (Conservation) Act 1967 (power to restrict fishing for sea fish) there shall be inserted—

"Powers to restrict fishing for marine environmental purposes.

    5A.—(1) Any power to make an order under section 5 above may be exercised for marine environmental purposes.

    (2) The power to make an order under section 5 above by virtue of this section is in addition to, and not in derogation from, the power to make an order under that section otherwise than by virtue of this section.

    (3) In this section "marine environmental purposes" means the purposes—

        (a) of conserving or enhancing the natural beauty or amenity of marine or coastal areas (including their geological or physiographical features) or of any features of archaeological or historic interest in such areas; or

        (b) of conserving flora or fauna which are dependent on, or associated with, a marine or coastal environment."

1984 c. 26.

    (2) After section 2 of the Inshore Fishing (Scotland) Act 1984 there shall be inserted—

"Powers to restrict fishing, or to prohibit the carriage of specified types of net, for marine environmental purposes.

    2A.—(1) Any power to make an order under section 1 or 2 above may be exercised for marine environmental purposes.

    (2) The power to make an order under section 1 or 2 above by virtue of this section is in addition to, and not in derogation from, the power to make an order under that section otherwise than by virtue of this section.

    (3) In this section "marine environmental purposes" means the purposes—

        (a) of conserving or enhancing the natural beauty or amenity of marine or coastal areas (including their geological or physiographical features) or of any features of archaeological or historic interest in such areas; or

(b) of conserving flora or fauna which are dependent on, or associated with, a marine or coastal environment."

(3) In Schedule 25 to the Water Resources Act 1991 (byelaw making powers) after paragraph 6 (byelaws for purposes of fisheries functions) there shall be inserted— 1991 c. 57.

"Fisheries byelaws for marine or aquatic environmental purposes

6A.—(1) Any power to make byelaws conferred by paragraph 6 above may be exercised for marine or aquatic environmental purposes.

(2) The power to make byelaws under paragraph 6 above by virtue of this paragraph is in addition to, and not in derogation from, the power to make byelaws under that paragraph otherwise than by virtue of this paragraph.

(3) In this paragraph "marine or aquatic environmental purposes" means—

(a) the conservation or enhancement of the natural beauty or amenity of marine or coastal, or aquatic or waterside, areas (including their geological or physiographical features) or of any features of archaeological or historic interest in such areas; or

(b) the conservation of flora or fauna which are dependent on, or associated with, a marine or coastal, or aquatic or waterside, environment."

104.—(1) After section 37 of the Salmon and Freshwater Fisheries Act 1975 there shall be inserted— *Fixed penalty system for certain fisheries offences.*
1975 c. 51.

"Fixed penalty notices for certain offences.

37A.—(1) Where on any occasion a water bailiff or other officer of the Agency finds a person who he has reason to believe is committing, or has on that occasion committed, a fixed penalty offence, he may give to that person a notice (in this section referred to as a "fixed penalty notice") offering him the opportunity of discharging any liability to conviction for that offence by payment of a fixed penalty.

(2) Where a person is given a fixed penalty notice in respect of a fixed penalty offence—

(a) no proceedings shall be instituted for that offence before the expiration of the period for paying the fixed penalty; and

(b) he shall not be convicted of that offence if the fixed penalty is paid before the expiration of that period.

(3) The Agency may extend the period for paying the fixed penalty in any particular case if it considers it appropriate to do so in all the circumstances of the case.

(4) If, in any particular case, the Agency considers that a fixed penalty notice which has been given ought not to have been given, it may give to the person to whom the

fixed penalty notice was given a notice withdrawing the fixed penalty notice; and where notice under this subsection is given—

(a) the Agency shall repay any amount which has been paid by way of fixed penalty in pursuance of the fixed penalty notice; and

(b) no proceedings shall be instituted or continued against that person for the offence in question.

(5) The amount by which the sums received by the Agency by way of fixed penalties exceed the sums repaid by it under subsection (4)(a) above shall be paid into the Consolidated Fund.

(6) In any proceedings, a certificate purporting to be signed by or on behalf of the Chief Executive of the Agency and stating either—

(a) that payment of a fixed penalty was, or (as the case may be) was not, received by the Agency on or before a date specified in the certificate, or

(b) that an envelope containing an amount sent by post in payment of a fixed penalty was marked as posted on a date specified in the certificate,

shall be received as evidence of the matters so stated and shall be treated, without further proof, as being so signed unless the contrary is shown.

(7) A fixed penalty notice shall give such reasonable particulars of the circumstances alleged to constitute the fixed penalty offence to which the notice relates as are necessary for giving reasonable information of the offence and shall state—

(a) the monetary amount of the fixed penalty which may be paid;

(b) the person to whom and the address at which—

(i) the fixed penalty may be paid, and

(ii) any correspondence relating to the fixed penalty notice may be sent;

(c) the method or methods by which payment of the fixed penalty may be made;

(d) the period for paying the fixed penalty;

(e) the consequences of the fixed penalty not being paid before the expiration of that period.

(8) A fixed penalty notice may also contain such other information relating to, or for the purpose of facilitating, the administration of the fixed penalty system as the Agency considers necessary or desirable.

(9) Regulations may—

(a) make provision with respect to the giving of fixed penalty notices, including, in particular, provision with respect to—

(i) the methods by which,

(ii) the officers, servants or agents by, to or on whom, and

(iii) the places at which,

fixed penalty notices may be given by, or served on behalf of, a water bailiff or other officer of the Agency;

(b) prescribe the method or methods by which fixed penalties may be paid;

(c) make provision for or with respect to the issue of prescribed documents to persons to whom fixed penalty notices are or have been given.

(10) In this section—

"fixed penalty" means a penalty of such amount as may be prescribed (whether by being specified in, or made calculable under, regulations);

"fixed penalty offence" means, subject to subsection (11) below, any offence—

(a) under this Act,

(b) under the Salmon Act 1986,   1986 c. 62.

(c) under or by virtue of regulations or orders made under section 115, 116 or 142 of the Water Resources Act 1991, or   1991 c. 57.

(d) under section 211(3) of that Act, so far as relating to byelaws made by virtue of paragraph 6 of Schedule 25 to that Act,

which is for the time being prescribed for the purpose;

"the fixed penalty system" means the system implementing this section and regulations made under it;

"the Ministers" means the Secretary of State and the Minister;

"notice" means notice in writing;

"the period for paying", in relation to any fixed penalty, means such period as may be prescribed for the purpose;

"prescribed" means prescribed by regulations;

"regulations" means regulations made under this section by the Ministers.

(11) The provision that may be made by regulations prescribing fixed penalty offences includes provision for an offence to be a fixed penalty offence—

(a) only if it is committed in such circumstances or manner as may be prescribed; or

(b) except if it is committed in such circumstances or manner as may be prescribed.

(12) Regulations may provide for any offence which is a fixed penalty offence to cease to be such an offence.

(13) An offence which, in consequence of regulations made by virtue of subsection (12) above, has ceased to be a fixed penalty offence shall be eligible to be prescribed as such an offence again.

(14) Regulations may—

(a) make different provision in relation to different cases or classes of case; or

(b) provide for such exceptions, limitations and conditions, or make such incidental, supplemental, consequential or transitional provision, as the Ministers consider necessary or expedient.

(15) Any power to make regulations under this section shall be exercisable by statutory instrument made by the Ministers; and a statutory instrument containing any such regulations shall be subject to annulment pursuant to a resolution of either House of Parliament."

(2) In section 35 of that Act (which, among other things, creates an offence of failing to state one's name and address when required to do so under that section) in subsection (1) (water bailiffs and constables), for the words from "A water bailiff" to "any constable" there shall be substituted the words "A water bailiff or other officer of the Agency, or any constable,".

(3) After that subsection there shall be inserted—

"(1A) Without prejudice to subsection (1) above, a water bailiff or other officer of the Agency who on any occasion finds a person who he has reason to believe is committing, or has on that occasion committed, a fixed penalty offence, within the meaning of section 37A below, may require that person to state his name and address."

(4) In section 41(1) of that Act (definitions), before the definition of "authorised officer" there shall be inserted—

""the Agency" means the Environment Agency;".

Minor and consequential amendments relating to fisheries.

105. Schedule 15 to this Act (which makes minor and consequential amendments relating to fisheries) shall have effect.

New provisions for Scotland

Control of pollution of water in Scotland.

106. Schedule 16 to this Act (which amends the Control of Pollution Act 1974 as respects the control of pollution of rivers and coastal waters in Scotland) shall have effect.

Statutory nuisances: Scotland.

107. Schedule 17 to this Act (which makes provision with respect to statutory nuisances in Scotland) shall have effect.

Powers of entry

Powers of enforcing authorities and persons authorised by them.

108.—(1) A person who appears suitable to an enforcing authority may be authorised in writing by that authority to exercise, in accordance with the terms of the authorisation, any of the powers specified in subsection (4) below for the purpose—

(a) of determining whether any provision of the pollution control enactments in the case of that authority is being, or has been, complied with;

(b) of exercising or performing one or more of the pollution control functions of that authority; or

(c) of determining whether and, if so, how such a function should be exercised or performed.

(2) A person who appears suitable to the Agency or SEPA may be authorised in writing by the Agency or, as the case may be, SEPA to exercise, in accordance with the terms of the authorisation, any of the powers specified in subsection (4) below for the purpose of enabling the Agency or, as the case may be, SEPA to carry out any assessment or prepare any report which the Agency or, as the case may be, SEPA is required to carry out or prepare under section 5(3) or 33(3) above.

(3) Subsection (2) above only applies where the Minister who required the assessment to be carried out, or the report to be prepared, has, whether at the time of making the requirement or at any later time, notified the Agency or, as the case may be, SEPA that the assessment or report appears to him to relate to an incident or possible incident involving or having the potential to involve—

(a) serious pollution of the environment,

(b) serious harm to human health, or

(c) danger to life or health.

(4) The powers which a person may be authorised to exercise under subsection (1) or (2) above are—

(a) to enter at any reasonable time (or, in an emergency, at any time and, if need be, by force) any premises which he has reason to believe it is necessary for him to enter;

(b) on entering any premises by virtue of paragraph (a) above, to take with him—

(i) any other person duly authorised by the enforcing authority and, if the authorised person has reasonable cause to apprehend any serious obstruction in the execution of his duty, a constable; and

(ii) any equipment or materials required for any purpose for which the power of entry is being exercised;

(c) to make such examination and investigation as may in any circumstances be necessary;

(d) as regards any premises which he has power to enter, to direct that those premises or any part of them, or anything in them, shall be left undisturbed (whether generally or in particular respects) for so long as is reasonably necessary for the purpose of any examination or investigation under paragraph (c) above;

(e) to take such measurements and photographs and make such recordings as he considers necessary for the purpose of any examination or investigation under paragraph (c) above;

(f) to take samples, or cause samples to be taken, of any articles or substances found in or on any premises which he has power to enter, and of the air, water or land in, on, or in the vicinity of, the premises;

(g) in the case of any article or substance found in or on any premises which he has power to enter, being an article or substance which appears to him to have caused or to be likely to cause pollution of the environment or harm to human health, to cause it to be dismantled or subjected to any process or test (but not so as to damage or destroy it, unless that is necessary);

(h) in the case of any such article or substance as is mentioned in paragraph (g) above, to take possession of it and detain it for so long as is necessary for all or any of the following purposes, namely—

(i) to examine it, or cause it to be examined, and to do, or cause to be done, to it anything which he has power to do under that paragraph;

(ii) to ensure that it is not tampered with before examination of it is completed;

(iii) to ensure that it is available for use as evidence in any proceedings for an offence under the pollution control enactments in the case of the enforcing authority under whose authorisation he acts or in any other proceedings relating to a variation notice, enforcement notice or prohibition notice under those enactments;

(j) to require any person whom he has reasonable cause to believe to be able to give any information relevant to any examination or investigation under paragraph (c) above to answer (in the absence of persons other than a person nominated by that person to be present and any persons whom the authorised person may allow to be present) such questions as the authorised person thinks fit to ask and to sign a declaration of the truth of his answers;

(k) to require the production of, or where the information is recorded in computerised form, the furnishing of extracts from, any records—

(i) which are required to be kept under the pollution control enactments for the enforcing authority under whose authorisation he acts, or

(ii) which it is necessary for him to see for the purposes of an examination or investigation under paragraph (c) above,

and to inspect and take copies of, or of any entry in, the records;

(l) to require any person to afford him such facilities and assistance with respect to any matters or things within that person's control or in relation to which that person has responsibilities as are necessary to enable the authorised person to exercise any of the powers conferred on him by this section;

(m) any other power for—

(i) a purpose falling within any paragraph of subsection (1) above, or

(ii) any such purpose as is mentioned in subsection (2) above,

which is conferred by regulations made by the Secretary of State.

(5) The powers which by virtue of subsections (1) and (4) above are conferred in relation to any premises for the purpose of enabling an

enforcing authority to determine whether any provision of the pollution control enactments in the case of that authority is being, or has been, complied with shall include power, in order to obtain the information on which that determination may be made,—

> (a) to carry out experimental borings or other works on those premises; and

> (b) to install, keep or maintain monitoring and other apparatus there.

(6) Except in an emergency, in any case where it is proposed to enter any premises used for residential purposes, or to take heavy equipment on to any premises which are to be entered, any entry by virtue of this section shall only be effected—

> (a) after the expiration of at least seven days' notice of the proposed entry given to a person who appears to the authorised person in question to be in occupation of the premises in question, and

> (b) either—

>> (i) with the consent of a person who is in occupation of those premises; or

>> (ii) under the authority of a warrant by virtue of Schedule 18 to this Act.

(7) Except in an emergency, where an authorised person proposes to enter any premises and—

> (a) entry has been refused and he apprehends on reasonable grounds that the use of force may be necessary to effect entry, or

> (b) he apprehends on reasonable grounds that entry is likely to be refused and that the use of force may be necessary to effect entry,

any entry on to those premises by virtue of this section shall only be effected under the authority of a warrant by virtue of Schedule 18 to this Act.

(8) In relation to any premises belonging to or used for the purposes of the United Kingdom Atomic Energy Authority, subsections (1) to (4) above shall have effect subject to section 6(3) of the Atomic Energy Authority Act 1954 (which restricts entry to such premises where they have been declared to be prohibited places for the purposes of the Official Secrets Act 1911). *1954 c. 32.* *1911 c. 28.*

(9) The Secretary of State may by regulations make provision as to the procedure to be followed in connection with the taking of, and the dealing with, samples under subsection (4)(f) above.

(10) Where an authorised person proposes to exercise the power conferred by subsection (4)(g) above in the case of an article or substance found on any premises, he shall, if so requested by a person who at the time is present on and has responsibilities in relation to those premises, cause anything which is to be done by virtue of that power to be done in the presence of that person.

(11) Before exercising the power conferred by subsection (4)(g) above in the case of any article or substance, an authorised person shall consult—

(a) such persons having duties on the premises where the article or substance is to be dismantled or subjected to the process or test, and

(b) such other persons,

as appear to him appropriate for the purpose of ascertaining what dangers, if any, there may be in doing anything which he proposes to do or cause to be done under the power.

(12) No answer given by a person in pursuance of a requirement imposed under subsection (4)(j) above shall be admissible in evidence in England and Wales against that person in any proceedings, or in Scotland against that person in any criminal proceedings.

(13) Nothing in this section shall be taken to compel the production by any person of a document of which he would on grounds of legal professional privilege be entitled to withhold production on an order for discovery in an action in the High Court or, in relation to Scotland, on an order for the production of documents in an action in the Court of Session.

(14) Schedule 18 to this Act shall have effect with respect to the powers of entry and related powers which are conferred by this section.

(15) In this section—

"authorised person" means a person authorised under subsection (1) or (2) above;

"emergency" means a case in which it appears to the authorised person in question—

(a) that there is an immediate risk of serious pollution of the environment or serious harm to human health, or

(b) that circumstances exist which are likely to endanger life or health,

and that immediate entry to any premises is necessary to verify the existence of that risk or those circumstances or to ascertain the cause of that risk or those circumstances or to effect a remedy;

"enforcing authority" means—

(a) the Secretary of State;

(b) the Agency;

(c) SEPA; or

(d) a local enforcing authority;

"local enforcing authority" means—

(a) a local enforcing authority, within the meaning of Part I of the Environmental Protection Act 1990;

(b) a local authority, within the meaning of Part IIA of that Act, in its capacity as an enforcing authority for the purposes of that Part;

(c) a local authority for the purposes of Part IV of this Act or regulations under that Part;

"mobile plant" means plant which is designed to move or to be moved whether on roads or otherwise;

1990 c. 43.

"pollution control enactments", in relation to an enforcing authority, means the enactments and instruments relating to the pollution control functions of that authority;

"pollution control functions", in relation to the Agency or SEPA, means the functions conferred or imposed on it by or under—

(a) the Alkali, &c, Works Regulation Act 1906; 1906 c. 14.

(b) Part III of the Rivers (Prevention of Pollution) (Scotland) Act 1951; 1951 c. 66.

(c) the Rivers (Prevention of Pollution) (Scotland) Act 1965; 1965 c. 13.

(d) Part I of the Health and Safety at Work etc. Act 1974; 1974 c. 37.

(e) Parts I, IA and II of the Control of Pollution Act 1974; 1974 c. 40.

(f) the Control of Pollution (Amendment) Act 1989; 1989 c. 14.

(g) Parts I, II and IIA of the Environmental Protection Act 1990 (integrated pollution control, waste on land and contaminated land); 1990 c. 43.

(h) Chapter III of Part IV of the Water Industry Act 1991 (special category effluent); 1991 c. 56.

(j) Part III and sections 161 to 161D of the Water Resources Act 1991; 1991 c. 57.

(k) section 19 of the Clean Air Act 1993; 1993 c. 11.

(l) the Radioactive Substances Act 1993; 1993 c. 12.

(m) regulations made by virtue of section 2(2) of the European Communities Act 1972, to the extent that the regulations relate to pollution; 1972 c. 68.

"pollution control functions", in relation to a local enforcing authority, means the functions conferred or imposed on, or transferred to, that authority—

(a) by or under Part I or IIA of the Environmental Protection Act 1990;

(b) by or under regulations made by virtue of Part IV of this Act; or

(c) by or under regulations made by virtue of section 2(2) of the European Communities Act 1972, to the extent that the regulations relate to pollution;

"pollution control functions", in relation to the Secretary of State, means any functions which are conferred or imposed upon him by or under any enactment or instrument and which relate to the control of pollution;

"premises" includes any land, vehicle, vessel or mobile plant.

(16) Any power to make regulations under this section shall be exercisable by statutory instrument; and a statutory instrument containing any such regulations shall be subject to annulment pursuant to a resolution of either House of Parliament.

109.—(1) Where, in the case of any article or substance found by him on any premises which he has power to enter, an authorised person has reasonable cause to believe that, in the circumstances in which he finds it,

Power to deal with cause of imminent danger of serious pollution etc.

the article or substance is a cause of imminent danger of serious pollution of the environment or serious harm to human health, he may seize it and cause it to be rendered harmless (whether by destruction or otherwise).

(2) As soon as may be after any article or substance has been seized and rendered harmless under this section, the authorised person shall prepare and sign a written report giving particulars of the circumstances in which the article or substance was seized and so dealt with by him, and shall—

   (a) give a signed copy of the report to a responsible person at the premises where the article or substance was found by him; and

   (b) unless that person is the owner of the article or substance, also serve a signed copy of the report on the owner;

and if, where paragraph (b) above applies, the authorised person cannot after reasonable inquiry ascertain the name or address of the owner, the copy may be served on him by giving it to the person to whom a copy was given under paragraph (a) above.

(3) In this section, "authorised person" has the same meaning as in section 108 above.

Offences.

110.—(1) It is an offence for a person intentionally to obstruct an authorised person in the exercise or performance of his powers or duties.

(2) It is an offence for a person, without reasonable excuse,—

   (a) to fail to comply with any requirement imposed under section 108 above;

   (b) to fail or refuse to provide facilities or assistance or any information or to permit any inspection reasonably required by an authorised person in the execution of his powers or duties under or by virtue of that section; or

   (c) to prevent any other person from appearing before an authorised person, or answering any question to which an authorised person may require an answer, pursuant to subsection (4) of that section.

(3) It is an offence for a person falsely to pretend to be an authorised person.

(4) A person guilty of an offence under subsection (1) above shall be liable—

   (a) in the case of an offence of obstructing an authorised person in the execution of his powers under section 109 above—

      (i) on summary conviction, to a fine not exceeding the statutory maximum;

      (ii) on conviction on indictment, to a fine or to imprisonment for a term not exceeding two years, or to both;

   (b) in any other case, on summary conviction, to a fine not exceeding level 5 on the standard scale.

(5) A person guilty of an offence under subsection (2) or (3) above shall be liable on summary conviction to a fine not exceeding level 5 on the standard scale.

(6) In this section—

"authorised person" means a person authorised under section 108 above and includes a person designated under paragraph 2 of Schedule 18 to this Act;

"powers and duties" includes powers or duties exercisable by virtue of a warrant under Schedule 18 to this Act.

Evidence

111.—(1) The following provisions (which restrict the admissibility in evidence of information obtained from samples) shall cease to have effect—

Evidence in connection with certain pollution offences.

(a) section 19(2) to (2B) of the Rivers (Prevention of Pollution) (Scotland) 1951;

1951 c. 66.

(b) section 49 of the Sewerage (Scotland) Act 1968;

1968 c. 47.

(c) section 171(4) and (5) of the Water Industry Act 1991; and

1991 c. 56.

(d) section 209(1), (2) and (4) of the Water Resources Act 1991.

1991 c. 57.

(2) Information provided or obtained pursuant to or by virtue of a condition of a relevant licence (including information so provided or obtained, or recorded, by means of any apparatus) shall be admissible in evidence in any proceedings, whether against the person subject to the condition or any other person.

(3) For the purposes of subsection (2) above, apparatus shall be presumed in any proceedings to register or record accurately, unless the contrary is shown or the relevant licence otherwise provides.

(4) Where—

(a) by virtue of a condition of a relevant licence, an entry is required to be made in any record as to the observance of any condition of the relevant licence, and

(b) the entry has not been made,

that fact shall be admissible in any proceedings as evidence that that condition has not been observed.

(5) In this section—

"apparatus" includes any meter or other device for measuring, assessing, determining, recording or enabling to be recorded, the volume, temperature, radioactivity, rate, nature, origin, composition or effect of any substance, flow, discharge, emission, deposit or abstraction;

"condition of a relevant licence" includes any requirement to which a person is subject under, by virtue of or in consequence of a relevant licence;

"environmental licence" has the same meaning as it has in Part I above as it applies in relation to the Agency or SEPA, as the case may be;

"relevant licence" means—

(a) any environmental licence;

(b) any consent under Part II of the Sewerage (Scotland) Act 1968 to make discharges of trade effluent;

(c) any agreement under section 37 of that Act with respect to, or to any matter connected with, the reception, treatment or disposal of such effluent;

(d) any consent under Chapter III of Part IV of the Water Industry Act 1991 to make discharges of special category effluent; or

(e) any agreement under section 129 of that Act with respect to, or to any matter connected with, the reception or disposal of such effluent.

(6) In section 25 of the Environmental Protection Act, after subsection (2) (which makes similar provision to subsection (4) above) there shall be inserted—

"(3) Subsection (2) above shall not have effect in relation to any entry required to be made in any record by virtue of a condition of a relevant licence, within the meaning of section 111 of the Environment Act 1995 (which makes corresponding provision in relation to such licences)."

Offences

112. Schedule 19 to this Act shall have effect.

Information

113.—(1) Notwithstanding any prohibition or restriction imposed by or under any enactment or rule of law, information of any description may be disclosed—

(a) by a new Agency to a Minister of the Crown, the other new Agency or a local enforcing authority,

(b) by a Minister of the Crown to a new Agency, another Minister of the Crown or a local enforcing authority, or

(c) by a local enforcing authority to a Minister of the Crown, a new Agency or another local enforcing authority,

for the purpose of facilitating the carrying out by either of the new Agencies of any of its functions, by any such Minister of any of his environmental functions or by any local enforcing authority of any of its relevant functions; and no person shall be subject to any civil or criminal liability in consequence of any disclosure made by virtue of this subsection.

(2) Nothing in this section shall authorise the disclosure to a local enforcing authority by a new Agency or another local enforcing authority of information—

(a) disclosure of which would, in the opinion of a Minister of the Crown, be contrary to the interests of national security; or

(b) which was obtained under or by virtue of the Statistics of Trade Act 1947 and which was disclosed to a new Agency or any of its officers by the Secretary of State.

(3) No information disclosed to any person under or by virtue of this section shall be disclosed by that person to any other person otherwise than in accordance with the provisions of this section, or any provision of any other enactment which authorises or requires the disclosure, if that information is information—

(a) which relates to a trade secret of any person or which otherwise is or might be commercially confidential in relation to any person; or

(b) whose disclosure otherwise than under or by virtue of this section would, in the opinion of a Minister of the Crown, be contrary to the interests of national security.

(4) Any authorisation by or under this section of the disclosure of information by or to any person shall also be taken to authorise the disclosure of that information by or, as the case may be, to any officer of his who is authorised by him to make the disclosure or, as the case may be, to receive the information.

(5) In this section—

"new Agency" means the Agency or SEPA;

"the environment" has the same meaning as in Part I of the Environmental Protection Act 1990;

1990 c. 43.

"environmental functions", in relation to a Minister of the Crown, means any function of that Minister, whether conferred or imposed under or by virtue of any enactment or otherwise, relating to the environment; and

"local enforcing authority" means—

(a) any local authority within the meaning of Part IIA of the Environmental Protection Act 1990, and the "relevant functions" of such an authority are its functions under or by virtue of that Part;

(b) any local authority within the meaning of Part IV of this Act, and the "relevant functions" of such an authority are its functions under or by virtue of that Part;

(c) in relation to England, any county council for an area for which there are district councils, and the "relevant functions" of such a county council are its functions under or by virtue of Part IV of this Act; or

(d) in relation to England and Wales, any local enforcing authority within the meaning of section 1(7) of the Environmental Protection Act 1990, and the "relevant functions" of such an authority are its functions under or by virtue of Part I of that Act.

Appeals

114.—(1) The Secretary of State may—

(a) appoint any person to exercise on his behalf, with or without payment, any function to which this paragraph applies; or

(b) refer any item to which this paragraph applies to such person as the Secretary of State may appoint for the purpose, with or without payment.

Power of Secretary of State to delegate his functions of determining, or to refer matters involved in, appeals.

(2) The functions to which paragraph (a) of subsection (1) above applies are any of the Secretary of State's functions of determining—

(a) an appeal under—

(i) section 31A(2)(b), 42B(5), 46C or 49B of the Control of Pollution Act 1974,

1974 c. 40.

(ii) section 4 of the Control of Pollution (Amendment) Act 1989,

1989 c. 14.

1990 c. 43.

1991 c. 28.

1991 c. 57.

1993 c. 12.

S.I. 1994/1056.

1974 c. 40.

         (iii) section 15, 22(5), 43, 62(3)(c), 66(5), 78L or 78T of the Environmental Protection Act 1990,

         (iv) paragraph 2 or paragraph 3(3) of Schedule 6 to the Natural Heritage (Scotland) Act 1991,

         (v) section 43, 91, 92, 96, 161C or 191B(5) of the Water Resources Act 1991,

         (vi) section 26 of the Radioactive Substances Act 1993 against any decision of, or notice served by, SEPA,

         (vii) paragraph 6 of Schedule 5 to the Waste Management Licensing Regulations 1994,

or any matter involved in such an appeal;

    (b) the questions, or any of the questions, which fall to be determined by the Secretary of State under section 39(1) or section 49(4) of the Control of Pollution Act 1974.

(3) The items to which paragraph (b) of subsection (1) above applies are—

    (a) any matter involved in an appeal falling within subsection (2)(a) above;

    (b) any of the questions which fall to be determined by the Secretary of State under section 39(1) or section 49(4) of the Control of Pollution Act 1974.

(4) Schedule 20 to this Act shall have effect with respect to appointments under subsection (1)(a) above.

Crown application

Application of this Act to the Crown.

115.—(1) Subject to the provisions of this section, this Act shall bind the Crown.

(2) Part III of this Act and any amendments, repeals and revocations made by other provisions of this Act (other than those made by Schedule 21, which shall bind the Crown) bind the Crown to the extent that the enactments to which they relate bind the Crown.

(3) No contravention by the Crown of any provision made by or under this Act shall make the Crown criminally liable; but the High Court or, in Scotland, the Court of Session may, on the application of the Agency or, in Scotland, SEPA, declare unlawful any act or omission of the Crown which constitutes such a contravention.

(4) Notwithstanding anything in subsection (3) above, any provision made by or under this Act shall apply to persons in the public service of the Crown as it applies to other persons.

(5) If the Secretary of State certifies that it appears to him, as respects any Crown premises and any powers of entry exercisable in relation to them specified in the certificate, that it is requisite or expedient that, in the interests of national security, the powers should not be exercisable in relation to those premises, those powers shall not be exercisable in relation to those premises; and in this subsection "Crown premises" means premises held or used by or on behalf of the Crown.

(6) Nothing in this section shall be taken as in any way affecting Her Majesty in her private capacity; and this subsection shall be construed as

if section 38(3) of the Crown Proceedings Act 1947 (interpretation of
references to Her Majesty in her private capacity) were contained in
this Act.

116. Schedule 21 to this Act shall have effect.

Application of
certain other
enactments to the
Crown.

Isles of Scilly

117.—(1) Subject to sections 77, 80 and 89 above and the provisions of
any order under this section or section 89 above, nothing in this Act shall
require or authorise any function, duty or power to be carried out,
performed or exercised in relation to the Isles of Scilly by the Agency; and
references in the other provisions of this Act (apart from Part III) to
England and Wales shall not include references to those Isles.

Application of this
Act to the Isles of
Scilly.

(2) The Secretary of State may, after consultation with the Council of
the Isles of Scilly, by order make provision with respect to the carrying
out in those Isles of functions (other than functions under or by virtue of
Part III or IV of this Act) falling to be carried out in relation to other parts
of England and Wales by the Agency.

(3) Without prejudice to the generality of the power conferred by
subsection (2) above, an order under this section may apply any provision
of this Act (other than a provision contained in Part III or IV) in relation
to the Isles of Scilly with or without modifications.

(4) An order under this section may—

(a) make different provision for different cases, including different
provision in relation to different persons, circumstances or
localities; and

(b) contain such supplemental, consequential and transitional
provision as the Secretary of State considers appropriate,
including provision saving provision repealed by or under any
enactment.

(5) The power of the Secretary of State to make an order under this
section shall be exercisable by statutory instrument; and a statutory
instrument containing such an order shall be subject to annulment in
pursuance of a resolution of either House of Parliament.

118.—(1) After section 10 of the Control of Pollution (Amendment)
Act 1989 there shall be inserted—

Application of
certain other
enactments to the
Isles of Scilly.

1989 c. 14.

"Application to
the Isles of
Scilly.

    10A.—(1) Subject to the provisions of any order under
this section, this Act shall not apply in relation to the Isles
of Scilly.

    (2) The Secretary of State may, after consultation with
the Council of the Isles of Scilly, by order provide for the
application of any provisions of this Act to the Isles of
Scilly; and any such order may provide for the application
of those provisions to those Isles with such modifications
as may be specified in the order.

    (3) An order under this section may—

        (a) make different provision for different cases,

including different provision in relation to different persons, circumstances or localities; and

(b) contain such supplemental, consequential and transitional provision as the Secretary of State considers appropriate, including provision saving provision repealed by or under any enactment.

(4) The power of the Secretary of State to make an order under this section shall be exercisable by statutory instrument; and a statutory instrument containing such an order shall be subject to annulment in pursuance of a resolution of either House of Parliament."

1974 c. 40.

(2) In section 11 of that Act, subsection (3) (which provides for section 107 of the Control of Pollution Act 1974 to have effect in relation to the application and modification of that Act to the Isles of Scilly) shall cease to have effect.

1990 c. 43.

(3) For section 76 of the Environmental Protection Act 1990 (which provides for Part II of that Act to have effect in its application to the Isles of Scilly with modifications specified by order) there shall be substituted—

"Application to the Isles of Scilly.

76.—(1) Subject to the provisions of any order under this section, this Part shall not apply in relation to the Isles of Scilly.

(2) The Secretary of State may, after consultation with the Council of the Isles of Scilly, by order provide for the application of any provisions of this Part to the Isles of Scilly; and any such order may provide for the application of those provisions to those Isles with such modifications as may be specified in the order.

(3) An order under this section may—

(a) make different provision for different cases, including different provision in relation to different persons, circumstances or localities; and

(b) contain such supplemental, consequential and transitional provision as the Secretary of State considers appropriate, including provision saving provision repealed by or under any enactment."

1991 c. 56.

(4) For section 222 of the Water Industry Act 1991 (application to Isles of Scilly) there shall be substituted—

"Application to the Isles of Scilly.

222.—(1) Subject to the provisions of any order under this section, this Act shall not apply in relation to the Isles of Scilly.

(2) The Secretary of State may, after consultation with the Council of the Isles of Scilly, by order provide for the application of any provisions of this Act to the Isles of Scilly; and any such order may provide for the application of those provisions to those Isles with such modifications as may be specified in the order.

(3) An order under this section may—

(a) make different provision for different cases, including different provision in relation to different persons, circumstances or localities; and

(b) contain such supplemental, consequential and transitional provision as the Secretary of State considers appropriate, including provision saving provision repealed by or under any enactment.

(4) The power of the Secretary of State to make an order under this section shall be exercisable by statutory instrument subject to annulment in pursuance of a resolution of either House of Parliament."

(5) For section 224 of the Water Resources Act 1991 (application to Isles of Scilly) there shall be substituted—

1991 c. 57.

"Application to the Isles of Scilly.

224.—(1) Subject to the provisions of any order under this section, this Act shall not apply in relation to the Isles of Scilly.

(2) The Secretary of State may, after consultation with the Council of the Isles of Scilly, by order provide for the application of any provisions of this Act to the Isles of Scilly; and any such order may provide for the application of those provisions to those Isles with such modifications as may be specified in the order.

(3) An order under this section may—

(a) make different provision for different cases, including different provision in relation to different persons, circumstances or localities; and

(b) contain such supplemental, consequential and transitional provision as the Secretary of State considers appropriate, including provision saving provision repealed by or under any enactment.

(4) The power of the Secretary of State to make an order under this section shall be exercisable by statutory instrument subject to annulment in pursuance of a resolution of either House of Parliament."

(6) For section 75 of the Land Drainage Act 1991 (application to the Isles of Scilly) there shall be substituted—

1991 c. 59.

"Application to the Isles of Scilly.

75.—(1) Subject to the provisions of any order under this section, this Act shall not apply in relation to the Isles of Scilly.

(2) The Secretary of State may, after consultation with the Council of the Isles of Scilly, by order provide for the application of any provisions of this Act to the Isles of Scilly; and any such order may provide for the application of those provisions to those Isles with such modifications as may be specified in the order.

(3) An order under this section may—

> (a) make different provision for different cases, including different provision in relation to different persons, circumstances or localities; and

> (b) contain such supplemental, consequential and transitional provision as the Secretary of State considers appropriate, including provision saving provision repealed by or under any enactment.

(4) The power of the Secretary of State to make an order under this section shall be exercisable by statutory instrument subject to annulment in pursuance of a resolution of either House of Parliament."

Miscellaneous and supplemental

Stamp duty.

119.—(1) No transfer effected by Part I of this Act shall give rise to any liability to stamp duty.

(2) Stamp duty shall not be chargeable—

> (a) on any transfer scheme; or

> (b) on any instrument or agreement which is certified to the Commissioners of Inland Revenue by the Secretary of State as made in pursuance of a transfer scheme.

(3) No transfer scheme, and no instrument which is certified as mentioned in subsection (2)(b) above, shall be taken to be duly stamped unless—

1891 c. 39.

> (a) it has, in accordance with section 12 of the Stamp Act 1891, been stamped with a particular stamp denoting that it is not chargeable with that duty or that it is duly stamped; or

> (b) it is stamped with the duty to which it would be liable, apart from this section.

(4) In this section "transfer scheme" means a scheme made or approved by the Secretary of State under section 3 or 22 above for the transfer of property, rights or liabilities to the Agency or to SEPA.

Minor and consequential amendments, transitional and transitory provisions, savings and repeals.

120.—(1) The enactments mentioned in Schedule 22 to this Act shall have effect with the amendments there specified (being minor amendments and amendments consequential on provisions of this Act); and, without prejudice to any power conferred by any other provision of this Act, the Secretary of State and the Minister shall each have power by regulations to make such additional consequential amendments—

> (a) of public general enactments passed before, or in the same Session as, this Act, and

> (b) of subordinate legislation made before the passing of this Act,

as he considers necessary or expedient by reason of the coming into force of any provision of this Act.

(2) The transitional provisions, transitory provisions and savings contained in Schedule 23 to this Act shall have effect; but those provisions are without prejudice to sections 16 and 17 of the Interpretation Act 1978 (effect of repeals).

1978 c. 30.

(3) The enactments mentioned in Schedule 24 to this Act (which include some that are spent or no longer of practical utility) are hereby repealed to the extent specified in the third column of that Schedule.

(4) The power to make regulations under subsection (1) above shall be exercisable by statutory instrument; and a statutory instrument containing any such regulations shall be subject to annulment in pursuance of a resolution of either House of Parliament.

(5) The power to make regulations under subsection (1) above includes power to make such incidental, supplemental, consequential and transitional provision as the Secretary of State or the Minister thinks necessary or expedient.

(6) In this section—

"the Minister" means the Minister of Agriculture, Fisheries and Food;

"subordinate legislation" has the same meaning as in the Interpretation Act 1978.

1978 c. 30.

121.—(1) If it appears to the Secretary of State or the Minister to be appropriate to do so—

Local statutory provisions: consequential amendments etc.

(a) for the purposes of, or in consequence of, the coming into force of any enactment contained in this Act; or

(b) in consequence of the effect or operation at any time after the transfer date of any such enactment or of anything done under any such enactment,

he may by order repeal, amend or re-enact (with or without modifications) any local statutory provision, including, in the case of an order by virtue of paragraph (b) above, a provision amended by virtue of paragraph (a) above.

(2) An order made by the Secretary of State or the Minister under subsection (1) above may—

(a) make provision applying generally in relation to local statutory provisions of a description specified in the order;

(b) make different provision for different cases, including different provision in relation to different persons, circumstances or localities;

(c) contain such supplemental, consequential and transitional provision as the Secretary of State or, as the case may be, the Minister considers appropriate; and

(d) in the case of an order made after the transfer date, require provision contained in the order to be treated as if it came into force on that date.

(3) The power under this section to repeal or amend a local statutory provision shall include power to modify the effect in relation to any local statutory provision of any provision of Schedule 23 to this Act.

(4) Nothing in any order under this section may abrogate or curtail the effect of so much of any local statutory provision as confers any right of way or confers on or preserves for the public—

(a) any right of enjoyment of air, exercise or recreation on land; or

(b) any right of access to land for the purposes of exercise or recreation.

(5) The power to make an order under subsection (1) above shall be exercisable by statutory instrument subject to annulment in pursuance of a resolution of either House of Parliament.

(6) The power to make an order under subsection (1) above shall be without prejudice to any power conferred by any other provision of this Act.

(7) In this section—

"local statutory provision" means—

> (a) a provision of a local Act (including an Act confirming a provisional order);

> (b) a provision of so much of any public general Act as has effect with respect to a particular area, with respect to particular persons or works or with respect to particular provisions falling within any paragraph of this definition;

> (c) a provision of an instrument made under any provision falling within paragraph (a) or (b) above; or

> (d) a provision of any other instrument which is in the nature of a local enactment;

"the Minister" means the Minister of Agriculture, Fisheries and Food;

"the transfer date" has the same meaning as in Part I of this Act.

Directions.

122.—(1) Any direction given under this Act shall be in writing.

(2) Any power conferred by this Act to give a direction shall include power to vary or revoke the direction.

(3) Subsections (4) and (5) below apply to any direction given—

(a) to the Agency or SEPA under any provision of this Act or any other enactment, or

(b) to any other body or person under any provision of this Act,

being a direction to any extent so given for the purpose of implementing any obligations of the United Kingdom under the Community Treaties.

(4) A direction to which this subsection applies shall not be varied or revoked unless, notwithstanding the variation or revocation, the obligations mentioned in subsection (3) above, as they have effect for the time being, continue to be implemented, whether by directions or any other instrument or by any enactment.

(5) Any variation or revocation of a direction to which this subsection applies shall be published in such manner as the Minister giving it considers appropriate for the purpose of bringing the matters to which it relates to the attention of persons likely to be affected by them; and—

(a) copies of the variation or revocation shall be made available to the public; and

(b) notice of the variation or revocation, and of where a copy of the variation or revocation may be obtained, shall be given—

> (i) if the direction has effect in England and Wales, in the London Gazette;

(ii) if the direction has effect in Scotland, in the Edinburgh Gazette.

123.—(1) Without prejudice to paragraph 17(2)(d) of Schedule 7 to this Act, any notice required or authorised by or under this Act to be served (whether the expression "serve" or the expression "give" or "send" or any other expression is used) on any person may be served by delivering it to him, or by leaving it at his proper address, or by sending it by post to him at that address.

Service of documents.

(2) Any such notice may—

(a) in the case of a body corporate, be served on the secretary or clerk of that body;

(b) in the case of a partnership, be served on a partner or a person having the control or management of the partnership business.

(3) For the purposes of this section and of section 7 of the Interpretation Act 1978 (service of documents by post) in its application to this section, the proper address of any person on whom any such notice is to be served shall be his last known address, except that—

1978 c. 30.

(a) in the case of a body corporate or their secretary or clerk, it shall be the address of the registered or principal office of that body;

(b) in the case of a partnership or person having the control or the management of the partnership business, it shall be the principal office of the partnership;

and for the purposes of this subsection the principal office of a company registered outside the United Kingdom or of a partnership carrying on business outside the United Kingdom shall be their principal office within the United Kingdom.

(4) If the person to be served with any such notice has specified an address in the United Kingdom other than his proper address within the meaning of subsection (3) above as the one at which he or someone on his behalf will accept notices of the same description as that notice, that address shall also be treated for the purposes of this section and section 7 of the Interpretation Act 1978 as his proper address.

(5) Where under any provision of this Act any notice is required to be served on a person who is, or appears to be, in occupation of any premises then—

(a) if the name or address of such a person cannot after reasonable inquiry be ascertained, or

(b) if the premises appear to be or are unoccupied,

that notice may be served either by leaving it in the hands of a person who is or appears to be resident or employed on the premises or by leaving it conspicuously affixed to some building or object on the premises.

(6) This section shall not apply to any notice in relation to the service of which provision is made by rules of court.

(7) The preceding provisions of this section shall apply to the service of a document as they apply to the service of a notice.

(8) In this section—

"premises" includes any land, vehicle, vessel or mobile plant;

"serve" shall be construed in accordance with subsection (1) above.

PART V

General
interpretation.

124.—(1) In this Act, except in so far as the context otherwise requires—

"the Agency" means the Environment Agency;

"financial year" means a period of twelve months ending with 31st March;

"functions" includes powers and duties;

"modifications" includes additions, alterations and omissions and cognate expressions shall be construed accordingly;

"notice" means notice in writing;

"records", without prejudice to the generality of the expression, includes computer records and any other records kept otherwise than in a document;

"SEPA" means the Scottish Environment Protection Agency.

(2) The amendment by this Act of any provision contained in subordinate legislation shall not be taken to have prejudiced any power to make further subordinate legislation amending or revoking that provision.

1978 c. 30.

(3) In subsection (2) above, "subordinate legislation" has the same meaning as in the Interpretation Act 1978.

Short title,
commencement,
extent, etc.

125.—(1) This Act may be cited as the Environment Act 1995.

(2) Part III of this Act, except for section 78, paragraph 7(2) of Schedule 7 and Schedule 10, shall come into force at the end of the period of two months beginning with the day on which this Act is passed.

(3) Except as provided in subsection (2) above and except for this section, section 74 above and paragraphs 76(8)(a) and 135 of Schedule 22 to this Act (which come into force on the passing of this Act) and the repeal of sub-paragraph (1) of paragraph 22 of Schedule 10 to this Act (which comes into force in accordance with sub-paragraph (7) of that paragraph) this Act shall come into force on such day as the Secretary of State may specify by order made by statutory instrument; and different days may be so specified for different provisions or for different purposes of the same provision.

(4) Without prejudice to the provisions of Schedule 23 to this Act, an order under subsection (3) above may make such transitional provisions and savings as appear to the Secretary of State necessary or expedient in connection with any provision brought into force by the order.

(5) The power conferred by subsection (4) above includes power to modify any enactment contained in this or any other Act.

1974 c. 28.

(6) An Order in Council under paragraph 1(1)(b) of Schedule 1 to the Northern Ireland Act 1974 (legislation for Northern Ireland in the interim period) which states that it is made only for purposes corresponding to those of section 98 of this Act—

(a) shall not be subject to paragraph 1(4) and (5) of that Schedule (affirmative resolution of both Houses of Parliament); but

(b) shall be subject to annulment in pursuance of a resolution of either House of Parliament.

(7) Except for this section and any amendment or repeal by this Act of any provision contained in—

(a) the Parliamentary Commissioner Act 1967,

(b) the Sea Fish (Conservation) Act 1967,

(c) the House of Commons Disqualification Act 1975, or

(d) the Northern Ireland Assembly Disqualification Act 1975,

1967 c. 13.
1967 c. 84.
1975 c. 24.
1975 c. 35.

this Act shall not extend to Northern Ireland.

(8) Part III of this Act, and Schedule 24 to this Act so far as relating to that Part, extends to England and Wales only.

(9) Section 106 of, and Schedule 16 to, this Act extend to Scotland only.

(10) Subject to the foregoing provisions of this section and to any express provision made by this Act to the contrary, any amendment, repeal or revocation made by this Act shall have the same extent as the enactment or instrument to which it relates.

SCHEDULES

SCHEDULE 1

THE ENVIRONMENT AGENCY

Membership

1.—(1) Subject to the following provisions of this paragraph, a member shall hold and vacate office in accordance with the terms of his appointment and shall, on ceasing to be a member, be eligible for re-appointment.

(2) A member may at any time resign his office by giving notice to the appropriate Minister.

(3) The appropriate Minister may remove a member from that office if he is satisfied—

(a) that the member has been absent from meetings of the Agency for a period of more than three months without the permission of the Agency;

(b) that the member has been adjudged bankrupt, that his estate has been sequestrated or that he has made a composition or arrangement with, or granted a trust deed for, his creditors; or

(c) that the member is unable or unfit to carry out the functions of a member.

Chairman and deputy chairman

2. The chairman or deputy chairman of the Agency shall hold office as such unless and until—

(a) he resigns that office by giving notice to the Secretary of State, or

(b) he ceases to be a member,

and shall, on ceasing to be the chairman or deputy chairman, be eligible for further designation as such in accordance with section 1(3) of this Act at any time when he is a member.

Remuneration, pensions, etc.

3.—(1) The Agency shall pay to its members such remuneration, and such travelling and other allowances, as may be determined by the appropriate Minister.

(2) The Agency shall, if so required by the appropriate Minister,—

(a) pay such pension, allowances or gratuities as may be determined by that Minister to or in respect of a person who is or has been a member;

(b) make such payments as may be determined by that Minister towards provision for the payment of a pension, allowances or gratuities to or in respect of a person who is or has been a member; or

(c) provide and maintain such schemes (whether contributory or not) as may be determined by that Minister for the payment of pensions, allowances or gratuities to or in respect of persons who are or have been members.

(3) If, when any member ceases to hold office, the appropriate Minister determines that there are special circumstances which make it right that that member should receive compensation, the Agency shall pay to him a sum by way of compensation of such amount as may be so determined.

Staff

4.—(1) The Agency may appoint such officers and employees as it may determine.

(2) No member or other person shall be appointed by the Agency to act as chief executive of the Agency unless the Secretary of State has consented to the appointment of that person.

(3) The Agency may—

(a) pay such pensions, allowances or gratuities to or in respect of any persons who are or have been its officers or employees as it may, with the approval of the Secretary of State, determine;

(b) make such payments as it may so determine towards provision for the payment of pensions, allowances or gratuities to or in respect of any such persons;

(c) provide and maintain such schemes as it may so determine (whether contributory or not) for the payment of pensions, allowances or gratuities to or in respect of any such persons.

(4) Any reference in sub-paragraph (3) above to pensions, allowances or gratuities to or in respect of any such persons as are mentioned in that sub-paragraph includes a reference to pensions, allowances or gratuities by way of compensation to or in respect of any of the Agency's officers or employees who suffer loss of office or employment or loss or diminution of emoluments.

Proceedings of the Agency

5. Subject to the following provisions of this Schedule and to section 106 of the 1991 Act (obligation to carry out flood defence functions through committees), the Agency may regulate its own procedure (including quorum).

Delegation of powers

6. Subject to section 106 of the 1991 Act, anything authorised or required by or under any enactment to be done by the Agency may be done—

(a) by any member, officer or employee of the Agency who has been authorised for the purpose, whether generally or specially, by the Agency; or

(b) by any committee or sub-committee of the Agency which has been so authorised.

Members' interests

7.—(1) A member who is in any way directly or indirectly interested in any matter that is brought up for consideration at a meeting of the Agency shall disclose the nature of his interest to the meeting; and, where such a disclosure is made—

(a) the disclosure shall be recorded in the minutes of the meeting; and

(b) the member shall not take any part in any deliberation or decision of the Agency, or of any of its committees or sub-committees, with respect to that matter.

(2) For the purposes of sub-paragraph (1) above, a general notification given at a meeting of the Agency by a member to the effect that he—

(a) is a member of a specified company or firm, and

(b) is to be regarded as interested in any matter involving that company or firm,

shall be regarded as a sufficient disclosure of his interest in relation to any such matter.

(3) A member need not attend in person at a meeting of the Agency in order to make a disclosure which he is required to make under this paragraph if he takes reasonable steps to secure that the disclosure is made by a notice which is read and considered at the meeting.

(4) The Secretary of State may, subject to such conditions as he considers appropriate, remove any disability imposed by virtue of this paragraph in any case where the number of members of the Agency disabled by virtue of this paragraph at any one time would be so great a proportion of the whole as to impede the transaction of business.

(5) The power of the Secretary of State under sub-paragraph (4) above includes power to remove, either indefinitely or for any period, a disability which would otherwise attach to any member, or members of any description, by reason of such interests, and in respect of such matters, as may be specified or described by the Secretary of State.

(6) Nothing in this paragraph precludes any member from taking part in the consideration or discussion of, or voting on, any question whether an application should be made to the Secretary of State for the exercise of the power conferred by sub-paragraph (4) above.

(7) Any reference in this paragraph to a meeting of the Agency includes a reference to a meeting of any committee or sub-committee of the Agency.

Vacancies and defective appointments

8. The validity of any proceedings of the Agency shall not be affected by a vacancy amongst the members or by a defect in the appointment of a member.

Minutes

9.—(1) Minutes shall be kept of proceedings of the Agency, of its committees and of its sub-committees.

(2) Minutes of any such proceedings shall be evidence of those proceedings if they are signed by a person purporting to have acted as chairman of the proceedings to which the minutes relate or of any subsequent proceedings in the course of which the minutes were approved as a correct record.

(3) Where minutes of any such proceedings have been signed as mentioned in sub-paragraph (2) above, those proceedings shall, unless the contrary is shown, be deemed to have been validly convened and constituted.

Application of seal and proof of instruments

10.—(1) The application of the seal of the Agency shall be authenticated by the signature of any member, officer or employee of the Agency who has been authorised for the purpose, whether generally or specially, by the Agency.

(2) In this paragraph the reference to the signature of a person includes a reference to a facsimile of a signature by whatever process reproduced; and, in paragraph 11 below, the word "signed" shall be construed accordingly.

Documents served etc. by or on the Agency

11.—(1) Any document which the Agency is authorised or required by or under any enactment to serve, make or issue may be signed on behalf of the Agency by any member, officer or employee of the Agency who has been authorised for the purpose, whether generally or specially, by the Agency.

(2) Every document purporting to be an instrument made or issued by or on behalf of the Agency and to be duly executed under the seal of the Agency, or to be signed or executed by a person authorised by the Agency for the purpose, shall be received in evidence and be treated, without further proof, as being so made or issued unless the contrary is shown.

(3) Any notice which is required or authorised, by or under any provision of any other Act, to be given, served or issued by, to or on the Agency shall be in writing.

Interpretation

12. In this Schedule—

"the appropriate Minister", in relation to any person who is or has been a member, means the Minister or the Secretary of State, according to whether that person was appointed as a member by the Minister or by the Secretary of State; and

"member", except where the context otherwise requires, means any member of the Agency (including the chairman and deputy chairman).

SCHEDULE 2

Sections 3 and 22.

TRANSFERS OF PROPERTY ETC: SUPPLEMENTAL PROVISIONS

PART I

INTRODUCTORY

Interpretation

1. In this Schedule—

"the chief inspector"—

(a) in the application of this Schedule in relation to transfers by or under section 3 of this Act, means any of the inspectors or chief inspectors mentioned in section 2(1) of this Act;

(b) in the application of this Schedule in relation to transfers by or under section 22 of this Act, means any of the inspectors or chief inspectors mentioned in section 21(1) of this Act;

and any reference to the chief inspector for England and Wales or the chief inspector for Scotland shall be construed accordingly;

"the relevant new Agency" means—

(a) in the application of this Schedule in relation to transfers by or under section 3 of this Act, the Agency; and

(b) in the application of this Schedule in relation to transfers by or under section 22 of this Act, SEPA;

"transfer scheme" means a scheme under section 3 or 22 of this Act;

"the transferor", in relation to transfers by or under section 3 of this Act, means—

(a) in the case of any transfer by section 3(1)(a) of this Act, the National Rivers Authority or the London Waste Regulation Authority, as the case may be; or

(b) in the case of any transfer scheme, or any transfer by transfer scheme—

(i) the Secretary of State,

(ii) the chief inspector, or

(iii) any waste regulation authority,

(as the case may be) from whom any property, rights or liabilities are, or are to be, transferred by that scheme;

"the transferor", in relation to transfers by or under section 22 of this Act, means—

(a) in the case of any transfer by section 22(1)(a) of this Act, the river purification board in question; or

(b) in the case of any transfer scheme, or any transfer by transfer scheme—

(i) the Secretary of State;

(ii) the chief inspector; or

(iii) any local authority,

1994 c. 39.

(as the case may be) from whom any property, rights or liabilities are, or are to be, transferred by that scheme; and, as respects any such local authority which is a district or islands council, includes, in relation to any time on or after 1st April 1996, the council for any local government area named in column 1 of Schedule 1 to the Local Government etc. (Scotland) Act 1994 which is wholly or partly conterminous with the area of that council.

The property etc. which may be transferred

2.—(1) The property, rights and liabilities which are transferred by, or may be transferred by transfer scheme under, section 3 or 22 of this Act include—

(a) property, rights and liabilities that would not otherwise be capable of being transferred or assigned by the transferor;

(b) in the case of a transfer scheme, such property, rights and liabilities to which the transferor may become entitled or subject after the making of the scheme and before the transfer date as may be specified in the scheme;

(c) property situated anywhere in the United Kingdom or elsewhere;

(d) rights and liabilities under enactments;

(e) rights and liabilities under the law of any part of the United Kingdom or of any country or territory outside the United Kingdom.

(2) The transfers authorised by paragraph (a) of sub-paragraph (1) above include transfers which, by virtue of that paragraph, are to take effect as if there were no such contravention, liability or interference with any interest or right as there would be, in the case of a transfer or assignment otherwise than by or under section 3 or 22 of this Act, by reason of any provision having effect (whether under any enactment or agreement or otherwise) in relation to the terms on which the transferor is entitled or subject to the property, right or liability in question.

(3) This paragraph is subject to paragraph 3 below.

Contracts of employment

3.—(1) The rights and liabilities that may be transferred by and in accordance with a transfer scheme include (subject to the following provisions of this paragraph) any rights or liabilities of the employer under the contract of employment of any person—

(a) who is employed—

(i) in the civil service of the State;

(ii) by a body which is a waste regulation authority in England or Wales; or

(iii) by a local authority in Scotland;

(b) who appears to the appropriate authority to be employed for the purposes of, or otherwise in connection with, functions which are by virtue of this Act to become functions of a new Agency; and

(c) whom the appropriate authority considers it necessary or expedient to transfer into the employment of that new Agency;

and in the following provisions of this paragraph any reference to a "qualifying employee" is a reference to such a person.

(2) A transfer scheme which provides for the transfer of rights or liabilities under the contracts of employment of qualifying employees must identify those employees—

   (a) by specifying them;

   (b) by referring to persons of a description specified in the scheme (with or without exceptions); or

   (c) partly in the one way and partly in the other.

(3) A transfer scheme shall not operate to transfer rights or liabilities under so much of a contract of employment as relates to an occupational pension scheme, other than any provisions of such a pension scheme which do not relate to benefits for old age, invalidity or survivors.

(4) Where a transfer scheme provides for the transfer of rights or liabilities under the contract of employment of a qualifying employee—

   (a) all the employer's rights, powers, duties and liabilities under or in connection with the contract of employment shall be transferred to the relevant new Agency on the transfer date by and in accordance with the scheme, and

   (b) anything done by or in relation to the employer in respect of the qualifying employee before the transfer date shall be treated on and after that date as done by or in relation to the relevant new Agency,

except in a case where objection is made by the qualifying employee as mentioned in sub-paragraph (8)(b) below.

(5) Sub-paragraphs (6) and (7) below shall have effect in any case where rights or liabilities under the contract of employment of a qualifying employee are transferred by and in accordance with a transfer scheme.

(6) In a case falling within sub-paragraph (5) above—

   (a) the transfer shall be regarded for the purposes of section 84 of the Employment Protection (Consolidation) Act 1978 (renewal of contract or re-engagement) as a renewal of the qualifying employee's contract of employment, or a re-engagement of the qualifying employee, falling within subsection (1) of that section; and   1978 c. 44.

   (b) the qualifying employee shall accordingly not be regarded as having been dismissed by virtue of the transfer.

(7) In a case falling within sub-paragraph (5) above, for the purposes of Schedule 13 to the Employment Protection (Consolidation) Act 1978 (ascertainment of the length of an employee's period of employment and whether that employment is continuous)—

   (a) so much of the qualifying employee's period of continuous employment as ends with the day preceding the transfer date shall be treated on and after that date as a period of employment with the relevant new Agency; and

   (b) the continuity of the period of employment of the qualifying employee shall be treated as not having been broken by the transfer.

(8) Sub-paragraph (9) below shall have effect in any case where—

   (a) a transfer scheme contains provision for the transfer of rights or liabilities under the contract of employment of a qualifying employee, but

(b) the qualifying employee informs the appropriate authority or the relevant new Agency that he objects to becoming employed by that new Agency.

(9) In a case falling within sub-paragraph (8) above—

(a) the transfer scheme—

(i) shall not operate to transfer any rights, powers, duties or liabilities under or in connection with the contract of employment; but

(ii) shall operate so as to terminate that contract on the day preceding the transfer date; and

(b) the qualifying employee shall not, by virtue of that termination, be treated for any purpose as having been dismissed.

(10) In this paragraph—

"the appropriate authority" means—

(a) in the case of a person employed in the civil service of the State, the Secretary of State;

(b) in the case of a transfer scheme under section 3 of this Act and a person employed by a body which is a waste regulation authority, that body;

(c) in the case of a transfer scheme under section 22 of this Act and a person employed by a local authority, that authority;

"occupational pension scheme" has the meaning given by section 1 of the Pension Schemes Act 1993.

1993 c. 48.

(11) This paragraph shall apply in relation to any qualifying employee as if, as respects any time before the transfer date,—

(a) any reference to a person's contract of employment included a reference to his employment in the civil service of the State or to the terms of that employment, as the case may require; and

(b) any reference to the dismissal of a person included a reference to the termination of his employment in that service.

Part II

Transfer schemes

Description of the property etc. to be transferred by scheme

4. A transfer scheme may define the property, rights and liabilities to be transferred by the scheme—

(a) by specifying or describing the property, rights and liabilities in question;

(b) by referring to all (or all but so much as may be excepted) of the property, rights and liabilities comprised in a specified part of the undertaking of the transferor; or

(c) partly in the one way and partly in the other.

Division of property etc. to be transferred by scheme: creation of new rights and interests

5.—(1) For the purpose of making any division of property, rights or liabilities which it is considered appropriate to make in connection with the transfer of property, rights and liabilities by and in accordance with a transfer scheme, any such scheme may—

(a) create in favour of the transferor an interest in, or right over, any property transferred by the scheme;

(b) create in favour of the relevant new Agency an interest in, or right over, any property retained by the transferor;

(c) create new rights and liabilities as between the relevant new Agency and the transferor; or

(d) in connection with any provision made by virtue of paragraph (a), (b) or (c) above, make incidental provision as to the interests, rights and liabilities of persons other than the transferor and the relevant new Agency with respect to the subject-matter of the transfer scheme;

and references in the other provisions of Part I of this Act to the transfer of property, rights or liabilities (so far as relating to transfers by and in accordance with transfer schemes) shall accordingly be construed as including references to the creation of any interest, right or liability by virtue of paragraph (a), (b) or (c) above or the making of provision by virtue of paragraph (d) above.

(2) The provision that may be made by virtue of paragraph (c) of sub-paragraph (1) above includes—

(a) provision for treating any person who is entitled by virtue of a transfer scheme to possession of a document as having given another person an acknowledgement in writing of the right of that other person to the production of the document and to delivery of copies of it; and

(b) in the case of a transfer scheme under section 3 of this Act, provision applying section 64 of the Law of Property Act 1925 (production and safe custody of documents) in relation to any case in relation to which provision falling within paragraph (a) above has effect.

1925 c. 20.

Transfer schemes: incidental, supplemental and consequential provision

6.—(1) A transfer scheme may make such incidental, supplemental and consequential provision—

(a) as the Secretary of State considers appropriate, in the case of a scheme made by him,

(b) as a body which is a waste regulation authority considers appropriate, in the case of a scheme made by that body under section 3 of this Act, or

(c) as a local authority considers appropriate, in the case of a scheme made by that authority under section 22 of this Act.

(2) Without prejudice to the generality of sub-paragraph (1) above, a transfer scheme may provide—

(a) that disputes as to the effect of the scheme between the transferor and the relevant new Agency are to be referred to such arbitration as may be specified in or determined under the transfer scheme;

(b) that determinations on such arbitrations and certificates given jointly by the transferor and the relevant new Agency as to the effect of the scheme as between them are to be conclusive for all purposes.

Modification of transfer schemes

7.—(1) If at any time after a transfer scheme has come into force the Secretary of State considers it appropriate to do so, he may by order provide that the scheme shall for all purposes be deemed to have come into force with such modifications as may be specified in the order.

(2) An order under sub-paragraph (1) above—

(a) may make, with effect from the coming into force of the transfer scheme in question, such provision as could have been made by the scheme; and

(b) in connection with giving effect to that provision from that time, may contain such supplemental, consequential or transitional provision as the Secretary of State considers appropriate.

(3) The Secretary of State shall not make an order under sub-paragraph (1) above except after consultation with—

(a) the relevant new Agency; and

(b) if the transfer scheme in question is—

(i) a scheme under section 3 of this Act which transferred property, rights or liabilities of a waste regulation authority, or

(ii) a scheme under section 22 of this Act which transferred property, rights or liabilities of a local authority,

the body which was the transferor in the case of that scheme.

(4) The power to make an order under sub-paragraph (1) above shall be exercisable by statutory instrument; and a statutory instrument containing any such order shall be subject to annulment in pursuance of a resolution of either House of Parliament.

Provision of information and assistance to the Secretary of State and the new Agencies in connection with transfer schemes

8.—(1) It shall be the duty of each of the following, that is to say—

(a) the chief inspector for England and Wales,

(b) any body which is a waste regulation authority in England or Wales, and

(c) any officer of such a body,

to provide the Secretary of State or the Agency with such information or assistance as the Secretary of State or, as the case may be, the Agency may reasonably require for the purposes of, or in connection with, the exercise of any powers of the Secretary of State or the Agency in relation to transfer schemes.

(2) It shall be the duty of each of the following, that is to say—

(a) the chief inspector for Scotland,

(b) any local authority, and

(c) any officer of a local authority,

to provide the Secretary of State or SEPA with such information or assistance as the Secretary of State or, as the case may be, SEPA may reasonably require for the purposes of, or in connection with, the exercise of any powers of the Secretary of State or SEPA in relation to transfer schemes.

Pᴀʀᴛ III

Gᴇɴᴇʀᴀʟ ᴘʀᴏᴠɪsɪᴏɴs ᴡɪᴛʜ ʀᴇsᴘᴇᴄᴛ ᴛᴏ ᴛʀᴀɴsғᴇʀs ʙʏ ᴏʀ ᴜɴᴅᴇʀ sᴇᴄᴛɪᴏɴ 3 ᴏʀ 22

Consideration

9. No consideration shall be provided in respect of the transfer of any property, rights or liabilities by or under section 3 or 22 of this Act; but—

(a) a transfer scheme may contain provision for consideration to be provided by the relevant new Agency in respect of the creation of interests, rights or liabilities by means of the transfer scheme; and

(b) any such provision shall be enforceable in the same way as if the interests, rights or liabilities had been created, and (if the case so requires) had been capable of being created, by agreement between the parties.

Continuity

10.—(1) This paragraph applies in relation to—

(a) any transfer of property, rights or liabilities by section 3 or 22 of this Act; or

(b) subject to any provision to the contrary in the transfer scheme in question, any transfer of property, rights or liabilities by a transfer scheme.

(2) Where this paragraph applies in relation to a transfer, then, so far as may be necessary for the purposes of, or in connection with, the transfer—

(a) any agreements made, transactions effected or other things done by or in relation to the transferor shall be treated as made, effected or done by or in relation to the relevant new Agency;

(b) references (whether express or implied and, if express, however worded) to the transferor in any agreement (whether in writing or not) or in any deed, bond, instrument or other document relating to the property, rights or liabilities transferred shall, as respects anything falling to be done on or after the transfer date, have effect as references to the relevant new Agency.

Remedies

11.—(1) Without prejudice to the generality of paragraph 10 above, a new Agency and any other person shall, as from the transfer date, have the same rights, powers and remedies (and, in particular, the same rights and powers as to the taking or resisting of legal proceedings or the making or resisting of applications to any authority) for ascertaining, perfecting or enforcing any right or liability transferred to that new Agency by or under this Act as that new Agency or that person would have had if that right or liability had at all times been a right or liability of that new Agency.

(2) Without prejudice to the generality of paragraph 10 above, any legal proceedings or applications to any authority pending immediately before the transfer date by or against a transferor, in so far as they relate to any property, right or liability transferred to the relevant new Agency by or under this Act or to any agreement relating to any such property, right or liability, shall be continued by or against the relevant new Agency to the exclusion of the transferor.

Perfection of vesting of foreign property, rights and liabilities

12.—(1) This paragraph applies in the case of any transfer by or under section 3 or 22 of this Act of any foreign property, rights or liabilities.

(2) It shall be the duty of the transferor and the relevant new Agency to take, as and when that new Agency considers it appropriate, all such steps as may be requisite to secure that the vesting in that new Agency by, or by transfer scheme under, section 3 or 22 of this Act of any foreign property, right or liability is effective under the relevant foreign law.

(3) Until the vesting in the relevant new Agency by, or by transfer scheme under, section 3 or 22 of this Act of any foreign property, right or liability is effective under the relevant foreign law, it shall be the duty of the transferor to hold that property or right for the benefit of, or to discharge that liability on behalf of, the relevant new Agency.

(4) Nothing in sub-paragraphs (2) and (3) above shall be taken as prejudicing the effect under the law of any part of the United Kingdom of the vesting in the relevant new Agency by, or by transfer scheme under, section 3 or 22 of this Act of any foreign property, right or liability.

(5) The transferor shall have all such powers as may be requisite for the performance of his duty under this paragraph, but it shall be the duty of the relevant new Agency to act on behalf of the transferor (so far as possible) in performing the duty imposed on the transferor by this paragraph.

(6) References in this paragraph to any foreign property, right or liability are references to any property, right or liability as respects which any issue arising in any proceedings would have been determined (in accordance with the rules of private international law) by reference to the law of a country or territory outside the United Kingdom.

(7) Duties imposed on the transferor or the relevant new Agency by this paragraph shall be enforceable in the same way as if the duties were imposed by a contract between the transferor and that new Agency.

(8) Any expenses reasonably incurred by the transferor under this paragraph shall be met by the relevant new Agency.

Section 12.

SCHEDULE 3

ENVIRONMENT PROTECTION ADVISORY COMMITTEES

Introductory

1.—(1) In this Schedule, "scheme" means a scheme prepared under this Schedule.

(2) Subject to sub-paragraph (1) above, expressions used in this Schedule and in section 12 of this Act have the same meaning in this Schedule as they have in that section.

Duty of Agency to prepare and submit schemes for each region

2.—(1) It shall be the duty of the Agency, in accordance with such guidance as may be given for the purpose by the Secretary of State,—

    (a) to prepare, in respect of each region, a scheme with respect to the appointment of persons as members of the advisory committee for that region; and

    (b) to submit that scheme to the Secretary of State for his approval before such date as may be specified in the guidance.

(2) Every scheme shall—

    (a) specify descriptions of bodies which, or persons who, appear to the Agency likely to have a significant interest in matters likely to be affected by the manner in which it carries out its functions in the region to which the scheme relates;

    (b) indicate how the membership of the advisory committee is to reflect the different descriptions of bodies or persons so specified;

    (c) specify or describe bodies which, and persons whom, the Agency proposes to consult in connection with appointments of persons as members of the advisory committee; and

    (d) make provision with respect to such other matters as the Agency considers relevant to the membership of the advisory committee.

Approval of schemes

3.—(1) A scheme shall not come into force unless it has been approved by the Secretary of State or until such date as he may specify for the purpose in giving his approval.

(2) Where the Agency submits a scheme to the Secretary of State for his approval, it shall also submit to him—

(a) a statement of the Agency's reasons for considering that the scheme is one which it is appropriate for him to approve; and

(b) such information in support of those reasons as it considers necessary.

(3) On submitting a scheme to the Secretary of State for his approval, the Agency shall publish the scheme, in such manner as it considers appropriate for bringing it to the attention of persons likely to be interested in it, together with a notice specifying the period within which representations or objections with respect to the scheme may be made to the Secretary of State.

(4) Where a scheme has been submitted to the Secretary of State for his approval, it shall be the duty of the Secretary of State, in determining whether to—

(a) approve the scheme,

(b) reject the scheme, or

(c) approve the scheme subject to modifications,

to consider any representations or objections made to him within the period specified pursuant to sub-paragraph (3) above and not withdrawn.

(5) Where the Secretary of State approves a scheme, with or without modifications, it shall be the duty of the Agency to take such steps as it considers appropriate for bringing the scheme as so approved to the attention of persons whom it considers likely to be interested in it.

Replacement and variation of approved membership schemes

4.—(1) The Agency may from time to time, and if required to do so by the Secretary of State shall,—

(a) prepare in accordance with paragraph 2 above a fresh scheme with respect to the appointment of persons as members of the advisory committee for any particular region; and

(b) submit that scheme to the Secretary of State for his approval;

and paragraph 3 above shall have effect accordingly in relation to any such scheme.

(2) An approved membership scheme may from time to time be varied by the Agency with the approval of the Secretary of State.

(3) The provisions of paragraph 3 above shall have effect in relation to any variation of an approved membership scheme as they have effect in relation to a scheme.

Appointment of members

5.—(1) Before appointing a person to be a member of an advisory committee, the Agency—

(a) shall consult such of the associates for that advisory committee as it considers appropriate in the particular case; and

(b) may, if it considers it appropriate to do so, also consult bodies or persons who are not associates for that advisory committee.

(2) In this paragraph, "associates", in the case of any advisory committee, means those bodies and persons specified or described in the approved membership scheme for that advisory committee pursuant to paragraph 2(2)(c) above.

Vacancies, defective appointments etc.

6. The validity of any proceedings of an advisory committee shall not be affected by—

(a) any vacancy amongst the members;

(b) any defect in the appointment of a member; or

(c) any temporary breach of the terms of the approved membership scheme for the advisory committee.

Remuneration and allowances

7.—(1) The Agency shall pay to the chairman of an advisory committee such remuneration, and such travelling and other allowances, as the Secretary of State may determine.

(2) The Agency shall pay to the members of an advisory committee other than the chairman such sums by way of reimbursement (whether in whole or in part) for loss of remuneration, for travelling expenses and for other out-of-pocket expenses as the Secretary of State may determine.

Section 14.

SCHEDULE 4

Boundaries of Regional Flood Defence Areas

Power to make order

1.—(1) The relevant Minister may by order made by statutory instrument—

(a) alter the boundaries of the area of any regional flood defence committee; or

(b) provide for the amalgamation of any two or more such areas.

(2) Where an order under this Schedule makes provision by reference to anything shown on a main river map, that map shall be conclusive evidence for the purposes of the order of what is shown on the map.

(3) The power to make an order under this Schedule shall include power to make such supplemental, consequential and transitional provision as the relevant Minister considers appropriate.

(4) In the case of an order under this Schedule amalgamating the areas of any two or more regional flood defence committees, the provision made by virtue of sub-paragraph (3) above may include provision determining—

(a) the total number of members of the amalgamated committee; and

(b) the total number of such members to be appointed by the constituent councils of that committee;

and subsections (7) and (8) of section 16 of this Act shall apply in relation to so much of an order under this Schedule as is made by virtue of this sub-paragraph as they apply in relation to an order under subsection (5) of that section.

(5) In this paragraph and the following paragraphs of this Schedule "the relevant Minister" —

(a) in relation to any alteration of the boundaries of an area where the whole or any part of that area is in Wales, means the Ministers;

(b) in relation to the amalgamation of any two or more areas where the whole or any part of any one of those areas is in Wales, means the Ministers; and

(c) in any other case, means the Minister.

(6) In this paragraph—

"main river" means a main river within the meaning of Part IV of the 1991 Act; and

"main river map" has, subject to section 194 of the 1991 Act, the meaning given by section 193(2) of that Act.

Consultation and notice of intention to make order

2.—(1) Before making an order under this Schedule, the relevant Minister shall—

(a) consult such persons or representative bodies as he considers it appropriate to consult at that stage;

(b) prepare a draft order;

(c) publish a notice complying with sub-paragraph (2) below in the London Gazette and in such other manner as he considers appropriate for bringing the draft order to the attention of persons likely to be affected by it if it is made.

(2) A notice for the purposes of sub-paragraph (1)(c) above with respect to a draft order shall—

(a) state the relevant Minister's intention to make the order and its general effect;

(b) specify the places where copies of the draft order and of any map to which it refers may be inspected by any person free of charge at all reasonable times during the period of twenty-eight days beginning with the date on which the notice is first published otherwise than in the London Gazette; and

(c) state that any person may within that period by notice in writing to the relevant Minister object to the making of the order.

(3) The relevant Minister shall also cause copies of the notice and of the draft order to be served on every person carrying out functions under any enactment who appears to him to be concerned.

Objections to draft order and making of order

3.—(1) Before making an order under this Schedule, the relevant Minister—

(a) shall consider any representations or objections which are duly made with respect to the draft order and are not withdrawn; and

(b) may, if he thinks fit, cause a local inquiry to be held with respect to any such representations or objections.

(2) Where notice of a draft order has been published and given in accordance with paragraph 2 above and any representations or objections considered under sub-paragraph (1) above, the relevant Minister may make the order either in the terms of the draft or in those terms as modified in such manner as he thinks fit, or may decide not to make the order.

(3) The relevant Minister shall not make a modification of a draft order in so far as the modification is such as to include in the area of any regional flood defence committee any tidal waters which, if the order had been made in the form of the draft, would have been outside the area of every regional flood defence committee.

Procedure for making of order

4.—(1) Where the relevant Minister makes an order under this Schedule, he shall serve notice of the making of the order on every person (if any) who—

    (a) is a person on whom notice is required to have been served under paragraph 2(3) above; and

    (b) has duly made an objection to the making of the order that has not been withdrawn.

(2) Where a notice is required to be served under sub-paragraph (1) above with respect to any order, the order shall not have effect before the end of a period of twenty-eight days from the date of service of the last notice served under that sub-paragraph.

(3) If before an order takes effect under sub-paragraph (2) above—

    (a) any person who has been served with a notice under sub-paragraph (1) above with respect to that order serves notice objecting to the order on the Minister (or, in the case of an order made jointly by the Ministers, on either of them), and

    (b) the objection is not withdrawn,

the order shall be subject to special parliamentary procedure.

(4) A statutory instrument containing an order under this Schedule which is not subject to special parliamentary procedure under sub-paragraph (3) above shall be subject to annulment in pursuance of a resolution of either House of Parliament.

Notice after making of order

5.—(1) Subject to sub-paragraph (2) below, after making an order under this Schedule, the relevant Minister shall publish in the London Gazette, and in such other manner as he considers appropriate for bringing the order to the attention of persons likely to be affected by it, a notice—

    (a) stating that the order has been made; and

    (b) naming the places where a copy of the order may be inspected at all reasonable times.

(2) In the case of an order to which sub-paragraph (2) of paragraph 4 above applies, the notice—

    (a) shall not be published until the end of the period of twenty-eight days referred to in that sub-paragraph; and

    (b) shall state whether or not the order is to be subject to special parliamentary procedure.

Questioning of order in courts

6.—(1) Subject to sub-paragraph (3) below, if any person desires to question the validity of an order under this Schedule on the ground—

    (a) that it is not within the powers of this Schedule, or

    (b) that any requirement of this Schedule has not been complied with,

he may, within six weeks after the date of the first publication of the notice required by paragraph 5 above, make an application for the purpose to the High Court.

(2) On an application under this paragraph the High Court, if satisfied—

    (a) that the order is not within the powers of this Schedule, or

    (b) that the interests of the applicant have been substantially prejudiced by a failure to comply with any of the requirements of this Schedule,

may quash the order either generally or in so far as it affects the applicant.

(3) Sub-paragraph (1) above—

    (a) shall not apply to any order which is confirmed by Act of Parliament under section 6 of the Statutory Orders (Special Procedure) Act 1945; and

1945 c. 18.

    (b) shall have effect in relation to any other order which is subject to special parliamentary procedure by virtue of the provisions of this Schedule as if the reference to the date of the first publication of the notice required by paragraph 5 above were a reference to the date on which the order becomes operative under that Act of 1945.

(4) Except as provided by this paragraph the validity of an order under this Schedule shall not, either before or after the order has been made, be questioned in any legal proceedings whatsoever.

SCHEDULE 5

Section 19.

MEMBERSHIP AND PROCEEDINGS OF REGIONAL AND LOCAL FLOOD DEFENCE COMMITTEES

PART I

MEMBERSHIP OF FLOOD DEFENCE COMMITTEES

Terms of membership

1.—(1) Members of a flood defence committee (that is to say a regional flood defence committee or a local flood defence committee), other than those appointed by or on behalf of one or more constituent councils, shall hold and vacate office in accordance with the terms of their appointment.

(2) The first members of a local flood defence committee appointed by or on behalf of any one or more constituent councils—

    (a) shall come into office on the day on which the committee comes into existence or, in the case of a member who is for any reason appointed after that day, on the day on which the appointment is made; and

    (b) subject to the following provisions of this Schedule, shall hold office until the end of May in such year as may be specified for the purposes of this paragraph in the scheme establishing the committee.

(3) Any members of a flood defence committee appointed by or on behalf of any one or more constituent councils who are not members to whom sub-paragraph (2) above applies—

    (a) shall come into office at the beginning of the June next following the day on which they are appointed; and

    (b) subject to the following provisions of this Schedule, shall hold office for a term of four years.

(4) If for any reason any such member as is mentioned in sub-paragraph (3) above is appointed on or after the day on which he ought to have come into office, he shall—

    (a) come into office on the day on which he is appointed; and

    (b) subject to the following provisions of this Schedule, hold office for the remainder of the term.

(5) References in this paragraph and the following provisions of this Schedule to a member of a flood defence committee include references to the chairman of such a committee.

Membership of constituent council as qualification for membership of committee

2.—(1) Members of a flood defence committee appointed by or on behalf of any one or more constituent councils may be members of that council, or one of those councils, or other persons.

(2) Any member of a flood defence committee appointed by or on behalf of a constituent council who at the time of his appointment was a member of that council shall, if he ceases to be a member of that council, also cease to be a member of the committee with whichever is the earlier of the following—

    (a) the end of the period of three months beginning with the date when he ceases to be a member of the council; and

    (b) the appointment of another person in his place.

(3) For the purposes of sub-paragraph (2) above a member of a council shall not be deemed to have ceased to be a member of the council by reason of retirement if he has been re-elected a member of the council not later than the date of his retirement.

Disqualification for membership of committee

3.—(1) Subject to the following provisions of this paragraph, a person shall be disqualified for appointment as a member of a flood defence committee if he—

    (a) is a paid officer of the Agency; or

    (b) is a person who has been adjudged bankrupt, or whose estate has been sequestrated or who has made a composition or arrangement with, or granted a trust deed for, his creditors; or

    (c) within the period of five years before the day of his appointment, has been convicted, in the United Kingdom, the Channel Islands or the Isle of Man, of any offence and has had passed on him a sentence of imprisonment (whether suspended or not) for a period of not less than three months without the option of a fine; or

1982 c. 32.
1983 c. 2.

    (d) is disqualified for being elected or for being a member of a local authority under Part III of the Local Government Finance Act 1982 (accounts and audit) or Part III of the Representation of the People Act 1983 (legal proceedings).

(2) Where a person is disqualified under sub-paragraph (1) above by reason of having been adjudged bankrupt, the disqualification shall cease—

    (a) unless the bankruptcy order made against that person is previously annulled, on his discharge from bankruptcy; and

    (b) if the bankruptcy order is so annulled, on the date of the annulment.

(3) Where a person is disqualified under sub-paragraph (1) above by reason of having had his estate sequestrated, the disqualification shall cease—

1985 c. 66.

    (a) unless the sequestration is recalled or reduced, on the person's discharge under section 54 of the Bankruptcy (Scotland) Act 1985; and

    (b) if the sequestration is recalled or reduced, on the date of the recall or reduction.

(4) Where a person is disqualified under sub-paragraph (1) above by reason of his having made a composition or arrangement with, or having granted a trust deed for, his creditors, the disqualification shall cease—

    (a) if he pays his debts in full, on the date on which the payment is completed; and

    (b) in any other case, at the end of five years from the date on which the terms of the deed of composition or arrangement, or of the trust deed, are fulfilled.

(5) For the purposes of sub-paragraph (1)(c) above the date of the conviction shall be taken to be—

> (a) the ordinary date on which the period allowed for making an appeal or application with respect to the conviction expires; or

> (b) if such an appeal or application is made, the date on which it is finally disposed of or abandoned or fails by reason of non-prosecution.

(6) Section 92 of the Local Government Act 1972 (proceedings for disqualification) shall apply in relation to disqualification under this paragraph for appointment as a member of a flood defence committee as it applies in relation to disqualification for acting as a member of a local authority.

1972 c. 70.

Vacation of office by disqualifying event

4.—(1) The office of a member of a flood defence committee shall become vacant upon the fulfilment of any of the following conditions, that is to say—

> (a) the person holding that office is adjudged bankrupt, is a person whose estate is sequestrated or makes a composition or arrangement with, or grants a trust deed for, his creditors;

> (b) that person is convicted, in the United Kingdom, the Channel Islands or the Isle of Man, of any offence and has passed on him a sentence of imprisonment (whether suspended or not) for a period of not less than three months without the option of a fine;

> (c) that person is disqualified for being elected or for being a member of a local authority under Part III of the Local Government Finance Act 1982 (accounts and audit) or Part III of the Representation of the People Act 1983 (legal proceedings); or

1982 c. 32.
1983 c. 2.

> (d) that person has, for a period of six consecutive months been absent from meetings of the committee, otherwise than by reason of illness or some other cause approved during the period by the committee.

(2) For the purposes of sub-paragraph (1)(d) above, the attendance of a member of a flood defence committee—

> (a) at a meeting of any sub-committee of the committee of which he is a member, or

> (b) at any joint committee to which he has been appointed by that committee,

shall be treated as attendance at a meeting of the committee.

Resignation of office by members of regional committee

5.—(1) The chairman of a regional flood defence committee may resign his office at any time by giving notice to the chairman of the Agency and to one of the Ministers.

(2) Any other member of such a committee may resign his office at any time by giving notice to the chairman of the committee and also, if he was appointed by one of the Ministers, to that Minister.

Resignation of office by members of local committee

6.—(1) The chairman of a local flood defence committee may resign his office at any time by giving notice to the chairman of the regional flood defence committee.

(2) Any other member of a local flood defence committee may resign his office at any time by giving notice to the chairman of that local flood defence committee.

Appointments to fill casual vacancies

7.—(1) Where, for any reason whatsoever, the office of a member of a flood defence committee becomes vacant before the end of his term of office, the vacancy—

> (a) shall, if the unexpired portion of the term of office of the vacating member is six months or more, be filled by the appointment of a new member; and

> (b) may be so filled in any other case.

(2) A person appointed by virtue of sub-paragraph (1) above to fill a casual vacancy shall hold office for so long only as the former member would have held office.

Eligibility of previous members for re-appointment

8. Subject to the provisions of this Schedule, a member of a flood defence committee shall be eligible for reappointment.

Appointment of deputies

9.—(1) Subject to the following provisions of this paragraph, a person nominated by one or more constituent councils may act as deputy for a member of a flood defence committee appointed by or on behalf of that council or those councils and may, accordingly, attend and vote at a meeting of the committee, instead of that member.

(2) A person nominated under sub-paragraph (1) above as deputy for a member of a flood defence committee may, by virtue of that nomination, attend and vote at a meeting of a sub-committee of that committee which—

> (a) has been appointed by that committee under Part II of this Schedule; and

> (b) is a committee to which the member for whom he is a deputy belongs.

(3) A person acting as deputy for a member of a flood defence committee shall be treated for the purposes for which he is nominated as a member of that committee.

(4) A person shall not act as deputy for a member of a flood defence committee unless his nomination has been notified to such officer of the Agency as is appointed to receive such nominations.

(5) A nomination under this paragraph shall be in writing and may apply either to a particular meeting or to all meetings during a stated period or until the nomination is revoked.

(6) A person shall not act as deputy for more than one member of a flood defence committee.

(7) Nothing in this paragraph shall entitle a person to attend and vote at a meeting of a local flood defence committee by reason of his nomination as deputy for a member of a regional flood defence committee.

Payments to past and present chairmen and to members

10.—(1) The Agency shall pay to any person who is a chairman of a flood defence committee such remuneration and allowances as may be determined by the relevant Minister.

(2) If the relevant Minister so determines in the case of any person who is or has been chairman of a flood defence committee, the Agency shall pay or make arrangements for the payment of a pension in relation to that person in accordance with the determination.

(3) If a person ceases to be chairman of a flood defence committee and it appears to the relevant Minister that there are special circumstances which make it right that that person should receive compensation in respect of his ceasing to be chairman, the relevant Minister may require the Agency to pay to that person a sum of such amount as that Minister may determine.

(4) The Agency may pay to any person who is a member of a flood defence committee such allowances as may be determined by the relevant Minister.

(5) In this paragraph—

"pension", in relation to any person, means a pension (whether contributory or not) of any kind payable to or in respect of him, and includes an allowance, gratuity or lump sum so payable and a return of contributions with or without interest or any other addition; and

"the relevant Minister"—

(a) in relation to the regional flood defence committee for an area the whole or the greater part of which is in Wales and in relation to any local flood defence committee for any district comprised in the area of such a regional flood defence committee, means the Secretary of State; and

(b) in relation to any other flood defence committee, means the Minister.

PART II

PROCEEDINGS OF FLOOD DEFENCE COMMITTEES

Appointment of sub-committees, joint sub-committees etc.

11.—(1) For the purpose of carrying out any functions in pursuance of arrangements under paragraph 12 below—

(a) a flood defence committee may appoint a sub-committee of the committee;

(b) two or more regional or two or more local flood defence committees may appoint a joint sub-committee of those committees;

(c) any sub-committee may appoint one or more committees of that sub-committee ("under sub-committees").

(2) The number of members of any sub-committee and their terms of office shall be fixed by the appointing committee or committees or, in the case of an under sub-committee, by the appointing sub-committee.

(3) A sub-committee appointed under this paragraph may include persons who are not members of the appointing committee or committees or, in the case of an under sub-committee, the committee or committees of whom they are an under sub-committee; but at least two thirds of the members appointed to any such sub-committee shall be members of that committee or those committees, as the case may be.

(4) A person who is disqualified for being a member of a flood defence committee shall be disqualified also for being a member of a sub-committee or under sub-committee appointed under this paragraph.

Delegation of functions to sub-committees etc.

12.—(1) Subject to section 106 of the 1991 Act and to any other express provision contained in any enactment, a flood defence committee may arrange for the carrying out of any of their functions—

(a) by a sub-committee, or an under sub-committee of the committee or an officer of the Agency; or

(b) by any other regional or, as the case may be, local flood defence committee;

and two or more regional or two or more local flood defence committees may arrange to carry out any of their functions jointly or may arrange for the carrying out of any of their functions by a joint sub-committee of theirs.

(2) Where by virtue of this paragraph any functions of a flood defence committee or of two or more such committees may be carried out by a sub-committee, then, unless the committee or committees otherwise direct, the sub-committee may arrange for the carrying out of any of those functions by an under sub-committee or by an officer of the Agency.

(3) Where by virtue of this paragraph any functions of a flood defence committee or of two or more such committees may be carried out by an under sub-committee, then, unless the committee or committees or the sub-committee otherwise direct, the under sub-committee may arrange for the carrying out of any of those functions by an officer of the Agency.

(4) Any arrangements made by a flood defence committee under this paragraph for the carrying out of any function shall not prevent the committee from discharging their functions themselves.

(5) References in the preceding provisions of this paragraph to the carrying out of any functions of a flood defence committee include references to the doing of anything which is calculated to facilitate, or is conducive or incidental to, the carrying out of any of those functions.

(6) A regional flood defence committee shall not, under this paragraph, make arrangements for the carrying out in a local flood defence district of any functions which fall to be carried out there by the local flood defence committee.

Rules of procedure

13.—(1) A flood defence committee may, with the approval of the relevant Minister, make rules for regulating the proceedings of the committee.

(2) Nothing in section 6(4) of this Act or section 105 or 106 of the 1991 Act shall entitle the Agency to make any arrangements or give any directions for regulating the proceedings of any flood defence committee.

(3) In this paragraph "the relevant Minister" has the same meaning as in paragraph 10 above.

Declarations of interest etc.

14.—(1) Subject to the following provisions of this paragraph, the provisions of sections 94 to 98 of the Local Government Act 1972 (pecuniary interests of members of local authorities) shall apply in relation to members of a flood defence committee as those provisions apply in relation to members of local authorities.

1972 c. 70.

(2) In their application by virtue of this paragraph those provisions shall have effect in accordance with the following provisions—

(a) for references to meetings of the local authority there shall be substituted references to meetings of the committee;

(b) in section 94(4), for the reference to provision being made by standing orders of a local authority there shall be substituted a reference to provisions being made by directions of the committee;

(c) in section 96, for references to the proper officer of the local authority there shall be substituted a reference to an officer of the Agency appointed for the purposes of this paragraph; and

(d) section 97 shall apply as it applies to a local authority other than a parish or community council.

(3) Subject to sub-paragraph (4) below, a member of a flood defence committee shall be disqualified, for so long as he remains such a member and for twelve months after he ceases to be such a member, for appointment to any paid office by the Agency or any regional flood defence committee.

(4) Sub-paragraph (3) above shall not disqualify any person for appointment to the office of chairman of a local flood defence committee.

Authentication of documents

15.—(1) Any notice or other document which a flood defence committee are required or authorised to give, make or issue by or under any enactment may be signed on behalf of the committee by any member of the committee or any officer of the Agency who is generally or specifically authorised for that purpose by a resolution of the committee.

(2) Any document purporting to bear the signature of a person expressed to be authorised as mentioned in sub-paragraph (1) above shall be deemed, unless the contrary is shown, to be duly given, made or issued by authority of the committee.

(3) In this paragraph "signature" includes a facsimile of a signature by whatever process reproduced.

Proof and validity of proceedings

16.—(1) A minute of the proceedings of a meeting of a flood defence committee, purporting to be signed at that or the next ensuing meeting by—

(a) the chairman of the meeting to the proceedings of which the minute relates, or

(b) by the chairman of the next ensuing meeting,

shall be evidence of the proceedings and shall be received in evidence without further proof.

(2) Where a minute has been signed as mentioned in sub-paragraph (1) above in respect of a meeting of a committee or sub-committee, then, unless the contrary is shown—

(a) the meeting shall be deemed to have been duly convened and held;

(b) all the proceedings had at any such meeting shall be deemed to have been duly had; and

(c) that committee or sub-committee shall be deemed to have been duly constituted and have had power to deal with the matters referred to in the minute.

(3) The validity of any proceedings of a flood defence committee shall not be affected by any vacancy among the members of the committee or by any defect in the appointment of such a member.

SCHEDULE 6   Section 20.

THE SCOTTISH ENVIRONMENT PROTECTION AGENCY

Status

1. SEPA shall be a body corporate with a common seal.

2. Subject to section 38 of this Act, SEPA shall not—

(a) be regarded as a servant or agent of the Crown;

(b) have any status, immunity or privilege of the Crown;

(c) by virtue of its connection with the Crown, be exempt from any tax, duty, rate, levy or other charge whatsoever whether general or local,

and its property shall not be regarded as property of, or held on behalf of, the Crown.

Membership

3. SEPA shall consist of not less than eight, nor more than twelve, members appointed by the Secretary of State.

4. In making appointments under paragraph 3 above, the Secretary of State shall have regard to the desirability of appointing persons who have knowledge or experience in some matter relevant to the functions of SEPA.

5. Subject to paragraphs 7 and 8 below, each member—

(a) shall hold and vacate office in accordance with the terms of his appointment;

(b) may, by giving notice to the Secretary of State, resign his office; and

(c) after ceasing to hold office shall be eligible for reappointment as a member.

6. The Secretary of State may, by order made by statutory instrument subject to annulment in pursuance of a resolution of either House of Parliament, amend paragraph 3 above so as to substitute for the numbers for the time being specified as, respectively, the minimum and maximum membership such other numbers as he thinks fit.

7. The Secretary of State may remove a member from office if he is satisfied that the member—

(a) has been absent from meetings of SEPA for a period longer than three months without the permission of SEPA; or

(b) has been adjudged bankrupt, has made an arrangement with his creditors, has had his estate sequestrated or has granted a trust deed for his creditors or a composition contract; or

(c) is unable or unfit to carry out the functions of a member.

Chairman and deputy chairman

8.—(1) The Secretary of State shall appoint one of the members of SEPA to be chairman and another of those members to be deputy chairman.

(2) The chairman and deputy chairman shall hold and vacate office in terms of their appointments.

(3) A member who is chairman or deputy chairman may resign his office by giving notice to the Secretary of State; but if the chairman or deputy chairman ceases to be a member (whether or not on giving notice under paragraph 5(b) above) he shall cease to be chairman or, as the case may be, deputy chairman.

(4) A person who ceases to be chairman or deputy chairman shall be eligible for reappointment as such under sub-paragraph (1) above at any time when he is a member.

Remuneration, pensions, etc.

9.—(1) SEPA shall—

    (a) pay to its members such remuneration and such travelling and other allowances (if any); and

    (b) as regards any member or former member in whose case the Secretary of State may so determine—

        (i) pay such pension, allowance or gratuity to or in respect of him;

        (ii) make such payments towards the provision of such pension, allowance or gratuity; or

        (iii) provide and maintain such schemes (whether contributory or not) for the payment of pensions, allowances or gratuities,

as the Secretary of State may determine.

(2) If a person ceases to be a member, and it appears to the Secretary of State that there are special circumstances which make it right that he should receive compensation, the Secretary of State may require SEPA to pay to that person a sum of such amount as the Secretary of State may determine.

Staff

10.—(1) There shall be a chief officer of SEPA.

(2) The Secretary of State shall, after consultation with the chairman or person designated to be chairman (if there is a person holding or designated to hold that office), make the first appointment of chief officer on such terms and conditions as he may determine; and thereafter SEPA may, with the approval of the Secretary of State, make subsequent appointments to that office on such terms and conditions as it may with such approval determine.

11. SEPA may appoint such other employees as it thinks fit.

12.—(1) SEPA shall, in the case of such of its employees or former employees as it may, with the approval of the Secretary of State, determine—

    (a) pay such pensions, allowances or gratuities to or in respect of those employees;

    (b) make such payments towards provision of such pensions, allowances or gratuities; or

    (c) provide and maintain such schemes (whether contributory or not) for the payment of such pensions, allowances or gratuities,

as it may, with the approval of the Secretary of State, determine.

(2) References in sub-paragraph (1) above to pensions, allowances or gratuities in respect of employees of SEPA include references to pensions, allowances or gratuities by way of compensation to or in respect of any such employee who suffers loss of office or employment.

Proceedings

13.—(1) SEPA may regulate its own procedure and that of any committee established by it (including making provision in relation to the quorum for its meetings and the meetings of any such committee).

(2) The proceedings of SEPA and of any committee established by it shall not be invalidated by any vacancy amongst its members or the members of such committee or by any defect in the appointment of such member.

Committees

14.—(1) SEPA may appoint persons who are not members of it to be members of any committee established by it, but at least one member of any such committee shall be a member of SEPA.

(2) SEPA shall pay to a person so appointed such remuneration and allowances (if any) as the Secretary of State may determine.

(3) Any committee established by SEPA shall comply with any directions given to them by it.

Delegation of powers

15.—(1) Anything authorised or required by or under any enactment to be done by SEPA may be done by any of its committees which, or by any of its members or employees who, is authorised (generally or specifically) for the purpose by SEPA.

(2) Nothing in sub-paragraph (1) above shall prevent SEPA from doing anything that a committee, member or employee has been authorised or required to do.

Regional Boards

16.—(1) Without prejudice to the generality of its power to establish committees, SEPA shall establish committees (to be known as "Regional Boards") for the purposes of discharging in relation to such areas as it may, with the approval of the Secretary of State, determine, such of its functions as it may, with such approval, determine.

(2) A Regional Board shall have a chairman who shall be a member of SEPA and appointed to that office by SEPA.

(3) It shall be the duty of SEPA to comply with such guidance as the Secretary of State may from time to time give as to—

  (a) the number of persons to be appointed to a Regional Board;

  (b) the qualifications and experience which persons (other than members of SEPA) should have to be eligible for appointment to a Regional Board;

  (c) the descriptions of bodies which, or persons who, have a significant interest in matters likely to be affected by the discharge by a Regional Board of its functions; and

  (d) how the membership of a Regional Board is to reflect the different descriptions of bodies or persons referred to in paragraph (c) above.

(4) Anything authorised or required to be done by a Regional Board by virtue of sub-paragraph (1) above may be done by any member of the Board, or by any employee of SEPA, who is authorised (generally or specifically) for the purpose by the Board.

(5) Nothing in sub-paragraph (4) above shall prevent a Regional Board doing anything that a member or employee has been authorised or required to do.

Members' interests

17.—(1) A member who is in any way directly or indirectly interested in any matter that is brought up for consideration at a meeting of SEPA shall disclose the nature of his interest to the meeting; and, where such a disclosure is made—

  (a) the disclosure shall be recorded in the minutes of the meeting; and

  (b) the member shall not take any part in any deliberation or decision of SEPA or of any of its committees with respect to that matter.

(2) For the purposes of sub-paragraph (1) above, a general notification given at a meeting of SEPA by a member to the effect that he—

(a) is a member of a specified company or firm, and

(b) is to be regarded as interested in any matter involving that company or firm,

shall be regarded as a sufficient disclosure of his interest in relation to any such matter.

(3) A member need not attend in person at a meeting of SEPA in order to make a disclosure which he is required to make under this paragraph if he takes reasonable steps to secure that the disclosure is made by a notice which is read and considered at the meeting.

(4) The Secretary of State may, subject to such conditions as he considers appropriate, remove any disability imposed by virtue of this paragraph in any case where the number of members of SEPA disabled by virtue of this paragraph at any one time would be so great a proportion of the whole as to impede the transaction of business.

(5) The power of the Secretary of State under sub-paragraph (4) above includes power to remove, either indefinitely or for any period, a disability which would otherwise attach to any member, or members of any description, by reason of such interests, and in respect of such matters, as may be specified or described by the Secretary of State.

(6) Nothing in this paragraph precludes any member from taking part in the consideration or discussion of, or voting on, any question whether an application should be made to the Secretary of State for the exercise of the power conferred by sub-paragraph (4) above.

(7) In this paragraph—

(a) any reference to a meeting of SEPA includes a reference to a meeting of any of SEPA's committees; and

(b) any reference to a member includes a reference to a person who is not a member of SEPA but who is a member of any such committee.

Minutes

18.—(1) Minutes shall be kept of proceedings of SEPA and of its committees.

(2) Minutes of any such proceedings shall be evidence of those proceedings if they are signed by a person purporting to have acted as chairman of the proceedings to which the minutes relate or of any subsequent proceedings in the course of which the minutes were approved as a correct record.

(3) Where minutes of any such proceedings have been signed as mentioned in sub-paragraph (2) above, those proceedings shall, unless the contrary is shown, be deemed to have been validly convened and constituted.

SCHEDULE 7

Section 63.

Nᴀᴛɪᴏɴᴀʟ Pᴀʀᴋ ᴀᴜᴛʜᴏʀɪᴛɪᴇs

Status and constitution of authorities

1.—(1) A National Park authority shall be a body corporate.

(2) A National Park authority shall consist of—

(a) such number of local authority members as may be specified in the relevant order; and

(b) such number of members to be appointed by the Secretary of State as may be so specified.

(3) In the case of a National Park authority for a National Park in England, such number as may be specified in the relevant order of the number of members of the authority to be appointed by the Secretary of State shall be parish members.

(4) The number specified in the relevant order for any National Park authority as the number of members of that authority who are to be appointed by the Secretary of State shall—

    (a) as respects any National Park authority for a National Park in England, be two less than the number of local authority members specified in the order; and

    (b) as respects any National Park authority for a National Park in Wales, be equal to half the number of local authority members specified in the order.

(5) As respects any National Park authority for a National Park in England, the number specified in the relevant order as the number of parish members to be appointed by the Secretary of State shall be one less than one half of the total number of the members of the authority to be appointed by the Secretary of State.

(6) Accordingly—

    (a) in the case of a National Park authority for a National Park in England, the effect of the relevant order shall be such that the total number of members of the authority will be an even number which is not a whole number multiple of four; and

    (b) in the case of a National Park authority for a National Park in Wales, the number of local authority members specified in the relevant order shall be an even number.

Local authority members

2.—(1) The local authority members of a National Park authority shall be appointed by such of the councils for the principal areas wholly or partly comprised in the relevant Park as may be specified in or determined under the relevant order.

(2) Each of the councils who are to appoint the local authority members of a National Park authority shall be entitled to appoint such number of those members as may be so specified or determined and to make any appointment required by reason of a vacancy arising in respect of a member appointed by that council.

(3) Before making any provision by the relevant order as to—

    (a) the number of members of a National Park authority who are to be local authority members,

    (b) the councils by whom the local authority members of a National Park authority are to be appointed, or

    (c) the number of members to be appointed by each such council,

the Secretary of State shall consult the council for every principal area the whole or any part of which is comprised in the relevant Park; and the Secretary of State may make provision for excluding the council for any such area from the councils by whom the local authority members of a National Park authority are to be appointed only at the request of that council.

(4) A person shall not be appointed as a local authority member of a National Park authority unless he is a member of a principal council the area of which is wholly or partly comprised in the relevant Park; and, in appointing local authority members of a National Park authority, a principal council shall have

regard to the desirability of appointing members of the council who represent wards, or (in Wales) electoral divisions, situated wholly or partly within the relevant Park.

(5) Subject to the following provisions of this Schedule, where a person who qualifies for his appointment by virtue of his membership of any council is appointed as a local authority member of a National Park authority—

    (a) he shall hold office from the time of his appointment until he ceases to be a member of that council; but

    (b) his appointment may, before any such cessation, be terminated for the purposes of, and in accordance with, sections 15 to 17 of the Local Government and Housing Act 1989 (political balance). 1989 c. 42.

(6) Sub-paragraph (5)(a) above shall have effect so as to terminate the term of office of a person who, on retiring from any council, immediately becomes such a member again as a newly elected councillor; but a person who so becomes a member again shall be eligible for re-appointment to the National Park authority.

(7) The appointment of any person as a local authority member of a National Park authority may provide that he is not to be treated for the purposes of sub-paragraph (5) above as qualifying for his appointment by virtue of his membership of any council other than that specified in the appointment.

(8) In paragraph 2(1) of Schedule 1 to the Local Government and Housing Act 1989 (bodies to which appointments have to be made taking account of political balance), after paragraph (b) there shall be inserted the following paragraph—

    "(ba) a National Park authority;".

Parish members of English National Park authorities

3.—(1) The parish members of an English National Park authority shall be appointed by the Secretary of State.

(2) A person shall not be appointed as a parish member of an English National Park authority unless he is—

    (a) a member of the parish council for a parish the whole or any part of which is comprised in the relevant Park; or

    (b) the chairman of the parish meeting of a parish—

        (i) which does not have a separate parish council; and

        (ii) the whole or any part of which is comprised in the relevant Park.

(3) Subject to the following provisions of this Schedule, where a person who qualifies for his appointment by virtue of his membership of a parish council is appointed as a parish member of an English National Park authority, he shall hold office from the time of his appointment until he ceases to be a member of that parish council.

(4) Sub-paragraph (3) above shall have effect so as to terminate the term of office of a person who on retiring from any parish council immediately becomes such a member again as a newly elected councillor; but a person who so becomes a member again shall be eligible for re-appointment to the National Park authority.

(5) Subject to the following provisions of this Schedule, where a person who qualifies for his appointment by virtue of his being the chairman of a parish meeting is appointed as a parish member of an English National Park authority, he shall hold office from the time of his appointment until he ceases to be the chairman of that parish meeting.

(6) Sub-paragraph (5) above shall have effect so as to terminate the term of office of a person who is elected to succeed himself as chairman of any parish meeting; but a person who so becomes the chairman again shall be eligible for re-appointment to the National Park authority.

(7) Subject to the provisions of this Schedule, a parish member of an English National Park authority shall hold office in accordance with the terms of his appointment.

(8) In this paragraph, "English National Park authority" means a National Park authority for a National Park in England.

Members (other than parish members) appointed by the Secretary of State

4.—(1) Before appointing any person as a member of a National Park authority the Secretary of State shall consult, according to whether the relevant Park is in England or in Wales, either the Countryside Commission or the Countryside Council for Wales.

(2) Subject to the following provisions of this Schedule, a person appointed as a member of a National Park authority by the Secretary of State—

  (a) shall hold office for such period of not less than one year nor more than three years as may be specified in the terms of his appointment; but

  (b) on ceasing to hold office shall be eligible for re-appointment.

(3) The term of office of a person appointed by the Secretary of State to fill such a vacancy in the membership of a National Park authority as occurs where a person appointed by the Secretary of State ceases to be a member of the authority before the end of his term of office may be for a period of less than one year if it is made to expire with the time when the term of office of the person in respect of whom the vacancy has arisen would have expired.

(4) Subject to the provisions of this Schedule, a member of a National Park authority appointed by the Secretary of State shall hold office in accordance with the terms of his appointment.

(5) This paragraph shall not apply to persons appointed as parish members of a National Park authority for a National Park in England or to their appointment as such members.

Chairman and deputy chairman

5.—(1) The members of a National Park authority shall elect, from amongst their members, both a chairman and a deputy chairman of the authority.

(2) Subject to sub-paragraphs (3) and (4) below, the chairman and deputy chairman of a National Park authority shall be elected for a period not exceeding one year; but a person so elected shall, on ceasing to hold office at the end of his term of office as chairman or deputy chairman, be eligible for re-election.

(3) A person shall cease to hold office as chairman or deputy chairman of a National Park authority if he ceases to be a member of the authority.

(4) Where a vacancy occurs in the office of chairman or deputy chairman of a National Park authority, it shall be the duty of the members of that authority to secure that that vacancy is filled as soon as possible.

Removal of members

6.—(1) The Secretary of State may, by giving a local authority member of a National Park authority such written notice of the termination of his appointment as the Secretary of State considers appropriate, remove that member from office; but he shall do so only where he considers it appropriate to remove that member from office in consequence of the provisions of any order for varying either the area of the relevant Park or the number of local authority members of that authority .

(2) The Secretary of State may remove from office any member of a National Park authority appointed by him, other than any parish member of a National Park authority for a National Park in England, either—

    (a) by giving that member three months' written notice of the termination of the appointment; or

    (b) in such other manner as may be provided for in the terms of that member's appointment.

(3) The Secretary of State may remove from office any parish member of a National Park authority for a National Park in England either—

    (a) by giving that member such written notice of the termination of his appointment as the Secretary of State considers appropriate; or

    (b) in such other manner as may be provided for in the terms of that member's appointment;

but a parish member shall only be removed from office in the manner mentioned in paragraph (a) above where the Secretary of State considers it appropriate to do so in consequence of the provisions of any order for varying either the area of the relevant Park or the number of parish members of the National Park authority in question.

Disqualification of members

7.—(1) A person is disqualified for becoming or remaining a member of a National Park authority if he holds any paid office or employment appointments to which are or may be made or confirmed by—

    (a) the authority itself or any council by whom a local authority member of the authority is appointed;

    (b) any committee or sub-committee of the authority or of any such council;

    (c) any joint committee on which the authority or any such council is represented;

    (d) as respects a National Park authority for a National Park in England—

        (i) any parish council for, or parish meeting of, a parish the whole or any part of which is comprised in the relevant Park;

        (ii) any committee or sub-committee of any such parish council or any committee of any such parish meeting; or

        (iii) any joint committee on which any such parish council or parish meeting is represented; or

    (e) any person himself holding an office or employment which disqualifies him for becoming a member of the authority.

(2) A person is also disqualified for becoming or remaining a member of a National Park authority if he holds any employment in a company which, in accordance with Part V of the Local Government and Housing Act 1989 other than section 73, is under the control of that authority.

1989 c. 42.

(3) Section 92 of the 1972 Act (proceedings for disqualification) shall have effect in relation to a person who acts or claims to be entitled to act as a member of a National Park authority as it applies in relation to a person who acts or claims to be entitled to act as a member of a local authority, but as if—

    (a) references in that section to a local government elector for the area concerned were references to a local government elector for any principal area the whole or any part of which is comprised in the relevant Park; and

(b) in subsection (6)(b) of that section (failure to deliver declaration of acceptance of office), the words from "of failure" to "or by reason" were omitted.

1989 c. 42.

(4) Sections 1 to 3 of the Local Government and Housing Act 1989 (disqualification of persons holding politically restricted posts) shall have effect as if a National Park authority were a local authority for the purposes of Part I of that Act.

1975 c. 24.

(5) In Part III of Schedule 1 to the House of Commons Disqualification Act 1975 (other disqualifying offices), in the entry inserted by section 1(2) of that Act of 1989 (politically restricted post), after "that Part" there shall be inserted "or a National Park authority".

Vacation of office for failure to attend meetings

8. Section 85 of the 1972 Act (failure to attend meetings) shall have effect in relation to a National Park authority as it has effect in relation to a local authority.

Code of conduct for members

9. Section 31 of the Local Government and Housing Act 1989 (code of conduct for members of local authorities) shall have effect as if a National Park authority were a local authority for the purposes of that section.

Restrictions on voting on account of interests etc.

10.—(1) Sections 94 to 98 of the 1972 Act (restrictions on voting) shall have effect in relation to meetings of a National Park authority as they have effect in relation to meetings of a local authority.

(2) Section 19 of the Local Government and Housing Act 1989 (members' interests) shall have effect as if a National Park authority were a local authority for the purposes of Part I of that Act.

Allowances and time off for members

11.—(1) A National Park authority shall be a body to which sections 174 to 176 of the 1972 Act (allowances for travelling, conferences and visits) shall apply and shall also be deemed to be a relevant authority for the purposes of section 18 of the Local Government and Housing Act 1989 (basic attendance and special responsibility allowances).

(2) For the purposes of sub-paragraph (1) above references in section 18 of that Act of 1989 to a member of an authority who is a councillor shall be deemed, in relation to a National Park authority, to include references to a member of that authority who is appointed as such a member by the Secretary of State.

1978 c. 44.

(3) In section 29(1) of the Employment Protection (Consolidation) Act 1978 (time off for public duties), after paragraph (b) there shall be inserted the following paragraph—

"(ba) a National Park authority;"

but section 10 of that Act of 1989 (limit on paid leave for local authority duties) shall have effect as if a National Park authority were a relevant council for the purposes of that section.

Meetings and proceedings of the authority

12.—(1) The following provisions, that is to say—

(a) the provisions of Part VI of Schedule 12 to the 1972 Act (proceedings and meetings of local authorities) and of section 99 of that Act so far as it relates to that Part of that Schedule; and

(b) the provisions of section 100 of that Act (admission of the public and press),

shall have effect as if a National Park authority were a local authority for the purposes of those provisions.

(2) In section 100J of the 1972 Act (bodies in addition to principal councils to which provisions as to access to meetings etc. apply)—

(a) in subsection (1), after paragraph (cc) there shall be inserted the following paragraph—

"(cd) a National Park authority;"

(b) in subsection (3), after "(cc)" there shall be inserted "(cd)"; and

(c) in subsection (4)(aa)—

(i) after "Navigation Committee" there shall be inserted "or any National Park authority"; and

(ii) for "body which" there shall be substituted "person who".

(3) Section 20 of the Local Government and Housing Act 1989 (power to require adoption of certain procedural standing orders) shall have effect as if a National Park authority were a relevant authority for the purposes of that section.

1989 c. 42.

(4) The validity of any proceedings of a National Park authority shall not be affected by a vacancy amongst its members, by any defect in the appointment of a member of the authority or by the want of qualification, or the disqualification, of any such member.

Committees and sub-committees and officers

13.—(1) Sections 101 to 106 of the 1972 Act (arrangements for committees and sub-committees) shall have effect as if a National Park authority were a local authority for the purposes of those sections.

(2) Accordingly, section 13 of the Local Government and Housing Act 1989 (voting rights of members of certain committees) shall have effect as if a National Park authority were a relevant authority for the purposes of that section.

(3) It shall be the duty of a National Park authority, in relation to any committee or sub-committee to which this sub-paragraph applies, to secure—

(a) that the membership of the committee or sub-committee consists of or includes both local authority members of the authority and at least one member appointed to the authority by the Secretary of State;

(b) that the division of members of the authority who are members of the committee or sub-committee between—

(i) local authority members, and

(ii) members appointed to the authority by the Secretary of State,

is (as nearly as possible using whole numbers) in the same proportions as required, by virtue of paragraph 1(2) above, in the case of the authority itself; and

(c) that the quorum of the committee or sub-committee includes at least one local authority member of the authority and at least one member appointed to the authority by the Secretary of State.

(4) Sub-paragraph (3) above applies in the case of any National Park authority to the following committees and sub-committees, except those appointed under section 102(4) or (4A) of the 1972 Act (advisory committees), that is to say—

(a) any committee or sub-committee of the authority;

(b) any joint committee on which the authority is represented; and

(c) any sub-committee of such a joint committee.

(5) The proceedings of a committee or sub-committee to which sub-paragraph (3) above applies shall not be invalidated by any failure of a National Park authority to perform its duty under that sub-paragraph.

1976 c. 57.

(6) The provisions of sections 112 to 119 and 151 of the 1972 Act (staff of local authorities) and of section 30 of the Local Government (Miscellaneous Provisions) A~t 1976 (power to forgo repayment of remuneration) shall have effect as if a National Park authority were a local authority for the purposes of those provisions.

1989 c. 42.

(7) The following provisions of the Local Government and Housing Act 1989 shall apply in relation to a National Park authority as they apply in relation to the authorities which are relevant authorities for the purposes of those provisions, that is to say—

(a) section 4 (designation and reports of head of paid service);

(b) section 5 (designation and reports of monitoring officer); and

(c) with the omission of subsection (4)(d) (assistants for political groups), section 8 (standing orders with respect to staff);

and section 7 of that Act (staff to be appointed on merit) shall apply to any appointment to paid office or employment under a National Park authority as it applies to an appointment to paid office or employment under a body which is a local authority for the purposes of Part I of that Act.

(8) Section 12 of that Act of 1989 (conflict of interest in staff negotiations) shall have effect as if references in that section to a local authority included references to a National Park authority.

National Park Officer

14.—(1) Every National Park authority for a National Park shall secure that there is at all times an officer appointed by that authority to be responsible to the authority for the manner in which the carrying out of its different functions is co-ordinated.

(2) For the purposes of this paragraph a National Park authority may adopt—

(a) any appointment which an existing authority has made under paragraph 15 of Schedule 17 to the 1972 Act in relation to any area wholly or partly comprised in the relevant Park; or

(b) if the relevant Park is in Wales, any appointment—

(i) which was made under that paragraph in relation to any such area, and

(ii) which was adopted by a National Park planning board, as defined in section 64 of this Act, by virtue of an order under paragraph 3A of Schedule 17 to the 1972 Act or section 2(1B) of the Town and Country Planning Act 1990.

1990 c. 8.

(3) Before making or adopting an appointment under this paragraph or assigning additional responsibilities to a person holding such an appointment, a National Park authority shall consult, according to whether the Park in question is in England or in Wales, either the Countryside Commission or the Countryside Council for Wales.

(4) Sub-paragraph (3) above shall not apply in relation to the adoption of an appointment under this paragraph in relation to a National Park in Wales in any case where—

(a) the National Park authority in question is the National Park authority in relation to that National Park by virtue of an order under section 63 of this Act made by virtue of section 64(1) of this Act;

(b) the appointment in question was made or adopted by the body corporate which has so become that National Park authority, but in its capacity as the National Park planning board, as defined in section 64 of this Act, for the area of the National Park in question; and

(c) no additional responsibilities are, on the occasion of the adoption of the appointment, to be assigned to the person holding the appointment.

(5) A person who holds office with a National Park authority by virtue of an appointment made or adopted under this paragraph—

(a) may at the same time hold the office of head of that authority's paid service, the office of monitoring officer in relation to that authority or both those offices; but

(b) shall not at the same time be that authority's chief finance officer (within the meaning of section 5 of the Local Government and Housing Act 1989) or hold any office under any principal council. 　　1989 c. 42.

(6) An officer holding office with a National Park authority by virtue of an appointment made or adopted under this paragraph shall be known as a National Park officer.

Personal liability of members and officers

15. Section 265 of the Public Health Act 1875 (personal liability of members 　1875 c. 55. and officers of certain authorities) shall have effect as if—

(a) a National Park authority were an authority such as is mentioned in that section;

(b) the references in that section to a member of the authority included, in relation to a National Park authority, references to any person who is not such a member but for the time being serves as a member of a committee or sub-committee of such an authority;

(c) the references in that section to the purpose of executing that Act and to the purposes of that Act were each, in relation to a National Park authority, references to the purpose of carrying out the functions of that authority by virtue of Part III of this Act; and

(d) the words "or rate" were omitted.

Liaison with parish and community councils

16. A National Park authority shall make arrangements—

(a) in the case of a National Park in England, with each parish council the area of which is comprised wholly or partly within the Park, or

(b) in the case of a National Park in Wales, with each community council the area of which is so comprised,

for the purpose of informing and consulting that council about the authority's discharge of its functions.

Documents, notices, records, byelaws etc.

17.—(1) The Local Government (Records) Act 1962 shall have effect in 　1962 c. 56. relation to a National Park authority as if that authority were a local authority for the purposes of that Act.

(2) Subject to sub-paragraph (3) below, the following provisions of the 1972 Act, that is to say—

(a) sections 224 and 225(1) (custody and deposit of documents with a proper officer of the local authority),

(b) sections 228 and 229 (inspection of documents and photocopies),

(c) section 230 (reports and returns),

(d) sections 231 to 234 (service and authentication of documents), and

(e) without prejudice to their application by virtue of any other provision of Part III of this Act, sections 236 to 238 (byelaws),

shall have effect as if for the purposes of those provisions a National Park authority were a local authority or, in the case of section 224, a principal council.

(3) References in section 228 of the 1972 Act to a local government elector shall have effect for the purposes of that section as applied by sub-paragraph (2) above as if, in relation to a National Park authority, they were references to a local government elector for any principal area the whole or any part of which is comprised in the relevant Park.

1976 c. 57.

(4) Section 41 of the Local Government (Miscellaneous Provisions) Act 1976 (evidence of resolutions and minutes of proceedings) shall have effect as if a National Park authority were a local authority for the purposes of that Act.

(5) Where a National Park authority has made any byelaws and those byelaws have been confirmed, that authority shall send a copy of the byelaws as confirmed to every council for a principal area the whole or any part of which is comprised in the relevant Park.

Investigation in connection with maladministration etc.

1974 c. 7.

18.—(1) In section 25(1) of the Local Government Act 1974 (bodies subject to investigation under Part III of that Act), after paragraph (aa) there shall be inserted the following paragraph—

"(ab) a National Park authority;".

(2) In section 26(7) of that Act (no investigation where complaint relates to all or most of the inhabitants of an area), before paragraph (a) there shall be inserted the following paragraph—

"(aa) where the complaint relates to a National Park authority, the area of the Park for which it is such an authority;".

(3) In section 34(1) of that Act (interpretation), in the definition of "member", after "the joint board" there shall be inserted "and in relation to a National Park authority, includes a member of any of the councils by whom a local authority member of the authority is appointed".

Audit by Audit Commission auditor etc.

1982 c. 32.

19.—(1) In section 12(2) of the Local Government Finance Act 1982 (bodies whose accounts are subject to audit), after paragraph (ff) there shall be inserted the following paragraph—

"(fg) a National Park authority;"

1992 c. 19.

and sections 1 to 7 of the Local Government Act 1992 (performance standards and further provisions relating to audit) shall have effect accordingly.

(2) Sections 19 and 20 of that Act of 1982 (unlawful payments etc.) shall have effect as if references in those sections to a local authority included references to a National Park authority.

(3) In section 36 of that Act of 1982 (interpretation), after subsection (3) there shall be inserted the following subsection—

"(3A) In the application of Part III of this Act in relation to a National Park authority, any reference to a local government elector for the area of the authority shall be construed as a reference to a local government elector for any area the whole or any part of which is comprised in the Park for which that authority is the local planning authority."

Meaning of "relevant order"

20. In this Schedule "the relevant order", in relation to a National Park authority, means—

    (a) the order under section 63 of this Act establishing that authority;

    (b) any order under that section relating to that authority; or

    (c) any order made in relation to that authority in exercise of the power to amend an order under that section.

SCHEDULE 8

Section 65.

Supplemental and incidental powers of National Park authorities

Powers in relation to land etc.

1.—(1) Subject to sub-paragraph (2) below, the following provisions, that is to say—

    (a) sections 120, 122 and 123 of the 1972 Act (powers of local authorities to acquire and dispose of land), and

    (b) sections 128 to 131 of that Act (general provisions in relation to land transactions),

shall have effect as if, for the purposes of those provisions, a National Park authority were a principal council and the relevant Park were the authority's area.

(2) The following provisions of the Local Government (Miscellaneous Provisions) Act 1976, that is to say—

1976 c. 57.

    (a) section 13 (compulsory acquisition of rights over land),

    (b) section 15 (survey of land for the purposes of compulsory purchase),

    (c) section 16 (obtaining information about land), and

    (d) section 29 (repayment of unclaimed compensation),

shall apply in relation to a National Park authority as if the authority were a local authority for the purposes of that Act.

(3) Section 33 of the Local Government (Miscellaneous Provisions) Act 1982 (enforceability by local authorities of certain covenants relating to land) shall have effect as if references to a principal council included references to a National Park authority and as if the relevant Park were that authority's area; and for the purposes of this paragraph the reference in subsection (1) of that section to section 111 of the 1972 Act shall have effect as a reference to section 65 of this Act.

1982 c. 30.

(4) This paragraph shall be without prejudice to any power conferred on a National Park authority by virtue of paragraph 2 below.

2.—(1) After section 244 of the Town and Country Planning Act 1990 (powers of joint planning boards) there shall be inserted the following section—

1990 c. 8.

"Powers of National Park authorities under Part IX.

    244A.—(1) A National Park authority shall, on being authorised to do so by the Secretary of State, have the same power to acquire land compulsorily as the local authorities to whom section 226 applies have under that section.

    (2) A National Park authority shall have the same power to acquire land by agreement as the local authorities mentioned in subsection (1) of section 227 have under that subsection.

    (3) Sections 226(1) and (7), 227, 229, 230, 232, 233 and 235 to

242 shall apply with the necessary modifications as if a National Park authority were a local authority to which those sections applied and as if the Park in relation to which it carries out functions were the authority's area."

(2) Every such reference in that Act to the acquisition or appropriation of land for planning purposes as falls to be construed in accordance with section 246 of that Act shall be taken (so far as it would not otherwise do so) to include a reference to an acquisition or appropriation of land under any power conferred by virtue of sub-paragraph (1) above.

(3) The following provisions of that Act, that is to say—

(a) sections 251(1), 258(1), 260(1), 261, 271, 272 and 274 (extinguishing rights of way and other rights),

(b) sections 275 and 276 (extension and modification of functions of statutory undertakers), and

(c) section 324(6) (rights of entry),

shall have effect as if a National Park authority were a local authority for the purposes of that Act.

1990 c. 9.

1990 c. 8.

(4) The reference to a local authority in section 66(2) of the Planning (Listed Buildings and Conservation Areas) Act 1990 (which refers to the powers of a local authority under sections 232, 233 and 235(1) of the Town and Country Planning Act 1990) shall include a reference to a National Park authority.

Miscellaneous transactions and powers

3.—(1) The following provisions of the 1972 Act shall also have effect as if a National Park authority were a principal council for the purposes of that Act and as if the relevant Park were the authority's area, that is to say—

(a) section 132 (use of premises);

(b) section 135 (contracts of local authorities);

(c) section 136 (contributions towards expenditure on concurrent functions);

(d) section 139 (acceptance of gifts of property);

(e) sections 140, 140A and 140C (insurance);

(f) section 143 (subscriptions to local government associations); and

(g) sections 222 and 223 (conduct of prosecutions and participation in other legal proceedings).

1976 c. 57.

(2) Section 38 of the Local Government (Miscellaneous Provisions) Act 1976 (use of spare capacity of local authority computers) shall have effect as if a National Park authority were a local authority for the purposes of that Act.

1982 c. 30.

(3) Section 41 of the Local Government (Miscellaneous Provisions) Act 1982 (lost property) shall have effect as if a National Park authority were a local authority for the purposes of that Act.

1973 c. 50.

(4) Section 45 of that Act of 1982 (arrangements under the Employment and Training Act 1973) shall have effect as if a National Park authority were a local authority to which that section applies.

Transfer of securities on alteration of area

4. Section 146 of the 1972 Act (transfer of securities on alteration of area) shall have effect as if a National Park authority were a local authority for the purposes of that Act and as if the reference in subsection (1)(b) of that section to an enactment similar to a provision of the 1972 Act included a reference to any provision of Part III of this Act.

The Local Authorities (Goods and Services) Act 1970

5. The Local Authorities (Goods and Services) Act 1970 (supply of goods and services by local authorities) shall have effect as if a National Park authority were both a local authority and a public body for the purposes of that Act.   1970 c. 39.

Power to execute works outside Park

6. Any power to execute works which is conferred on a National Park authority by virtue of Part III of this Act or any other enactment shall be taken, except in so far as the contrary intention appears, to include power, for the purposes of the carrying out of the authority's functions in relation to the relevant Park, to execute works of the relevant description outside, as well as inside, that Park.

Power to promote Bills

7.—(1) Section 239 of the 1972 Act (power of local authority to promote local or personal Bills) shall have effect in relation to a National Park authority as if it were a local authority for the purposes of that Act and as if the relevant Park were the authority's area.

(2) A National Park authority shall have no power by virtue of Part III of this Act to promote a Bill for—

(a) modifying the area of any National Park or any local government area;

(b) modifying the authority's own constitution or that of any other National Park authority; or

(c) modifying the status or the electoral arrangements of any such local government area.

(3) In sub-paragraph (2) above—

"electoral arrangements" means any electoral arrangements within the meaning of section 14(4) of the Local Government Act 1992 or any corresponding arrangements in relation to any area in Wales; and   1992 c. 19.

"local government area" means any local government area within the meaning of that Act or any area in Wales for which any council carries out functions of local government.

Competitive tendering etc.

8.—(1) Part III of the Local Government, Planning and Land Act 1980 (direct labour organisations) shall have effect in relation to a National Park authority as if such an authority were a local authority for the purposes of that Part.   1980 c. 65.

(2) In section 1(1) of the Local Government Act 1988 (defined authorities for the purposes of the provisions of that Act relating to competition), after paragraph (a) there shall be inserted the following paragraph—   1988 c. 9.

"(aa) a National Park authority;".

(3) In Schedule 2 to that Act of 1988 (bodies to which Part II of that Act applies), after the entry relating to the Broads Authority there shall be inserted—

"Any National Park authority".

(4) In section 18 of that Act of 1988 (race relations matters), after subsection (7) there shall be inserted the following subsection —

"(7A) Any reference in this section to a local authority shall be deemed to include a reference to a National Park authority."

(5) In section 33(3)(c) of that Act of 1988 (definition of "relevant public body" for the purposes of provisions relating to contracts with associated companies), after "within" there shall be inserted "paragraph (aa) or".

(6) References in sections 8 to 10 of the Local Government Act 1992 (competition) to any provisions of that Act of 1980 or of that Act of 1988 shall include references to those provisions as they have effect by virtue of this paragraph.

Restrictions on publicity

1986 c. 10.

9. Part II of the Local Government Act 1986 (restrictions on publicity) shall have effect as if a National Park authority were a local authority for the purposes of that Part.

Provisions applying in relation to companies in which authorities have interests

1989 c. 42.

10. In section 67(3) of the Local Government and Housing Act 1989 (local authorities for the purposes of Part V of that Act), after paragraph (m) there shall be inserted the following paragraph—

"(ma) a National Park authority;".

Provisions as to charges

11. In section 152(2) of that Act of 1989 (provisions as to charges), after paragraph (j) there shall be inserted the following paragraph—

"(ja) a National Park authority;"

and section 151 of that Act (power to amend existing provisions as to charges) shall have effect as if references to an existing provision included references to any such provision as applied by Part III of this Act.

Service agency agreements

1994 c. 19.

12. Section 25 of the Local Government (Wales) Act 1994 (service agency agreements) shall have effect as if a National Park authority for any National Park in Wales were a new principal council for the purposes of that section.

Contracting out

1994 c. 40.

13. Part II of the Deregulation and Contracting Out Act 1994 (contracting out) shall have effect as if a National Park authority were a local authority for the purposes of that Part.

Section 70.

SCHEDULE 9

MISCELLANEOUS STATUTORY FUNCTIONS OF NATIONAL PARK AUTHORITIES

Common land etc.

1.—(1) The enactments specified in sub-paragraph (2) below shall have effect in relation to any registered common which—

(a) is within any National Park for which a National Park authority is the local planning authority, and

(b) is not owned by, or vested in, any other body which is a local authority,

as if the National Park authority were a local authority for the purposes of those enactments and as if the relevant Park were that authority's area.

(2) The enactments mentioned in sub-paragraph (1) above are—

1899 c. 30.

(a) section 1 of the Commons Act 1899 (scheme for regulation);

1925 c. 20.

(b) section 194(2) of the Law of Property Act 1925 (application for removal of works);

(c) section 23 of and Schedule 2 to the Caravan Sites and Control of Development Act 1960 (power of district council to prohibit caravans on commons); and — 1960 c. 62.

(d) section 9 of the Commons Registration Act 1965 (protection of unclaimed common land). — 1965 c. 64.

(3) In the Commons Act 1899 references to the council by which a scheme is made under section 1 of that Act shall be construed accordingly; and the powers conferred by sections 7 and 12 of that Act (acquisition of land and contributions to expenses) shall be exercisable by a National Park authority in relation to the relevant Park as they are exercisable by a district council in relation to their district. — 1899 c. 30.

(4) A National Park authority shall have the same power to make an application under section 18 of the Commons Act 1899 (modification of provisions for recreation grounds) as a local authority.

(5) References in this paragraph, in relation to an enactment specified in sub-paragraph (2) above or to any enactment contained in section 18 of the Commons Act 1899, to a local authority are references to any such local authority, within the meaning of the 1972 Act, as has functions conferred on it by or by virtue of that enactment.

(6) In this paragraph "registered common" means any land registered as common land or as a town or village green under the Commons Registration Act 1965.

Open spaces

2. The Open Spaces Act 1906 shall have effect as if references in that Act to a local authority included references to a National Park authority. — 1906 c. 25.

Nature reserves

3. Sections 21 and 22 of the National Parks and Access to the Countryside Act 1949 (establishment of nature reserves and application of enactments to local authority reserves) shall have effect as if the bodies on whom powers are conferred by section 21 of that Act included every National Park authority and as if the relevant Park were the authority's area; and references in those sections to a local authority and to their area shall be construed accordingly. — 1949 c. 97.

Caravan sites

4. In the Caravan Sites and Control of Development Act 1960—

(a) section 24 (power to provide sites for caravans), and

(b) paragraph 11 of Schedule 1 to that Act (no licence required for land occupied by a local authority),

shall have effect as if a National Park authority were a local authority for the purposes of that Act and as if the relevant Park were that authority's area.

Country Parks

5. The Countryside Act 1968 shall have effect as if a National Park authority were a local authority for the purposes of— — 1968 c. 41.

(a) sections 6 to 8 of that Act (country parks);

(b) section 9 of that Act (powers exercisable over or near common land); and

(c) section 41 of that Act (byelaws) in so far as it has the effect in relation to—

(i) any country park provided under section 7 of that Act, or

(ii) any land as respects which any powers under section 9 of that Act have been exercised,

1949 c. 97.

of conferring powers on a local authority or of applying provisions of section 92 of the National Parks and Access to the Countryside Act 1949 (wardens);

and the references to a local authority in sections 43 to 45 of that Act of 1968 (general provisions as to the powers of local authorities) shall have effect accordingly.

Provision of information and encouragement of visitors

6. Sections 142 and 144 of the 1972 Act (provision of information about local services and encouragement of visitors) shall have effect (subject to paragraph 9 of Schedule 8 to this Act) as if a National Park authority were a local authority for the purposes of that Act and as if the relevant Park were the authority's area.

Derelict land etc.

1975 c. 70.
1982 c. 42.

7. The provisions of section 16 of the Welsh Development Agency Act 1975 and of section 1 of the Derelict Land Act 1982 (powers for the improvement of land) shall have effect in relation to land in a National Park for which a National Park authority is the local planning authority as if references in those provisions to a local authority included references to the National Park authority and as if the relevant Park were the authority's area.

Recreational facilities

1976 c. 57.

8. Section 19 of the Local Government (Miscellaneous Provisions) Act 1976 (recreational facilities) shall have effect as if the powers conferred by that section on local authorities were also conferred, so as to be exercisable within a National Park for which a National Park authority is the local planning authority, on that authority.

Refuse Disposal

1978 c. 3.

9.—(1) Subject to sub-paragraph (2) below, references to a local authority in the Refuse Disposal (Amenity) Act 1978 shall have effect in relation to land in a National Park for which a National Park authority is the local planning authority as if they included references to that authority and as if the relevant Park were the authority's area.

(2) Sub-paragraph (1) above shall not apply, in relation to any time before the coming into force of the repeal of section 1 of that Act, to any reference in that section.

Ancient Monuments and Archaeological Areas

1979 c. 46.

10.—(1) Subject to sub-paragraph (2) below, Parts I and II of the Ancient Monuments and Archaeological Areas Act 1979 shall have effect as if in relation—

(a) to any monument in a National Park for which a National Park authority is the local planning authority, or

(b) to any area the whole or any part of which is comprised in such a Park,

the references in those Parts to a local authority included references to that National Park authority.

(2) Section 35 of that Act (notice of operations affecting area of archaeological importance) shall have effect in relation to land in such a National Park as is mentioned in sub-paragraph (1) above as if—

(a) any notice required to be served on a local authority under that section were required, instead, to be served on the National Park authority; and

(b) the functions conferred on a local authority by virtue of that section had been conferred instead on the National Park authority.

(3) Section 45(2) and (3) of that Act (assistance for archaeological investigations) shall have effect as if a National Park authority were a local authority for the purposes of that Act and as if the relevant Park were the authority's area.

Footpaths and bridleways

11. The following provisions of the the Highways Act 1980, that is to say— 1980 c. 66.

(a) sections 25 to 29 (footpaths and bridleways),

(b) section 72(2) (widening of public paths),

(c) sections 118 to 121 (stopping up and diversion of public paths), and

(d) Schedule 6 (procedure for orders),

shall have effect as if references in those sections to a local authority or council included references to a National Park authority and as if the relevant Park were the authority's area.

Litter

12. The following provisions, that is to say—

(a) section 4 of the Litter Act 1983 (consultations and proposals for the 1983 c. 35. abatement of litter), and

(b) section 88 of the Environmental Protection Act 1990 (fixed penalty 1990 c. 43. notices for leaving litter),

shall have effect as if a National Park authority were a litter authority for the purposes of those provisions, as if the relevant Park were the authority's area and as if the reference in that section 4 to the authority's area were a reference to any part of the relevant Park.

Listed and historic buildings

13. —(1) In the case of a building situated in a National Park for which a National Park authority is the local planning authority, that authority and no other authority shall be the appropriate authority for the purposes of sections 47 to 51 of the Planning (Listed Buildings and Conservation Areas) Act 1990 1990 c. 9. (purchase of listed buildings etc in need of repair); and the reference to a local authority in section 88(5) of that Act (rights of entry) and in section 6 of the Historic Buildings and Ancient Monuments Act 1953 (under which grants for 1953 c. 49. the acquisition of buildings in Wales may be made) shall have effect accordingly.

(2) In relation to any building or land in any such National Park, the powers conferred on a county council or county borough council by section 52 of that Act of 1990 (power to acquire building and land by agreement) shall be exercisable by the National Park authority, and not (without prejudice to their powers apart from that section) by any other authority; and subsection (2) of that section shall have effect accordingly.

(3) Section 53(1) of that Act (management of listed buildings etc. acquired under the Act) shall apply in relation to the powers conferred by virtue of this paragraph on a National Park authority as it applies in relation to the powers conferred by sections 47 and 52 of that Act on a local authority.

(4) That Act shall have effect as if a National Park authority were a local authority for the purposes of—

    (a) sections 54 and 55 of that Act (urgent works to preserve listed buildings etc.), and

    (b) sections 57 and 58 of that Act (power of local authorities to contribute towards preservation of listed buildings etc.),

and, in relation to those provisions, as if the relevant Park were the authority's area.

    (5) In relation to the powers conferred on a National Park authority by virtue of this paragraph, section 88 of that Act (powers of entry) shall have effect as if references in that section to a local authority included references to a National Park authority.

    (6) References to a local authority in section 90(1) to (4) of that Act (financial provisions) shall be deemed to include references to a National Park authority.

Hazardous substances

1990 c. 10.

    14.—(1) For the purposes of the Planning (Hazardous Substances) Act 1990, where a National Park authority is the local planning authority for any National Park, that authority, and no other authority, shall be the hazardous substances authority for land in the relevant Park.

    (2) References to a local authority in sections 12 and 38(1) to (4) of that Act (government consent to local authority activities and financial provisions) shall be deemed to include references to a National Park authority.

Local Charities

1993 c. 10.

    15. Sections 76 to 78 of the Charities Act 1993 (local charities) shall have effect as if the references to a council for any area included references to a National Park authority and as if the relevant Park were the authority's area.

Overseas Assistance

1993 c. 25.

    16. The Local Government (Overseas Assistance) Act 1993 shall have effect as if a National Park authority were a local authority for the purposes of that Act.

Section 78.

SCHEDULE 10

MINOR AND CONSEQUENTIAL AMENDMENTS RELATING TO NATIONAL PARKS

The Finance Act 1931 (c. 28)

    1. In Schedule 2 to the Finance Act 1931 (requirements in connection with production of instruments of transfer), in paragraph (viii), for "local authority" there shall be substituted "local planning authority".

The National Parks and Access to the Countryside Act 1949 (c. 97)

    2.—(1) In section 6 of the National Parks and Access to the Countryside Act 1949 (general duties of Countryside Commission and the Countryside Council for Wales as respects the National Parks)—

    (a) in subsection (3)—

        (i) in paragraph (a), before "local authorities" there shall be inserted "National Park authorities and"; and

        (ii) in paragraph (b), before "local authority" there shall be inserted "National Park authority";

    and

(b) in subsection (6), after "means" there shall be inserted the words "a National Park authority or".

(2) In section 7 of that Act—

(a) in subsection (5) (bodies consulted about variation of the area of a National Park), after "consult with" there shall be inserted "any National Park authority for the Park in question and with"; and

(b) in subsection (6) (notices), after "as the case may be" there shall be inserted "at the offices (where the order is for the variation of an order designating a Park) of any National Park authority for the Park in question".

(3) In section 9(1) of that Act (local planning authority to consult Countryside Commission or Countryside Council for Wales about proposals for a development plan affecting a National Park), for "the local planning authority" there shall be substituted "the authority or authorities who are required to prepare the plan or, as the case may be, who are entitled to alter or add to it".

(4) In section 12(1) of that Act (provision in a National Park of facilities) for "provision in" there shall be substituted "provision for".

(5) In subsection (4) of section 51 of that Act (consultation as to proposals for a long distance route)—

(a) after the word "every", in the first place where it occurs, there shall be inserted "National Park authority,";

(b) after "whose" there shall be inserted "Park or"; and

(c) after "every such" there shall be inserted "authority,";

and in subsection (5) of that section (report to contain estimates of capital outlay by local authorities), after "local authorities" there shall be inserted "and National Park authorities".

(6) In section 52(2) of that Act (notice of determination as to any proposals on long distance routes)—

(a) after "every" there shall be inserted "National Park authority"; and

(b) after "whose" there shall be inserted "Park or".

(7) For section 88 of that Act (application to areas of outstanding natural beauty of provisions relating to National Parks) there shall be substituted—

"Functions of certain bodies in relation to areas of outstanding natural beauty.

88.—(1) The following provisions of this Act, that is to say—

(a) paragraph (e) of subsection (4) of section six,

(b) section nine,

(c) subsection (1) of section sixty-two,

(d) subsection (5) of section sixty-four, and

(e) subsections (5) and (5A) of section sixty-five,

shall apply in relation to areas of outstanding natural beauty as they apply in relation to National Parks.

(2) In paragraph (e) of subsection (4) of section six of this Act as it applies by virtue of the last foregoing subsection, the expression "appropriate planning authority" means a local planning authority whose area consists of or includes the whole or any part of an area of outstanding natural beauty and includes a local authority, not being a local planning authority, by whom any powers of a local planning authority as respects an area of outstanding natural beauty are exercisable, whether under this Act or otherwise.

(3) The provisions of section 4A of this Act shall apply to the provisions mentioned in paragraphs (a) and (b) of subsection

SCH. 10

(1) of this section for the purposes of their application to areas of outstanding natural beauty as the provisions of the said section 4A apply for the purposes of Part II of this Act.

(4) A local planning authority whose area consists of or includes the whole or any part of an area of outstanding natural beauty shall have power, subject to the following provisions of this section, to take all such action as appears to them expedient for the accomplishment of the purpose of conserving and enhancing the natural beauty of the area of outstanding natural beauty or so much thereof as is included in their area.

(5) Nothing in this Act shall be construed as limiting the generality of the last foregoing subsection; but in so far as the provisions of this Act confer specific powers falling within that subsection those powers shall be exercised in accordance with those provisions and subject to any limitations expressed or implied therein.

(6) Without prejudice to the powers conferred by this Act, subsection (4) of this section shall have effect only for the purpose of removing any limitation imposed by law on the capacity of a local planning authority by virtue of its constitution, and shall not authorise any act or omission on the part of such an authority which apart from that subsection would be actionable at the suit of any person on any ground other than such a limitation."

(8) In section 114(2) of that Act (construction of references to the preservation of the natural beauty of an area) after the word "preservation"—

   (a) in the first place where it occurs, there shall be inserted the words ", or the conservation,", and

   (b) in the second place where it occurs, there shall be inserted the words "or, as the case may be, the conservation".

(9) In Schedule 1 to that Act (procedure for certain orders)—

   (a) in paragraph 1, after sub-paragraph (3) there shall be inserted the following sub-paragraph—

"(3A) Where under this paragraph any notice is required to be given by any person in respect of any land which is already in a National Park for which a National Park authority is the local planning authority, that person shall serve a copy of that notice on that authority.";

   (b) in paragraph 2(5), after "the Council" there shall be inserted "a National Park authority,";

   (c) in paragraph 3(a), after "under sub-paragraph" there shall be inserted "(3A) or"; and

   (d) after paragraph 3 there shall be inserted the following paragraph—

"3A. An order designating a National Park shall have effect as from such time as may be determined by the Minister and specified in the notice of the confirmation of that order."

The Landlord and Tenant Act 1954 (c. 56)

3. In section 69(1) of the Landlord and Tenant Act 1954 (interpretation), in the definition of "local authority", for the words from "has the same meaning" to "Broads Authority" there shall be substituted "means any local authority within the meaning of the Town and Country Planning Act 1990, any National Park authority, the Broads Authority or".

1990 c. 8.

The Land Compensation Act 1961 (c. 33)

4.—(1) Paragraph 55(2) of Schedule 16 to the 1972 Act (which relates to the operation of section 17 of the Land Compensation Act 1961 in a National Park) shall not apply in the case of a National Park for which a National Park authority is the local planning authority.

(2) In section 39(1) of that Act of 1961 (interpretation), for the definition of "local planning authority" there shall be substituted the following definition—

> "'local planning authority' shall be construed in accordance with Part I of the Town and Country Planning Act 1990;".   1990 c. 8.

The Trustee Investments Act 1961 (c. 62)

5. In section 11 of the Trustee Investments Act 1961 (local authority investment schemes), in subsection (4)(a), after "the Broads Authority" there shall be inserted "a National Park authority".

The Agriculture Act 1967 (c. 22)

6. In section 50(3) of the Agriculture Act 1967 (bodies transfers to whom are not subject to section 49), after paragraph (a) there shall be inserted the following paragraph—

> "(aa) a National Park authority;".

The Leasehold Reform Act 1967 (c. 88)

7. In section 28 of the Leasehold Reform Act 1967 (retention or resumption of land required for public purposes), in subsection (5), after paragraph (aa) there shall be inserted the following paragraph—

> "(ab) to any National Park authority; and".

The Countryside Act 1968 (c. 41)

8.—(1) In section 4(1) of the Countryside Act 1968 (experimental projects and schemes) after "local authorities" there shall be inserted "National Park authorities".

(2) In section 12(1) of that Act (provision in National Park of facilities), for "provision in" there shall be substituted "provision for".

(3) In section 13(12) of that Act (enforcement of byelaws), for "in the area of that other local authority" there shall be substituted "for an area that includes any part of the National Park in question".

The Employers Liability (Compulsory Insurance) Act 1969 (c. 57)

9. In section 3 of the Employers Liability (Compulsory Insurance) Act 1969 (employers exempted from insurance), in subsection (2), after "the Broads Authority" there shall be inserted "a National Park authority".

The 1972 Act

10.—(1) In subsection (1)(a) of section 80 of the 1972 Act (disqualification for persons holding appointments made or confirmed by a local authority or connected authority), after "joint committee" there shall be inserted "or National Park authority"; and after subsection (2) of that section there shall be inserted the following subsections—

> "(2A) Subsection (2) above shall have effect as if the reference to a joint board included a reference to a National Park authority.

(2B) For the purposes of this section a local authority shall be treated as represented on a National Park authority if it is entitled to make any appointment of a local authority member of the National Park authority."

(2) In section 184 of the 1972 Act (functions under countryside legislation)—

(a) at the beginning of subsection (1) there shall be inserted the words "Subject to section 68 of the Environment Act 1995 (planning authority functions under National Parks legislation to be functions of National Park authorities in certain cases),"; and

(b) in paragraph (b) of that subsection, for the words "subsections (6) to (8) below" there shall be substituted the words "subsections (7) and (8) below".

(3) In subsection (3) of that section, for the words "sections 9 and 11" there shall be substituted the words "section 9".

The Employment Agencies Act 1973 (c. 35)

11. In section 13(7) of the Employment Agencies Act 1973 (cases in which Act does not apply), after paragraph (ff) there shall be inserted the following paragraph —

"(fg) the exercise by a National Park authority of any of its functions;".

The Health and Safety at Work etc. Act 1974 (c. 37)

12. In section 28 of the Health and Safety at Work etc. Act 1974 (restrictions on disclosure of information), for subsection (10) there shall be substituted the following subsection—

"(10) The Broads Authority and every National Park authority shall be deemed to be local authorities for the purposes of this section."

The Welsh Development Agency Act 1975 (c. 70)

13.—(1) In section 1(14) of the Welsh Development Agency Act 1975 (consultation by Agency with local authorities and other bodies), after "local authorities" there shall be inserted "National Park authorities".

(2) In subsections (1) and (2) of section 5 of that Act (assistance to the Agency from other bodies), after "local authority", in each case, there shall be inserted "a National Park authority".

(3) In section 15(1) of that Act (which refers to consultation under section 1(14)), after "local authorities" there shall be inserted "National Park authorities".

Local Land Charges Act 1975 (c. 76)

14. In sections 1 and 2 of the Local Land Charges Act 1975 (obligations that are and are not local land charges), after the words "local authority", in each place where they occur, there shall be inserted "or National Park authority".

The Race Relations Act 1976 (c. 74)

15.—(1) In section 19A of the Race Relations Act 1976 (discrimination in planning), in subsection (2)(a) (definition of "planning authority"), after "the Broads Authority" there shall be inserted "a National Park authority or".

(2) In section 71 of that Act (general statutory duty of local authorities), after "the Broads Authority" there shall be inserted "and every National Park authority".

The Development of Rural Wales Act 1976 (c. 75)

16.—(1) In section 1(4) of the Development of Rural Wales Act 1976 (consultation as to orders varying area for which the Board is responsible), after paragraph (b) there shall be inserted the following paragraph—

> "(ba) every National Park authority which is the local planning authority for a National Park any part of which will be included in the area for which the Board is responsible if the order is made or which (whether the proposal is for an order under subsection (2) or for an order under subsection (3)) is included in the area for which it is responsible at the time of the proposal;".

(2) In section 4(1)(d)(i) of that Act (power to finance measures taken by local authorities), after "local authority" there shall be inserted "National Park authority".

(3) In subsections (1) and (3) of section 8 of that Act (assistance to the Board from other bodies), after "local authority", in each case, there shall be inserted "National Park authority".

(4) In paragraph 3(3) of Schedule 1 to that Act (consultation as to membership of Board), after paragraph (a) there shall be inserted the following paragraph—

> "(aa) every National Park authority which is the local planning authority for a National Park any part of which is included in the area for which the Board is responsible; and".

(5) In Schedule 3 to that Act (the New Towns code), in paragraph 14 (special parliamentary procedure for compulsory purchase of local authority property), after the words "local authority", in each place where they occur, there shall be inserted "or National Park authority".

The Rent (Agriculture) Act 1976 (c. 80)

17. In section 5(3) of the Rent (Agriculture) Act 1976 (no statutory tenancy where landlord's interest belongs to Crown or local authority etc.), after paragraph (bc) there shall be inserted the following paragraph—

> "(bd) any National Park authority;".

The Rent Act 1977 (c. 42)

18. In section 14 of the Rent Act 1977 (exemption from protection for lettings by local authorities etc.), after paragraph (bb) there shall be inserted the following paragraph—

> "(bc) a National Park authority;".

The Justices of the Peace Act 1979 (c. 55)

19. In section 64 of the Justices of the Peace Act 1979 (which disqualifies in certain circumstances justices who are members of local authorities), in subsection (2A), for the words "shall be treated as a local authority" there shall be substituted "and every National Park authority shall be deemed to be local authorities."

The Local Government, Planning and Land Act 1980 (c. 65)

20.—(1) In section 103 of the Local Government, Planning and Land Act 1980—

(a) in subsection (2)(c) (consultation with local authorities as to acquisition of land by the Land Authority for Wales), the word "and" immediately preceding sub-paragraph (ii) shall be omitted and after that sub-paragraph there shall be inserted "and

(iii) any National Park authority which is the local planning authority for a National Park in which the land, or any part of the land, is situated"; and

(b) after subsection (8) there shall be inserted the following subsection—

"(8A) Subsections (6) to (8) above shall have effect as if any reference to a council included a reference to a National Park authority for a National Park in Wales and the references to the area of a council were to be construed accordingly."

(2) In paragraph 1 of Schedule 19 to that Act (public authorities who may be assisted by that Authority), after sub-paragraph (f) there shall be inserted the following sub-paragraph—

"(fa) a National Park authority;".

(3) In paragraph 4 of Schedule 20 to that Act (notice to and objections by local authorities in the case of compulsory purchase by that Authority), at the end there shall be inserted—

"For the purposes of this paragraph the references to a local authority within whose area the land is situated shall be deemed to include references to any National Park authority which is the local planning authority for a National Park in which the land is situated."

(4) In paragraph 9 of Schedule 21 to that Act (notice of planning applications) in sub-paragraph (1), after "Wales" there shall be inserted "and every National Park authority for a National Park in Wales".

The Acquisition of Land Act 1981 (c. 67)

21.—(1) In section 17(3) of the Acquisition of Land Act 1981 (special Parliamentary procedure not to apply to compulsory acquisition by certain bodies), after "subsection (4) below)" there shall be inserted ", a National Park authority".

(2) In paragraph 4(3) of Schedule 3 to that Act (which makes similar provision in relation to the acquisition of rights), after "sub-paragraph (4) below)" there shall be inserted ", a National Park authority".

The Wildlife and Countryside Act 1981 (c. 69)

22.—(1) In section 39(5)(a) of the Wildlife and Countryside Act 1981 (definition of "relevant authority"), before "in a National Park" there shall be inserted "which is not in an area for which a National Park authority is the local planning authority but is".

(2) In section 41(5A) of that Act (duties of agriculture Ministers with respect to the countryside to have effect in relation to the Broads as if the Broads were a National Park), at the end there shall be inserted "(and, as respects land within the Broads, any reference in this section to the relevant authority is accordingly a reference to the Broads Authority)."

(3) In section 42 of that Act (notification of agricultural operations on moor and heath), for the words "local planning authority", wherever they occur, there shall be substituted "National Park authority".

(4) In section 44 of that Act (grants and loans for National Parks purposes)—

(a) in subsection (2), for "a local planning authority" there shall be substituted "the authority in question";

(b) in subsection (3), for "A local planning authority" there shall be substituted "The authority in question"; and

(c) in subsection (4), for the words from "county planning authority" onwards there shall be substituted "National Park authority and the Broads as a National Park for which it is the local planning authority".

(5) In section 51(2)(c) of that Act (definition of "relevant authority" in relation to the exercise of powers of entry for the purposes of section 42), for "local planning authority" there shall be substituted "National Park authority".

(6) In section 52(2) of that Act (construction of references to a local planning authority), after "except as respects" there shall be inserted "a National Park for which a National Park authority is the local planning authority,".

(7) Sub-paragraph (1) above shall cease to have effect with the coming into force of the repeal by this Act of section 39(5)(a) of that Act of 1981.

The County Courts Act 1984 (c. 28)

23. In section 60(3) of the County Courts Act 1984 (right of audience for proper officer of local authority in certain circumstances), after "the Broads Authority" there shall be inserted "any National Park authority,".

The Housing Act 1985 (c. 68)

24.—(1) In section 43 of the Housing Act 1985 (consent of the Secretary of State required for certain disposals by local authorities), after subsection (5) there shall be inserted the following subsection—

   "(5A) References in this section and in section 44 to a local authority shall include references to a National Park authority."

(2) In section 45(2)(b) of that Act (definition of "public sector authority" for the purposes of provisions relating to service charges after disposal), after "a local authority" there shall be inserted—

   "a National Park authority".

(3) In section 573 of that Act (definition of "public sector authority" for the purposes of assisting the owners of defective housing), after the entry relating to joint boards there shall be inserted the following entry—

   "a National Park authority (or a predecessor of such an authority),".

The Landlord and Tenant Act 1985 (c. 70)

25.—(1) In sections 14(4) and 26(1) of, and in paragraph 9(1) of the Schedule to, the Landlord and Tenant Act 1985 (provisions excluding operation of certain provisions in the case of public sector housing), after "a local authority", in each case, there shall be inserted—

   "a National Park authority".

(2) In section 28(6) of that Act (meaning of "qualified accountant" in the case of public sector landlords), after "local authority" there shall be inserted "National Park authority".

(3) In section 31(3) of that Act (reserve powers to limit rents), in the definition of "rent", after "local authorities" there shall be inserted "National Park authorities".

The Landlord and Tenant Act 1987 (c. 31)

26. In section 58(1) of the Landlord and Tenant Act 1987 (exempt landlords), after paragraph (dd) there shall be inserted the following paragraph—

   "(de) a National Park authority;".

The Norfolk and Suffolk Broads Act 1988 (c. 4)

27. In Schedule 3 to the Norfolk and Suffolk Broads Act 1988 (functions of the Broads authority), in paragraph 43, for the words from "as a local authority" onwards there shall be substituted "for the purposes of the Derelict Land Act 1982 as a National Park authority and the Broads as a National Park for which it is the local planning authority".

The Housing Act 1988 (c. 50)

28. In paragraph 12(2) of Schedule 1 to the Housing Act 1988 (meaning of "local authority" for the purposes of determining the tenancies to be treated as local authority tenancies), after paragraph (d) there shall be inserted the following paragraph—

"(da) a National Park authority;".

The Road Traffic Act 1988 (c. 52)

29. In section 144(2)(a)(i) of the Road Traffic Act 1988 (exemptions from requirement of third party insurance or security), after "London borough" there shall be inserted "a National Park authority".

The Electricity Act 1989 (c. 29)

30.—(1) Paragraph 2(6) of Schedule 8 to the Electricity Act 1989 (definition of "relevant planning authority" for the purposes of consents under that Act) shall be amended in accordance with the following provisions of this paragraph.

(2) In this paragraph "the 1994 amendment" means the omission of the words "and Wales" in paragraph (a) of the said paragraph 2(6) by paragraph 22 of Schedule 6 to the Local Government (Wales) Act 1994.

(3) If the 1994 amendment comes into force after this paragraph, then—

(a) in paragraph (a) of the said paragraph 2(6), for the words "England and Wales" there shall be substituted the words "land in England and Wales which is not in a National Park for which a National Park authority is the local planning authority";

(b) after that paragraph (a) there shall be inserted the following paragraph—

"(aa) in relation to land in England and Wales which is in a National Park for which a National Park authority is the local planning authority, means that National Park authority; and"; and

(c) the 1994 amendment shall have effect in relation to the said paragraph (a) as amended by paragraph (a) above, and on the coming into force of the 1994 amendment the words "and Wales" shall also be omitted from the paragraph (aa) inserted by paragraph (b) above.

(4) If the 1994 amendment comes into force before this paragraph, then—

(a) in paragraph (a) of the said paragraph 2(6), for the word "England" there shall be substituted the words "land in England which is not in a National Park for which a National Park authority is the local planning authority"; and

(b) after that paragraph (a) there shall be inserted the following paragraph—

"(aa) in relation to land in England which is in a National Park for which a National Park authority is the local planning authority, means that National Park authority; and".

(5) If the 1994 amendment comes into force on the same day as this paragraph, the 1994 amendment shall be deemed to have come into force immediately before this paragraph (and sub-paragraph (4) above shall have effect accordingly).

(6) The paragraph (aa) inserted by paragraph 22 of Schedule 6 to the Local Government (Wales) Act 1994 shall be re-numbered "(ab)". 1994 c. 19.

The Local Government and Housing Act 1989 (c. 42)

31.—(1) In section 21(1) of the Local Government and Housing Act 1989 (interpretation of Part I) the word "and" immediately preceding paragraph (m) shall be omitted and after that paragraph there shall be added "and

> (n) a joint planning board constituted for an area in Wales outside a National Park by an order under section 2(1B) of the Town and 1990 c. 8. Country Planning Act 1990."

(2) In section 39(1) of that Act (application of Part IV), after paragraph (h) there shall be inserted—

> "(hh) a joint planning board constituted for an area in Wales outside a National Park by an order under section 2(1B) of the Town and Country Planning Act 1990;".

(3) In section 67(3) of that Act (local authorities for the purposes of Part V) the word "and" at the end of paragraph (o) shall be omitted and after that paragraph there shall be inserted—

> "(oo) a joint planning board constituted for an area in Wales outside a National Park by an order under section 2(1B) of the Town and Country Planning Act 1990; and".

(4) In section 152(2) of that Act (relevant authorities for the purposes of imposing certain charges) the word "and" immediately preceding paragraph (l) shall be omitted and after that paragraph there shall be added "and

> (m) a joint planning board constituted for an area in Wales outside a National Park by an order under section 2(1B) of the Town and Country Planning Act 1990."

(5) In paragraph 2(1)(b) of Schedule 1 to that Act (bodies to which appointments are made taking account of political balance) for "paragraphs (k) and (m)" there shall be substituted "paragraphs (k), (m) and (n)".

The Town and Country Planning Act 1990 (c. 8)

32.—(1) In paragraph (a) of section 1(5) of the Town and Country Planning Act 1990 (provisions to which subsections (1) to (4) are subject)—

(a) for "sections 5 to" there shall be substituted "sections 4A to"; and

(b) at the end there shall be inserted "and".

(2) In section 2 of that Act (joint planning boards), before subsection (2) of that section there shall be inserted the following subsection—

> "(1D) The areas that may be constituted as a united district for the purposes of this section shall not include the whole or any part of an area which is comprised in a National Park for which there is a National Park authority."

(3) In section 4 of that Act (National Parks), after subsection (4) there shall be inserted the following subsection—

> "(5) This section shall have effect subject to section 4A below."

(4) In sections 90(1) and 101(2)(c) of that Act (development with government authorisation), after the words "local authority", in each place where they occur, there shall be inserted "or National Park authority".

(5) In sections 169 and 170(2)(b) of that Act (provisions in relation to blighted land), after "local authority" there shall be inserted "National Park authority".

(6) In section 209(5) of that Act (regulations for charging expenses of a local authority which is a local planning authority on land), after "local authority" there shall be inserted "or National Park authority".

(7) In section 252 of that Act (procedure for making certain orders)—

(a) in subsection (2) (bodies to be given notice), after paragraph (a) there shall be inserted the following paragraph—

"(aa) on any National Park authority which is the local planning authority for the area in which any highway or, as the case may be, any land to which the order relates is situated, and";

(b) in subsection (4) (objections), after "local authority" there shall be inserted "National Park authority".

(8) In section 253(2)(a) of that Act (procedure in anticipation of planning permission)—

(a) in subsections (2)(a) and (3)(a), after "local authority", in each case, there shall be inserted "National Park authority"; and

(b) in subsection (4), after "London borough" there shall be inserted "a National Park authority".

(9) In section 305(1)(a) of that Act (contribution by Ministers towards compensation paid by local authorities), after "local authority" there shall be inserted "or National Park authority".

(10) In section 306 of that Act (contributions by local authorities and statutory undertakers), after subsection (5) there shall be inserted the following subsection—

"(6) This section shall have effect as if the references to a local authority included references to a National Park authority."

(11) In section 330 of that Act (power to require information as to interests in land), after subsection (5) there shall be inserted the following subsection—

"(6) This section shall have effect as if the references to a local authority included references to a National Park authority."

(12) In section 333(1) of that Act (regulations as to form of notice etc.), after "local authority" there shall be inserted "or National Park authority".

(13) In section 336(1) of that Act (interpretation), in the definition of "local authority" after "subsection (10)" there shall be inserted "below and section 71(7) of the Environment Act 1995".

(14) In Schedule 1 to that Act (distribution of planning functions)—

(a) in paragraph 4(2) (consultation with district planning authorities)—

(i) after "determined by a" there shall be inserted "National Park authority or"; and

(ii) before "the district planning authority" there shall be inserted "any authority which (but for section 4A) would be or, as the case may be, which is"; and

(b) in paragraph 13(1), for "A county planning authority" there shall be substituted "In the case of any area for which there is both a district planning authority and a county planning authority, the county planning authority";

(c) in sub-paragraph (2) of paragraph 19, after "Park" there shall be inserted "to which section 4 applies", and after that sub-paragraph there shall be inserted the following sub-paragraph—

"(2A) As respects the area of any National Park for which a National Park authority is the local planning authority those functions shall be exercised by that authority."

(d) in paragraph 20(4)—

(i) in paragraph (a), for "outside a metropolitan county" there shall be substituted "which is land in an area the local planning authority for which comprises both a county planning authority and a district planning authority"; and

(ii) in paragraph (b), for "elsewhere" there shall be substituted "other land in an area the local planning authority for which comprises both a county planning authority and a district planning authority".

(15) In paragraph 4(5)(b) of Schedule 8 to that Act (which refers to directions under section 90(1) of that Act), after "local authority" there shall be inserted "National Park authority".

(16) In Schedule 13 to that Act (blighted land), in paragraph 1(a)(i), after "local authority" there shall be inserted "National Park authority".

(17) In Schedule 14 to that Act (procedure for footpaths and bridleways orders)—

(a) after paragraph 1(2)(b)(ii) (persons on whom notice served) there shall be inserted the following sub-paragraph—

"(iia) any National Park authority for a National Park which includes any of that land; and";

(b) in paragraph 1(6) (cases where owner, occupier or lessee is local authority), after "local authority" there shall be inserted "National Park authority"; and

(c) in paragraph 3(2) (local inquiry to be held if objection by local authority), after "local authority" there shall be inserted "or a National Park authority".

(18) So much of any provision of this paragraph as amends an enactment repealed by this Act shall cease to have effect with the coming into force of the repeal.

The Planning (Listed Buildings and Conservation Areas) Act 1990 (c. 9)

33.—(1) The Planning (Listed Buildings and Conservation Areas) Act 1990 shall be amended as follows.

(2) In section 32 (purchase notice), after subsection (4) there shall be inserted the following subsection—

"(4A) This section and sections 33 to 37 shall have effect as if—

(a) the bodies on whom a listed building purchase notice may be served under this section included any National Park authority which is the local planning authority for the area in which the building and land in question are situated; and

(b) a National Park authority were a local authority for the purposes of this Act and the Park for which it is the local planning authority were its area;

and the references in those sections and in section 63(7)(a) to a council and to a local authority shall be construed accordingly."

(3) In subsection (3) of section 79 (definition of "local authority" for the purposes of town scheme agreements), after paragraph (c) there shall be inserted the following paragraph—

"(ca) in relation to any building in a National Park for which a National Park authority is the local planning authority, that authority;".

(4) In section 93(1)(a) (regulations as to form of notice etc.), after "local authority" there shall be inserted "or National Park authority".

(5) In paragraph 4 of Schedule 2, after sub-paragraph (3) (expenses of various persons and bodies with respect to listed building enforcement) there shall be inserted the following sub-paragraph—

"(4) The reference to a local authority in sub-paragraph (3) above includes a reference to any National Park authority which is the local planning authority for any area."

(6) In paragraph 2 of Schedule 4 (provision as to exercise of functions by different authorities), after "4" there shall be inserted "4A".

(7) In paragraph 3 of Schedule 4—

(a) after "determined by a" there shall be inserted "National Park authority or"; and

(b) in sub-paragraph (a), before "the district planning authority" there shall be inserted "any authority which (but for section 4A) would be or, as the case may be, which is";

(c) in sub-paragraph (b), for "the district planning" there shall be substituted "any such".

(8) In paragraph 4 of Schedule 4—

(a) in sub-paragraph (1)—

(i) in paragraph (a), after "a metropolitan county" there shall be inserted "or in any National Park for which a National Park authority is the local planning authority"; and

(ii) in paragraph (b), for "outside a metropolitan county" there shall be substituted "to which paragraph (a) above does not apply"; and

(b) in sub-paragraph (2), after "county planning authority" there shall be inserted "or National Park authority".

Water consolidation legislation

34.—(1) The references to a National Park authority in the following provisions (which impose environmental duties), that is to say—

1991 c. 56.   (a) section 4 of the Water Industry Act 1991,

1991 c. 57.   (b) section 17 of the Water Resources Act 1991, and

1991 c. 59.   (c) section 61C of the Land Drainage Act 1991,

shall have effect, until the coming into force of the repeal by this Act of the definition for the purposes of those provisions of the expression "National Park authority", as if they included references to a National Park authority established under Part III of this Act which has become the local planning authority for the National Park in question; and thereafter those references shall have effect as if they were references to a National Park authority so established.

(2) The references to a National Park planning authority—

(a) in sections 34 and 45 of the Water Resources Act 1991 (regulations with respect to notice to be given of particulars of certain licence applications), and

(b) in any regulations under those sections,

shall have effect, until the coming into force of the repeal by this Act of subsection (5) of section 34 of that Act, as if they included references to a National Park authority established under Part III of this Act which has become the local planning authority for the National Park in question; and thereafter those references shall have effect as if they were references to a National Park authority so established.

The Local Government Finance Act 1992 (c. 14)

35. In section 35 of the Local Government Finance Act 1992 (definition of "special items") in subsection (5) (expenses of a billing authority not to be special expenses if they are expenses of meeting a levy from a National Park planning board) paragraphs (a) and (b) shall be omitted and at the end of that subsection there shall be added the words "or

> (c) a National Park authority in relation to a National Park in Wales."

The Local Government (Overseas Assistance) Act 1993 (c. 25)

36. In section 1(10) of the Local Government (Overseas Assistance) Act 1993 (certain bodies on which powers are conferred by the Act), at the end there shall be added—

> "(h) a joint planning board constituted for an area in Wales outside a National Park by an order under section 2(1B) of the Town and Country Planning Act 1990."

1990 c. 8.

The Welsh Language Act 1993 (c. 38)

37. In section 6(1) of the Welsh Language Act 1993 (bodies which are public bodies for the purposes of the provisions of that Act about Welsh language schemes), after paragraph (c) there shall be inserted the following paragraph—

> "(ca) a National Park authority;".

The Local Government (Wales) Act 1994 (c. 19)

38.—(1) In Schedule 6 to the Local Government (Wales) Act 1994 (minor and consequential amendments relating to planning) in paragraph 1, at the beginning of the subsection which that paragraph substitutes for subsection (1) of section 184 of the 1972 Act, there shall be inserted the words "Subject to section 68 of the Environment Act 1995 (planning authority functions under National Parks legislation to be functions of National Park authorities in certain cases),".

(2) In paragraph 2 of that Schedule, for the words "paragraphs 3 to 14" there shall be substituted the words "paragraphs 13 and 14".

SCHEDULE 11

Section 90.

Air Quality: Supplemental Provisions

Consultation requirements

1.—(1) A local authority in carrying out its functions in relation to—

(a) any air quality review,

(b) any assessment under section 82 or 84 of this Act, or

(c) the preparation of an action plan or any revision of an action plan,

shall consult such other persons as fall within sub-paragraph (2) below.

(2) Those persons are—

(a) the Secretary of State;

(b) the appropriate new Agency;

(c) in England and Wales, the highway authority for any highway in the area to which the review or, as the case may be, the action plan or revision relates;

(d) every local authority whose area is contiguous to the authority's area;

(e) any county council in England whose area consists of or includes the whole or any part of the authority's area;

(f) any National Park authority for a National Park whose area consists of or includes the whole or any part of the authority's area;

(g) such public authorities exercising functions in, or in the vicinity of, the authority's area as the authority may consider appropriate;

(h) such bodies appearing to the authority to be representative of persons with business interests in the area to which the review or action plan in question relates as the authority may consider appropriate;

(j) such other bodies or persons as the authority considers appropriate.

(3) In this paragraph "National Park authority", subject to sub-paragraph (4) below, means a National Park authority established under section 63 of this Act which has become the local planning authority for the National Park in question.

(4) As respects any period before a National Park authority established under section 63 of this Act in relation to a National Park becomes the local planning authority for that National Park, any reference in sub-paragraph (2) above to a National Park authority shall be taken as a reference to the National Park Committee or joint or special planning board for that National Park.

Exchange of information with county councils in England

2.—(1) This paragraph applies in any case where a district in England for which there is a district council is comprised in an area for which there is a county council; and in this paragraph—

(a) any reference to the county council is a reference to the council of that area; and

(b) any reference to a district council is a reference to the council of a district comprised in that area.

(2) It shall be the duty of the county council to provide a district council with all such information as is reasonably requested by the district council for purposes connected with the carrying out of its functions under or by virtue of this Part.

(3) It shall be the duty of a district council to provide the county council with all such information as is reasonably requested by the county council for purposes connected with the carrying out of any of its functions relating to the assessment or management of the quality of air.

(4) Information provided to a district council or county council under sub-paragraph (2) or (3) above shall be provided in such form and in such manner and at such times as the district council or, as the case may be, the county council may reasonably require.

(5) A council which provides information under sub-paragraph (2) or (3) above shall be entitled to recover the reasonable cost of doing so from the council which requested the information.

(6) The information which a council may be required to provide under this paragraph shall include information which, although it is not in the possession of the council or would not otherwise come into the possession of the council, is information which it is reasonable to require the council to obtain.

Joint exercise of local authority functions

3.—(1) The appropriate authority may give directions to any two or more local authorities requiring them to exercise the powers conferred by—

(a) section 101(5) of the Local Government Act 1972 (power of two or more local authorities to discharge functions jointly), or

(b) section 56(5) of the Local Government (Scotland) Act 1973 (which makes similar provision for Scotland),

in relation to functions under or by virtue of this Part in accordance with the directions.

(2) The appropriate authority may give directions to a local authority requiring it—

(a) not to exercise those powers, or

(b) not to exercise those powers in a manner specified in the directions,

in relation to functions under or by virtue of this Part.

(3) Where two or more local authorities have exercised those powers in relation to functions under or by virtue of this Part, the appropriate authority may give them directions requiring them to revoke, or modify in accordance with the directions, the arrangements which they have made.

(4) In this paragraph, "the appropriate authority" means—

(a) in relation to England and Wales, the Secretary of State; and

(b) in relation to Scotland, SEPA acting with the approval of the Secretary of State.

Public access to information about air quality

4.—(1) It shall be the duty of every local authority—

(a) to secure that there is available at all reasonable times for inspection by the public free of charge a copy of each of the documents specified in sub-paragraph (2) below; and

(b) to afford to members of the public facilities for obtaining copies of those documents on payment of a reasonable charge.

(2) The documents mentioned in sub-paragraph (1)(a) above are—

(a) a report of the results of any air quality review which the authority has caused to be conducted;

(b) a report of the results of any assessment which the authority has caused to be made under section 82 or 84 of this Act;

(c) any order made by the authority under section 83 of this Act;

(d) any action plan prepared by the authority;

(e) any proposals or statements submitted to the authority pursuant to subsection (3) or (4) of section 86 of this Act;

(f) any directions given to the authority under this Part;

(g) in a case where section 86 of this Act applies, any directions given to the county council under this Part.

Fixed penalty offences

5.—(1) Without prejudice to the generality of paragraph (o) of subsection (2) of section 87 of this Act, regulations may, in particular, make provision—

(a) for the qualifications, appointment or authorisation of persons who are to issue fixed penalty notices;

(b) for the offences in connection with which, the cases or circumstances in which, the time or period at or within which, or the manner in which fixed penalty notices may be issued;

(c) prohibiting the institution, before the expiration of the period for paying the fixed penalty, of proceedings against a person for an offence in connection with which a fixed penalty notice has been issued;

(d) prohibiting the conviction of a person for an offence in connection with which a fixed penalty notice has been issued if the fixed penalty is paid before the expiration of the period for paying it;

(e) entitling, in prescribed cases, a person to whom a fixed penalty notice is issued to give, within a prescribed period, notice requesting a hearing in respect of the offence to which the fixed penalty notice relates;

(f) for the amount of the fixed penalty to be increased by a prescribed amount in any case where the person liable to pay the fixed penalty fails to pay it before the expiration of the period for paying it, without having given notice requesting a hearing in respect of the offence to which the fixed penalty notice relates;

(g) for or in connection with the recovery of an unpaid fixed penalty as a fine or as a civil debt or as if it were a sum payable under a county court order;

(h) for or in connection with execution or other enforcement in respect of an unpaid fixed penalty by prescribed persons;

(j) for a fixed penalty notice, and any prescribed proceedings or other prescribed steps taken by reference to the notice, to be rendered void in prescribed cases where a person makes a prescribed statutory declaration, and for the consequences of any notice, proceedings or other steps being so rendered void (including extension of any time limit for instituting criminal proceedings);

(k) for or in connection with the extension, in prescribed cases or circumstances, by a prescribed person of the period for paying a fixed penalty;

(l) for or in connection with the withdrawal, in prescribed circumstances, of a fixed penalty notice, including—

(i) repayment of any amount paid by way of fixed penalty in pursuance of a fixed penalty notice which is withdrawn; and

(ii) prohibition of the institution or continuation of proceedings for the offence in connection with which the withdrawn notice was issued;

(m) for or in connection with the disposition of sums received by way of fixed penalty;

(n) for a certificate purporting to be signed by or on behalf of a prescribed person and stating either—

(i) that payment of a fixed penalty was, or (as the case may be) was not, received on or before a date specified in the certificate, or

(ii) that an envelope containing an amount sent by post in payment of a fixed penalty was marked as posted on a date specified in the certificate,

to be received as evidence of the matters so stated and to be treated, without further proof, as being so signed unless the contrary is shown;

(o) requiring a fixed penalty notice to give such reasonable particulars of the circumstances alleged to constitute the fixed penalty offence to which the notice relates as are necessary for giving reasonable information of the offence and to state—

(i) the monetary amount of the fixed penalty which may be paid;

(ii) the person to whom, and the address at which, the fixed penalty may be paid and any correspondence relating to the fixed penalty notice may be sent;

(iii) the method or methods by which payment of the fixed penalty may be made;

(iv) the period for paying the fixed penalty;

(v) the consequences of the fixed penalty not being paid before the expiration of that period;

(p) similar to any provision made by section 79 of the Road Traffic Offenders Act 1988 (statements by constables in fixed penalty cases);

(q) for presuming, in any proceedings, that any document of a prescribed description purporting to have been signed by a person to whom a fixed penalty notice has been issued has been signed by that person;

(r) requiring or authorising a fixed penalty notice to contain prescribed information relating to, or for the purpose of facilitating, the administration of the fixed penalty system;

(s) with respect to the giving of fixed penalty notices, including, in particular, provision with respect to—

   (i) the methods by which,

   (ii) the officers, servants or agents by, to or on whom, and

   (iii) the places at which,

fixed penalty notices may be given by, or served on behalf of, a prescribed person;

(t) prescribing the method or methods by which fixed penalties may be paid;

(u) for or with respect to the issue of prescribed documents to persons to whom fixed penalty notices are or have been given;

(w) for a fixed penalty notice to be treated for prescribed purposes as if it were an information or summons or any other document of a prescribed description.

(2) The provision that may be made by regulations prescribing fixed penalty offences includes provision for an offence to be a fixed penalty offence—

(a) only if it is committed in such circumstances or manner as may be prescribed; or

(b) except if it is committed in such circumstances or manner as may be prescribed.

(3) Regulations may provide for any offence which is a fixed penalty offence to cease to be such an offence.

(4) An offence which, in consequence of regulations made by virtue of sub-paragraph (3) above, has ceased to be a fixed penalty offence shall be eligible to be prescribed as such an offence again.

(5) Regulations may make provision for such exceptions, limitations and conditions as the Secretary of State considers necessary or expedient.

(6) In this paragraph—

"fixed penalty" means a penalty of such amount as may be prescribed (whether by being specified in, or made calculable under, regulations);

"fixed penalty notice" means a notice offering a person an opportunity to discharge any liability to conviction for a fixed penalty offence by payment of a penalty of a prescribed amount;

"fixed penalty offence" means, subject to sub-paragraph (2) above, any offence (whether under or by virtue of this Part or any other enactment) which is for the time being prescribed as a fixed penalty offence;

"the fixed penalty system" means the system implementing regulations made under or by virtue of paragraph (o) of subsection (2) of section 87 of this Act;

"the period for paying", in relation to any fixed penalty, means such period as may be prescribed for the purpose;

"regulations" means regulations under or by virtue of paragraph (o) of subsection (2) of section 87 of this Act.

Section 92.   SCHEDULE 12

SCHEDULE 2A TO THE ENVIRONMENTAL PROTECTION ACT 1990

Sections 44A and
44B.   "SCHEDULE 2A

OBJECTIVES FOR THE PURPOSES OF THE NATIONAL WASTE STRATEGY

1. Ensuring that waste is recovered or disposed of without endangering human health and without using processes or methods which could harm the environment and, in particular, without—

(a) risk to water, air, soil, plants or animals;

(b) causing nuisance through noise or odours; or

(c) adversely affecting the countryside or places of special interest.

2. Establishing an integrated and adequate network of waste disposal installations, taking account of the best available technology not involving excessive costs.

3. Ensuring that the network referred to in paragraph 2 above enables—

(a) the European Community as a whole to become self-sufficient in waste disposal, and the Member States individually to move towards that aim, taking into account geographical circumstances or the need for specialised installations for certain types of waste; and

(b) waste to be disposed of in one of the nearest appropriate installations, by means of the most appropriate methods and technologies in order to ensure a high level of protection for the environment and public health.

4. Encouraging the prevention or reduction of waste production and its harmfulness, in particular by—

(a) the development of clean technologies more sparing in their use of natural resources;

(b) the technical development and marketing of products designed so as to make no contribution or to make the smallest possible contribution, by the nature of their manufacture, use or final disposal, to increasing the amount or harmfulness of waste and pollution hazards; and

(c) the development of appropriate techniques for the final disposal of dangerous substances contained in waste destined for recovery.

5. Encouraging—

(a) the recovery of waste by means of recycling, reuse or reclamation or any other process with a view to extracting secondary raw materials; and

(b) the use of waste as a source of energy."

SCHEDULE 13

REVIEW OF OLD MINERAL PLANNING PERMISSIONS

Interpretation

1.—(1) In this Schedule—

"dormant site" means a Phase I or Phase II site in, on or under which no minerals development has been carried out to any substantial extent at any time in the period beginning on 22nd February 1982 and ending with 6th June 1995 otherwise than by virtue of a planning permission which is not a relevant planning permission relating to the site;

"first list", in relation to a mineral planning authority, means the list prepared by them pursuant to paragraph 3 below;

"mineral planning authority"—

(a) as respects England and Wales, means a mineral planning authority within the meaning of the 1990 Act, and

(b) as respects Scotland, means a planning authority for the purposes of the 1972 Act;

"mineral site" has the meaning given by sub-paragraph (2) below;

"National Park" means an area designated as such under section 5(3) of the National Parks and Access to the Countryside Act 1949;

1949 c. 97.

"old mining permission" has the meaning given—

(a) as respects England and Wales, by section 22(1) of the 1991 Act, and

(b) as respects Scotland, by section 49H(1) of the 1972 Act;

"owner", in relation to any land—

(a) as respects England and Wales, means any person who—

(i) is the estate owner in respect of the fee simple, or

(ii) is entitled to a tenancy granted or extended for a term of years certain of which not less than seven years remains unexpired; and

(b) as respects Scotland, has the meaning given by paragraph 10(1) of Schedule 10A to the 1972 Act;

"Phase I site" and "Phase II site" have the meaning given by paragraph 2 below;

"relevant planning permission" means any planning permission, other than an old mining permission or a planning permission granted by a development order, granted after 30th June 1948 for minerals development; and

"second list", in relation to a mineral planning authority, means the list prepared by them pursuant to paragraph 4 below.

(2) For the purposes of this Schedule, but subject to sub-paragraph (3) below, "mineral site" means—

(a) in a case where it appears to the mineral planning authority to be expedient to treat as a single site the aggregate of the land to which any two or more relevant planning permissions relate, the aggregate of the land to which those permissions relate; and

(b) in any other case, the land to which a relevant planning permission relates.

(3) In determining whether it appears to them to be expedient to treat as a single site the aggregate of the land to which two or more relevant planning permissions relate a mineral planning authority shall have regard to any guidance issued for the purpose by the Secretary of State.

(4) Any reference (however expressed) in this Schedule to an old mining permission or a relevant planning permission relating to a mineral site is a reference to the mineral site, or some part of it, being the land to which the permission relates; and where any such permission authorises the carrying out of development consisting of the winning and working of minerals but only in respect of any particular mineral or minerals, that permission shall not be taken, for the purposes of this Schedule, as relating to any other mineral in, on or under the land to which the permission relates.

(5) For the purposes of this Schedule, a mineral site which is a Phase I site or a Phase II site is active if it is not a dormant site.

(6) For the purposes of this Schedule, working rights are restricted in respect of a mineral site if any of—

(a) the size of the area which may be used for the winning and working of minerals or the depositing of mineral waste;

(b) the depth to which operations for the winning and working of minerals may extend;

(c) the height of any deposit of mineral waste;

(d) the rate at which any particular mineral may be extracted;

(e) the rate at which any particular mineral waste may be deposited;

(f) the period at the expiry of which any winning or working of minerals or depositing of mineral waste is to cease; or

(g) the total quantity of minerals which may be extracted from, or of mineral waste which may be deposited on, the site,

is restricted or reduced in respect of the mineral site in question.

(7) For the purposes of this Schedule, where an application is made under paragraph 9 below for the determination of the conditions to which the relevant planning permissions relating to the mineral site to which the application relates are to be subject, those conditions are finally determined when—

(a) the proceedings on the application, including any proceedings on or in consequence of an application under section 288 of the 1990 Act or, as the case may be, section 233 of the 1972 Act, have been determined, and

(b) any time for appealing under paragraph 11(1) below, or applying or further applying under paragraph 9 below, (where there is a right to do so) has expired.

Phase I and II sites

2.—(1) This paragraph has effect for the purposes of determining which mineral sites are Phase I sites, which are Phase II sites, and which are neither Phase I nor Phase II sites.

(2) A mineral site is neither a Phase I site nor a Phase II site where—

(a) all the relevant planning permissions which relate to the site have been granted after 21st February 1982; or

(b) some only of the relevant planning permissions which relate to the site have been granted after 21st February 1982, and the parts of the site to which those permissions relate constitute the greater part of that site.

(3) With the exception of those mineral sites which, by virtue of sub-paragraph (2) above, are neither Phase I nor Phase II sites, every mineral site is either a Phase I site or a Phase II site.

SCH. 13

(4) Subject to sub-paragraph (2) above, where any part of a mineral site is situated within—

(a) a National Park;

(b) a site in respect of which a notification under section 28 of the Wildlife   1981 c. 69.
and Countryside Act 1981 (sites of special scientific interest) is in force;

(c) an area designated under section 87 of the National Parks and Access to   1949 c. 97.
the Countryside Act 1949 as an area of outstanding natural beauty;

(d) an area designated as a National Scenic Area under section 262C of the
1972 Act; or

(e) an area designated as a Natural Heritage Area under section 6 of the
Natural Heritage (Scotland) Act 1991,   1991 c. 28.

that site is a Phase I site.

(5) Subject to sub-paragraphs (2) and (4) above, where—

(a) all the relevant planning permissions which relate to a mineral site, and
which were not granted after 21st February 1982, were granted after the
relevant day in 1969; or

(b) the parts of a mineral site to which relate such of the relevant planning
permissions relating to the site as were granted after the relevant day in
1969 but before 22nd February 1982 constitute a greater part of the site
than is constituted by those parts of the site to which no such relevant
planning permission relates but to which a relevant planning
permission granted on or before the relevant day in 1969 does relate,

the mineral site is a Phase II site.

(6) In sub-paragraph (5) above, "the relevant day in 1969" means—

(a) as respects England and Wales, 31st March 1969; and

(b) as respects Scotland, 7th December 1969.

(7) Every other mineral site, that is to say any mineral site other than one—

(a) which is, by virtue of sub-paragraph (2) above, neither a Phase I nor a
Phase II site; or

(b) which is a Phase I site by virtue of sub-paragraph (4) above; or

(c) which is a Phase II site by virtue of sub-paragraph (5) above,

is a Phase I site.

(8) In ascertaining, for the purposes of sub-paragraph (2) or (5) above,
whether any parts of a mineral site constitute the greater part of that site, or
whether a part of a mineral site is greater than any other part, that mineral site
shall be treated as not including any part of the site—

(a) to which an old mining permission relates; or

(b) which is a part where minerals development has been (but is no longer
being) carried out and which has, in the opinion of the mineral planning
authority, been satisfactorily restored;

but no part of a site shall be treated, by virtue of paragraph (b) above, as being
not included in the site unless the mineral planning authority are satisfied that
any aftercare conditions which relate to that part have, so far as relating to that
part, been complied with.

The "first list"

3.—(1) A mineral planning authority shall, in accordance with the following
provisions of this paragraph, prepare a list of mineral sites in their area ("the
first list").

(2) A site shall, but shall only, be included in the first list if it is a mineral site
in the area of the mineral planning authority and is either—

(a) an active Phase I site;

(b) an active Phase II site; or

(c) a dormant site.

(3) In respect of each site included in the first list, the list shall indicate whether the site is an active Phase I site, an active Phase II site or a dormant site.

(4) In respect of each active Phase I site included in the first list, that list shall specify the date by which an application is to be made to the mineral planning authority under paragraph 9 below.

(5) Any date specified pursuant to sub-paragraph (4) above shall be a date—

(a) not earlier than the date upon which expires the period of 12 months from the date on which the first list is first advertised in accordance with paragraph 5 below, and

(b) not later than the date upon which expires the period of three years from the date upon which the provisions of this Schedule come into force.

(6) The preparation of the first list shall be completed before the day upon which it is first advertised in accordance with paragraph 5 below.

The "second list"

4.—(1) A mineral planning authority shall, in accordance with the following provisions of this paragraph, prepare a list of the active Phase II sites in their area ("the second list").

(2) The second list shall include each mineral site in the mineral planning authority's area which is an active Phase II site.

(3) In respect of each site included in the second list, that list shall indicate the date by which an application is to be made to the mineral planning authority under paragraph 9 below.

(4) Subject to paragraph (5) below, any date specified pursuant to sub-paragraph (3) above shall be a date—

(a) not earlier than the date upon which expires the period of 12 months from the date on which the second list is first advertised in accordance with paragraph 5 below, and

(b) not later than the date upon which expires the period of six years from the date upon which the provisions of this Schedule come into force.

(5) The Secretary of State may by order provide that sub-paragraph (4)(b) above shall have effect as if for the period of six years referred to in that paragraph there were substituted such longer period specified in the order.

(6) The power of the Secretary of State to make an order under sub-paragraph (5) above shall be exercisable by statutory instrument; and any statutory instrument containing such an order shall be subject to annulment in pursuance of a resolution of either House of Parliament.

(7) The preparation of the second list shall be completed before the day upon which it is first advertised in accordance with paragraph 5 below.

Advertisement of the first and second lists

5.—(1) This paragraph makes provision for the advertisement of the first and second lists prepared by a mineral planning authority.

(2) The mineral planning authority shall advertise each of the first and second lists by causing to be published, in each of two successive weeks, in one or more newspapers circulating in its area, notice of the list having been prepared.

(3) In respect of each of those lists, such notice shall—

(a) state that the list has been prepared by the authority; and

(b) specify one or more places within the area of the authority at which the list may be inspected, and in respect of each such place specify the times (which shall be reasonable times) during which facilities for inspection of the list will be afforded.

(4) In respect of the first list, such notice shall—

(a) be first published no later than the day upon which expires the period of three months from the date upon which the provisions of this Schedule come into force;

(b) explain the general effect of a mineral site being classified as a dormant site or, as the case may be, as an active Phase I site or an active Phase II site;

(c) explain the consequences which will occur if no application is made under paragraph 9 below in respect of an active Phase I site included in the list by the date specified in the list for that site;

(d) explain the effects for any dormant or active Phase I or II site not included in the list of its not being included in the list and—

(i) set out the right to make an application to the authority for that site to be included in the list;

(ii) set out the date by which such an application must be made; and

(iii) state that the owner of such a site has a right of appeal against any decision of the authority upon such an application; and

(e) explain that the owner of an active Phase I site has a right to apply for postponement of the date specified in the list for the making of an application under paragraph 9 below, and set out the date by which an application for such postponement must be made.

(5) In respect of the second list, such notice shall—

(a) be first published no later than the day upon which expires the period of three years, or such longer period as the Secretary of State may by order specify, from the date upon which the provisions of this Schedule come into force; and

(b) explain the consequences which will occur if no application is made under paragraph 9 below in respect of an active Phase II site included in the list by the date specified in the list for that site.

(6) The power of the Secretary of State to make an order under sub-paragraph (5) above shall be exercisable by statutory instrument; and any statutory instrument containing such an order shall be subject to annulment in pursuance of a resolution of either House of Parliament.

Applications for inclusion in the first list of sites not included in that list as originally prepared and appeals from decisions upon such applications

6.—(1) Any person who is the owner of any land, or is entitled to an interest in a mineral, may, if that land or interest is not a mineral site included in the first list and does not form part of any mineral site included in that list, apply to the mineral planning authority for that land or interest to be included in that list.

(2) An application under sub-paragraph (1) above shall be made no later than the day upon which expires the period of three months from the day when the first list was first advertised in accordance with paragraph 5 above.

(3) Where the mineral planning authority consider that—

(a) the land or interest is, or forms part of, any dormant or active Phase I or II site, they shall accede to the application; or

(b) part only of the land or interest is, or forms part of, any dormant or active Phase I or II site, they shall accede to the application so far as it relates to that part of the land or interest,

but shall otherwise refuse the application.

(4) On acceding, whether in whole or in part, to an application made under sub-paragraph (1) above, the mineral planning authority shall amend the first list as follows—

(a) where they consider that the land or interest, or any part of the land or interest, is a dormant site or an active Phase I or II site, they shall add the mineral site consisting of the land or interest or, as the case may be, that part, to the first list and shall cause the list to indicate whether the site is an active Phase I site, an active Phase II site or a dormant site;

(b) where they consider that the land or interest, or any part of the land or interest, forms part of any mineral site included in the first list, they shall amend the entry in the first list for that site accordingly.

(5) Where the mineral planning authority amend the first list in accordance with sub-paragraph (4) above, they shall also—

(a) in a case where an active Phase I site is added to the first list pursuant to paragraph (a) of that sub-paragraph, cause that list to specify, in respect of that site, the date by which an application is to be made to the mineral planning authority under paragraph 9 below;

(b) in a case where—

(i) the entry for an active Phase I site included in the first list is amended pursuant to paragraph (b) of that sub-paragraph; and

(ii) the date specified in that list in respect of that site as the date by which an application is to be made to the mineral planning authority under paragraph 9 below is a date falling less than 12 months after the date upon which the authority make their decision upon the application in question,

cause that date to be amended so as to specify instead the date upon which expires the period of 12 months from the date on which the applicant is notified under sub-paragraph (10) below of the authority's decision upon his application.

(6) Any date specified pursuant to sub-paragraph (5)(a) above shall be a date—

(a) not earlier than the date upon which expires the period of 12 months from the date on which the applicant is notified under sub-paragraph (10) below of the mineral planning authority's decision upon his application, and

(b) not later than the later of—

(i) the date upon which expires the period of three years from the date upon which the provisions of this Schedule come into force; and

(ii) the date mentioned in paragraph (a) above.

(7) On acceding, whether in whole or in part, to an application made under sub-paragraph (1) above, the mineral planning authority shall, if the second list has been first advertised in accordance with paragraph 5 above prior to the time at which they make their decision on the application, amend the second list as follows—

(a) where they consider that the land or interest, or any part of the land or interest, is an active Phase II site, they shall add the mineral site consisting of the land or interest or, as the case may be, that part, to the second list;

(b) where they consider that the land or interest, or any part of the land or interest, forms part of any active Phase II site included in the second list, they shall amend the entry in that list for that site accordingly.

(8) Where the mineral planning authority amend the second list in accordance with sub-paragraph (7) above, they shall also—

(a) in a case where an active Phase II site is added to the second list pursuant to paragraph (a) of that sub-paragraph, cause that list to specify, in respect of that site, the date by which an application is to be made to the authority under paragraph 9 below;

(b) in a case where—

(i) the entry for an active Phase II site included in the second list is amended pursuant to paragraph (b) of that sub-paragraph; and

(ii) the date specified in that list in respect of that site as the date by which an application is to be made to the authority under paragraph 9 below is a date falling less than 12 months after the date upon which the authority make their decision upon the application in question,

cause that date to be amended so as to specify instead the date upon which expires the period of 12 months from the date on which the applicant is notified under sub-paragraph (10) below of the authority's decision upon his application.

(9) Any date specified pursuant to sub-paragraph (8)(a) above shall be a date—

(a) not earlier than the date upon which expires the period of 12 months from the date on which the applicant is notified under sub-paragraph (10) below of the mineral planning authority's decision upon his application, and

(b) not later than the later of—

(i) the date upon which expires the period of six years from the date upon which the provisions of this Schedule come into force; and

(ii) the date mentioned in paragraph (a) above.

(10) When a mineral planning authority determine an application made under sub-paragraph (1) above, they shall notify the applicant in writing of their decision and, in a case where they have acceded to the application, whether in whole or in part, shall supply the applicant with details of any amendment to be made to the first or second list in accordance with sub-paragraph (4) or (8) above.

(11) Where a mineral planning authority—

(a) refuse an application made under sub-paragraph (1) above; or

(b) accede to such an application only so far as it relates to part of the land or interest in respect of which it was made,

the applicant may by notice appeal to the Secretary of State.

(12) A person who has made such an application may also appeal to the Secretary of State if the mineral planning authority have not given notice to the applicant of their decision on the application within eight weeks of their having received the application or within such extended period as may at any time be agreed upon in writing between the applicant and the authority.

(13) An appeal under sub-paragraph (11) or (12) above must be made by giving notice of appeal to the Secretary of State before the end of the period of six months beginning with—

(a) in the case of an appeal under sub-paragraph (11) above, the determination; or

(b) in the case of an appeal under sub-paragraph (12) above, the end of the period of eight weeks mentioned in that sub-paragraph or, as the case may be, the end of the extended period mentioned in that sub-paragraph.

Postponement of the date specified in the first or second list for review of the permissions relating to a Phase I or II site in cases where the existing conditions are satisfactory

7.—(1) Any person who is the owner of any land, or of any interest in any mineral, comprised in—

(a) an active Phase I site included in the first list; or

(b) an active Phase II site included in the second list,

may apply to the mineral planning authority for the postponement of the date specified in that list in respect of that site as the date by which an application is to be made to the authority under paragraph 9 below (in this paragraph referred to as "the specified date").

(2) Subject to sub-paragraph (3) below, an application under sub-paragraph (1) above shall be made no later than the day upon which expires the period of three months from the day when—

(a) in the case of an active Phase I site, the first list; or

(b) in the case of an active Phase II site, the second list,

was first advertised in accordance with paragraph 5 above.

(3) In the case of—

(a) an active Phase I site—

(i) added to the first list in accordance with paragraph 6(4)(a) above; or

(ii) in respect of which the entry in the first list was amended in accordance with paragraph 6(4)(b) above;

or

(b) an active Phase II site—

(i) added to the second list in accordance with paragraph 6(7)(a) above; or

(ii) in respect of which the entry in the second list was amended in accordance with paragraph 6(7)(b) above,

an application under sub-paragraph (1) above shall be made no later than the day upon which expires the period of three months from the day on which notice was given under paragraph 6(10) above of the mineral planning authority's decision to add the site to or, as the case may be, so to amend the list in question.

(4) An application under sub-paragraph (1) above shall be in writing and shall—

(a) set out the conditions to which each relevant planning permission relating to the site is subject;

(b) set out the applicant's reasons for considering those conditions to be satisfactory;

(c) set out the date which the applicant wishes to be substituted for the specified date; and

(d) be accompanied by the appropriate certificate (within the meaning of sub-paragraph (5) or (6) below).

(5) For the purposes of sub-paragraph (4) above, as respects England and Wales the appropriate certificate is such a certificate—

(a) as would be required, under section 65 of the 1990 Act (notice etc. of applications for planning permission) and any provision of a development order made by virtue of that section, to accompany the application if it were an application for planning permission for minerals development, but

(b) with such modifications as are required for the purposes of this paragraph,

and section 65(6) of that Act (offences) shall also have effect in relation to any certificate purporting to be the appropriate certificate.

(6) For the purposes of sub-paragraph (4) above, the appropriate certificate is, as respects Scotland, each of the certificates which would be required, under or by virtue of sections 23 and 24 of the 1972 Act (notice etc. of applications for planning permission), to accompany the application if it were an application for planning permission for minerals development, but with such modifications as are required for the purposes of this paragraph; and sections 23(3) and 24(5) of that Act (offences) shall have effect in relation to any certificate purporting to be the appropriate certificate.

(7) Where the mineral planning authority receive an application made under sub-paragraph (1) above—

(a) if they consider the conditions referred to in sub-paragraph (4)(a) above to be satisfactory they shall agree to the specified date being postponed in which event they shall determine the date to be substituted for that date;

(b) in any other case they shall refuse the application.

(8) Where the mineral planning authority agree to the specified date being postponed they shall cause the first or, as the case may be, the second list to be amended accordingly.

(9) When a mineral planning authority determine an application made under sub-paragraph (1) above, they shall notify the applicant in writing of their decision and, in a case where they have agreed to the postponement of the specified date, shall notify the applicant of the date which they have determined should be substituted for the specified date.

(10) Where, within three months of the mineral planning authority having received an application under sub-paragraph (1) above, or within such extended period as may at any time be agreed upon in writing between the applicant and the authority, the authority have not given notice, under sub-paragraph (9) above, to the applicant of their decision upon the application, the authority shall be treated as—

(a) having agreed to the specified date being postponed; and

(b) having determined that the date referred to in sub-paragraph (4)(c) above be substituted for the specified date,

and sub-paragraph (8) above shall apply accordingly.

Service on owners etc. of notice of preparation of the first and second lists

8.—(1) The mineral planning authority shall, no later than the date upon which the first list is first advertised in accordance with paragraph 5 above, serve notice in writing of the first list having been prepared on each person appearing to them to be the owner of any land, or entitled to an interest in any mineral, included within a mineral site included in the first list, but this sub-paragraph is subject to sub-paragraph (7) below.

(2) A notice required to be served by sub-paragraph (1) above shall—

(a) indicate whether the mineral site in question is a dormant site or an active Phase I or II site; and

(b) where that site is an active Phase I site—

(i) indicate the date specified in the first list in relation to that site as the date by which an application is to be made to the mineral planning authority under paragraph 9 below;

(ii) explain the consequences which will occur if such an application is not made by the date so specified; and

(iii) explain the right to apply to have that date postponed, and indicate the date by which such an application must be made.

(3) Where, in relation to any land or mineral included in an active Phase I site, the mineral planning authority—

(a) has served notice on any person under sub-paragraph (1) above; and

(b) has received no application under paragraph 9 below from that person by the date falling eight weeks before the date specified in the first list as the date by which such applications should be made in respect of the site in question,

the authority shall serve a written reminder on that person, and such a reminder shall—

(i) indicate that the land or mineral in question is included in an active Phase I site;

(ii) comply with the requirements of sub-paragraph (2)(b)(i) and (ii) above; and

(iii) be served on that person on or before the date falling four weeks before the date specified in the first list in respect of that site as the date by which an application is to be made to the authority under paragraph 9 below.

(4) The mineral planning authority shall, no later than the date upon which the second list is first advertised in accordance with paragraph 5 above, serve notice in writing of the second list having been prepared on each person appearing to them to be the owner of any land, or entitled to an interest in any mineral, included within an active Phase II site included in the second list, but this sub-paragraph is subject to sub-paragraph (7) below.

(5) A notice required to be served by sub-paragraph (4) above shall—

(a) indicate that the mineral site in question is an active Phase II site; and

(b) indicate the date specified in the second list in relation to that site as the date by which an application is to be made to the mineral planning authority under paragraph 9 below;

(c) explain the consequences which will occur if such an application is not made by the date so specified; and

(d) explain the right to apply to have that date postponed, and indicate the date by which such an application must be made.

(6) Where, in relation to any land or mineral included in an active Phase II site, the mineral planning authority—

(a) has served notice on any person under sub-paragraph (4) above; and

(b) has received no application under paragraph 9 below from that person by the date falling eight weeks before the date specified in the second list as the date by which such applications should be made in respect of the site in question,

the authority shall serve a written reminder on that person, and such a reminder shall—

(i) comply with the requirements of sub-paragraph (5)(a) to (c) above; and

(ii) be served on that person on or before the date falling four weeks before the date specified in the second list in respect of that site as the date by which an application is to be made to the authority under paragraph 9 below.

(7) Sub-paragraph (1) or (4) above shall not require the mineral planning authority to serve notice under that sub-paragraph upon any person whose identity or address for service is not known to and cannot practicably, after reasonable inquiry, be ascertained by them, but in any such case the authority shall cause to be firmly affixed, to each of one or more conspicuous objects on

the land or, as the case may be, on the surface of the land above the interest in question, a copy of the notice which they would (apart from the provisions of this sub-paragraph) have had to serve under that sub-paragraph on the owner of that land or interest.

(8) If, in a case where sub-paragraph (7) above applies, no person makes an application to the authority under paragraph 9 below in respect of the active Phase I or II site which includes the land or interest in question by the date falling eight weeks before the date specified in the first or, as the case may be, the second list as the date by which such applications should be made in respect of that site, the authority shall cause to be firmly affixed, to each of one or more conspicuous objects on the land or, as the case may be, on the surface of the land above the interest in question, a copy of the written reminder that would, in a case not falling within sub-paragraph (7) above, have been served under sub-paragraph (3) or (6) above.

(9) Where by sub-paragraph (7) or (8) above a copy of any notice is required to be affixed to an object on any land that copy shall—

   (a) be displayed in such a way as to be easily visible and legible;

   (b) be first displayed—

      (i) in a case where the requirement arises under sub-paragraph (7) above, no later than the date upon which the first or, as the case may be, the second list is first advertised in accordance with paragraph 5 above; or

      (ii) in a case where the requirement arises under sub-paragraph (8) above, no later than the date falling four weeks before the date specified in the first or, as the case may be, the second list in respect of the site in question as the date by which an application is to be made to the authority under paragraph 9 below; and

   (c) be left in position for at least the period of 21 days from the date when it is first displayed, but where the notice is, without fault or intention of the authority, removed, obscured or defaced before that period has elapsed, that requirement shall be treated as having been complied with if the authority has taken reasonable steps for protection of the notice and, if need be, its replacement.

(10) In sub-paragraphs (7) and (8) above, any reference to a conspicuous object on any land includes, in a case where the person serving a notice considers that there are no or insufficient such objects on the land, a reference to a post driven into or erected upon the land by the person serving the notice for the purpose of having affixed to it the notice in question.

(11) Where the mineral planning authority, being required—

   (a) by sub-paragraph (3) or (6) above to serve a written reminder on any person; or

   (b) by sub-paragraph (8) above to cause a copy of such a reminder to be displayed in the manner set out in that sub-paragraph,

fail to comply with that requirement by the date specified for the purpose, they may at any later time serve or, as the case may be, cause to be displayed, such a written reminder and, in any such case, the date by which an application in relation to the mineral site in question is to be made under paragraph 9 below is the date upon which expires the period of three months from the date when the reminder was served or posted in accordance with the provisions of this sub-paragraph.

Applications for approval of conditions and appeals in cases where the conditions approved are not those proposed

9.—(1) Any person who is the owner of any land, or who is entitled to an interest in a mineral, may, if that land or mineral is or forms part of a dormant site or an active Phase I or II site, apply to the mineral planning authority to determine the conditions to which the relevant planning permissions relating to that site are to be subject.

(2) An application under this paragraph shall be in writing and shall—

    (a) identify the mineral site to which the application relates;

    (b) specify the land or minerals comprised in the site of which the applicant is the owner or, as the case may be, in which the applicant is entitled to an interest;

    (c) identify any relevant planning permissions relating to the site;

    (d) identify, and give an address for, each other person that the applicant knows or, after reasonable inquiry, has cause to believe to be an owner of any land, or entitled to any interest in any mineral, comprised in the site;

    (e) set out the conditions to which the applicant proposes the permissions referred to in paragraph (c) above should be subject; and

    (f) be accompanied by the appropriate certificate (within the meaning of sub-paragraph (3) or (4) below).

(3) For the purposes of sub-paragraph (2) above, as respects England and Wales the appropriate certificate is such a certificate—

    (a) as would be required, under section 65 of the 1990 Act (notice etc. of applications for planning permission) and any provision of a development order made by virtue of that section, to accompany the application if it were an application for planning permission for minerals development, but

    (b) with such modifications as are required for the purposes of this paragraph,

and section 65(6) of that Act (offences) shall also have effect in relation to any certificate purporting to be the appropriate certificate.

(4) For the purposes of sub-paragraph (2) above, the appropriate certificate is, as respects Scotland, each of the certificates which would be required, under or by virtue of sections 23 and 24 of the 1972 Act (notice etc. of applications for planning permission), to accompany the application if it were an application for planning permission for minerals development, but with such modifications as are required for the purposes of this paragraph; and sections 23(3) and 24(5) of that Act (offences) shall have effect in relation to any certificate purporting to be the appropriate certificate.

(5) Section 65 of the 1990 Act or, as respects Scotland, section 24 of the 1972 Act (by virtue of which a development order may provide for publicising applications for planning permission) shall have effect, with any necessary modifications, as if subsection (1) of that section also authorised a development order to provide for publicising applications under this paragraph.

(6) Where the mineral planning authority receive an application under this paragraph in relation to a dormant site or an active Phase I or II site they shall determine the conditions to which each relevant planning permission relating to the site is to be subject; and any such permission shall, from the date when the conditions to which it is to be subject are finally determined, have effect subject to the conditions which are determined under this Schedule as being the conditions to which it is to be subject.

(7) The conditions imposed by virtue of a determination under sub-paragraph (6) above—

   (a) may include any conditions which may be imposed on a grant of planning permission for minerals development;

   (b) may be in addition to, or in substitution for, any existing conditions to which the permission in question is subject.

(8) In determining that a relevant planning permission is to be subject to any condition relating to development for which planning permission is granted by a development order, the mineral planning authority shall have regard to any guidance issued for the purpose by the Secretary of State.

(9) Subject to sub-paragraph (10) below, where, within the period of three months from the mineral planning authority having received an application under this paragraph, or within such extended period as may at any time be agreed upon in writing between the applicant and the authority, the authority have not given notice to the applicant of their decision upon the application, the authority shall be treated as having at the end of that period or, as the case may be, that extended period, determined that the conditions to which any relevant planning permission to which the application relates is to be subject are those specified in the application as being proposed in relation to that permission; and any such permission shall, from that time, have effect subject to those conditions.

(10) Where a mineral planning authority, having received an application under this paragraph, are of the opinion that they are unable to determine the application unless further details are supplied to them, they shall within the period of one month from having received the application give notice to the applicant—

   (a) stating that they are of such opinion; and

   (b) specifying the further details which they require,

and where the authority so serve such a notice the period of three months referred to in sub-paragraph (9) above shall run not from the authority having received the application but from the time when the authority have received all the further details specified in the notice.

(11) Without prejudice to the generality of sub-paragraph (10) above, the further details which may be specified in a notice under that sub-paragraph include any—

   (a) information, plans or drawings; or

   (b) evidence verifying any particulars of details supplied to the authority in respect of the application in question,

which it is reasonable for the authority to request for the purpose of enabling them to determine the application.

Notice of determination of conditions to be accompanied by additional information in certain cases

10.—(1) This paragraph applies in a case where—

   (a) on an application made to the mineral planning authority under paragraph 9 above in respect of an active Phase I or II site the authority determine under that paragraph the conditions to which the relevant planning permissions relating to the site are to be subject;

   (b) those conditions differ in any respect from the proposed conditions set out in the application; and

   (c) the effect of the conditions, other than any restoration or aftercare conditions, so determined by the authority, as compared with the effect of the conditions, other than any restoration or aftercare conditions, to which the relevant planning permissions in question were subject immediately prior to the authority making the determination, is to restrict working rights in respect of the site.

(2) In a case where this paragraph applies, the mineral planning authority shall, upon giving to the applicant notice of the conditions determined by the authority under paragraph 9 above, also give to the applicant notice—

    (a) stating that the conditions determined by the authority differ in some respect from the proposed conditions set out in the application;

    (b) stating that the effect of the conditions, other than any restoration or aftercare conditions, determined by the authority, as compared with the effect of the conditions, other than any restoration or aftercare conditions, to which the relevant planning permissions relating to the site in question were subject immediately prior to the making of the authority's determination, is to restrict working rights in respect of the site;

    (c) identifying the working rights so restricted; and

    (d) stating whether, in the opinion of the authority, the effect of that restriction of working rights would be such as to prejudice adversely to an unreasonable degree—

        (i) the economic viability of operating the site; or

        (ii) the asset value of the site.

(3) In determining whether, in their opinion, the effect of that restriction of working rights would be such as is mentioned in sub-paragraph (2)(d) above, a mineral planning authority shall have regard to any guidance issued for the purpose by the Secretary of State.

(4) In this paragraph, "the applicant" means the person who made the application in question under paragraph 9 above.

Right to appeal against mineral planning authority's determination of conditions etc.

11.—(1) Where the mineral planning authority—

    (a) on an application under paragraph 9 above determine under that paragraph conditions that differ in any respect from the proposed conditions set out in the application; or

    (b) give notice, under paragraph (d) of paragraph 10(2) above, stating that, in their opinion, the restriction of working rights in question would not be such as to prejudice adversely to an unreasonable degree either of the matters referred to in sub-paragraphs (i) and (ii) of the said paragraph (d),

the person who made the application may appeal to the Secretary of State.

(2) An appeal under sub-paragraph (1) above must be made by giving notice of appeal to the Secretary of State before the end of the period of six months beginning with the date on which the authority give notice to the applicant of their determination or, as the case may be, stating their opinion.

Permissions ceasing to have effect

12.—(1) Subject to paragraph 8(11) above, where no application under paragraph 9 above in respect of an active Phase I or II site has been served on the mineral planning authority by the date specified in the first or, as the case may be, the second list as the date by which applications under that paragraph in respect of that site are to be made, or by such later date as may at any time be agreed upon in writing between the applicant and the authority, each relevant planning permission relating to the site shall cease to have effect, except insofar as it imposes any restoration or aftercare condition, on the day following the last date on which such an application may be made.

(2) The reference in sub-paragraph (1) above to the date specified in the first or, as the case may be, the second list as the date by which applications under

paragraph 9 above are to be made in respect of any Phase I or II site is a reference to the date specified for that purpose in respect of that site in that list as prepared by the mineral planning authority or, where that date has been varied by virtue of any provision of this Schedule, to that date as so varied.

(3) Subject to sub-paragraph (4) below, no relevant planning permission which relates to a dormant site shall have effect to authorise the carrying out of minerals development unless—

>   (a) an application has been made under paragraph 9 above in respect of that site; and

>   (b) that permission has effect in accordance with sub-paragraph (6) of that paragraph.

(4) A relevant planning permission which relates to a Phase I or II site not included in the first list shall cease to have effect, except insofar as it imposes any restoration or aftercare condition, on the day following the last date on which an application under sub-paragraph (1) of paragraph 6 above may be made in respect of that site unless an application has been made under that sub-paragraph by that date in which event, unless the site is added to that list, such a permission shall cease to have effect when the following conditions are met—

>   (a) the proceedings on that application, including any proceedings on or in consequence of the application under section 288 of the 1990 Act or, as the case may be, section 233 of the 1972 Act, have been determined, and

>   (b) any time for appealing under paragraph 6(11) or (12) above, or applying or further applying under paragraph 6(1) above, (where there is a right to do so) has expired.

Reference of applications to the Secretary of State

13.—(1) The Secretary of State may give directions requiring applications under paragraph 9 above to any mineral planning authority to be referred to him for determination instead of being dealt with by the authority.

(2) Any such direction may relate either to a particular application or to applications of a class specified in the direction.

(3) Where an application is referred to the Secretary of State in accordance with such a direction—

>   (a) subject to paragraph (b) below, the following provisions of this Schedule—

>>   (i) paragraph 9(6) and (7),

>>   (ii) paragraph 10, and

>>   (iii) paragraph 14 so far as relating to applications under paragraph 9 above,

>   shall apply, with any necessary modifications, as they apply to applications which fall to be determined by the mineral planning authority;

>   (b) before determining the application the Secretary of State must, if either the applicant or the mineral planning authority so wish, give each of them an opportunity of appearing before and being heard by a person appointed by the Secretary of State for the purpose; and

>   (c) the decision of the Secretary of State on the application shall be final.

Two or more applicants

14.—(1) Where a mineral planning authority has received from any person a duly made application under paragraph 7(1) or 9 above—

>   (a) that person may not make any further application under the paragraph in question in respect of the same site; and

    (b) if the application has been determined, whether or not in the case of an application under paragraph 9 above it has been finally determined, no other person may make an application under the paragraph in question in respect of the same site.

(2) Where—

    (a) a mineral planning authority has received from any person in respect of a mineral site a duly made application under paragraph 7(1) or 9 above; and

    (b) the authority receives from another person a duly made application under the paragraph in question in respect of the same site,

then for the purpose of the determination of the applications and any appeal against such a determination, this Schedule shall have effect as if the applications were a single application received by the authority on the date on which the later application was received by the authority and references to the applicant shall be read as references to either or any of the applicants.

Compensation

15.—(1) This paragraph applies in a case where—

    (a) an application made under paragraph 9 above in respect of an active Phase I or II site is finally determined; and

    (b) the requirements of either sub-paragraph (2) or (3) below are satisfied.

(2) The requirements, referred to in sub-paragraph (1)(b) above, of this sub-paragraph are—

    (a) that the conditions to which the relevant planning permissions relating to the site are to be subject were determined by the mineral planning authority;

    (b) no appeal was made under paragraph 11(1)(a) above in respect of that determination or any such appeal was withdrawn or dismissed; and

    (c) the authority gave notice under paragraph (d) of paragraph 10(2) above and either—

        (i) that notice stated that, in the authority's opinion, the restriction of working rights in question would be such as to prejudice adversely to an unreasonable degree either of the matters referred to in sub-paragraphs (i) and (ii) of the said paragraph (d); or

        (ii) that notice stated that, in the authority's opinion, the restriction in question would not be such as would so prejudice either of those matters but an appeal under paragraph 11(1) above in respect of the giving of the notice has been allowed.

(3) The requirements, referred to in sub-paragraph (1)(b) above, of this sub-paragraph are that the conditions to which the relevant planning permissions are to be subject were determined by the Secretary of State (whether upon an appeal under paragraph 11(1)(a) above or upon a reference under paragraph 13 above) and—

    (a) in a case where those conditions were determined upon an appeal under paragraph 11(1)(a) above either—

        (i) the mineral planning authority gave notice under paragraph (d) of paragraph 10(2) above stating that, in their opinion, the restriction of working rights in question would be such as to prejudice adversely to an unreasonable degree either of the matters referred to in sub-paragraphs (i) and (ii) of the said paragraph (d), or

   (ii) the authority gave a notice under the said paragraph (d) stating that, in their opinion, the restriction in question would not be such as would so prejudice either of those matters but an appeal under paragraph 11(1)(b) above in respect of the giving of that notice has been allowed;

  or

 (b) in a case where those conditions were determined upon a reference under paragraph 13 above, the Secretary of State gave notice under paragraph (d) of paragraph 10(2) above stating that, in his opinion, the restriction of working rights in question would be such as to prejudice adversely to an unreasonable degree either of the matters referred to in sub-paragraphs (i) and (ii) of the said paragraph (d).

(4) In a case to which this paragraph applies—

 (a) as respects England and Wales, Parts IV and XI of the 1990 Act, or

 (b) as respects Scotland, Parts VIII and XI of the 1972 Act,

shall have effect as if an order made under section 97 of the 1990 Act or, as the case may be, section 42 of the 1972 Act, had been confirmed by the Secretary of State under section 98 of the 1990 Act or, as the case may be, section 42 of the 1972 Act at the time when the application in question was finally determined and, as so confirmed, had effect to modify those permissions to the extent specified in sub-paragraph (5) below.

(5) For the purposes of sub-paragraph (4) above, the order which is treated by virtue of that sub-paragraph as having been made under section 97 of the 1990 Act or section 42 of the 1972 Act is one whose only effect adverse to the interests of any person having an interest in the land or minerals comprised in the mineral site is to restrict working rights in respect of the site to the same extent as the relevant restriction.

(6) For the purposes of section 116 of the 1990 Act and section 167A of the 1972 Act and of any regulations made under those sections, the permissions treated as being modified by the order mentioned in sub-paragraph (4) above shall be treated as if they were planning permissions for development which neither consists of nor includes any minerals development.

Appeals: general procedural provisions

16.—(1) This paragraph applies to appeals under any of the following provisions of this Schedule—

 (a) paragraph 6(11) or (12) above; or

 (b) paragraph 11(1) above.

(2) Notice of appeal in respect of an appeal to which this paragraph applies shall be given on a form supplied by or on behalf of the Secretary of State for use for that purpose, and giving, so far as reasonably practicable, the information required by that form.

(3) Paragraph 6 of Schedule 2 to the 1991 Act (determination of appeals) shall, as respects England and Wales, apply to an appeal to which this paragraph applies as it applies to an appeal under paragraph 5 of that Schedule.

(4) As respects England and Wales, sections 284 to 288 of the 1990 Act (validity of certain decisions and proceedings for questioning their validity) shall have effect as if the action mentioned in section 284(3) of that Act included any decision of the Secretary of State—

 (a) on an appeal to which this paragraph applies; or

 (b) on an application under paragraph 9 above referred to him under paragraph 13 above.

(5) Paragraph 6 of Schedule 10A to the 1972 Act (determination of appeals) shall, as respects Scotland, apply to an appeal to which this paragraph applies as it applies to appeals under paragraph 5 of that Schedule.

(6) As respects Scotland, sections 231 to 233 of the 1972 Act (validity of certain decisions and proceedings for questioning their validity) shall have effect as if the action mentioned in section 231(3) included any decision of the Secretary of State—

(a) on an appeal to which this paragraph applies; or

(b) on an application under paragraph 9 above referred to him under paragraph 13 above.

(7) As respects Scotland, Schedule 7 to the 1972 Act shall apply to appeals to which this paragraph applies.

Section 96.

SCHEDULE 14

Periodic Review of Mineral Planning Permissions

Duty to carry out periodic reviews

1. The mineral planning authority shall, in accordance with the provisions of this Schedule, cause periodic reviews to be carried out of the mineral permissions relating to a mining site.

Interpretation

2.—(1) For the purposes of this Schedule—

"first review date", in relation to a mining site, shall, subject to paragraph 5 below, be ascertained in accordance with paragraph 3 below;

"mineral permission" means any planning permission, other than a planning permission granted by a development order, for minerals development;

"mineral planning authority"—

(a) as respects England and Wales, means a mineral planning authority within the meaning of the 1990 Act, and

(b) as respects Scotland, means a planning authority for the purposes of the 1972 Act;

"mining site" means—

(a) in a case where it appears to the mineral planning authority to be expedient to treat as a single site the aggregate of the land to which any two or more mineral permissions relate, the aggregate of the land to which those permissions relate; and

(b) in any other case, the land to which a mineral permission relates;

"old mining permission" has the meaning given—

(a) as respects England and Wales, by section 22(1) of the 1991 Act, and

(b) as respects Scotland, by section 49H(1) of the 1972 Act; and

"owner", in relation to any land—

(a) as respects England and Wales, means any person who—

(i) is the estate owner in respect of the fee simple, or

(ii) is entitled to a tenancy granted or extended for a term of years certain of which not less than seven years remains unexpired; and

(b) as respects Scotland, has the meaning given by paragraph 10(1) of Schedule 10A to the 1972 Act.

(2) In determining whether it appears to them to be expedient to treat as a single site the aggregate of the land to which two or more mineral permissions relate a mineral planning authority shall have regard to any guidance issued for the purpose by the Secretary of State.

(3) Any reference (however expressed) in this Schedule to a mining site being a site to which relates—

(a) an old mining permission; or

(b) a mineral permission,

is a reference to the mining site, or some part of it, being the land to which the permission relates.

(4) For the purposes of this Schedule, an application made under paragraph 6 below is finally determined when—

(a) the proceedings on the application, including any proceedings on or in consequence of an application under section 288 of the 1990 Act or section 233 of the 1972 Act, have been determined, and

(b) any time for appealing under paragraph 9(1) below, or applying or further applying under paragraph 6 below, (where there is a right to do so) has expired.

The first review date

3.—(1) Subject to sub-paragraph (7) below, in a case where the mineral permissions relating to a mining site include an old mining permission, the first review date means—

(a) the date falling fifteen years after the date upon which, pursuant to an application made under paragraph 2 of Schedule 2 to the 1991 Act or, as the case may be, paragraph 2 of Schedule 10A to the 1972 Act, the conditions to which that old mining permission is to be subject are finally determined under that Schedule; or

(b) where there are two or more old mining permissions relating to that site, and the date upon which those conditions are finally determined is not the same date for each of those permissions, the date falling fifteen years after the date upon which was made the last such final determination to be so made in respect of any of those permissions,

and paragraph 10(2) of Schedule 2 to the 1991 Act or, as the case may be, paragraph 10(2) of Schedule 10A to the 1972 Act (meaning of "finally determined") shall apply for the purposes of this sub-paragraph as it applies for the purposes of section 22 of and Schedule 2 to the 1991 Act or, as the case may be, section 49H of and Schedule 10A to the 1972 Act.

(2) Subject to sub-paragraph (7) below, in the case of a mining site which is a Phase I or II site within the meaning of Schedule 13 to this Act, the first review date means the date falling fifteen years after the date upon which, pursuant to an application made under paragraph 9 of that Schedule, there is determined under that paragraph the conditions to which the relevant planning permissions (within the meaning of that Schedule) relating to the site are to be subject.

(3) Subject to sub-paragraphs (4) and (7) below, in the case of a mining site—

(a) which is not a Phase I or II site within the meaning of Schedule 13 to this Act; and

(b) to which no old mining permission relates,

the first review date is the date falling fifteen years after the date upon which was granted the most recent mineral permission which relates to the site.

(4) Where, in the case of a mining site falling within sub-paragraph (3) above, the most recent mineral permission relating to that site relates, or the most recent such permissions (whether or not granted on the same date) between them relate, to part only of the site, and in the opinion of the mineral planning authority it is expedient, for the purpose of ascertaining, under that sub-paragraph, the first review date in respect of that site, to treat that permission or those permissions as having been granted at the same time as the last of the other mineral permissions relating to the site, the first review date for that site shall be ascertained under that sub-paragraph accordingly.

(5) A mineral planning authority shall, in deciding whether they are of such an opinion as is mentioned in sub-paragraph (4) above, have regard to any guidance issued by the Secretary of State for the purpose.

(6) Subject to sub-paragraph (7) below, in the case of a mining site—

(a) to which relates a mineral permission in respect of which an order has been made under section 97 of the 1990 Act or section 42 of the 1972 Act, or

(b) in respect of which, or any part of which, an order has been made under paragraph 1 of Schedule 9 to the 1990 Act or section 49 of the 1972 Act,

the first review date shall be the date falling fifteen years after the date upon which the order took effect or, in a case where there is more than one such order, upon which the last of those orders to take effect took effect.

(7) In the case of a mining site for which the preceding provisions of this paragraph have effect to specify two or more different dates as the first review date, the first review date shall be the latest of those dates.

Service of notice of first periodic review

4.—(1) The mineral planning authority shall, in connection with the first periodic review of the mineral permissions relating to a mining site, no later than 12 months before the first review date, serve notice upon each person appearing to them to be the owner of any land, or entitled to an interest in any mineral, included in that site.

(2) A notice required to be served under sub-paragraph (1) above shall—

(a) specify the mining site to which it relates;

(b) identify the mineral permissions relating to that site;

(c) state the first review date;

(d) state that the first review date is the date by which an application must be made for approval of the conditions to which the mineral permissions relating to the site are to be subject and explain the consequences which will occur if no such application is made by that date; and

(e) explain the right to apply for postponement of the first review date and give the date by which such an application has to be made.

(3) Where, in relation to any land or mineral included in a mining site, the mineral planning authority—

(a) has served notice on any person under sub-paragraph (1) above; and

(b) has received no application under paragraph 6 below from that person by the date falling eight weeks before the first review date,

the authority shall serve a written reminder on that person.

(4) A reminder required to be served under sub-paragraph (3) above shall—

(a) indicate that the land or mineral in question is included in a mining site;

(b) comply with the requirements of sub-paragraph (2)(a) to (d) above; and

(c) be served on the person in question on or before the date falling four weeks before the first review date.

(5) Sub-paragraph (1) above shall not require the mineral planning authority to serve notice under that sub-paragraph upon any person whose identity or address for service is not known to and cannot practicably, after reasonable inquiry, be ascertained by them, but in any such case the authority shall cause to be firmly affixed, to each of one or more conspicuous objects on the land or, as the case may be, on the surface of the land above the interest in question, a copy of the notice which they would (apart from the provisions of this sub-paragraph) have had to serve under that sub-paragraph on the owner of that land or interest.

(6) If, in a case where sub-paragraph (5) above applies, no person makes an application to the authority under paragraph 6 below in respect of the mining site which includes the land or interest in question by the date falling eight weeks before the first review date, the authority shall cause to be firmly affixed, to each of one or more conspicuous objects on the land or, as the case may be, on the surface of the land above the interest in question, a copy of the written reminder that would, in a case not falling within sub-paragraph (5) above, have been served under sub-paragraph (3) above.

(7) Where by sub-paragraph (5) or (6) above a copy of any notice is required to be affixed to an object on any land that copy shall—

(a) be displayed in such a way as to be easily visible and legible;

(b) be first displayed—

(i) in a case where the requirement arises under sub-paragraph (5) above, no later than 12 months before the first review date; or

(ii) in a case where the requirement arises under sub-paragraph (6) above, no later than the date falling four weeks before the first review date;

and

(c) be left in position for at least the period of 21 days from the date when it is first displayed, but where the notice is, without fault or intention of the authority, removed, obscured or defaced before that period has elapsed, that requirement shall be treated as having been complied with if the authority has taken reasonable steps for protection of the notice and, if need be, its replacement.

(8) In sub-paragraphs (5) and (6) above, any reference to a conspicuous object on any land includes, in a case where the person serving a notice considers that there are no or insufficient such objects on the land, a reference to a post driven into or erected upon the land by the person serving the notice for the purpose of having affixed to it a copy of the notice in question.

Application for postponement of the first review date

5.—(1) Any person who is the owner of any land, or of any interest in any mineral, comprised in a mining site may, no later than the day upon which expires the period of three months from the day upon which notice was served upon him under paragraph 4 above, apply under this paragraph to the mineral planning authority for the postponement of the first review date.

(2) An application under this paragraph shall be in writing and shall set out—

(a) the conditions to which each mineral permission relating to the site is subject;

(b) the applicant's reasons for considering those conditions to be satisfactory; and

(c) the date which the applicant wishes to have substituted for the first review date.

(3) Where the mineral planning authority receive an application made under this paragraph—

    (a) if they consider the conditions referred to in sub-paragraph (2)(a) above to be satisfactory they shall agree to the first review date being postponed in which event they shall determine the date to be substituted for that date;

    (b) in any other case they shall refuse the application.

(4) When a mineral planning authority determine an application made under this paragraph, they shall notify the applicant in writing of their decision and, in a case where they have agreed to the postponement of the first review date, shall notify the applicant of the date which they have determined should be substituted for the first review date.

(5) Where, within the period of three months of the mineral planning authority having received an application under this paragraph, or within such extended period as may at any time be agreed upon in writing between the applicant and the authority, the authority have not given notice, under sub-paragraph (4) above, to the applicant of their decision upon the application, the authority shall be treated as having, at the end of that period or, as the case may be, that extended period—

    (a) agreed to the first review date being postponed; and

    (b) determined that the date referred to in sub-paragraph (2)(c) above be substituted for the first review date.

Application to determine the conditions to which the mineral permissions relating to a mining site are to be subject

6.—(1) Any person who is the owner of any land, or who is entitled to an interest in a mineral, may, if that land or mineral is or forms part of a mining site, apply to the mineral planning authority to determine the conditions to which the mineral permissions relating to that site are to be subject.

(2) An application under this paragraph shall be in writing and shall—

    (a) identify the mining site in respect of which the application is made and state that the application is made in connection with the first periodic review of the mineral permissions relating to that site;

    (b) specify the land or minerals comprised in the site of which the applicant is the owner or, as the case may be, in which the applicant is entitled to an interest;

    (c) identify the mineral permissions relating to the site;

    (d) identify, and give an address for, each other person that the applicant knows or, after reasonable inquiry, has cause to believe to be an owner of any land, or entitled to any interest in any mineral, comprised in the site;

    (e) set out the conditions to which the applicant proposes the permissions referred to in paragraph (c) above should be subject; and

    (f) be accompanied by the appropriate certificate (within the meaning of sub-paragraph (3) or (4) below).

(3) For the purposes of sub-paragraph (2) above, as respects England and Wales the appropriate certificate is such a certificate—

    (a) as would be required, under section 65 of the 1990 Act and any provision of a development order made by virtue of that section, to accompany the application if it were an application for planning permission for minerals development, but

(b) with such modifications as are required for the purposes of this paragraph,

and section 65(6) of the 1990 Act shall also have effect in relation to any certificate purporting to be the appropriate certificate.

(4) For the purposes of sub-paragraph (2) above, the appropriate certificate is, as respects Scotland, each of the certificates which would be required, under or by virtue of sections 23 and 24 of the 1972 Act (notice etc. of applications for planning permission), to accompany the application if it were an application for planning permission for minerals development, but with such modifications as are required for the purposes of this paragraph; and sections 23(3) and 24(5) of that Act (offences) shall have effect in relation to any certificate purporting to be the appropriate certificate.

(5) Where the mineral planning authority receive an application under this paragraph in relation to a mining site they shall determine the conditions to which each mineral permission relating to the site is to be subject.

(6) The conditions imposed by virtue of a determination under sub-paragraph (5) above—

(a) may include any conditions which may be imposed on a grant of planning permission for minerals development;

(b) may be in addition to, or in substitution for, any existing conditions to which the permission in question is subject.

(7) In determining that a mineral permission is to be subject to any condition relating to development for which planning permission is granted by a development order, the mineral planning authority shall have regard to any guidance issued for the purpose by the Secretary of State.

(8) Subject to sub-paragraph (9) below, where, within the period of three months of the mineral planning authority having received an application under this paragraph, or within such extended period as may at any time be agreed upon in writing between the applicant and the authority, the authority have not given notice to the applicant of their decision upon the application, the authority shall be treated as having at the end of that period or, as the case may be, that extended period, determined that the conditions to which any mineral permission to which the application relates is to be subject are those specified in the application as being proposed in relation to that permission; and any such permission shall, from that time, have effect subject to those conditions.

(9) Where a mineral planning authority, having received an application under this paragraph, are of the opinion that they are unable to determine the application unless further details are supplied to them, they shall within the period of one month from having received the application give notice to the applicant—

(a) stating that they are of such opinion; and

(b) specifying the further details which they require,

and where the authority so serve such a notice the period of three months referred to in sub-paragraph (8) above shall run not from the authority having received the application but from the time when the authority have received all the further details specified in the notice.

(10) Without prejudice to the generality of sub-paragraph (9) above, the further details which may be specified in a notice under that sub-paragraph include any—

(a) information, plans or drawings; or

(b) evidence verifying any particulars of details supplied to the authority in respect of the application in question,

which it is reasonable for the authority to request for the purpose of enabling them to determine the application.

Permissions ceasing to have effect

7. Where no application under paragraph 6 above in respect of a mining site has been served on the mineral planning authority by the first review date, or by such later date as may at any time be agreed upon in writing between the applicant and the authority, each mineral permission—

    (a) relating to the site; and

    (b) identified in the notice served in relation to the site under paragraph 4 above,

shall cease to have effect, except insofar as it imposes any restoration or aftercare condition, on the day following the first review date or, as the case may be, such later agreed date.

Reference of applications to the Secretary of State

8.—(1) The Secretary of State may give directions requiring applications made under paragraph 6 above to any mineral planning authority to be referred to him for determination instead of being dealt with by the authority.

(2) A direction under sub-paragraph (1) above may relate either to a particular application or to applications of a class specified in the direction.

(3) Where an application is referred to the Secretary of State in accordance with a direction under sub-paragraph (1) above—

    (a) subject to paragraph (b) below, paragraph 6(5) and (6) above, and paragraph 11 below so far as relating to applications under paragraph 6 above, shall apply, with any necessary modifications, to his determination of the application as they apply to the determination of applications by the mineral planning authority;

    (b) before determining the application the Secretary of State must, if either the applicant or the mineral planning authority so wish, give each of them an opportunity of appearing before and being heard by a person appointed by the Secretary of State for the purpose; and

    (c) the decision of the Secretary of State on the application shall be final.

Appeals

9.—(1) Where on an application under paragraph 6 above the mineral planning authority determine conditions that differ in any respect from the proposed conditions set out in the application, the applicant may appeal to the Secretary of State.

(2) An appeal under sub-paragraph (1) above must be made by giving notice of appeal to the Secretary of State, before the end of the period of six months beginning with the determination, on a form supplied by or on behalf of the Secretary of State for use for that purpose, and giving, so far as reasonably practicable, the information required by that form.

(3) Paragraph 6 of Schedule 2 to the 1991 Act (determination of appeals) shall, as respects England and Wales, apply to appeals under sub-paragraph (1) above as it applies to appeals under paragraph 5 of that Schedule.

(4) As respects England and Wales, sections 284 to 288 of the 1990 Act shall have effect as if the action mentioned in section 284(3) of that Act included any decision of the Secretary of State—

    (a) on an appeal under sub-paragraph (1) above; or

    (b) on an application under paragraph 6 above referred to him under paragraph 8 above.

(5) Paragraph 6 of Schedule 10A to the 1972 Act (determination of appeals) shall, as respects Scotland, apply to appeals under sub-paragraph (1) above as it applies to appeals under paragraph 5 of that Schedule.

(6) As respects Scotland, sections 231 to 233 of the 1972 Act shall have effect as if the action mentioned in section 231(3) included any decision of the Secretary of State—

(a) on an appeal under sub-paragraph (1) above; or

(b) on an application under paragraph 6 above referred to him under paragraph 8 above.

(7) As respects Scotland, Schedule 7 to the 1972 Act shall apply to appeals under sub-paragraph (1) above.

Time from which conditions determined under this Schedule are to take effect

10.—(1) Where an application has been made under paragraph 6 above in respect of a mining site, each of the mineral permissions relating to the site shall, from the time when the application is finally determined, have effect subject to the conditions to which it is determined under this Schedule that that permission is to be subject.

(2) Sub-paragraph (1) above is without prejudice to paragraph 6(8) above.

Two or more applicants

11.—(1) Where a mineral planning authority have received from any person a duly made application under paragraph 5 or 6 above—

(a) that person may not make any further application under the paragraph in question in respect of the same site; and

(b) if the application has been determined, whether or not in the case of an application under paragraph 6 above it has been finally determined, no other person may make an application under the paragraph in question in respect of the same site.

(2) Where—

(a) a mineral planning authority have received from any person in respect of a mineral site a duly made application under paragraph 5 or 6 above; and

(b) the authority receives from another person a duly made application under the paragraph in question in respect of the same site,

then for the purpose of the determination of the applications and any appeal against such a determination, this Schedule shall have effect as if the applications were a single application received by the authority on the date on which the later application was received by the authority and references to the applicant shall be read as references to either or any of the applicants.

Second and subsequent periodic reviews

12.—(1) In this paragraph, in relation to a mining site, but subject to paragraph 5 above as applied by sub-paragraph (2) below, "review date" means—

(a) in the case of the second periodic review, the date falling fifteen years after the date upon which was finally determined an application made under paragraph 6 above in respect of the site; and

(b) in the case of subsequent periodic reviews, the date falling fifteen years after the date upon which there was last finally determined under this Schedule an application made in respect of that site under paragraph 6 above as applied by sub-paragraph (2) below.

(2) Paragraphs 4 to 11 above shall apply in respect of the second or any subsequent periodic review of the mineral permissions relating to a mining site as they apply to the first such periodic review, but as if—

(a) any reference in those paragraphs to the "first review date" were a reference to the review date; and

(b) the references in paragraphs 4(1) and 6(2)(a) above to the first periodic review were references to the periodic review in question.

Compensation

13.—(1) This paragraph applies where—

(a) an application made under paragraph 6 above in respect of a mining site is finally determined; and

(b) the conditions to which the mineral permissions relating to the site are to be subject, as determined under this Schedule, differ in any respect from the proposed conditions set out in the application; and

(c) the effect of the new conditions, except insofar as they are restoration or aftercare conditions, as compared with the effect of the existing conditions, except insofar as they were restoration or aftercare conditions, is to restrict working rights in respect of the site.

(2) For the purposes of this paragraph—

"the new conditions", in relation to a mining site, means the conditions, determined under this Schedule, to which the mineral permissions relating to the site are to be subject; and

"the existing conditions", in relation to a mining site, means the conditions to which the mineral permissions relating to the site were subject immediately prior to the final determination of the application made under paragraph 6 above in respect of that site.

(3) For the purposes of this paragraph, working rights are restricted in respect of a mining site if any of—

(a) the size of the area which may be used for the winning and working of minerals or the depositing of mineral waste;

(b) the depth to which operations for the winning and working of minerals may extend;

(c) the height of any deposit of mineral waste;

(d) the rate at which any particular mineral may be extracted;

(e) the rate at which any particular mineral waste may be deposited;

(f) the period at the expiry of which any winning or working of minerals or depositing of mineral waste is to cease; or

(g) the total quantity of minerals which may be extracted from, or of mineral waste which may be deposited on, the site,

is restricted or reduced in respect of the mining site in question.

(4) In a case to which this paragraph applies, but subject to sub-paragraph (6) below, as respects England and Wales, Parts IV and XI of the 1990 Act and, as respects Scotland, Parts VIII and XI of the 1972 Act, shall have effect as if an order made under section 97 of the 1990 Act or, as the case may be, section 42 of the 1972 Act—

(a) had been confirmed by the Secretary of State under section 98 of the 1990 Act or, as the case may be, section 42 of the 1972 Act at the time when the application in question was finally determined; and

(b) as so confirmed, had effect to modify those permissions to the extent specified in sub-paragraph (6) below.

(5) For the purposes of this paragraph, the order referred to in sub-paragraph (4) above is one whose only effect adverse to the interests of any person having an interest in the land or minerals comprised in the mineral site is to restrict working rights in respect of the site to the same extent as the relevant restriction.

(6) For the purposes of section 116 of the 1990 Act and section 167A of the 1972 Act and of any regulations made under those sections, the permissions treated as being modified by the order mentioned in sub-paragraph (4) above shall be treated as if they were planning permissions for development which neither consists of nor includes any minerals development.

SCHEDULE 15

MINOR AND CONSEQUENTIAL AMENDMENTS RELATING TO FISHERIES

Interpretation

1. In this Schedule—

"local statutory provision" means—

    (a) a provision of a local Act (including an Act confirming a provisional order);

    (b) a provision of so much of any public general Act as has effect with respect to particular persons or works or with respect to particular provisions falling within any paragraph of this definition;

    (c) a provision of an instrument made under any provision falling within paragraph (a) or (b) above;

    (d) a provision of any other instrument which is in the nature of a local enactment;

"the Minister" means the Minister of Agriculture, Fisheries and Food;

"subordinate legislation" has the same meaning as in the Interpretation Act 1978;

                                              1978 c. 30.

"the transfer date" has the same meaning as in Part I of this Act.

General modifications of references to the National Rivers Authority

2.—(1) Subject to—

(a) the following provisions of this Schedule,

(b) the provisions of sections 102 to 104 of this Act, and

(c) any repeal made by this Act,

any provision to which this paragraph applies which contains, or falls to be construed as containing, a reference (however framed and whether or not in relation to an area) to the National Rivers Authority shall have effect on and after the transfer date as if that reference were a reference to the Agency.

(2) Sub-paragraph (1) above is subject to paragraph 1(2)(a) of Schedule 17 to the Water Act 1989 (references in certain local statutory provisions or subordinate legislation to the area of a particular water authority to have effect as references to the area which, immediately before the transfer date within the meaning of that Act, was the area of that authority for the purposes of their functions relating to fisheries).

                                              1989 c. 15.

(3) Subject as mentioned in sub-paragraph (1) above, any provision to which this paragraph applies which contains, or falls to be construed as containing, a reference (however framed) to the whole area in relation to which the National Rivers Authority carries out its functions in relation to fisheries shall have effect on and after the transfer date as if that reference were a reference to the whole area in relation to which the Agency carries out its functions relating to fisheries.

(4) The provisions to which this paragraph applies are the provisions of—

(a) the Sea Fisheries Regulation Act 1966;   1966 c. 38.

(b) the Salmon and Freshwater Fisheries Act 1975; and   1975 c. 51.

(c) any local statutory provision or subordinate legislation which is in force immediately before the transfer date and—

 (i) relates to the carrying out by the National Rivers Authority of any function relating to fisheries; or

1937 c. 33. (ii) in the case of subordinate legislation, was made by virtue of any provision to which this paragraph applies or under the Diseases of Fish Act 1937.

(5) The modifications made by this paragraph shall be subject to any power by subordinate legislation to revoke or amend any provision to which this paragraph applies; and, accordingly, any such power, including the powers conferred by section 121 of this Act and paragraph 3 below, shall be exercisable so as to exclude the operation of this paragraph in relation to the provisions in relation to which the power is conferred.

Power to amend subordinate legislation etc.

3.—(1) If it appears to the Minister or the Secretary of State to be appropriate to do so for the purposes of, or in consequence of, the coming into force of any provision of this Schedule, he may by order revoke or amend any subordinate legislation.

(2) An order under this paragraph may—

(a) make different provision for different cases, including different provision in relation to different persons, circumstances or localities; and

(b) contain such supplemental, consequential and transitional provision as the Minister or the Secretary of State considers appropriate.

(3) The power conferred by virtue of this paragraph in relation to subordinate legislation made under any enactment shall be without prejudice to any other power to revoke or amend subordinate legislation made under that enactment, but—

(a) no requirement imposed with respect to the exercise of any such other power shall apply in relation to any revocation or amendment of that legislation by an order under this paragraph; and

(b) the power to make an order under this paragraph shall be exercisable (instead of in accordance with any such requirement) by statutory instrument subject to annulment in pursuance of a resolution of either House of Parliament.

The Diseases of Fish Act 1937

4.—(1) Subject to sub-paragraph (2) below, in the Diseases of Fish Act 1937—

(a) any reference which to any extent is, or falls to be construed as, a reference to the National Rivers Authority shall have effect, in relation to the area which by virtue of section 6(7) of this Act is the area in relation to which the Agency carries out functions under that Act, as a reference to the Agency; and

1991 c. 57. (b) references to an area (including references which fall to be construed as references to the area which by virtue of subsection (6) of section 2 of the Water Resources Act 1991 is the area in relation to which the National Rivers Authority carries out functions under the said Act of 1937), in relation to the Agency, shall have effect as references to the area described in paragraph (a) above.

(2) In section 8(3) of the said Act of 1937 (offences in relation to the Esk) for the words "National Rivers Authority" there shall be substituted the words "Environment Agency".

(3) Nothing in this paragraph or in that Act shall authorise the Agency to take legal proceedings in Scotland in respect of any offence.

The Sea Fisheries Regulation Act 1966

5.—(1) The provisions of section 1 of the Sea Fisheries Regulation Act 1966 (establishment of fisheries committees) which provide that an order under that section modifying a previous such order is to be made only on such an application and after such consultation as is mentioned in that section shall not apply to an order under that section which contains a statement that the only provision made by the order is provision which appears to the Minister making the order to be appropriate in consequence of any of the provisions of this Act. {1966 c. 38.}

(2) In section 2(2) of that Act (constitution of local fisheries committee) for the words "the National Rivers Authority" there shall be substituted the words "the Environment Agency".

(3) In section 18(3) of that Act (provision where a water authority or harbour authority have the powers of a local fisheries committee) for the words "National Rivers Authority)" there shall be substituted the words "Environment Agency)".

The Sea Fish (Conservation) Act 1967

6. In section 18(1) of the Sea Fish (Conservation) Act 1967 (enforcement of orders relating to salmon and migratory trout)— {1967 c. 84.}

    (a) for the words "subsection (6) of section 2 of the Water Resources Act 1991" there shall be substituted the words "subsection (7) of section 6 of the Environment Act 1995"; and

    (b) for the words "the National Rivers Authority" there shall be substituted the words "the Environment Agency".

The Salmon and Freshwater Fisheries Act 1975

7. In section 5 of the Salmon and Freshwater Fisheries Act 1975 (prohibition of use of explosives, poisons, electrical devices etc) in subsection (2), the words following paragraph (b) (which require Ministerial approval for the giving of permission to use noxious substances) shall be omitted. {1975 c. 51.}

8. In section 6(3) of that Act (definition of "unauthorised fixed engine") in paragraph (d) for the words "the National Rivers Authority" there shall be substituted the words "the Agency".

9. In section 8(2) of that Act (fishing mill dams to have attached to them fish passes of form and dimensions approved by the Minister) for the words "the Minister" there shall be inserted the words "the Agency".

10. In section 9(1) of that Act (owner or occupier of certain dams or other obstructions to make fish passes of form and dimensions approved by the Minister) for the words "the Minister" there shall be substituted the words "the Agency".

11.—(1) In section 10 of that Act, in subsection (1) (power of the National Rivers Authority, with the written consent of the Minister, to construct and maintain fish passes of form and dimensions approved by the Minister)—

    (a) the words "with the written consent of the Minister," shall be omitted; and

    (b) for the words "as the Minister may approve" there shall be substituted the words "as it may determine".

(2) In subsection (2) of that section (power of the National Rivers Authority, with the consent of the Minister, to alter etc fish passes and free gaps) the words "with the written consent of the Minister," shall be omitted.

12.—(1) In section 11 of that Act (Minister's consents and approvals for fish passes) for subsection (1) there shall be substituted—

"(1) Any approval given by the Agency to or in relation to a fish pass may, if in giving it the Agency indicates that fact, be provisional until the Agency notifies the applicant for approval that the pass is functioning to its satisfaction.

(1A) The applicant for any such approval—

(a) shall be liable to meet any costs incurred (whether by him or by the Agency or any other person) for the purposes of, or otherwise in connection with, the performance of the Agency's function of determining for the purposes of subsection (1) above whether or not the fish pass in question is functioning to its satisfaction; and

(b) shall provide the Agency with such information or assistance as it may require for the purpose of performing that function."

(2) In subsection (2) of that section (Minister's power to revoke approval or consent while still provisional)—

(a) for the words "or consent is provisional, the Minister" there shall be substituted the words "is provisional, the Agency"; and

(b) for the words from "his intention" onwards there shall be substituted the words "its intention to do so, revoke the approval".

(3) In subsection (3) of that section (Minister's power, when revoking provisional approval, to extend period for making fish pass)—

(a) for the words "the Minister" there shall be substituted the words "the Agency"; and

(b) for the word "he" there shall be substituted the word "it".

(4) In subsection (4) of that section (Minister's power to approve and certify fish pass if he is of the opinion that it is efficient)—

(a) for the words "The Minister" there shall be substituted the words "The Agency"; and

(b) for the word "he" there shall be substituted the word "it".

(5) In subsection (5) of that section (fish passes approved by the Minister deemed to be in conformity with the Act) for the words "the Minister" there shall be substituted the words "the Agency".

13. For section 14 of that Act (gratings) there shall be substituted—

"Screens.

14.—(1) This section applies in any case where—

(a) by means of any conduit or artificial channel, water is diverted from waters frequented by salmon or migratory trout; and

(b) any of the water so diverted is used for the purposes of a water or canal undertaking or for the purposes of any mill or fish farm;

and in this section "the responsible person" means the owner of the water or canal undertaking or (as the case may be) the occupier of the mill or the owner or occupier of the fish farm.

(2) Where this section applies, the responsible person shall, unless an exemption from the obligation is granted by the Agency, ensure (at his own cost) that there is placed and maintained at the entrance of, or within, the conduit or channel a screen which—

(a) subject to subsection (4) below, prevents the descent of the salmon or migratory trout; and

(b) in a case where any of the water diverted is used for the purposes of a fish farm, prevents the egress of farmed fish from the fish farm by way of the conduit or channel.

(3) Where this section applies, the responsible person shall also, unless an exemption from the obligation is granted by the Agency, ensure (at his own cost) that there is placed and maintained across any outfall of the conduit or channel a screen which—

(a) prevents salmon or migratory trout from entering the outfall; and

(b) in a case where any of the water diverted is used for the purposes of a fish farm, prevents the egress of farmed fish from the fish farm by way of the outfall.

(4) Where a screen is placed within any conduit or channel pursuant to subsection (2) above, the responsible person shall ensure that a continuous by-wash is provided immediately upstream of the screen, by means of which salmon or migratory trout may return by as direct a route as practicable to the waters from which they entered the conduit or channel (and accordingly nothing in subsection (2) or (3) above applies in relation to a by-wash provided for the purposes of this subsection).

(5) Any screen placed, or by-wash provided, in pursuance of this section shall be so constructed and located as to ensure, so far as reasonably practicable, that salmon or migratory trout are not injured or damaged by it.

(6) No such screen shall be so placed as to interfere with the passage of boats on any navigable canal.

(7) Any exemption under subsection (2) or (3) above may be granted subject to conditions.

(8) If any person who is required to do so by this section fails to ensure that a screen is placed or maintained, or that a by-wash is provided, in accordance with the provisions of this section, he shall be guilty of an offence.

(9) In any proceedings for an offence under subsection (8) above, it shall, subject to subsection (10) below, be a defence for the person charged to prove that he took all reasonable precautions and exercised all due diligence to avoid the commission of the offence by himself or a person under his control.

(10) If in any case the defence provided by subsection (9) above involves the allegation that the commission of the offence was due to an act or default of another person, or to reliance on information supplied by another person, the person charged shall not, without leave of the court, be entitled to rely on that defence unless—

(a) at least seven clear days before the hearing, and

(b) where he has previously appeared before a court in connection with the alleged offence, within one month of his first such appearance,

he has served on the prosecutor a notice in writing giving such information identifying or assisting in the identification of that other person as was then in his possession.

(11) Any reference in subsection (10) above to appearing before a court includes a reference to being brought before a court.

(12) The obligations imposed by subsections (2) to (6) above, except so far as relating to farmed fish, shall not be in force during such period (if any) in each year as may be prescribed by byelaw.

(13) The obligations imposed by subsections (2) to (6) above on the occupier of a mill shall apply only where the conduit or channel was constructed on or after 18th July 1923.

(14) Any reference in this section to ensuring that a screen is placed and maintained includes, in a case where the screen takes the form of apparatus the operation of which prevents the passage of fish of the descriptions in question, a reference to ensuring that the apparatus is kept in continuous operation.

(15) In this section "by-wash" means a passage through which water flows."

14.—(1) In section 15 of that Act (power of National Rivers Authority, with the consent of the Minister, to use gratings etc. to limit movements of salmon and trout) for the word "grating" or "gratings", wherever occurring (including in the side-note), there shall be substituted respectively the word "screen" or "screens".

(2) In subsection (1) of that section (placing of gratings, deepening of channels etc.) the words "with the written consent of the Minister" shall be omitted.

(3) In subsection (3) of that section (use of such means as the Minister may approve for preventing ingress)—

   (a) the words "with the written consent of the Minister" shall be omitted; and

   (b) for the words "as the Minister may approve" there shall be substituted the words "as in its opinion are necessary".

(4) At the end of that section there shall be added—

   "(5) In this section "open", in relation to a screen which consists of apparatus, includes the doing of anything which interrupts, or otherwise interferes with, the operation of the apparatus."

15. In section 17 of that Act (restrictions on taking salmon or trout above or below an obstruction etc) in subsection (3) (section not to be enforced, in cases where the fish pass is approved by the Minister, until compensation has been paid) for the words "approved by the Minister" there shall be substituted—

   "(a) approved by the Agency, or

   (b) constructed and maintained by the Agency in accordance with section 10(1) above,".

16. In section 18 of that Act (provisions supplementary to Part II) for subsection (2) (notice of application for Ministerial consent to the doing of certain acts to be given to the owner and occupier of the dam etc in question) there shall be substituted—

   "(2) The Agency shall not—

   (a) construct, abolish or alter any fish pass, or abolish or alter any free gap, in pursuance of section 10 above, or

   (b) do any work under section 15 above,

unless reasonable notice of its intention to do so (specifying the section in question) has been served on the owner and occupier of the dam, fish pass or free gap, watercourse, mill race, cut, leat, conduit or other channel, with a plan and specification of the proposed work; and the Agency shall take into consideration any objections by the owner or occupier, before doing the proposed work."

17. In section 30 of that Act, the paragraph defining "fish farm" (which is superseded by amendments made by this Schedule) shall be omitted.

18.—(1) In section 35 of that Act (power to require production of fishing licences) in subsection (3), for the words "the National Rivers Authority" there shall be substituted the words "the Agency".

(2) For subsection (4) of that section (definition of "the appropriate office of the National Rivers Authority") there shall be substituted—

"(4) In subsection (3) above, "the appropriate office of the Agency" means—

(a) in a case where the person requiring the production of the licence or other authority specifies a particular office of the Agency for its production, that office; and

(b) in any other case, any office of the Agency;

and for the purposes of that subsection where a licence or other authority which any person has been required to produce is sent by post to an office of the Agency that licence or other authority shall be treated as produced by that person at that office."

19. After subsection (1A) of section 39 of that Act (application of Act to River Esk in Scotland) there shall be inserted—

"(1B) Sections 31 to 34 and 36(2) of this Act shall, subject to the modifications set out in subsection (1C) below, apply throughout the catchment area of the River Esk in Scotland but a water bailiff shall exercise his powers under those sections as so applied only in relation to an offence—

(a) against this Act;

(b) against section 1 of the Salmon and Freshwater Fisheries (Protection) (Scotland) Act 1951; or

1951 c. 26.

(c) which is deemed to be an offence under this Act by virtue of section 211(6) of the Water Resources Act 1991,

1991 c. 57.

which he has reasonable cause to suspect has been committed in a place to which this Act applies by virtue of subsection (1)(b) above.

(1C) The modifications referred to in subsection (1B) above are—

(a) references in sections 31 to 34 of this Act to "this Act" shall be construed as including references to section 1 of the Salmon and Freshwater Fisheries (Protection) (Scotland) Act 1951 (as applied to the River Esk by section 21 of that Act); and

(b) in section 33—

(i) references to a justice of the peace shall be construed as including references to a sheriff; and

(ii) in subsection (2), the reference to an information on oath shall be construed as including a reference to evidence on oath.".

20. In section 41(1) of that Act (general definitions) the following definitions shall be inserted at the appropriate places, that is to say—

(a) ""fish farm" has the same meaning as in the Diseases of Fish Act 1937;"; and

1937 c. 33.

(b) ""screen" means a grating or other device which, or any apparatus the operation of which, prevents—

(a) the passage of salmon or migratory trout, and

(b) if the screen is required in connection with a fish farm, the passage of any fish farmed at that fish farm,

or any combination of devices or apparatus which, taken together, achieve that result;";

and the definition of "grating" shall be omitted.

21. In subsection (3) of section 43 of that Act (extent of Act to Scotland), after the words "(1A)" there shall be inserted the words ", (1B), (1C)".

22. In paragraph 1 of Schedule 1 to that Act (close seasons and close times) for the words "the National Rivers Authority" there shall be substituted the words "the Agency".

The Diseases of Fish Act 1983

1983 c. 30.

23. In section 9(1)(d) of the Diseases of Fish Act 1983 (disclosure of information for the purpose of enabling the National Rivers Authority to carry out any of its functions) for the words "the National Rivers Authority" there shall be substituted the words "the Environment Agency".

The Salmon Act 1986

1986 c. 62.

24. In section 37(3) of the Salmon Act 1986 (byelaws requiring consent of the National Rivers Authority) for the words "the National Rivers Authority has" there shall be substituted the words "the Environment Agency has".

The Water Resources Act 1991

1991 c. 57.

25. In section 115 of the Water Resources Act 1991, in subsection (1) (power by order to make provision in relation to an area defined by the order for the modification, in relation to the fisheries in that area, of the enactments specified in the paragraphs of that subsection) for paragraph (b) there shall be substituted—

"(b) of section 142 or 156 below or paragraph 6 or 7 of Schedule 25 to this Act; or"

26.—(1) In paragraph 6 of Schedule 25 to that Act (powers to make byelaws in relation to any part or parts of the area in relation to which the National Rivers Authority carries out its functions in relation to fisheries under Part V of that Act) in sub-paragraphs (1) to (5) for the words "in relation to any part or parts", in each place where they occur, there shall be substituted the words "in relation to the whole or any part or parts".

1975 c. 51.

(2) In sub-paragraph (3)(c) of that paragraph (byelaws for the purpose of determining for the purposes of the Salmon and Freshwater Fisheries Act 1975 the period of the year during which gratings need not be maintained) for the word "gratings" there shall be substituted the word "screens".

Section 106.

SCHEDULE 16

POLLUTION OF RIVERS AND COASTAL WATERS IN SCOTLAND: AMENDMENT OF THE CONTROL OF POLLUTION ACT 1974

1974 c.40.

1. The Control of Pollution Act 1974, as it has effect in Scotland, shall be amended in accordance with the following paragraphs.

2. After section 30E there shall be inserted the following sections—

"Control of entry of polluting matter and effluents into water

Pollution offences.

30F.—(1) A person contravenes this section if he causes or knowingly permits any poisonous, noxious or polluting matter or any solid waste matter to enter any controlled waters.

(2) A person contravenes this section if he causes or knowingly permits any matter, other than trade effluent or sewage effluent, to enter controlled waters by being discharged from a sewer or from a drain in contravention of a prohibition imposed under section 30G below.

(3) A person contravenes this section if he causes or knowingly permits any trade effluent or sewage effluent to be discharged—

    (a) into any controlled waters; or

    (b) from land in Scotland, through a pipe, into the sea outside the seaward limits of controlled waters.

(4) A person contravenes this section if he causes or knowingly permits any trade effluent or sewage effluent to be discharged, in contravention of any prohibition imposed under section 30G below, from a building or from any plant—

    (a) on to or into any land; or

    (b) into any waters of a loch or pond which are not inland waters.

(5) A person contravenes this section if he causes or knowingly permits any matter whatever to enter any inland waters so as to tend (either directly or in combination with other matter which he or another person causes or permits to enter those waters) to impede the proper flow of the waters in a manner leading, or likely to lead, to a substantial aggravation of—

    (a) pollution due to other causes; or

    (b) the consequences of such pollution.

(6) Subject to the following provisions of this Part, a person who contravenes this section shall be guilty of an offence and liable—

    (a) on summary conviction, to imprisonment for a term not exceeding three months or to a fine not exceeding £20,000 or to both;

    (b) on conviction on indictment, to imprisonment for a term not exceeding two years or to a fine or to both.

Prohibition of certain discharges by notice or regulations.

30G.—(1) For the purposes of section 30F above a discharge of any effluent or other matter is, in relation to any person, in contravention of a prohibition imposed under this section if, subject to the following provisions of this section—

    (a) SEPA has given that person notice prohibiting him from making or, as the case may be, continuing the discharge; or

    (b) SEPA has given that person notice prohibiting him from making or, as the case may be, continuing the discharge unless specified conditions are observed, and those conditions are not observed.

(2) For the purposes of section 30F above a discharge of any effluent or other matter is also in contravention of a prohibition imposed under this section if the effluent or matter discharged—

    (a) contains a prescribed substance or a prescribed concentration of such a substance; or

    (b) derives from a prescribed process or from a process involving the use of prescribed substances or the use of such substances in quantities which exceed the prescribed amounts.

(3) Nothing in subsection (1) above shall authorise the giving of a notice for the purposes of that subsection in respect of discharges from a vessel; and nothing in any regulations made by virtue of subsection (2) above shall require any discharge from a vessel to be treated as a discharge in contravention of a prohibition imposed under this section.

(4) A notice given for the purposes of subsection (1) above shall expire at such time as may be specified in the notice.

(5) The time specified for the purposes of subsection (4) above shall not be before the end of the period of three months beginning with the day on which the notice is given, except in a case where SEPA is satisfied that there is an emergency which requires the prohibition in question to come into force at such time before the end of that period as may be so specified.

(6) Where, in the case of such a notice for the purposes of subsection (1) above as (but for this subsection) would expire at a time at or after the end of the said period of three months, an application is made before that time for a consent in pursuance of section 34 of this Act in respect of the discharge to which the notice relates, that notice shall be deemed not to expire until the result of the application becomes final—

    (a) on the grant or withdrawal of the application;

    (b) on the expiration, without the bringing of an appeal with respect to the decision on the application, of any period prescribed by virtue of section 39(2) below as the period within which any such appeal must be brought; or

    (c) on the withdrawal or determination of any such appeal.

Discharges into and from sewers etc.

30H.—(1) For the purposes of section 30F above where—

    (a) any sewage effluent is discharged as mentioned in subsection (3) or (4) of that section from any sewer or works—

        (i) vested in a sewerage authority; or

        (ii) vested in a person other than a sewerage authority and forming (or forming part of) a system provided by him such as is mentioned in section 98(1)(b) of the Local Government etc. (Scotland) Act 1994; and

1994 c.39.

(b) the authority or, as the case may be, the person did not cause or knowingly permit the discharge but was bound (either unconditionally or subject to conditions which were observed) to receive into the sewer or works matter included in the discharge,

the authority or person shall be deemed to have caused the discharge.

(2) A sewerage authority shall not be guilty of an offence under section 30F of this Act by reason only of the fact that a discharge from a sewer or works vested in the authority contravenes conditions of a consent relating to the discharge if—

(a) the contravention is attributable to a discharge which another person caused or permitted to be made into the sewer or works; and

(b) the authority either was not bound to receive the discharge into the sewer or works or was bound to receive it there subject to conditions but the conditions were not observed; and

(c) the authority could not reasonably have been expected to prevent the discharge into the sewer or works;

and a person shall not be guilty of such an offence in consequence of a discharge which he caused or permitted to be made into a sewer or works vested in a sewerage authority if the authority was bound to receive the discharge there either unconditionally or subject to conditions which were observed.

(3) A person in whom any such sewer or works as is described in subsection (1)(a)(ii) above is vested (such person being in this subsection referred to as a "relevant person") shall not be guilty of an offence under section 30F of this Act by reason only of the fact that a discharge from the sewer or works contravenes conditions of a consent relating to the discharge if—

(a) the contravention is attributable to a discharge which another person caused or permitted to be made into the sewer or works; and

(b) the relevant person either was not bound to receive the discharge into the sewer or works or was bound to receive it there subject to conditions but the conditions were not observed; and

(c) the relevant person could not reasonably have been expected to prevent the discharge into the sewer or works;

and another person shall not be guilty of such an offence in consequence of a discharge which he caused or permitted to be made into a sewer or works vested in a relevant person if the relevant person was bound to receive the discharge there either unconditionally or subject to conditions which were observed.

Defence to principal offences in respect of authorised discharges.

30I.—(1) Subject to the following provisions of this section, a person shall not be guilty of an offence under section 30F above in respect of the entry of any matter into any waters or any discharge if the entry occurs or the discharge is made under and in accordance with, or as a result of, any act or omission under and in accordance with—

(a) a consent in pursuance of section 34 of this Act or

1991 c. 57.

under Chapter II of Part III of the Water Resources Act 1991 (which makes corresponding provision for England and Wales);

(b) an authorisation for a prescribed process designated for central control granted under Part I of the Environmental Protection Act 1990;

1990 c. 43.

(c) a waste management or disposal licence;

1985 c. 48.

(d) a licence granted under Part II of the Food and Environment Protection Act 1985;

1980 c. 45.

(e) section 33 of the Water (Scotland) Act 1980 (temporary discharge by authorities in connection with the construction of works);

(f) any provision of a local Act or statutory order which expressly confers power to discharge effluent into water; or

(g) any prescribed enactment.

(2) Nothing in any disposal licence shall be treated for the purposes of subsection (1) above as authorising—

(a) any such entry or discharge as is mentioned in subsections (2) to (4) of section 30F above; or

(b) any act or omission so far as it results in any such entry or discharge.

(3) In this section—

"disposal licence" means a licence issued in pursuance of section 5 of this Act;

"local Act" includes enactments in a public general Act which amend a local Act;

"statutory order" means an order, byelaw, scheme or award made under an Act of Parliament, including an order or scheme confirmed by Parliament or brought into operation in accordance with special parliamentary procedure; and

"waste management licence" means such a licence granted under Part II of the Environmental Protection Act 1990.

Other defences to principal offences.

30J.—(1) A person shall not be guilty of an offence under section 30F above in respect of the entry of any matter into any waters or any discharge if—

(a) the entry is caused or permitted, or the discharge is made, in an emergency in order to avoid danger to life or health;

(b) that person takes all such steps as are reasonably practicable in the circumstances for minimising the extent of the entry or discharge and of its polluting effects; and

(c) particulars of the entry or discharge are furnished to SEPA as soon as reasonably practicable after the entry occurs.

(2) A person shall not be guilty of an offence under section 30F above by reason of his causing or permitting any discharge of trade or sewage effluent from a vessel.

(3) A person shall not be guilty of an offence under section 30F above by reason only of his permitting water from an abandoned mine or an abandoned part of a mine to enter controlled waters.

(4) Subsection (3) above shall not apply to the owner or former operator of any mine or part of a mine if the mine or part in question became abandoned after 31st December 1999.

(5) In determining for the purposes of subsection (4) above whether a mine or part of a mine became abandoned before, on or after 31st December 1999 in a case where the mine or part has become abandoned on two or more occasions, of which—

(a) at least one falls on or before that date, and

(b) at least one falls after that date,

the mine or part shall be regarded as becoming abandoned after that date (but without prejudice to the operation of subsection (3) above in relation to that mine or part at, or in relation to, any time before the first of those occasions which falls after that date).

(6) Where, immediately before a part of a mine becomes abandoned, that part is the only part of the mine not falling to be regarded as abandoned for the time being, the abandonment of that part shall not be regarded for the purposes of subsection (4) or (5) above as constituting the abandonment of the mine, but only of that part of it.

(7) A person shall not, otherwise than in respect of the entry of any poisonous, noxious or polluting matter into any controlled waters, be guilty of an offence under section 30F above by reason of his depositing the solid refuse of a mine or quarry on any land so that it falls or is carried into inland waters if—

(a) he deposits the refuse on the land with the consent of SEPA;

(b) no other site for the deposit is reasonably practicable; and

(c) he takes all reasonably practicable steps to prevent the refuse from entering those inland waters.

(8) A roads authority obliged or entitled to keep open a drain by virtue of section 31 of the Roads (Scotland) Act 1984 shall not be guilty of an offence under section 30F above by reason of its causing or permitting any discharge to be made from a drain kept open by virtue of that section unless the discharge is made in contravention of a prohibition imposed under section 30G above."

1984 c. 54.

3. Sections 31(1), (2), (3), (7) and (10) (offences relating to pollution of rivers and coastal waters) and 32 (control of discharges of trade and effluent etc. into rivers and coastal waters etc.) shall cease to have effect.

4. In section 31(8) (maximum penalties) for the words "paragraphs (a) and (b) of the preceding subsection" there shall be substituted the words "section 30F(6) above".

5. In section 31B(4)(d) (nitrate sensitive areas: maximum penalties) for the words "subsection (7) of section 31 above" there shall be substituted the words "subsection (6) of section 30F above".

6. In section 34(3) (consents for discharges of trade and effluent) for the words "section 32(1)" there shall be substituted the words "section 30F(2) to (4)".

7. In section 39(1)(a) (appeals to the Secretary of State) for the words "section 31(3)" there shall be substituted the words "section 30J(4)".

8. In section 56(1) (interpretation etc of Part II) the following definitions shall be inserted in the appropriate places—

1968 c. 47.   ""drain" has the same meaning as in the Sewerage (Scotland) Act 1968;"; and

""sewer" has the same meaning as in the Sewerage (Scotland) Act 1968;".

9. In section 87(3) (time-bar in relation to legal proceedings)—

    (a) the words from the beginning to "offence; and" shall cease to have effect;

1954 c. 48.   (b) for the words "section 23 of the Summary Jurisdiction (Scotland) Act
1975 c. 21.   1954" there shall be substituted the words "section 331 of the Criminal Procedure (Scotland) Act 1975";

    (c) for the words "such offence" there shall be substituted the words "offence under section 30F of this Act or regulations or byelaws made in pursuance of section 31 of this Act"; and

    (d) for the words "subsection (2) of section 23 of the said Act of 1954" there shall be substituted the words "subsection (3) of section 331 of the said Act of 1975";

    (e) the words "in its application to Scotland" shall cease to have effect.

Section 107.

SCHEDULE 17

Statutory nuisances: Scotland

Amendments of the Environmental Protection Act 1990

1990 c. 43.   1. The Environmental Protection Act 1990 shall be amended in accordance with the provisions of paragraphs 2 to 7 of this Schedule.

2. In section 79 (statutory nuisances etc)—

    (a) in subsection (1)(ga) after the word "street" there shall be inserted the words "or in Scotland, road";

    (b) in subsection (7)—

        (i) in the definition of "local authority", before the word "outside" in paragraph (b) there shall be inserted "in England and Wales", the word "and" after paragraph (b) shall cease to have effect, and after paragraph (c) there shall be inserted "and

1994 c. 39.   (d) in Scotland, a district or islands council or a council constituted under section 2 of the Local Government etc (Scotland) Act 1994;";

        (ii) in the definition of "premises" after the word "and" where it second occurs there shall be inserted the words ", in relation to England and Wales,";

        (iii) at the appropriate place there shall be inserted—

""road" has the same meaning as in Part IV of the New Roads and Street Works Act 1991;";

    (c) in subsection (8)—

(i) after the words "port health district" where they first occur there shall be inserted the words "or in Scotland where by an order under section 172 of the Public Health (Scotland) Act 1897 a port local authority or a joint port local authority has been constituted for the whole or part of a port,";

(ii) after the words "port health authority" where they second occur there shall be inserted the words ", port local authority or joint port local authority, as the case may be";

(d) in subsection (10) after the words "or (e)" there shall be inserted "and, in relation to Scotland, paragraph (g) or (ga),";

(e) in subsection (11) after the words "subsection (12) and" there shall be inserted the words ", in relation to England and Wales,".

3. In section 80 (summary proceedings) in subsection (3) after the words "magistrate's court" there shall be inserted the words "or in Scotland, the sheriff";

4. In section 81 (supplementary provisions)—

(a) in subsection (2) after the words "magistrate's court" there shall be inserted the words "or in Scotland, the sheriff";

(b) in subsection (3) after the word "offence" there shall be inserted the words "or, in Scotland, whether or not proceedings have been taken for an offence,";

(c) in subsection (4) after the word "court" where it first occurs there shall be inserted the word "or sheriff" and after the words "court consider" there shall be inserted the words "or sheriff considers";

(d) in subsection (5) after the words "High Court" there shall be inserted the words "or, in Scotland, in any court of competent jurisdiction,".

5. In section 81A at the end, as subsection (10), and in section 81B at the end, as subsection (6), there shall be added—

"( ) This section does not apply to Scotland.".

6. In section 82 (proceedings by persons aggrieved)—

(a) in subsection (1) after the word "complaint" there shall be inserted the words "or, in Scotland, the sheriff may act under this section on a summary application,";

(b) in subsection (2)—

(i) after the words "magistrate's court" there shall be inserted the words "or, in Scotland, the sheriff";

(ii) after the word "street" there shall be inserted the words "or, in Scotland, road";

(iii) after the words "the court" there shall be inserted the words "or the sheriff";

(iv) in paragraph (a) after the word "defendant" there shall be inserted the words "or, in Scotland, defender";

(v) in paragraph (b) after the word "defendant" there shall be inserted the words "or defender";

(vi) after the word "and" where it third occurs there shall be inserted the words ", in England and Wales,";

(c) in subsection (3), after the words "magistrate's court" there shall be inserted the words "or the sheriff" and after the words "of the court" in both places where they occur there shall be inserted the words "or of the sheriff";

(d) in subsection (11), after the words "magistrate's court" there shall be inserted the words "or the sheriff";

(e) in subsection (12) after the word "complaint" there shall be inserted the words "or summary application", after the words "the court" in both places where they occur there shall be inserted the words "or the sheriff" and for the words "defendant (or defendants" there shall be substituted the words "defendant or defender (or defendants or defenders)";

(f) in subsection (13), after the words "magistrate's court" there shall be inserted the words "or to the sheriff" and after the words "the court" in both place where they occur there shall be inserted the words "or the sheriff".

7. In Schedule 3 (statutory nuisance; supplementary provisions)—

(a) after paragraph 1 there shall be inserted—

"Appeals to Sheriff

1A.—(1) This paragraph applies in relation to appeals to the sheriff under section 80(3) against an abatement notice.

(2) An appeal to which this paragraph applies shall be by way of a summary application.

(3) The Secretary of State may make regulations as to appeals to which this paragraph applies and the regulations may in particular include or prescribe any of the matters referred to in sub-paragraphs (4)(a) to (d) of paragraph 1 above.";

(b) in paragraph 2 at the end there shall be added—

"(8) In the application of this paragraph to Scotland, a reference to a justice of the peace or to a justice includes a reference to the sheriff.";

(c) in paragraph 2A(1)(b) after the word "street" there shall be inserted the words "or, in Scotland, road";

(d) in paragraph 4 at the end there shall be added—

"(9) This paragraph does not apply to Scotland.";

(e) in paragraph 6 after the words "magistrate's court" there shall be inserted the words "or, in Scotland, the sheriff".

Amendments of the Radioactive Substances Act 1993

1993 c. 12.

8. In the Radioactive Substances Act 1993, in Part II of Schedule 3—

(a) in paragraph 12, for the words "Sections 16 and 17" there shall be substituted the words "Section 16";

(b) at the end there shall be added—

1990 c. 43.

"17A. Part III of the Environmental Protection Act 1990.".

Section 108.

SCHEDULE 18

SUPPLEMENTAL PROVISIONS WITH RESPECT TO POWERS OF ENTRY

Interpretation

1.—(1) In this Schedule—

"designated person" means an authorised person, within the meaning of section 108 of this Act and includes a person designated by virtue of paragraph 2 below;

"relevant power" means a power conferred by section 108 of this Act, including a power exercisable by virtue of a warrant under this Schedule.

(2) Expressions used in this Schedule and in section 108 of this Act have the same meaning in this Schedule as they have in that section.

Issue of warrants

2.—(1) If it is shown to the satisfaction of a justice of the peace or, in Scotland, the sheriff or a justice of the peace, on sworn information in writing—

(a) that there are reasonable grounds for the exercise in relation to any premises of a relevant power; and

(b) that one or more of the conditions specified in sub-paragraph (2) below is fulfilled in relation to those premises,

the justice or sheriff may by warrant authorise an enforcing authority to designate a person who shall be authorised to exercise the power in relation to those premises, in accordance with the warrant and, if need be, by force.

(2) The conditions mentioned in sub-paragraph (1)(b) above are—

(a) that the exercise of the power in relation to the premises has been refused;

(b) that such a refusal is reasonably apprehended;

(c) that the premises are unoccupied;

(d) that the occupier is temporarily absent from the premises and the case is one of urgency; or

(e) that an application for admission to the premises would defeat the object of the proposed entry.

(3) In a case where subsection (6) of section 108 of this Act applies, a justice of the peace or sheriff shall not issue a warrant under this Schedule by virtue only of being satisfied that the exercise of a power in relation to any premises has been refused, or that a refusal is reasonably apprehended, unless he is also satisfied that the notice required by that subsection has been given and that the period of that notice has expired.

(4) Every warrant under this Schedule shall continue in force until the purposes for which the warrant was issued have been fulfilled.

Manner of exercise of powers

3. A person designated as the person who may exercise a relevant power shall produce evidence of his designation and other authority before he exercises the power.

Information obtained to be admissible in evidence

4.—(1) Subject to section 108(12) of this Act, information obtained in consequence of the exercise of a relevant power, with or without the consent of any person, shall be admissible in evidence against that or any other person.

(2) Without prejudice to the generality of sub-paragraph (1) above, information obtained by means of monitoring or other apparatus installed on any premises in the exercise of a relevant power, with or without the consent of any person in occupation of the premises, shall be admissible in evidence in any proceedings against that or any other person.

Duty to secure premises

5. A person who, in the exercise of a relevant power enters on any premises which are unoccupied or whose occupier is temporarily absent shall leave the premises as effectually secured against trespassers as he found them.

Compensation

6.—(1) Where any person exercises any power conferred by section 108(4)(a) or (b) or (5) of this Act, it shall be the duty of the enforcing authority under whose authorisation he acts to make full compensation to any person who has sustained loss or damage by reason of—

    (a) the exercise by the designated person of that power; or

    (b) the performance of, or failure of the designated person to perform, the duty imposed by paragraph 5 above.

  (2) Compensation shall not be payable by virtue of sub-paragraph (1) above in respect of any loss or damage if the loss or damage—

    (a) is attributable to the default of the person who sustained it; or

    (b) is loss or damage in respect of which compensation is payable by virtue of any other provision of the pollution control enactments.

  (3) Any dispute as to a person's entitlement to compensation under this paragraph, or as to the amount of any such compensation, shall be referred to the arbitration of a single arbitrator or, in Scotland, arbiter appointed by agreement between the enforcing authority in question and the person who claims to have sustained the loss or damage or, in default of agreement, by the Secretary of State.

  (4) A designated person shall not be liable in any civil or criminal proceedings for anything done in the purported exercise of any relevant power if the court is satisfied that the act was done in good faith and that there were reasonable grounds for doing it.

SCHEDULE 19

OFFENCES RELATING TO FALSE OR MISLEADING STATEMENTS OR FALSE ENTRIES

The Control of Pollution Act 1974

1.—(1) The Control of Pollution Act 1974 shall be amended in accordance with the following provisions of this paragraph.

  (2) For subsection (5) of section 34 (offences relating to consents for discharge of effluent etc) there shall be substituted—

    "(5) A person who, in an application for consent in pursuance of this section, makes any statement which he knows to be false or misleading in a material particular or recklessly makes any statement which is false or misleading in a material particular shall be guilty of an offence and shall be liable—

        (a) on summary conviction, to a fine not exceeding the statutory maximum;

        (b) on conviction on indictment, to a fine or to imprisonment for a term not exceeding two years, or to both.".

  (3) For subsection (3) of section 93 (offences relating to power of authorities to obtain information) there shall be substituted—

    "(3) A person who—

(a) fails without reasonable excuse to comply with the requirements of a notice served on him in pursuance of this section; or

(b) in furnishing any information in compliance with such a notice, makes any statement which he knows to be false or misleading in a material particular or recklessly makes any statement which is false or misleading in a material particular,

shall be guilty of an offence.

(3A) A person guilty of an offence under this section shall be liable—

(a) on summary conviction, to a fine not exceeding the statutory maximum; or

(b) on conviction on indictment, to a fine or to imprisonment for a term not exceeding two years, or to both.".

The Water (Scotland) Act 1980

2.—(1) The Water (Scotland) Act 1980 shall be amended in accordance with the following provisions of this paragraph. 1980 c. 45.

(2) In section 93 (obtaining of information as to underground water) after subsection (7) there shall be inserted—

"(8) Any person who in keeping a journal under subsection (1) or in furnishing information under subsection (2) or (3) makes any statement which he knows to be false or misleading in a material particular or recklessly makes any statement which is false or misleading in a material particular shall be guilty of an offence and shall be liable—

(a) on summary conviction, to a fine not exceeding the statutory maximum;

(b) on conviction on indictment, to a fine or to imprisonment for a term not exceeding two years, or to both.".

(3) In section 94 (false information) after the word "Act" there shall be inserted the words "(other than by or under section 93)".

The Control of Pollution (Amendment) Act 1989

3. In section 7(3)(b) of the Control of Pollution (Amendment) Act 1989 (offences of making false statements), after the word "false" in each place where it occurs there shall be inserted the words "or misleading". 1989 c. 14.

The Environmental Protection Act 1990

4.—(1) For section 44 of the Environmental Protection Act 1990 (offences of making false statements) there shall be substituted— 1990 c. 43.

"Offences of making false or misleading statements or false entries.

44.—(1) A person who—

(a) in purported compliance with a requirement to furnish any information imposed by or under any provision of this Part, or

(b) for the purpose of obtaining for himself or another any grant of a licence, any modification of the conditions of a licence, any acceptance of the surrender of a licence or any transfer of a licence,

makes a statement which he knows to be false or misleading in a material particular, or recklessly makes any statement which is false or misleading in a material particular, commits an offence.

262

c. 25c. **25**

Environment Act 1995

(2) A person who intentionally makes a false entry in any record required to be kept by virtue of a licence commits an offence.

(3) A person who commits an offence under this section shall be liable—

(a) on summary conviction, to a fine not exceeding the statutory maximum;

(b) on conviction on indictment, to a fine or to imprisonment for a term not exceeding two years, or to both."

(2) In section 71(3) of that Act, paragraph (b) (offence of making false or misleading statements) shall cease to have effect.

The Water Resources Act 1991

1991 c. 57.5.—(1) Section 206 of the Water Resources Act 1991 (making of false statements etc) shall be amended in accordance with the following provisions of this paragraph.

(2) For subsection (1), there shall be substituted—

"(1) If, in furnishing any information or making any application under or for the purposes of any provision of this Act, any person makes a statement which he knows to be false or misleading in a material particular, or recklessly makes any statement which is false or misleading in a material particular, he shall be guilty of an offence under this section."

(3) Subsection (2) (which is superseded by the amendment made by sub-paragraph (2) above) shall be omitted.

(4) After subsection (3) (offences relating to the use of meters in connection with licences under Chapter II of Part II) there shall be inserted—

"(3A) If a person intentionally makes a false entry in any record required to be kept by virtue of a licence under Chapter II of Part II of this Act, or a consent under Chapter II of Part III of this Act, he shall be guilty of an offence under this section."

(5) For subsections (5) to (7) (which require consent to the prosecution of certain offences and provide different penalties for different offences) there shall be substituted—

"(5) A person who is guilty of an offence under this section shall be liable—

(a) on summary conviction, to a fine not exceeding the statutory maximum;

(b) on conviction on indictment, to a fine or to imprisonment for a term not exceeding two years, or to both."

The Radioactive Substances Act 1993

1993 c. 12.6. After section 34 of the Radioactive Substances Act 1993 (offences relating to disclosure of information about trade secrets etc) there shall be inserted—

"Offences of making false or misleading statements or false entries.

34A.—(1) Any person who—

(a) for the purpose of obtaining for himself or another any registration under section 7 or 10, any authorisation under section 13 or 14 or any variation of such an authorisation under section 17, or

(b) in purported compliance with a requirement to furnish information imposed under section 31(1)(d),

makes a statement which he knows to be false or misleading in a material particular, or recklessly makes a statement which is false or misleading in a material particular, shall be guilty of an offence.

(2) Any person who intentionally makes a false entry in any record—

(a) which is required to be kept by virtue of a registration under section 7 or 10 or an authorisation under section 13 or 14, or

(b) which is kept in purported compliance with a condition which must be complied with if a person is to have the benefit of an exemption under section 8, 11 or 15,

shall be guilty of an offence.

(3) A person guilty of an offence under this section shall be liable—

(a) on summary conviction, to a fine not exceeding the statutory maximum;

(b) on conviction on indictment, to a fine or to imprisonment for a term not exceeding two years, or to both."

SCHEDULE 20

Section 114.

DELEGATION OF APPELLATE FUNCTIONS OF THE SECRETARY OF STATE

Interpretation

1. In this Schedule—

"appointed person" means a person appointed under section 114(1)(a) of this Act; and

"appointment", in the case of any appointed person, means appointment under section 114(1)(a) of this Act.

Appointments

2. An appointment under section 114(1)(a) of this Act must be in writing and—

(a) may relate to any particular appeal, matters or questions specified in the appointment or to appeals, matters or questions of a description so specified;

(b) may provide for any function to which it relates to be exercisable by the appointed person either unconditionally or subject to the fulfilment of such conditions as may be specified in the appointment; and

(c) may, by notice in writing given to the appointed person, be revoked at any time by the Secretary of State in respect of any appeal, matter or question which has not been determined by the appointed person before that time.

Powers of appointed person

3. Subject to the provisions of this Schedule, an appointed person shall, in relation to any appeal, matter or question to which his appointment relates, have the same powers and duties as the Secretary of State, other than—

    (a) any function of making regulations;

    (b) any function of holding an inquiry or other hearing or of causing an inquiry or other hearing to be held; or

    (c) any function of appointing a person for the purpose—

        (i) of enabling persons to appear before and be heard by the person so appointed; or

        (ii) of referring any question or matter to that person.

Holding of local inquiries and other hearings by appointed persons

4.—(1) If either of the parties to an appeal, matter or question expresses a wish to appear before and be heard by the appointed person, the appointed person shall give both of them an opportunity of appearing and being heard.

(2) Whether or not a party to an appeal, matter or question has asked for an opportunity to appear and be heard, the appointed person—

    (a) may hold a local inquiry or other hearing in connection with the appeal, matter or question, and

    (b) shall, if the Secretary of State so directs, hold a local inquiry in connection with the appeal, matter or question,

but this sub-paragraph is subject to sub-paragraph (3) below.

(3) No local inquiry shall be held by virtue of this Schedule in connection with an appeal under—

1974 c. 40.
    (a) section 42B(5) of the Control of Pollution Act 1974,

1990 c. 43.
    (b) section 22(5), 66(5) or 78T(3) of the Environmental Protection Act 1990, or

1991 c. 57.
    (c) section 191B(5) of the Water Resources Act 1991,

(appeals against decisions that information is not commercially confidential), or any matter involved in such an appeal, and any hearing held by virtue of this Schedule in connection with any such appeal or matter must be held in private.

(4) Where an appointed person holds a local inquiry or other hearing by virtue of this Schedule, an assessor may be appointed by the Secretary of State to sit with the appointed person at the inquiry or hearing and advise him on any matters arising, notwithstanding that the appointed person is to determine the appeal, matter or question.

(5) Subject to paragraph 5 below, the costs of a local inquiry held under this Schedule shall be defrayed by the Secretary of State.

Local inquiries under this Schedule: evidence and costs

1972 c. 70.
5.—(1) In relation to England and Wales, subsections (2) to (5) of section 250 of the Local Government Act 1972 (local inquiries: evidence and costs) shall apply to local inquiries or other hearings held under this Schedule by an appointed person as they apply to inquiries caused to be held under that section by a Minister, but with the following modifications, that is to say—

    (a) with the substitution in subsection (2) (evidence) for the reference to the person appointed to hold the inquiry of a reference to the appointed person;

    (b) with the substitution in subsection (4) (recovery of costs of holding the inquiry) for the references to the Minister causing the inquiry to be held of references to the Secretary of State;

(c) taking the reference in that subsection to a local authority as including the Agency; and

(d) with the substitution in subsection (5) (orders as to the costs of the parties) for the reference to the Minister causing the inquiry to be held of a reference to the appointed person or the Secretary of State.

(2) In relation to Scotland, subsections (3) to (8) of section 210 of the Local Government (Scotland) Act 1973 (which relate to the costs of and holding of local inquiries) shall apply to local inquiries or other hearings held under this Schedule as they apply to inquiries held under that section, but with the following modifications, that is to say—

1973 c. 65.

(a) with the substitution in subsection (3) (notice of inquiry) for the reference to the person appointed to hold the inquiry of a reference to the appointed person;

(b) with the substitution in subsection (4) (evidence) for the reference to the person appointed to hold the inquiry and, in paragraph (b), the reference to the person holding the inquiry of references to the appointed person;

(c) with the substitution in subsection (6) (expenses of witnesses etc.) for the references to the Minister causing the inquiry to be held of a reference to the appointed person or the Secretary of State;

(d) with the substitution in subsection (7) (expenses) for the references to the Minister of references to the appointed person or the Secretary of State;

(e) with the substitution in subsection (7A) (recovery of entire administrative expense)—

(i) for the first reference to the Minister of a reference to the appointed person or the Secretary of State;

(ii) in paragraph (a), for the reference to the Minister of a reference to the Secretary of State; and

(iii) in paragraph (b), for the reference to the Minister holding the inquiry of a reference to the Secretary of State;

(f) with the substitution in subsection (7B) (power to prescribe daily amount)—

(i) for the first reference to the Minister of a reference to the Secretary of State;

(ii) in paragraphs (a) and (c), for the references to the person appointed to hold the inquiry of references to the appointed person; and

(iii) in paragraph (d), for the reference to the Minister of a reference to the appointed person or the Secretary of State; and

(g) with the substitution in subsection (8) (certification of expenses) for the reference to the Minister, the reference to him and the reference to the Crown of references to the appointed person or the Secretary of State.

Revocation of appointments and making of new appointments

6.—(1) Where under paragraph 2(c) above the appointment of the appointed person is revoked in respect of any appeal, matter or question, the Secretary of State shall, unless he proposes to determine the appeal, matter or question himself, appoint another person under section 114(1)(a) of this Act to determine the appeal, matter or question instead.

(2) Where such a new appointment is made, the consideration of the appeal, matter or question, or any hearing in connection with it, shall be begun afresh.

(3) Nothing in sub-paragraph (2) above shall require any person to be given an opportunity of making fresh representations or modifying or withdrawing any representations already made.

Certain acts and omissions of appointed person to be treated as those of the Secretary of State

7.—(1) Anything done or omitted to be done by an appointed person in, or in connection with, the exercise or purported exercise of any function to which the appointment relates shall be treated for all purposes as done or omitted to be done by the Secretary of State in his capacity as such.

(2) Sub-paragraph (1) above shall not apply—

(a) for the purposes of so much of any contract made between the Secretary of State and the appointed person as relates to the exercise of the function; or

(b) for the purposes of any criminal proceedings brought in respect of anything done or omitted to be done as mentioned in that sub-paragraph.

Section 116.

SCHEDULE 21

APPLICATION OF CERTAIN ENACTMENTS TO THE CROWN

PART I

ENACTMENTS RELATING TO ENGLAND AND WALES

The Water Industry Act 1991

1991 c. 56.

1.—(1) For section 221 of the Water Industry Act 1991 (Crown application) there shall be substituted—

"Crown application.

221.—(1) Subject to the provisions of this section, this Act shall bind the Crown.

(2) No contravention by the Crown of any provision made by or under this Act shall make the Crown criminally liable; but the High Court may, on the application of the Environment Agency, a water undertaker or a sewerage undertaker, declare unlawful any act or omission of the Crown which constitutes such a contravention.

(3) Notwithstanding anything in subsection (2) above, any provision made by or under this Act shall apply to persons in the public service of the Crown as it applies to other persons.

(4) If the Secretary of State certifies that it appears to him, as respects any Crown premises and any powers of entry exercisable in relation to them specified in the certificate, that it is requisite or expedient that, in the interests of national security, the powers should not be exercisable in relation to those premises, those powers shall not be exercisable in relation to those premises.

1947 c. 44.

(5) Nothing in this section shall be taken as in any way affecting Her Majesty in her private capacity; and this subsection shall be construed as if section 38(3) of the Crown Proceedings Act 1947 (interpretation of references to Her Majesty in her private capacity) were contained in this Act.

(6) Subject to subsections (4) and (5) above, the powers conferred by sections 155, 159, 161(2) and 167 above shall be exercisable in relation to land in which there is a Crown or Duchy interest only with the consent of the appropriate authority.

(7) In this section—

"the appropriate authority" has the same meaning as it has in Part XIII of the Town and Country Planning Act 1990 by virtue of section 293(2) of that Act;

1990 c. 8.

"Crown or Duchy interest" means an interest which belongs to Her Majesty in right of the Crown or of the Duchy of Lancaster, or to the Duchy of Cornwall, or belonging to a government department or held in trust for Her Majesty for the purposes of a government department;

"Crown premises" means premises held by or on behalf of the Crown.

(8) The provisions of subsection (3) of section 293 of the Town and Country Planning Act 1990 (questions relating to Crown application) as to the determination of questions shall apply for the purposes of this section."

The Water Resources Act 1991

2.—(1) The Water Resources Act 1991 shall be amended in accordance with the following provisions of this paragraph.

1991 c. 57.

(2) In section 115 (fisheries orders) in subsection (7) (orders affecting Crown or Duchy property) in paragraph (a), after the words "an order under this section" there shall be inserted the words "making provision, by virtue of subsection (1)(b) above, for the modification of section 156 below in relation to fisheries in an area".

(3) In section 142 (orders providing for the imposition and collection of fisheries contributions), in subsection (2) (which applies, in relation to orders under that section, the provisions of subsections (2) to (9) of section 115 of that Act) for the words "(2) to (9)" there shall be substituted the words "(2) to (6)".

(4) For section 222 (Crown application) there shall be substituted—

"Crown application.

222.—(1) Subject to the provisions of this section, this Act binds the Crown.

(2) No contravention by the Crown of any provision made by or under this Act shall make the Crown criminally liable; but the High Court may, on the application of the Agency, declare unlawful any act or omission of the Crown which constitutes such a contravention.

(3) Notwithstanding anything in subsection (2) above, the provisions of this Act shall apply to persons in the public service of the Crown as they apply to other persons.

(4) If the Secretary of State certifies that it appears to him, as respects any Crown premises and any powers of entry exercisable in relation to them specified in the certificate, that it is requisite or expedient that, in the interests of national security, the powers should not be exercisable in relation to those premises, those powers shall not be exercisable in relation to those premises.

(5) Subject to subsection (4) above, the powers conferred by sections 154, 156, 160, 162(3) and 168 above shall be exercisable in relation to land in which there is a Crown or Duchy interest only with the consent of the appropriate authority.

(6) Nothing in this section shall be taken as in any way affecting Her Majesty in her private capacity; and this

subsection shall be construed as if section 38(3) of the Crown Proceedings Act 1947 (interpretation of references to Her Majesty in her private capacity) were contained in this Act.

(7) Nothing in this Act, as read with the other provisions of this section, shall be construed as conferring any power of levying drainage charges in respect of lands below the high-water mark of ordinary spring tides.

(8) Section 74 of the Land Drainage Act 1991 (Crown application), so far as it relates to land in which there is a Crown or Duchy interest, shall apply in relation to the flood defence provisions of this Act as it applies in relation to that Act; but nothing in this subsection shall affect any power conferred by this Act for the purposes both of the Agency's functions under those provisions and of other functions of the Agency.

(9) In this section—

"the appropriate authority" has the same meaning as it has in Part XIII of the Town and Country Planning Act 1990 by virtue of section 293(2) of that Act;

"Crown or Duchy interest" means an interest which belongs to Her Majesty in right of the Crown or of the Duchy of Lancaster, or to the Duchy of Cornwall, or belonging to a government department or held in trust for Her Majesty for the purposes of a government department;

"Crown premises" means premises held by or on behalf of the Crown.

(10) The provisions of subsection (3) of section 293 of the Town and Country Planning Act 1990 (questions relating to Crown application) as to the determination of questions shall apply for the purposes of this section."

PART II

ENACTMENTS RELATING TO SCOTLAND

The Sewerage (Scotland) Act 1968

3. For section 55 of the Sewerage (Scotland) Act 1968 (Crown application) there shall be substituted—

"Application of
Act to Crown.

55.—(1) Subject to the provisions of this section, this Act shall bind the Crown.

(2) No contravention by the Crown of any provision made by or under this Act shall make the Crown criminally liable; but the Court of Session may, on the application of a sewerage authority, declare unlawful any act or omission of the Crown which constitutes such a contravention.

(3) Notwithstanding anything in subsection (2) above, any provision made by or under this Act shall apply to persons in the public service of the Crown as it applies to other persons.

(4) If the Secretary of State certifies that it appears to him, as respects any Crown premises and any powers of entry exercisable in relation to them specified in the certificate, that it is requisite or expedient that, in the interests of national security, the powers should not be exercisable in relation to those premises, those powers shall not be exercisable in relation to those premises.

(5) Nothing in this section shall be taken as in any way affecting Her Majesty in her private capacity.

(6) In this section "Crown premises" means premises held by or on behalf of the Crown.".

The Control of Pollution Act 1974

4. For subsection (3) of section 105 of the Control of Pollution Act 1974 (application to Crown) as it has effect in relation to Scotland, there shall be substituted the following subsections—

1974 c. 40.

"(3) Subject to subsections (3A) to (3D) below, this Act shall bind the Crown.

(3A) No contravention by the Crown of any provision made by or under this Act shall make the Crown criminally liable; but the Court of Session may, on the application of—

(a) the Scottish Environment Protection Agency; or

(b) any other public or local authority charged with enforcing that provision,

declare unlawful any act or omission of the Crown which constitutes such a contravention.

(3B) Notwithstanding anything in subsection (3A) above, any provision made by or under this Act shall apply to persons in the public service of the Crown as it applies to other persons.

(3C) If the Secretary of State certifies that it appears to him, as respects any Crown premises and any powers of entry exercisable in relation to them specified in the certificate, that it is requisite or expedient that, in the interests of national security, the powers should not be exercisable in relation to those premises, those powers shall not be exercisable in relation to those premises; and in this subsection "Crown premises" means premises held or used by or on behalf of the Crown.

(3D) Nothing in this section shall be taken as in any way affecting Her Majesty in her private capacity."

The Water (Scotland) Act 1980

5. After section 110 of the Water (Scotland) Act 1980 there shall be inserted—

1980 c. 45.

"Application of Act to Crown.

110A.—(1) Subject to the provisions of this section, this Act shall bind the Crown.

(2) No contravention by the Crown of any provision made by or under this Act shall make the Crown criminally liable; but the Court of Session may, on the application of a water authority, declare unlawful any act or omission of the Crown which constitutes such a contravention.

(3) Notwithstanding anything in subsection (2) above, any provision made by or under this Act shall apply to persons in the public service of the Crown as it applies to other persons.

(4) If the Secretary of State certifies that it appears to him, as respects any Crown premises and any powers of entry exercisable in relation to them specified in the certificate, that it is requisite or expedient that, in the interests of national security, the powers should not be exercisable in relation to those premises, those powers shall not be exercisable in relation to those premises.

(5) Nothing in this section shall be taken as in any way affecting Her Majesty in her private capacity.

(6) Subject to subsections (4) and (5) above, the powers conferred by sections 16 to 18 above shall be exercisable in relation to land in which there is a Crown interest only with the consent of the appropriate authority.

(7) In this section—

1972 c. 52.

"the appropriate authority" has the same meaning as it has in section 253(7) of the Town and Country Planning (Scotland) Act 1972;

"Crown interest" means an interest belonging to Her Majesty in right of the Crown, or belonging to a government department or held in trust for Her Majesty for the purposes of a government department;

"Crown premises" means premises held by or on behalf of the Crown.

(8) The provisions of subsection (7) of section 253 of the Town and Country Planning (Scotland) Act 1972 (questions relating to Crown application) as to the determination of questions shall apply for the purposes of this section.".

The Local Government etc. (Scotland) Act 1994

1994 c. 39.

6. After section 125 of the Local Government etc. (Scotland) Act 1994 there shall be inserted—

"Application of Part II to Crown.

125A.—(1) Subject to the provisions of this section, this Part of this Act shall bind the Crown.

(2) No contravention by the Crown of any provision made by or under this Part of this Act shall make the Crown criminally liable; but the Court of Session may, on the application of a new water and sewerage authority, declare unlawful any act or omission of the Crown which constitutes such a contravention.

(3) Notwithstanding anything in subsection (2) above, any provision made by or under this Part of this Act shall apply to persons in the public service of the Crown as it applies to other persons.

(4) Nothing in this section shall be taken as in any way affecting Her Majesty in her private capacity.

(5) Subject to subsection (4) above, the powers conferred by section 99 above shall be exercisable in relation to land in which there is a Crown interest only with the consent of the appropriate authority.

(6) In this section—

"the appropriate authority" has the same meaning as it has in section 253(7) of the Town and Country Planning (Scotland) Act 1972;

"Crown interest" means an interest belonging to Her Majesty in right of the Crown, or belonging to a government department or held in trust for Her Majesty for the purposes of a government department;

"Crown premises" means premises held by or on behalf of the Crown.

(7) The provisions of subsection (7) of section 253 of the Town and Country Planning (Scotland) Act 1972 (questions relating to Crown application) as to the determination of questions shall apply for the purposes of this section.".   1972 c. 52.

SCHEDULE 22   Section 120.

MINOR AND CONSEQUENTIAL AMENDMENTS

The Alkali, &c., Works Regulation Act 1906

1.—(1) The Alkali, &c, Works Regulation Act 1906 shall be amended in   1906 c. 14.
accordance with the following provisions of this paragraph.

(2) In section 1(1) (alkali work to be carried on so as to secure that the condensation of hydrochloric acid gas, to the satisfaction of the chief inspector, falls below certain levels) for the words "the chief inspector" there shall be substituted the words "the appropriate Agency".

(3) In section 2(1) (no objection to be taken by an inspector to certain discharges) for the words "an inspector" there shall be substituted the words "the appropriate Agency".

(4) In section 9—

(a) in subsection (5) (condition of issue of certificate on first registration that the work is furnished with such appliances as appear to the chief inspector or, on appeal, the Secretary of State to be necessary for certain purposes) for the words "the chief inspector" there shall be substituted the words "the appropriate Agency";

(b) the proviso to that subsection (power of Secretary of State to dispense with certain requirements) shall cease to have effect; and

(c) in subsection (7) (notice of certain changes to be sent to the Secretary of State) for the words which are to be construed as a reference to the Secretary of State, there shall be substituted the words "the appropriate Agency".

(5) In section 22(1) (power of Secretary of State, after inquiring into a complaint, to direct proceedings to be taken by an inspector) for the words "an inspector" there shall be substituted the words "the appropriate Agency".

(6) In section 23(2) (damages not recoverable under the section from a person with a certificate of compliance from the chief inspector) for the words "the chief inspector" there shall be substituted the words "the appropriate Agency".

(7) Section 25 (basis on which the chief inspector may determine questions) shall cease to have effect.

(8) In section 27(1) (interpretation of terms)—

(a) after the definition of the expression "alkali works" there shall be inserted—

"The expression "the appropriate Agency" means—

(a) in relation to England and Wales, the Environment Agency; and

(b) in relation to Scotland, the Scottish Environment Protection Agency:"; and

(b) the definitions of the expressions "chief inspector" and "inspector" shall be omitted.

(9) In paragraph (b) of section 28 (application to Scotland)—

(a) the words "other than offences under subsection four of section twelve of this Act",

(b) in sub-paragraph (ii) (prosecution not to be instituted without consent) the words from "without the consent" to "direct, nor", and

(c) sub-paragraph (iii) (person taking proceedings presumed to be inspector),

shall cease to have effect.

The Statistics of Trade Act 1947

1947 c. 39.

2. In the Statistics of Trade Act 1947, after section 9 (restrictions on disclosure of information) there shall be inserted—

"Exceptions from section 9.

9A.—(1) Nothing in section nine of this Act shall prevent or penalise the disclosure by the Secretary of State of information obtained under this Act—

(a) to the Environment Agency or the Scottish Environment Protection Agency; or

(b) to an officer of either of those Agencies authorised by that Agency to receive the information.

(2) A person to whom information is disclosed in pursuance of the last foregoing subsection shall not use the information for any purpose other than the purposes of any functions of the Agency in question."

The Rivers (Prevention of Pollution) (Scotland) Act 1951

1951 c. 66.

3.—(1) The Rivers (Prevention of Pollution) (Scotland) Act 1951 shall be amended in accordance with the following provisions of this paragraph.

(2) Part II (river purification boards) (so far as unrepealed) and section 17 (duties of river purification authorities) shall cease to have effect.

(3) In section 18 (provision and obtaining of information)—

(a) in subsection (1) (power to obtain information)—

(i) for the word "them" in each place where it occurs there shall be substituted the word "it";

(ii) for the words "a river purification authority" there shall be substituted the words "SEPA"; and

(iii) the words "of their area", "in their area" (where first occurring) and "in their area or any part thereof" shall cease to have effect;

(b) in subsection (2) (Secretary of State's power to give directions) for the words "any river purification authority" and "the authority" there shall be substituted the words "SEPA", and for the word "them" there shall be substituted the word "it"; and

(c) in subsection (3) (duty to provide reasonable facilities for inspection of records)—

(i) for the words "Every river purification authority" and "the river purification authority" there shall be substituted the words "SEPA";

(ii) for the word "them" there shall be substituted the word "it"; and

(iii) the words "in their area" and the words from "whose" to "authority" where it next occurs shall cease to have effect; and

(d) in subsection (6) (interpretation of "stream") for the words "the river purification authority's" there shall be substituted the words "SEPA's".

(4) In section 19 (power to take samples of effluents)—

(a) in subsection (1) (power to obtain and take away samples of water from any stream or effluent)—

(i) for the words "A river purification authority" there shall be substituted the words "SEPA"; and

(ii) the words "in the area of the authority" shall cease to have effect; and

(b) in subsection (3) (interpretation of "stream") for the words "the river purification authority's" there shall be substituted the words "SEPA's".

(5) In section 35 (interpretation)—

(a) the definitions of "river purification authority", "river purification board" and "river purification board area" shall cease to have effect; and

(b) there shall be inserted at the appropriate place—

""SEPA" means the Scottish Environment Protection Agency;".

The Public Records Act 1958

4. In the First Schedule to the Public Records Act 1958 (definition of public records) in Part II of the Table at the end of paragraph 3 (organisations whose records are public records) there shall be inserted at the appropriate place the entry— 1958 c. 51.

"The Environment Agency.".

The Opencast Coal Act 1958

5.—(1) In section 7(8) of the Opencast Coal Act 1958 (definitions etc. for the purposes of section 7) in paragraph (i) of the definition of "statutory water undertakers" for the words "National Rivers Authority" there shall be substituted the words "Environment Agency". 1958 c. 69.

(2) In section 52(3) of that Act (general application to Scotland) for the words "a river purification authority within the meaning of the Rivers (Prevention of Pollution) (Scotland) Act 1951" there shall be substituted the words "the Scottish Environment Protection Agency". 1951 c. 66.

The Rivers (Prevention of Pollution) (Scotland) Act 1965

6. In section 10 of the Rivers (Prevention of Pollution) (Scotland) Act 1965 (samples of effluent)— 1965 c. 13.

(a) in subsection (2)—

(i) for the words "A river purification authority" there shall be substituted the words "the Scottish Environment Protection Agency (in this section referred to as "SEPA")"; and

(ii) for the words "the river purification authority's" there shall be substituted the words "SEPA's"; and

(b) in subsections (3) to (5), for the words "the river purification authority", in each place where they occur, and "Every river purification authority" there shall be substituted the words "SEPA".

The Nuclear Installations Act 1965

1965 c. 57.

7.—(1) In section 3 of the Nuclear Installations Act 1965, after subsection (1) (grant of nuclear site licences) there shall be inserted—

"(1A) The Health and Safety Executive shall consult the appropriate Agency before granting a nuclear site licence in respect of a site in Great Britain."

(2) In subsection (3) of that section (consultation with certain bodies), in paragraph (b), the words "the National Rivers Authority," shall cease to have effect.

(3) After subsection (6) of that section (variation of nuclear site licences) there shall be inserted—

1993 c. 12.

"(6A) The Health and Safety Executive shall consult the appropriate Agency before varying a nuclear site licence in respect of a site in Great Britain, if the variation relates to or affects the creation, accumulation or disposal of radioactive waste, within the meaning of the Radioactive Substances Act 1993."

8. In section 4 of that Act (attachment of conditions to licences) after subsection (3) there shall be inserted—

"(3A) The Health and Safety Executive shall consult the appropriate Agency—

(a) before attaching any condition to a nuclear site licence in respect of a site in Great Britain, or

(b) before varying or revoking any condition attached to such a nuclear site licence,

if the condition relates to or affects the creation, accumulation or disposal of radioactive waste, within the meaning of the Radioactive Substances Act 1993."

9. In section 5 of that Act (revocation and surrender of licences) after subsection (1) there shall be inserted—

"(1A) The Health and Safety Executive shall consult the appropriate Agency before revoking a nuclear site licence in respect of a site in Great Britain."

10. In section 26 (interpretation) in subsection (1), there shall be inserted at the appropriate place—

""the appropriate Agency" means—

(a) in the case of a site in England or Wales, the Environment Agency;

(b) in the case of a site in Scotland, the Scottish Environment Protection Agency;".

The Parliamentary Commissioner Act 1967

1967 c. 13.

11. In Schedule 2 to the Parliamentary Commissioner Act 1967 (departments and authorities subject to investigation)—

(a) there shall be inserted at the appropriate places the entries—

(i) "Environment Agency"; and

(ii) "Scottish Environment Protection Agency";

(b) after note 1, there shall be inserted—

1991 c. 57.

"1A. The reference to the Environment Agency is a reference to that Agency in relation to all its functions other than its flood defence functions, within the meaning of the Water Resources Act 1991."; and

(c) there shall be omitted—

  (i) the entry relating to the National Rivers Authority; and

  (ii) the note 9 inserted by paragraph 11 of Schedule 1 to the Water Act 1989 (which relates to that Authority). 1989 c. 15.

The Sewerage (Scotland) Act 1968

12.—(1) In section 38(3) of the Sewerage (Scotland) Act 1968 (duty of Secretary of State to consult on proposed extension of Part II to non-trade effluents)— 1968 c. 47.

(a) after the word "consult" where it first occurs there shall be inserted the words "the Scottish Environment Protection Agency and"; and

(b) the words "river purification authorities," shall cease to have effect.

(2) In section 59(1) of that Act (interpretation) the definition of "river purification authority" shall cease to have effect.

The Local Authorities (Goods and Services) Act 1970

13. The Local Authorities (Goods and Services) Act 1970 (supply of goods and services by local authorities to public bodies) shall have effect as if the Agency and SEPA were each both a local authority and a public body for the purposes of that Act other than section 2(2) (accounting requirements in relation to local authority agreements entered into in pursuance of section 1). 1970 c. 39.

The Agriculture Act 1970

14.—(1) The Agriculture Act 1970 shall be amended in accordance with the following provisions of this paragraph. 1970 c. 40.

(2) In section 92(1) (provision of flood warning systems)—

(a) for the words from the beginning to "may" where it first occurs there shall be substituted the words "The Scottish Environment Protection Agency may";

(b) the words "for their area" and "both within (and in the case of a river purification board) outwith, that area," shall cease to have effect;

(c) in sub-paragraph (i) of the proviso—

  (i) for the words "a river purification board" there shall be substituted the words "the Scottish Environment Protection Agency";

  (ii) for the word "them" there shall be substituted the word "it"; and

  (iii) for the words "that board" there shall be substituted the words "the Agency"; and

(d) in sub-paragraph (ia) of the proviso for the words following "exercise" to "shall" there shall be substituted the words ", the Agency shall".

(3) In section 92(2)—

(a) in paragraph (a)(iii) for the words "the authority providing the system" there shall be substituted the words "the Scottish Environment Protection Agency";

(b) paragraph (c) (definition of "river purification board") shall cease to have effect.

(4) In section 94 (co-operation with other persons as regards flood warning systems)—

(a) in subsection (1) for the words following "warning system" to "may" where it first occurs there shall be substituted the words "the Scottish Environment Protection Agency may" and for the words following "belonging to the" to "for" there shall be substituted the words "Agency for";

(b) in subsection (2) for the words from the beginning to "may" and for the words following "apparatus of" there shall be substituted the words "The Agency may" and " the Agency" respectively.

(5) In section 98 (extent of Part VI)—

(a) for the words from the beginning to "England" there shall be substituted the words "The Scottish Environment Protection Agency";

(b) for the words "section 92(1)(b)" there shall be substituted the words "section 92(1)"; and

(c) for the words "the National Rivers Authority" there shall be substituted the words "the Environment Agency".

The Prevention of Oil Pollution Act 1971

1971 c. 60.

15.—(1) The Prevention of Oil Pollution Act 1971 shall be amended in accordance with the following provisions of this paragraph.

(2) After section 11 (duty to report discharge of oil into waters of harbours) there shall be inserted—

"Certain provisions not to apply where a discharge or escape is authorised under Part I of the Environmental Protection Act 1990.

1990 c. 43.

11A.—(1) The provisions of sections 2(1) and (2A), 3(1) and 11(1) of this Act shall not apply to any discharge which is made under, and the provisions of section 11(1) of this Act shall not apply to any escape which is authorised by, an authorisation granted under Part I of the Environmental Protection Act 1990.

(2) This section does not extend to Northern Ireland."

(3) In section 25(1) (power to extend certain provisions of the Act to the Isle of Man etc.), after the words "other than section 3" there shall be inserted the word ", 11A".

The Town and Country Planning (Scotland) Act 1972

1972 c. 52.

16. In Schedule 7 to the Town and Country Planning (Scotland) Act 1972 (determination of certain appeals by persons appointed by the Secretary of State), in paragraph 2, after sub-paragraph (f) there shall be inserted—

"(g) in relation to appeals under paragraphs 6(11) and (12) and 11(1) of Schedule 13 and paragraph 9(1) of Schedule 14 to the Environment Act 1995, paragraph 6 of Schedule 10A to this Act.".

The Local Government Act 1972

1972 c. 70.

17. In section 223 of the Local Government Act 1972 (which includes provision for authorised members or officers of the National Rivers Authority to conduct certain magistrates' court proceedings on its behalf) in subsection (2)—

(a) after the words "joint authority" there shall be inserted the word "and"; and

(b) the words "and the National Rivers Authority" shall cease to have effect.

The Local Government Act 1974

18. In section 25(1) of the Local Government Act 1974 (authorities subject to investigation by Local Commissioners), for paragraph (d) there shall be substituted—   1974 c. 7.

"(d) in relation to the flood defence functions of the Environment Agency, within the meaning of the Water Resources Act 1991, the Environment Agency and any regional flood defence committee."   1991 c. 57.

The Control of Pollution Act 1974

19.—(1) Section 5 of the Control of Pollution Act 1974 (licences to dispose of waste) shall be amended in accordance with the following provisions of this paragraph.   1974 c. 40.

(2) In subsection (3) (duty of recipient of application for licence where planning permission is in force)—

(a) for the words "Where a disposal authority receives an application" there shall be substituted the words "Where an application has been received"; and

(b) for the words "the authority", where first occurring, there shall be substituted the words "the appropriate Agency" and, where secondly occurring, there shall be substituted the words "that Agency".

(3) In subsection (4) (duty of disposal authority to refer to National Rivers Authority etc proposals to issue licences)—

(a) for the words "a disposal authority" there shall be substituted the words "the appropriate Agency";

(b) for the words "the authority" there shall be substituted the words "that Agency";

(c) for paragraph (a), there shall be substituted—

"(a) to refer the proposal to any collection authority whose area includes any part of the relevant land; and";

(d) in paragraph (b), for the words "the disposal authority", in both places where they occur, there shall be substituted the words "that Agency"; and

(e) the words following paragraph (b) (reference of proposal to Secretary of State in certain cases) shall cease to have effect.

(4) Subsection (5) (separate provision for Scotland) shall cease to have effect.

20.—(1) Section 6 of that Act (provisions supplementary to section 5) shall be amended in accordance with the following provisions of this paragraph.

(2) In subsection (2) (conditions which may be included in disposal licences)—

(a) for the words "the disposal authority which issues it" there shall be substituted the words "the appropriate Agency"; and

(b) for the words "the authority" there shall be substituted the words "that Agency".

(3) In subsection (3) (offence of contravening a licence condition without reasonable excuse) for the words "the disposal authority which issued the licence" there shall be substituted the words "the Environment Agency".

(4) In subsection (4) (duty of each disposal authority to maintain registers etc)—

(a) for the words "each disposal authority" there shall be substituted the words "the Environment Agency and of SEPA";

(b) for paragraph (a) there shall be substituted—

"(a) to maintain a register containing copies of all disposal licences which are for the time being in force in respect of land in England and Wales or, as the case may be, Scotland;" and

(c) in paragraph (c), for the words "the authority" there shall be substituted the words "that Agency".

(5) In subsection (5) (applications deemed to be refused if not granted within two months of receipt)—

(a) for the words "a disposal authority receives an application duly made to it for a disposal licence" there shall be substituted the words "a duly made application for a disposal licence was received";

(b) for the words "the authority", in the first two places where they occur, there shall be substituted the words "the appropriate Agency"; and

(c) for the words "the authority", wherever else occurring, there shall be substituted the words "that Agency".

21.—(1) Section 7 of that Act (variation of conditions and revocation of licences) shall be amended in accordance with the following provisions of this paragraph.

(2) In subsection (1) (modification of conditions of disposal licences issued by disposal authorities)—

(a) the words "issued by a disposal authority" shall be omitted; and

(b) for the words "the authority", where first occurring, there shall be substituted the words "the appropriate Agency" and, wherever else occurring, there shall be substituted the words "that Agency".

(3) In subsection (2) (application of section 5(4))—

(a) the words "or, in relation to Scotland, subsection (5)" shall cease to have effect; and

(b) for paragraphs (a) and (b) there shall be substituted—

"(a) the Environment Agency or SEPA, as the case may be, may postpone the reference in pursuance of the said subsection (4) so far as it considers that by reason of an emergency it is appropriate to do so; and

(b) the Environment Agency or SEPA, as the case may be, may disregard any collection authority for the purposes of the preceding provisions of this subsection in relation to a modification which, in the opinion of that Agency, will not affect that authority."

(4) In subsection (4) (revocation of disposal licences issued by disposal authorities)—

(a) the words "issued by a disposal authority" shall be omitted;

(b) for the words "the authority", where first occurring, there shall be substituted the words "the appropriate Agency" and, in the other place where they occur, there shall be substituted the words "that Agency".

22.—(1) Section 8 of that Act (transfer and relinquishment of licences) shall be amended in accordance with the following provisions of this paragraph.

(2) In subsection (1) (transfer of licences)—

(a) for the words "the authority which issued the licence" there shall be substituted the words "the appropriate Agency"; and

(b) for the words "the authority", in both places where they occur, there shall be substituted the words "that Agency".

(3) In subsection (4) (cancellation of licences)—

(a) for the words "the authority which issued it" there shall be substituted the words "the appropriate Agency"; and

(b) for the words "the authority", in the other place where they occur, there shall be substituted the words "that Agency".

23.—(1) Section 9 of that Act (supervision of licensed activities) shall be amended in accordance with the following provisions of this paragraph.

(2) In subsection (1) (duties of the authority which issued the licence) for the words "the authority which issued the licence" there shall be substituted the words "the appropriate Agency".

(3) In subsection (2) (powers of entry of authorised officers to carry out works in an emergency)—

(a) for the words "a disposal authority" there shall be substituted the words "the Environment Agency or SEPA, as the case may be,"; and

(b) for the words "the authority", wherever occurring, there shall be substituted the words "that Agency".

(4) In subsection (3) (recovery of certain expenditure from licence holders)—

(a) for the words "a disposal authority" there shall be substituted the words "the Environment Agency or SEPA"; and

(b) for the words "the authority" there shall be substituted the word "it".

(5) In subsection (4) (breach of conditions of licences)—

(a) for the words "a disposal authority" there shall be substituted the words "the appropriate Agency";

(b) the words "issued by the authority" shall be omitted; and

(c) for the words "the authority", wherever else occurring, there shall be substituted the words "that Agency".

24.—(1) Section 10 of that Act (appeals to Secretary of State from decisions with respect to licences) shall be amended in accordance with the following provisions of this paragraph.

(2) In subsection (1) (duty of disposal authority concerned to implement Secretary of State's determination) for the words "the disposal authority concerned" there shall be substituted the words "the appropriate Agency".

(3) In subsection (3) (cases where the decision under appeal is effective pending the determination of the appeal)—

(a) for the words "to a decision of a disposal authority" there shall be substituted the words "if the decision in question is a decision";

(b) for the words "in the opinion of the authority" there shall be substituted the words "in the opinion of the body making the decision in question";

(c) for the words "the authority acted" there shall be substituted the words "that body acted"; and

(d) in paragraph (b), for the words "the authority" there shall be substituted the words "the appropriate Agency".

25. In section 11 of that Act (special provision for land occupied by disposal authorities: resolutions etc) subsections (1) to (11) shall cease to have effect.

26.—(1) Section 16 of that Act (removal of waste deposited in breach of licensing provisions) shall be amended in accordance with the following provisions of this paragraph.

(2) In subsection (1) (power of disposal or collection authority to serve notice on occupier of land in its area) for the words from "in the area" to "the authority may" there shall be substituted the words "in contravention of section 3(1) of this Act, any authority to which this section applies may".

(3) After subsection (7) there shall be added—

"(8) The authorities to which this section applies are—

(a) the appropriate Agency;

(b) any collection authority in whose area the land mentioned in subsection (1) above is situated."

27. In section 30 of that Act (interpretation of Part I) in subsection (1)—

(a) the following definition shall be inserted at the appropriate place—

""the appropriate Agency" means—

(a) in relation to England and Wales, the Environment Agency;

(b) in relation to Scotland, SEPA;";

(b) for the definition of "waste" there shall be substituted—

1990 c. 43.   ""waste" has the same meaning as it has in Part II of the Environmental Protection Act 1990 by virtue of section 75(2) of that Act;"; and

(c) the words from "and for the purposes" to the end (which provide a presumption that anything discarded is waste unless the contrary is proved) shall cease to have effect.

28. In section 62(2)(a) of that Act (exceptions to restrictions on the operation of loudspeakers in streets), as it has effect in relation to England and Wales, for the words "National Rivers Authority" there shall be substituted the words "Environment Agency".

1974 c. 40.   29.—(1) The Control of Pollution Act 1974, as it has effect in relation to Scotland, shall be amended in accordance with the following provisions of this paragraph.

(2) Subject to the amendments made by the following provisions of this paragraph, for the words "a river purification authority", "the river purification authority", "river purification authority", "river purification authorities", "the river purification authorities", "each river purification authority" and "any river purification authority", in each place where they occur in the undernoted provisions, there shall be substituted the words "SEPA"—

section 30A(2)(a) and (3);

section 30C(1);

section 30D;

section 31(4)(d) and (6);

section 31A(2);

section 33(1);

sections 34 to 39;

section 41;

sections 46 to 51;

section 96(3); and

Schedule 1A.

(3) In section 30A(2)(a) (Secretary of State to deposit maps showing fresh-water limits of every relevant river or watercourse) the words "in the area of that authority" shall cease to have effect.

(4) In section 30C (water quality objectives)—

(a) in subsection (1) (Secretary of State to establish water quality objectives), the words "within the area of that authority" shall cease to have effect;

(b) in subsection (3)(b) (Secretary of State to review water quality objectives) for the words "the river purification authority on which that notice has been served" there shall be substituted the words "SEPA";

(c) in subsection (4) (Secretary of State to give notice and consider representations when reviewing water quality objectives)—

(i) the words "in the area of a river purification authority" shall cease to have effect; and

(ii) in paragraph (a) for the words "that authority" there shall be substituted the words "SEPA";

(d) in subsection (5)(b) (form of notice to be given by the Secretary of State when varying water quality objectives) for the words "the authority" there shall be substituted the words "SEPA"; and

(e) in subsection (6) (Secretary of State to serve further notice where water quality objectives remain unchanged)—

(i) the words "in the area of a river purification authority" shall cease to have effect; and

(ii) for the words "that authority" there shall be substituted the words "SEPA".

(5) In section 30E (consultation and collaboration)—

(a) for the word "their" there shall be substituted the word "its";

(b) for the words "river purification authorities" there shall be substituted the words "SEPA"; and

(c) for the words "National Rivers Authority" there shall be substituted the words "Environment Agency".

(6) In section 31 (control of pollution of rivers and coastal waters etc.)—

(a) in subsection (4)(b) (Secretary of State power to restrict or prohibit prescribed activities in designated areas) for the words "the river purification authority in whose area the place is situated" there shall be substituted the words "SEPA"; and

(b) in subsection (6) (power to make byelaws to prohibit or regulate prescribed activities)—

(i) for the words "the authority" there shall be substituted the word "it"; and

(ii) the words "in its area" shall cease to have effect.

(7) Section 31D (powers of entry in relation to agreements under section 31B) shall cease to have effect.

(8) In section 33(1) (power to make byelaws regulating or prohibiting sanitary appliances on vessels)—

(a) for the words "the authority" where they first occur there shall be substituted the word "it"; and

(b) the words "in the area of the authority" shall cease to have effect.

(9) In section 34 (consents for discharges of trade and sewage effluent etc.)—

(a) for the words "the authority" and "the authority's" in each place where they occur (other than the last reference in subsection (2)) there shall be substituted the words "SEPA" and "SEPA's" respectively;

(b) in subsection (2) (disposal of application)—

(i) for the words "a river purification authority to which an application for consent is" there shall be substituted the words "SEPA, in relation to an application for consent";

(ii) for the word "three" there shall be substituted the word "four"; and

(iii) for the words "the authority shall be deemed to have refused the consent" there shall be substituted the words "the applicant may treat the consent applied for as having been refused"; and

(c) in subsection (3) (consent not to relate to discharges which occurred prior to consent) the words "in its area" shall cease to have effect.

(10) In the following provisions, for the words "an authority", "any authority", "the authority", "the authorities" and "the relevant river purification authority" in each place where they occur there shall be substituted the words "SEPA"—

sections 35 to 39;

section 41;

sections 46 to 49; and

Schedule 1A, paragraph 2.

(11) In section 36 (provisions supplementary to sections 34 and 35)—

(a) in subsection (1), after the word "shall" there shall be inserted the words ", subject to subsections (2A) and (2B) below,";

(b) after subsection (2) there shall be inserted the following subsections—

"(2A) A person who proposes to make, or has made, an application to SEPA for consent in pursuance of section 34 of this Act may apply to the Secretary of State within a prescribed period for a certificate providing that subsection (1) above shall not apply to that application.

(2B) If the Secretary of State is satisfied that—

(a) it would be contrary to the interests of national security; or

(b) it would prejudice to an unreasonable degree the commercial interests of any person,

not to issue a certificate applied for under subsection (2A) above, he may issue the certificate and, if he does so, subsection (1) above shall not apply to the application specified in the certificate."; and

(c) in subsection (6), for the word "three" there shall be substituted the word "four".

(12) In section 37(1) (revocation of consents and alteration and imposition of conditions), for the words from the beginning to "consent" in the second place where it occurs there shall be substituted the words "SEPA may from time to time review any consent given in pursuance of section 34 of this Act".

(13) In section 38 (restriction as to variation and revocation of consent and of previous variation), in each of subsections (1) and (2), for the word "two" there shall be substituted the word "four".

(14) After section 38 there shall be inserted—

"General review of consents.   38A.—(1) If it appears appropriate to the Secretary of State to do so he may at any time direct SEPA to review—

(a) the consents given under section 34 of this Act; or

(b) any description of such consents,

and the conditions (if any) to which those consents are subject.

(2) A direction given by virtue of subsection (1) above—

(a) shall specify the purpose for which; and

(b) may specify the manner in which,

the review is to be conducted.

(3) After carrying out the review, SEPA shall submit to the Secretary of State its proposals (if any) for—

(a) the modification of the conditions of any consent reviewed pursuant to the direction; or

(b) in the case of any such consent which is unconditional, subjecting the consent to conditions.

(4) Where the Secretary of State has received any proposals under subsection (3) above in relation to any consent he may, if it appears appropriate to him to do so, direct SEPA, in relation to that consent—

(a) to make modifications of the conditions of the consent; or

(b) in the case of an unconditional consent, to subject the consent to conditions.

(5) A direction given by virtue of subsection (4) above may direct SEPA to do, in relation to any such consent, only—

(a) any such thing as SEPA has proposed should be done in relation to that consent; or

(b) any such thing with such modifications as appear to the Secretary of State to be appropriate.".

(15) In section 39 (appeals to Secretary of State)—

(a) in subsection (1), in each of paragraphs (b) and (c), for the words "the preceding section" there shall be substituted the words "section 38 of this Act";

(b) in subsection (5), for the words "terms and period as are" there shall be substituted the words "period as is";

(c) after that subsection there shall be inserted the following subsections—

"(5A) Subject to subsection (5B) below, where a question is referred to the Secretary of State in pursuance of subsection (1)(b) above, the revocation of the consent or, as the case may be, the modification of the conditions of the consent or the provision that the consent (having been unconditional) shall be subject to conditions, shall not take effect while the reference is pending.

(5B) Subsection (5A) above shall not apply to a reference where the notice effecting the revocation, modification or provision in question includes a statement that in the opinion of SEPA it is necessary for the purpose of preventing or, where that is not practicable, minimising—

(a) the entry into controlled waters of any poisonous, noxious or polluting matter or any solid waste matter, or

(b) harm to human health,

that that subsection should not apply.

(5C) Where the reference falls within subsection (5B) above, if, on the application of the holder or former holder of the consent, the Secretary of State (or other person determining the question referred) determines that SEPA acted unreasonably in excluding the application of subsection (5A) above, then—

(a) if the reference is still pending at the end of the day on which that determination is made, subsection (5A) above shall apply to the reference from the end of that day; and

> (b) the holder or former holder of the consent shall be entitled to recover compensation from SEPA in respect of any loss suffered by him in consequence of the exclusion of the application of that subsection;
>
> and any dispute as to a person's entitlement to such compensation or as to the amount of it shall be determined by a single arbiter appointed, in default of agreement between the parties concerned, by the Secretary of State on the application of any of the parties."; and

(d) at the end there shall be added—

> ·"(7) This section is subject to section 114 of the Environment Act 1995 (delegation or reference of appeals).
>
> (8) In this section "the holder", in relation to a consent, is the person who has the consent."

(16) Section 40(4) (transitional provisions relating to consents) shall cease to have effect.

(17) In section 41(1) (maintenance of registers)—

(a) after the words "prescribed particulars of" there shall be inserted the words "or relating to";

(b) the following provisions shall cease to have effect—

> (i) in paragraph (c) (information contained in registers) the words "(except section 40(4))";
>
> (ii) in paragraph (d) (duty to maintain registers of samples of effluent), sub-paragraph (ii); and
>
> (iii) paragraph (e) (duty to register certain notices);

(c) there shall be added at the end the following paragraphs—

> "(f) enforcement notices served under section 49A of this Act;
>
> (g) directions given by the Secretary of State in relation to SEPA's functions under this Part of this Act;
>
> (h) convictions, for offences under this Part of this Act, of persons who have the benefit of consents under section 34 of this Act;
>
> (j) information obtained or furnished in pursuance of conditions of such consents;
>
> (k) works notices under section 46A of this Act;
>
> (l) appeals under section 46C of this Act;
>
> (m) convictions for offences under section 46D of this Act; and
>
> (n) such other matters relating to the quality of water as may be prescribed."

(18) In section 41(2) (registers to be available for inspection by, and facilities for obtaining copies of entries to be afforded to, the public), after paragraph (b) there shall be added the words—

> "and, for the purposes of this subsection, places may be prescribed at which any such registers or facilities as are mentioned in paragraph (a) or (b) above are to be available or afforded to the public in pursuance of the paragraph in question."

(19) At the end of section 41 there shall be added the following subsection—

> "(3) The Secretary of State may give SEPA directions requiring the removal from any register maintained by it under this section of any specified information which is not prescribed for inclusion under subsection (1) of this section or which, by virtue of section 42A or 42B of this Act, ought to have been excluded from the registers."

(20) For section 42, there shall be substituted the following sections—

"Exclusion from registers of information affecting national security.

42A.—(1) No information shall be included in a register kept or maintained by SEPA under section 41 of this Act if and so long as, in the opinion of the Secretary of State, the inclusion in such a register of that information, or information of that description, would be contrary to the interests of national security.

(2) The Secretary of State may, for the purposes of securing the exclusion from registers of information to which subsection (1) of this section applies, give SEPA directions—

> (a) specifying information, or descriptions of information, to be excluded from their registers; or

> (b) specifying descriptions of information to be referred to the Secretary of State for his determination;

and no information to be referred to the Secretary of State in pursuance of paragraph (b) of this subsection shall be included in any such register until the Secretary of State determines that it should be so included.

(3) SEPA shall notify the Secretary of State of any information it excludes from a register in pursuance of directions under subsection (2) of this section.

(4) A person may, as respects any information which appears to him to be information to which subsection (1) of this section may apply, give a notice to the Secretary of State specifying the information and indicating its apparent nature; and, if he does so—

> (a) he shall notify SEPA that he has done so; and

> (b) no information so notified to the Secretary of State shall be included in any such register until the Secretary of State has determined that it should be so included.

Exclusion from registers of certain confidential information.

42B.—(1) No information relating to the affairs of any individual or business shall, without the consent of that individual or the person for the time being carrying on that business, be included in a register kept or maintained by SEPA under section 41 of this Act, if and so long as the information—

> (a) is, in relation to him, commercially confidential; and

> (b) is not required to be included in the register in pursuance of directions under subsection (7) of this section;

but information is not commercially confidential for the purposes of this section unless it is determined under this section to be so by SEPA, or, on appeal, by the Secretary of State.

(2) Where information is furnished to SEPA for the purpose of—

> (a) an application for a consent under section 34 of this Act;

> (b) complying with any condition of such a consent; or

> (c) complying with a notice under section 93 of this Act,

then, if the person furnishing it applies to SEPA to have the information excluded from any register kept or maintained by SEPA under section 41 of this Act, on the ground that it is commercially confidential (as regards himself or another person), SEPA shall determine whether the information is or is not commercially confidential.

(3) A determination under subsection (2) of this section must be made within the period of fourteen days beginning with the date of the application and if SEPA fails to make a determination within that period it shall be treated as having determined that the information is commercially confidential.

(4) Where it appears to SEPA that any information (other than information furnished in circumstances within subsection (2) of this section) which has been obtained by SEPA under or by virtue of any provision of any enactment might be commercially confidential, SEPA shall—

(a) give to the person to whom or whose business it relates notice that that information is required to be included in a register kept or maintained by SEPA under section 41 of this Act, unless excluded under this section; and

(b) give him a reasonable opportunity—

(i) of objecting to the inclusion of the information on the ground that it is commercially confidential; and

(ii) of making representations to SEPA for the purpose of justifying any such objection;

and, if any representations are made, SEPA shall, having taken the representations into account, determine whether the information is or is not commercially confidential.

(5) Where, under subsection (2) or (4) of this section, SEPA determines that information is not commercially confidential—

(a) the information shall not be entered on the register until the end of the period of twenty-one days beginning with the date on which the determination is notified to the person concerned; and

(b) that person may appeal to the Secretary of State against the decision;

and, where an appeal is brought in respect of any information, the information shall not be entered on the register pending the final determination or withdrawal of the appeal.

(6) Subsections (2), (4) and (7) of section 49B of this Act shall apply in relation to appeals under subsection (5) of this section; but

(a) subsection (4) of that section shall have effect for the purposes of this subsection with the substitution for the words from ("which may" onwards of the words "(which must be held in private)"; and

(b) subsection (5) of this section is subject to section 114 of the Environment Act 1995 (delegation or reference of appeals etc).

(7) The Secretary of State may give SEPA directions as to specified information, or descriptions of information, which the public interest requires to be included in registers kept or maintained by SEPA under section 41 of this Act notwithstanding that the information may be commercially confidential.

(8) Information excluded from a register shall be treated as ceasing to be commercially confidential for the purposes of this section at the expiry of the period of four years beginning with the date of the determination by virtue of which it was excluded; but the person who furnished it may apply to SEPA for the information to remain excluded from the register on the ground that it is still commercially confidential and SEPA shall determine whether or not that is the case.

(9) Subsections (5) and (6) of this section shall apply in relation to a determination under subsection (8) of this section as they apply in relation to a determination under subsection (2) or (4) of this section.

(10) The Secretary of State may prescribe the substitution (whether in all cases or in such classes or descriptions of case as may be prescribed) for the period for the time being specified in subsection (3) above of such other period as he considers appropriate.

(11) Information is, for the purposes of any determination under this section, commercially confidential, in relation to any individual or person, if its being contained in register would prejudice to an unreasonable degree the commercial interests of that individual or person."

(21) In section 46 (operations to remedy or forestall pollution of water)—

(a) in subsection (1)—

(i) at the beginning there shall be inserted the words "Subject to subsection (1B) below,"; and

(ii) the words "in its area" where they first occur and "in its area or elsewhere" shall cease to have effect;

(b) after subsection (1) there shall be inserted—

"(1A) In either case mentioned in subsection (1) of this section, SEPA shall be entitled to carry out investigations for the purpose of establishing the source of the matter and the identity of the person who has caused or knowingly permitted it to be present in controlled waters or at a place from which it was likely, in the opinion of SEPA, to enter controlled waters.

(1B) Without prejudice to the power of SEPA to carry out investigations under subsection (1A) above, the power conferred by subsection (1) above to carry out operations shall be exercisable only in a case where—

(a) SEPA considers it necessary to carry out forthwith any operations falling within paragraph (a) or (b) of subsection (1) above; or

(b) it appears to SEPA, after reasonable inquiry, that no person can be found on whom to serve a works notice under section 46A of this Act.";

(c) in subsection (2) after the words "any operations" there shall be inserted the words "or investigations";

(d) in subsection (3)(b)—

(i) after the words "any operations" there shall be inserted the words "or investigations"; and

(ii) after the words "an abandoned mine" there shall be inserted the words "or an abandoned part of a mine"; and

(e) after subsection (3) there shall be inserted—

"(3A) Subsection (3)(b) of this section shall not apply to the owner or former operator of any mine or part of a mine if the mine or part in question became abandoned after 31st December 1999.

(3B) Subsections (5) and (6) of section 30J above shall apply in relation to subsections (3) and (3A) above as they apply in relation to subsections (3) and (4) of that section.".

(22) After section 46 there shall be inserted the following sections—

"Notices requiring persons to carry out anti-pollution operations.

46A.—(1) Subject to the following provisions of this section, where it appears to SEPA that any poisonous, noxious or polluting matter or any solid waste matter is likely to enter, or to be or to have been present in, any controlled waters, SEPA shall be entitled to serve a works notice on any person who, as the case may be,—

(a) caused or knowingly permitted the matter in question to be present at the place from which it is likely, in the opinion of SEPA, to enter any controlled waters; or

(b) caused or knowingly permitted the matter in question to be present in any controlled waters.

(2) For the purposes of this section, a "works notice" is a notice requiring the person on whom it is served to carry out such of the following operations as may be specified in the notice, that is to say—

(a) in a case where the matter in question appears likely to enter any controlled waters, operations for the purpose of preventing it from doing so; or

(b) in a case where the matter appears to be or to have been present in any controlled waters, operations for the purpose—

(i) of removing or disposing of the matter;

(ii) of remedying or mitigating any pollution caused by its presence in the waters; or

(iii) so far as it is reasonably practicable to do so, of restoring the waters, including any flora and fauna dependent on the aquatic environment of the waters, to their state immediately before the matter became present in the waters.

(3) A works notice—

(a) must specify the periods within which the person on whom it is served is required to do each of the things specified in the notice; and

(b) is without prejudice to the powers of SEPA by virtue of section 46(1B)(a) of this Act.

(4) Before serving a works notice on any person, SEPA shall reasonably endeavour to consult that person concerning the operations which are to be specified in the notice.

(5) The Secretary of State may by regulations make provision for or in connection with—

(a) the form or content of works notices;

(b) requirements for consultation, before the service of a works notice, with persons other than the person on whom that notice is to be served;

(c) steps to be taken for the purposes of any consultation required under subsection (4) above or regulations made by virtue of paragraph (b) above; and

(d) any other steps of a procedural nature which are to be taken in connection with, or in consequence of, the service of a works notice.

(6) A works notice shall not be regarded as invalid, or as invalidly served, by reason only of any failure to comply with the requirements of subsection (4) above or of regulations made by virtue of paragraph (b) of subsection (5) above.

(7) Nothing in subsection (1) above shall entitle SEPA to require the carrying out of any operations which would impede or prevent the making of any discharge in pursuance of a consent given by SEPA by virtue of section 34 of this Act.

(8) No works notice shall be served on any person requiring him to carry out any operations in respect of water from an abandoned mine or an abandoned part of a mine which that person permitted to reach such a place as is mentioned in subsection (1)(a) above or to enter any controlled waters.

(9) Subsection (8) above shall not apply to the owner or former operator of any mine or part of a mine if the mine or part in question became abandoned after 31st December 1999.

(10) Subsections (5) and (6) of section 30J of this Act shall apply in relation to subsections (8) and (9) above as they apply in relation to subsections (3) and (4) of that section.

(11) Where SEPA—

    (a) carries out any such investigations as are mentioned in section 46(1A) of this Act, and

    (b) serves a works notice on a person in connection with the matter to which the investigations relate,

it shall (unless the notice is quashed or withdrawn) be entitled to recover the costs or expenses reasonably incurred in carrying out those investigations from that person.

(12) The Secretary of State may, if he thinks fit in relation to any person, give directions to SEPA as to whether or how it should exercise its powers under this section.

Grant of, and compensation for, rights of entry etc.

46B.—(1) A works notice may require a person to carry out operations in relation to any land or waters notwithstanding that he is not entitled to carry out those operations.

(2) Any person whose consent is required before any operations required by a works notice may be carried out shall grant, or join in granting, such rights in relation to any land or waters as will enable the person on whom the works notice is served to comply with any requirements imposed by the works notice.

(3) Before serving a works notice, SEPA shall reasonably endeavour to consult every person who appears to it—

    (a) to be the owner or occupier of any relevant land, and

    (b) to be a person who might be required by subsection (2) above to grant, or join in granting, any rights,

concerning the rights which that person may be so required to grant.

(4) A works notice shall not be regarded as invalid, or as invalidly served, by reason only of any failure to comply with the requirements of subsection (3) above.

(5) A person who grants, or joins in granting, any rights pursuant to subsection (2) above shall be entitled, on making an application within such period as may be prescribed and in such manner as may be prescribed to such person as may be

prescribed, to be paid by the person on whom the works notice in question is served compensation of such amount as may be determined in such manner as may be prescribed.

(6) Without prejudice to the generality of the regulations that may be made by virtue of subsection (5) above, regulations by virtue of that subsection may make such provision in relation to compensation under this section as may be made by regulations by virtue of subsection (4) of section 35A of the Environmental Protection Act 1990 in relation to compensation under that section.

1990 c. 43.

(7) In this section—

"relevant land" means—

(a) any land or waters in relation to which the works notice in question requires, or may require, operations to be carried out; or

(b) any land adjoining or adjacent to that land or those waters;

"works notice" means a works notice under section 46A of this Act.

Appeals against works notices.

46C.—(1) A person on whom a works notice is served may, within the period of twenty-one days beginning with the day on which the notice is served, appeal against the notice to the Secretary of State.

(2) On any appeal under this section the Secretary of State—

(a) shall quash the notice, if he is satisfied that there is a material defect in the notice; but

(b) subject to that, may confirm the notice, with or without modification, or quash it.

(3) The Secretary of State may by regulations make provision with respect to—

(a) the grounds on which appeals under this section may be made; or

(b) the procedure on any such appeal.

(4) Regulations under subsection (3) above may (among other things)—

1936 c. 49.

(a) include provisions comparable to those in section 290 of the Public Health Act 1936 (appeals against notices requiring the execution of works);

(b) prescribe the cases in which a works notice is, or is not, to be suspended until the appeal is decided, or until some other stage in the proceedings;

(c) prescribe the cases in which the decision on an appeal may in some respects be less favourable to the appellant than the works notice against which he is appealing;

(d) prescribe the cases in which the appellant may claim that a works notice should have been served on some other person and prescribe the procedure to be followed in those cases;

(e) make provision as respects—

(i) the particulars to be included in the notice of appeal;

(ii) the persons on whom notice of appeal is to be served and the particulars, if any, which are to accompany the notice; or

(iii) the abandonment of an appeal.

(5) In this section "works notice" means a works notice under section 46A of this Act.

(6) This section is subject to section 114 of the Environment Act 1995 (delegation or reference of appeals).

Consequences of not complying with a works notice.
46D.—(1) If a person on whom SEPA serves a works notice fails to comply with any of the requirements of the notice, he shall be guilty of an offence.

(2) A person who commits an offence under subsection (1) above shall be liable—

(a) on summary conviction, to imprisonment for a term not exceeding three months or to a fine not exceeding £20,000 or to both;

(b) on conviction on indictment, to imprisonment for a term not exceeding two years or to a fine or to both.

(3) If a person on whom a works notice has been served fails to comply with any of the requirements of the notice, SEPA may do what that person was required to do and may recover from him any costs or expenses reasonably incurred by SEPA in doing it.

(4) If SEPA is of the opinion that proceedings for an offence under subsection (1) above would afford an ineffectual remedy against a person who has failed to comply with the requirements of a works notice, SEPA may take proceedings in any court of competent jurisdiction for the purpose of securing compliance with the notice.

(5) In this section "works notice" means a works notice under section 46A of this Act.".

(23) In section 47 (duty to deal with waste from vessels etc.)—

(a) in subsection (1) (duty), the words "in its area" shall cease to have effect; and

(b) in subsection (2) (provision of facilities), the words "in the authority's area" shall cease to have effect.

(24) In section 48(1) (power to exclude unregistered vessels from rivers etc.) the words "in its area" shall cease to have effect.

(25) In section 49 (deposit and vegetation in rivers etc) at the end there shall be added—

"(5) This section is subject to section 114 of the Environment Act 1995 (delegation or reference of appeals)."

(26) After that section there shall be inserted—

"Enforcement notices as respects discharge consents.
49A.—(1) If SEPA is of the opinion that the holder of a relevant consent is contravening any condition of the consent, or is likely to contravene any such condition, it may serve on him a notice (an "enforcement notice").

(2) An enforcement notice shall—

(a) state that SEPA is of the said opinion;

(b) specify the matters constituting the contravention or the matters making it likely that the contravention will arise;

(c) specify the steps that must be taken to remedy the contravention or, as the case may be, to remedy the matters making it likely that the contravention will arise; and

(d) specify the period within which those steps must be taken.

(3) Any person who fails to comply with any requirement imposed by an enforcement notice shall be guilty of an offence and liable—

(a) on summary conviction, to imprisonment for a term not exceeding three months or to a fine not exceeding £20,000 or to both;

(b) on conviction on indictment, to imprisonment for a term not exceeding two years or to a fine or to both.

(4) If SEPA is of the opinion that proceedings for an offence under subsection (3) above would afford an ineffectual remedy against a person who has failed to comply with the requirements of an enforcement notice, SEPA may take proceedings in any court of competent jurisdiction for the purpose of securing compliance with the notice.

(5) The Secretary of State may, if he thinks fit in relation to any person, give to SEPA directions as to whether it should exercise its powers under this section and as to the steps which must be taken.

(6) In this section—

"relevant consent" means a consent for the purposes of section 30J(7)(a), 34 or 49(1) of this Act; and

"the holder", in relation to a relevant consent, is the person who has the consent in question.

Appeals against enforcement notices.

49B.—(1) A person upon whom an enforcement notice has been served under section 49A of this Act may appeal to the Secretary of State.

(2) This section is subject to section 114 of the Environment Act 1995 (delegation or reference of appeals etc.).

(3) An appeal under this section shall, if and to the extent a requirement to do so is prescribed, be advertised in the manner prescribed.

(4) If either party to the appeal so requests or the Secretary of State so decides, an appeal shall be or continue in the form of a hearing (which may, if the person hearing the appeal so decides, be held, or held to any extent, in private).

(5) On the determination of an appeal under this section, the Secretary of State may either quash or affirm the enforcement notice and, if he affirms it, may do so either in its original form or with such modifications as he may in the circumstances think fit.

(6) The bringing of an appeal under this section shall not have the effect of suspending the operation of the notice appealed against.

(7) The period within which and the manner in which appeals under this section are to be brought and the manner in which they are to be considered shall be as prescribed."

(27) In section 50 (investigation of water pollution problems arising from closures of mines) the words "in its area" shall cease to have effect.

(28) Sections 53 (charges in respect of consents to certain discharges in Scotland), 54 (directions to the river purification authority), 55 (discharges by islands councils) and 56(4) (meaning of the area of a river purification authority) shall cease to have effect.

(29) In section 56(1) (interpretation of Part II), the following definition shall be inserted in the appropriate place in alphabetical order—

""operations" includes works;".

(30) In section 90(3) (establishment charges etc. in relation to Scotland), for the words from "a river" to the end there shall be substituted the words "SEPA".

(31) Section 91(5)(a) (application of that section to Scotland) shall cease to have effect.

(32) In section 96(3) (local inquiries) the words from "but as if" to the end shall cease to have effect.

(33) In section 98 (interpretation of Part V), for paragraph (b) of the definition of "relevant authority" there shall be substituted —

"(b) in Scotland—

(i) as respects sections 91 and 92, a council constituted under section 2 of the Local Government etc. (Scotland) Act 1994; and

1994 c. 39.

(ii) as respects this Part other than those sections, the Secretary of State, SEPA or a council constituted under section 2 of the Local Government etc. (Scotland) Act 1994.".

(34) In section 104(1) (orders and regulations) the words "59" shall cease to have effect.

(35) In section 105 (interpretation etc.— general) there shall be inserted in the appropriate place—

""SEPA" means the Scottish Environment Protection Agency;".

The Health and Safety at Work etc. Act 1974

30.—(1) The Health and Safety at Work etc. Act 1974 (in this paragraph referred to as "the 1974 Act") shall have effect in accordance with the following provisions of this paragraph.

1974 c. 37.

(2) The appropriate new Agency shall, in consequence of the transfer effected by virtue of section 2(2)(c) or, as the case may be, 21(2)(a) of this Act, be regarded for the purposes of Part I of the 1974 Act as the authority which is, by any of the relevant statutory provisions, made responsible in relation to England and Wales or, as the case may be, Scotland for the enforcement of the relevant enactments (and, accordingly, as the enforcing authority in relation to those enactments).

(3) Neither the Agency nor SEPA shall have power to appoint inspectors under section 19 of the 1974 Act.

(4) Sections 21 to 23 (improvement notices and prohibition notices) shall have effect in any case where the relevant statutory provision in question is any of the relevant enactments as if references in those sections to an inspector were references to the appropriate new Agency.

(5) Section 27 (obtaining of information by the Commission etc) shall have effect in relation to the appropriate new Agency, in its relevant capacity, as it has

effect in relation to the Health and Safety Commission (and not as it has effect in relation to an enforcing authority), except that the consent of the Secretary of State shall not be required to the service by the appropriate new Agency of a notice under subsection (1) of that section; and, accordingly, where that section has effect by virtue of this sub-paragraph—

(a) any reference in that section to the Commission shall be construed as a reference to the appropriate new Agency;

(b) any reference to an enforcing authority shall be disregarded; and

(c) in subsection (3) of that section, the words from "and also" onwards shall be disregarded.

(6) In section 28 (restrictions on disclosure of information)—

(a) in paragraph (a) of subsection (3) (exception for disclosure of information to certain bodies) after the words "the Executive," there shall be inserted the words "the Environment Agency, the Scottish Environment Protection Agency,";

(b) in paragraph (c)(ii) of that subsection (exception for disclosure to officers of certain bodies) as it applies to England and Wales—

(i) the words "of the National Rivers Authority or", and

(ii) the word "Authority," (where next occurring),

shall be omitted;

(c) for paragraph (c)(ii) of that subsection as it applies to Scotland there shall be substituted—

"(ii) an officer of a water undertaker, sewerage undertaker, sewerage authority or water authority who is authorised by that authority to receive it;";

(d) paragraph (c)(iii) of that subsection (exception for disclosure to officers of river purification boards) shall cease to have effect;

(e) in subsection (4) (references to certain bodies to include references to officers or inspectors), after the words "the Executive" (in the first place where they occur) there shall be inserted the words "the Environment Agency, the Scottish Environment Protection Agency,";

(f) in subsection (5) (information disclosed in pursuance of subsection (3) not to be used by recipient except for specified purposes)—

(i) in paragraph (a) (use for a purpose of the Executive etc) after the words "of the Executive or" there shall be inserted the words "of the Environment Agency or of the Scottish Environment Protection Agency or";

(ii) in paragraph (b) as it applies to England and Wales (use for the purposes of certain bodies of information given to officers of those bodies), the words "the National Rivers Authority" shall be omitted;

(iii) in the said paragraph (b) as it applies to Scotland, for the words from the beginning to "in connection" there shall be substituted the words "in the case of information given to an officer of a body which is a local authority, a water undertaker, a sewerage undertaker, a sewerage authority or a water authority the purposes of the body in connection".

(7) In section 38 (restriction on institution of proceedings in England and Wales) after the words "except by an inspector or" there shall be inserted the words "the Environment Agency or".

(8) In this paragraph—

"the appropriate new Agency" means—

(a) in relation to England and Wales, the Agency; and

(b) in relation to Scotland, SEPA;

"relevant capacity", in relation to the appropriate new Agency, means its capacity as the enforcing authority, for the purposes of Part I of the 1974 Act, which is responsible in relation to England and Wales or, as the case may be, Scotland for the enforcement of the relevant enactments;

"the relevant enactments" means the Alkali, &c, Works Regulation Act 1906 and section 5 of the 1974 Act;

"the relevant statutory provisions" has the same meaning as in Part I of the 1974 Act.

1906 c. 14.

The House of Commons Disqualification Act 1975 and the Northern Ireland Assembly Disqualification Act 1975

31. In Part II of Schedule 1 to the House of Commons Disqualification Act 1975 (bodies of which all members are disqualified for membership of the House of Commons) the following entries shall be inserted at the appropriate places—

(a) "The Environment Agency.";

(b) "The Scottish Environment Protection Agency.";

and the like insertions shall be made in Part II of Schedule 1 to the Northern Ireland Assembly Disqualification Act 1975 (bodies of which all members are disqualified for membership of the Northern Ireland Assembly).

1975 c. 24.

1975 c. 25.

The Local Government (Scotland) Act 1975

32.—(1) The Local Government (Scotland) Act 1975 shall be amended in accordance with the following provisions.

1975 c. 30.

(2) In section 16 (borrowing and lending by local authorities and certain other bodies)—

(a) after the words "local authorities" there shall be inserted the word "and";

(b) the words "and river purification boards" shall cease to have effect.

(3) In Schedule 3 (further provision relating to borrowing and lending by local authorities and certain other bodies) in paragraph 28—

(a) in sub-paragraph (1)—

(i) after the word "money" there shall be inserted the word "and";

(ii) the words "or a river purification board," shall cease to have effect;

(b) in sub-paragraph (2) for sub-paragraph (a) there shall be substituted—
"(a) a joint board; and".

The Local Government (Miscellaneous Provisions) Act 1976

33. In section 44 of the Local Government (Miscellaneous Provisions) Act 1976 (interpretation of Part I of that Act) after subsection (1A) (certain provisions of that Act, including section 16 (obtaining information about land), to have effect as if the Broads Authority were a local authority) there shall be inserted—

"(1B) Section 16 of this Act shall have effect as if the Environment Agency were a local authority.".

1976 c. 57.

The Water (Scotland) Act 1980

34.—(1) The Water (Scotland) Act 1980 shall be amended in accordance with the following provisions of this paragraph.

1980 c. 45.

(2) In section 31(1) (consultation where limits of water supply adjoin any part of England) for paragraph (b) there shall be substituted—

"(b) the Scottish Environment Protection Agency."

(3) In section 33(3)(a) (notice of temporary discharge of water into watercourses)—

(a) sub-paragraph (ii) and the preceding "and" shall cease to have effect ; and

(b) at the end of the paragraph there shall be inserted—

"and

(ii) to the Scottish Environment Protection Agency."

(4) In section 109(1) (interpretation) the definitions of "river purification authority" and "river purification board" shall cease to have effect.

(5) In Schedule 1—

(a) in paragraph 2(ii) for the words following "section 17(2)" to the end there shall be substituted the words " on the Scottish Environment Protection Agency";

(b) in paragraph 11(ii) the words "and any river purification authority" shall cease to have effect and at the end there shall be added the words "and on the Scottish Environment Protection Agency";

(c) in paragraph 19 for the words following "any fishery district" to the words "any public undertakers" there shall be substituted the words "any navigation authority exercising jurisdiction in relation to any watercourse from which water is proposed to be taken under the rights to be acquired, the Scottish Environment Protection Agency and any public undertakers".

The Criminal Justice (Scotland) Act 1980

1980 c. 62.

1974 c. 40.

35. In Schedule 1 to the Criminal Justice (Scotland) Act 1980 (sufficiency of evidence by certificate in certain routine matters) in the entry relating to the Control of Pollution Act 1974—

(a) for the words from "Section 31(1)" to "such waters etc)" there shall be substituted the words "Section 30F (pollution offences)"; and

(b) for the words "a river purification authority (within the meaning of that Act)" there shall be substituted the words "the Scottish Environment Protection Agency".

The Road Traffic Regulation Act 1984

1984 c. 27.

36.—(1) In section 1 of the Road Traffic Regulation Act 1984 (traffic regulation orders outside Greater London) in subsection (1), after paragraph (f) (which allows a traffic regulation order to be made for preserving or improving the amenities of the area through which the road runs) there shall be added "or

(g) for any of the purposes specified in paragraphs (a) to (c) of subsection (1) of section 87 of the Environment Act 1995 (air quality)."

(2) In section 6 of that Act (orders similar to traffic regulation orders in Greater London) in subsection (1)(b) (which allows orders in Greater London to be made for equivalent purposes to those in section 1(1)(a) to (f) of that Act) for the words "(a) to (f)" there shall be substituted the words "(a) to (g)".

(3) In section 122(2) of that Act (matters to which, so far as practicable, regard is to be had by local authorities in exercising their functions under the Act) after paragraph (b) there shall be inserted—

> "(bb) the strategy prepared under section 80 of the Environment Act 1995 (national air quality strategy);".

The Control of Pollution (Amendment) Act 1989

37.—(1) The Control of Pollution (Amendment) Act 1989 shall be amended in accordance with the following provisions of this paragraph.   1989 c. 14.

(2) In section 2 (registration of carriers)—

    (a) in subsection (3), without prejudice to the power of regulation authorities to impose a charge in respect of their consideration of any such application, paragraph (e) (power to require them to impose such charges) shall cease to have effect; and

    (b) after that subsection there shall be added—

> "(3A) Without prejudice to the generality of paragraphs (b) and (d) of subsection (3) above—
>
>   (a) the power to prescribe a form under paragraph (b) of that subsection includes power to require an application to be made on any form of any description supplied for the purpose by the regulation authority to which the application is to be made; and
>
>   (b) the power to impose requirements with respect to information under paragraph (d) of that subsection includes power to make provision requiring an application to be accompanied by such information as may reasonably be required by the regulation authority to which it is to be made.".

(3) In section 4 (appeals to the Secretary of State against refusal of registration etc) after subsection (8) there shall be added—

> "(9) This section is subject to section 114 of the Environment Act 1995 (delegation or reference of appeals etc).".

(4) In section 6 (seizure and disposal of vehicles used for illegal waste disposal) for subsection (6) there shall be substituted—

> "(6) Regulations under this section shall not authorise a regulation authority to sell or destroy any property or to deposit any property at any place unless—
>
>   (a) the following conditions are satisfied, that is to say—
>
>   (i) the authority have published such notice, and taken such other steps (if any), as may be prescribed for informing persons who may be entitled to the property that it has been seized and is available to be claimed; and
>
>   (ii) the prescribed period has expired without any obligation arising under the regulations for the regulation authority to return the property to any person; or
>
>   (b) the condition of the property requires it to be disposed of without delay.".

(5) In section 7 (further enforcement provisions) in subsection (1) (which applies certain provisions of the Environmental Protection Act 1990) for the words "sections 68(3), (4) and (5), 69, 70 and 71" there shall be substituted the words "section 71".   1990 c. 43.

(6) Subsection (2) of that section (disclosure of information between certain authorities) shall cease to have effect.

(7) Subsection (8) of that section (which applies section 72 of the 1990 Act) shall cease to have effect.

(8) In section 9, for the definition of "regulation authority" there shall be substituted—

""regulation authority" means—

(a) in relation to England and Wales, the Environment Agency; and

(b) in relation to Scotland, the Scottish Environment Protection Agency;

and any reference to the area of a regulation authority shall accordingly be construed as a reference to any area in England and Wales or, as the case may be, in Scotland;".

The Electricity Act 1989

1989 c. 29.

38.—(1) Section 3 of the Electricity Act 1989 (general duties of the Secretary of State and the Director General of Electricity Supply when exercising certain functions) shall be amended in accordance with the following provisions of this paragraph.

(2) In subsection (1)(c) (duty, subject to subsection (2), to promote competition), for the words "subsection (2)" there shall be substituted the words "subsections (2) and (2A)".

(3) After subsection (2) (duties as regards the supply of electricity in Scotland in certain cases) there shall be inserted—

"(2A) If an order under section 32(1) below requires a public electricity supplier to make, or produce evidence showing that he has made, arrangements or additional arrangements which will secure the result mentioned in subsection (2B) below, the order, so far as relating to any such requirement, may be made for the purpose of, or for purposes which include, promoting the supply to any premises of—

(a) heat produced in association with electricity, or

(b) steam produced from, or air or water heated by, such heat.

(2B) The result referred to in subsection (2A) above is that, for a period specified in the order, there will be available to the public electricity supplier—

(a) from combined heat and power stations; or

(b) from combined heat and power stations of any particular description,

an aggregate amount of generating capacity which is not less than that specified in relation to him in the order.

(2C) In subsection (2B) above, "combined heat and power station" has the meaning given by section 32(8) below.".

(4) In subsection (3) (further duties), for the words "and (2)" there shall be substituted the words ", (2) and (2A)".

39.—(1) Section 32 of that Act (electricity from non-fossil fuel sources) shall be amended in accordance with the following provisions of this paragraph.

(2) After subsection (2) (result to be secured by arrangements made pursuant to an order under subsection (1)) there shall be inserted—

"(2A) For the purposes of this section—

(a) combined heat and power stations generally; and

(b) combined heat and power stations of any particular description,

are to be taken as being particular descriptions of non-fossil fuel generating stations.

(2B) A particular description of combined heat and power stations may be described by reference to, or by reference to matters which include—

(a) the heat or, as the case may be, the steam or heated air or water to be supplied from the station to any premises;

(b) any premises to which any such heat, steam or heated air or water is to be supplied (including, without prejudice to the generality of the foregoing, the use to which any such premises are put);

(c) the means or method by which any such heat, steam or heated air or water is to be supplied to any premises (including, without prejudice to the generality of the foregoing, any system or network of supply or distribution); or

(d) the arrangements (including financial or contractual arrangements) under which any such heat, steam or heated air or water is to be supplied to any premises.

(2C) Subsections (2A) and (2B) above are without prejudice to—

(a) the generality of subsection (2)(b) above, or

(b) section 111(2) below;

and subsection (2B) above is without prejudice to the generality of subsection (2A)(b) above.".

(3) In subsection (8) (interpretation), after the definition of "coal products" there shall be inserted—

"combined heat and power station" means a non-fossil fuel generating station which is (or may be) operated for purposes including the supply to any premises of—

(a) heat produced in association with electricity, or

(b) steam produced from, or air or water heated by, such heat;".

40. In Schedule 4 to that Act (other powers etc. of licence holders) in paragraph 4(1)(b) (power for certain bodies to execute works involving alterations of electric lines or plant) for the words "National Rivers Authority" there shall be substituted the words "Environment Agency".

41. In Schedule 5 to that Act (water rights) in paragraph 8(b) for the words "river purification authority within whose area the watercourse or loch affected is situated" there shall be substituted the words "Scottish Environment Protection Agency".

The Town and Country Planning Act 1990

42. In section 2 of the Town and Country Planning Act 1990 (joint planning boards for National Parks and other areas) after subsection (6) there shall be inserted—

1990 c. 8.

"(6A) Section 241 of the Local Government Act 1972 shall be taken to authorise the application to a joint planning board, subject to any necessary modifications, of any provisions of Part III (accounts and audit) of the Local Government Finance Act 1982 (as well as of any provisions of the Local Government Act 1972) by such an order as is mentioned in subsection (6) above."

1972 c. 70.

1982 c. 32.

43. In Schedule 5 to that Act (conditions relating to mineral working) in paragraph 4 (consultations) after sub-paragraph (4) there shall be inserted—

"(4A) Without prejudice to the application of this paragraph in relation to consultation with the Forestry Commission, where the Minister is consulted pursuant to any provision of this paragraph—

>   (a) he is not required to inspect any land or to express a view on any matter or question; and

>   (b) he is not precluded from responding in general terms or otherwise in terms which are not specific to the land in question.".

44. In Schedule 6 to that Act (determination of certain appeals by person appointed by the Secretary of State) in paragraph 1(1) (power, in respect of appeals under certain provisions, to prescribe classes of appeals to be determined by an appointed person instead of by the Secretary of State), after "208," there shall be inserted "and paragraphs 6(11) and (12) and 11(1) of Schedule 13 and paragraph 9(1) of Schedule 14 to the Environment Act 1995,".

The Environmental Protection Act 1990

1990 c. 43.

45.—(1) Section 1 of the Environmental Protection Act 1990 (interpretation of Part I) shall be amended in accordance with the following provisions of this paragraph.

(2) In subsection (7) (definition of "enforcing authority" in relation to England and Wales), for the words "the chief inspector or the local authority by whom" there shall be substituted the words "the Environment Agency or the local authority by which".

(3) For subsection (8) (definition of "enforcing authority" in relation to Scotland) there shall be substituted—

"(8) In relation to Scotland, references to the "enforcing authority" and a "local enforcing authority" are references to the Scottish Environment Protection Agency (in this Part referred to as "SEPA")."

(4) After subsection (13) there shall be added—

"(14) In this Part "the appropriate Agency" means—

>   (a) in relation to England and Wales, the Environment Agency; and

>   (b) in relation to Scotland, SEPA."

46.—(1) Section 4 of that Act (determination of authority by whom functions are exercisable) shall be amended in accordance with the following provisions of this paragraph.

(2) In subsection (2) (functions of the chief inspector etc in relation to prescribed processes designated for central control) for the words "the chief inspector appointed for England and Wales by the Secretary of State under section 16 below and, in relation to Scotland, of the chief inspector so appointed for Scotland or of the river purification authority, as determined under regulations made under section 5(1) below" there shall be substituted the words "the appropriate Agency".

(3) In subsection (3) (discharge of functions designated for local control) for paragraphs (a) and (b) there shall be substituted—

>   "(a) in the case of a prescribed process carried on (or to be carried on) by means of a mobile plant, where the person carrying on the process has his principal place of business—

>   (i) in England and Wales, the local authority in whose area that place of business is;

>   (ii) in Scotland, SEPA;

>   (b) in any other cases, where the prescribed processes are (or are to be) carried on—

(i) in England and Wales, the local authority in whose area they are (or are to be) carried on;

(ii) in Scotland, SEPA;".

(4) In subsection (4) (directions transferring functions to the chief inspector) for the words "the chief inspector" there shall be substituted the words "the Environment Agency".

(5) After that subsection there shall be inserted—

"(4A) In England and Wales, a local authority, in exercising the functions conferred or imposed on it under this Part by virtue of subsection (3) above, shall have regard to the strategy for the time being published pursuant to section 80 of the Environment Act 1995."

(6) In subsection (5) (effect of such a transfer)—

(a) for the words "the chief inspector" there shall be substituted the words "the Environment Agency"; and

(b) for the word "him" there shall be substituted the words "that Agency".

(7) In subsection (8) (giving or withdrawal of directions)—

(a) for the words "the chief inspector" in each place where they occur there shall be substituted the words "the Environment Agency"; and

(b) the words "or, as the case may be, in the Edinburgh Gazette", in each place where they occur, shall be omitted.

(8) After subsection (8) there shall be inserted—

"(8A) The requirements of sub-paragraph (ii) of paragraph (a) or, as the case may be, of paragraph (b) of subsection (8) above shall not apply in any case where, in the opinion of the Secretary of State, the publication of notice in accordance with that sub-paragraph would be contrary to the interests of national security.

(8B) Subsections (4) to (8A) above shall not apply to Scotland."

(9) For subsection (9) (which, among other things, imposed a duty on the chief inspector etc to follow developments in technology etc and which is partly superseded by this Act) there shall be substituted—

"(9) It shall be the duty of local authorities to follow such developments in technology and techniques for preventing or reducing pollution of the environment due to releases of substances from prescribed processes as concern releases into the air of substances from prescribed processes designated for local control."

(10) In subsection (10) (duty of chief inspector etc to give effect to directions) for the words "the chief inspector, river purification authorities" there shall be substituted the words "the Environment Agency, SEPA".

(11) In subsection (11) (meaning of "local authority")—

(a) at the beginning of paragraph (b) there shall be inserted the words "in England and Wales," and

(b) paragraph (c) and the word "and" immediately preceding it shall cease to have effect.

47. Section 5 of that Act (further provision for Scotland as to discharge and scope of functions) shall cease to have effect.

48. In section 6 of that Act, in subsection (2) (fee payable on application for authorisation) after the words "shall be accompanied by" there shall be inserted—

"(a) in a case where, by virtue of section 41 of the Environment Act 1995, a charge prescribed by a charging scheme under that section is required to be paid to the appropriate Agency in respect of the application, the charge so prescribed; or

(b) in any other case,".

49.—(1) In section 7 of that Act (conditions of authorisations) in subsection (9) the words from "and, in relation to Scotland," to the end of the subsection shall be omitted.

(2) At the end of subsection (12) of that section (definition of "relevant enactments" for the purposes of subsection (2)) there shall be added "; and

(g) section 87 of the Environment Act 1995.".

50.—(1) Section 8 of that Act (fees and charges for authorisations) shall be amended in accordance with the following provisions of this paragraph.

(2) In subsection (1) (payments to be charged by, or paid to, the enforcing authority in accordance with schemes), for the words "enforcing authority" there shall be substituted the words "local enforcing authority".

(3) Subsection (4) (separate schemes for different descriptions of enforcing authority) shall cease to have effect.

(4) In subsection (7) (meaning of "relevant expenditure attributable to authorisations")—

(a) for the words "enforcing authorities" there shall be substituted the words "local enforcing authorities"; and

(b) the words from "together with the expenditure incurred by the National Rivers Authority" onwards shall be omitted.

(5) In subsection (8) (power to revoke authorisation for non-payment of charge), for the words "enforcing authority" there shall be substituted the words "local enforcing authority".

(6) Subsection (9) (payments by the Secretary of State to the National Rivers Authority) shall cease to have effect.

(7) For subsections (10) and (11) (special provision as respects Scotland) there shall be substituted—

"(10) The foregoing provisions of this section shall not apply to Scotland."

51.—(1) Section 10 of that Act (variation of authorisations by enforcing authority) shall be amended in accordance with the following provisions of this paragraph.

(2) In subsection (3) (which provides for the variation specified in a variation notice to take effect on the date so specified unless the notice is withdrawn) after the words "unless the notice is withdrawn" there shall be inserted the words "or is varied under subsection (3A) below".

(3) After that subsection there shall be inserted—

"(3A) An enforcing authority which has served a variation notice may vary that notice by serving on the holder of the authorisation in question a further notice—

(a) specifying the variations which the enforcing authority has decided to make to the variation notice; and

(b) specifying the date or dates on which the variations specified in the variation notice, as varied by the further notice, are to take effect;

and any reference in this Part to a variation notice, or to a variation notice served under subsection (2) above, includes a reference to such a notice as varied by a further notice served under this subsection."

(4) In subsection (4) of that section, for paragraph (b) (requirement to pay the fee prescribed under section 8 of that Act) there shall be substituted—

"(b) require the holder to pay, within such period as may be specified in the notice,—

(i) in a case where the enforcing authority is the Environment Agency or SEPA, the charge (if any) prescribed for the purpose by a charging scheme under section 41 of the Environment Act 1995; or

(ii) in any other case, the fee (if any) prescribed by a scheme under section 8 above."

(5) In subsection (8) of that section, in the definition of "vary", after the word ""vary"" there shall be inserted "(a)" and after the words "any of them;" there shall be added the words "and

(b) in relation to a variation notice, means adding to, or varying or rescinding the notice or any of its contents;".

52. In section 11 of that Act (application by holders of authorisations for variation of conditions etc) for subsection (9) (fees) there shall be substituted—

"(9) Any application to the enforcing authority under this section shall be accompanied—

(a) in a case where the enforcing authority is the Environment Agency or SEPA, by the charge (if any) prescribed for the purpose by a charging scheme under section 41 of the Environment Act 1995; or

(b) in any other case, by the fee (if any) prescribed by a scheme under section 8 above."

53. At the end of section 13 of that Act (enforcement notices) there shall be added—

"(4) The enforcing authority may, as respects any enforcement notice it has issued to any person, by notice in writing served on that person, withdraw the notice."

54.—(1) Section 15 of that Act (appeals against certain authorisations and notices) shall be amended in accordance with the following provisions of this paragraph.

(2) In subsection (2) (appeals against variation notices, enforcement notices or prohibition notices to the Secretary of State) after the words "to the Secretary of State" there shall be added the words "(except where the notice implements a direction of his)."

(3) For subsection (3) (reference of matters involved in appeals under that section to, and determination of such appeals by, persons appointed by the Secretary of State) there shall be substituted—

"(3) This section is subject to section 114 of the Environment Act 1995 (delegation or reference of appeals etc)."

(4) For subsection (5) (hearings) there shall be substituted—

"(5) Before determining an appeal under this section, the Secretary of State may, if he thinks fit—

(a) cause the appeal to take or continue in the form of a hearing (which may, if the person hearing the appeal so decides, be held, or held to any extent, in private); or

(b) cause a local inquiry to be held;

and the Secretary of State shall act as mentioned in paragraph (a) or (b) above if a request is made by either party to the appeal to be heard with respect to the appeal."

(5) In subsection (10) (regulations about appeals) after paragraph (b) there shall be added—

"and any such regulations may make different provision for different cases or different circumstances."

55. Sections 16 to 18 of that Act (appointment of inspectors, powers of inspectors and others and power to deal with cause of imminent danger of serious harm) shall cease to have effect.

56. In section 19 of that Act (obtaining of information from persons and authorities) in subsection (2) (power of specified authorities by notice in writing to require provision of information)—

(a) for paragraphs (c) and (d) (the chief inspector and river purification authorities) there shall be substituted—

"(c) the Environment Agency, and

(d) SEPA,"; and

(b) after the words "service of the notice" there shall be inserted the words ", or at such time,".

57.—(1) Section 20 of that Act (public registers of information) shall be amended in accordance with the following provisions of this paragraph.

(2) In subsection (2) (local registers also to contain prescribed particulars of relevance to the area which are contained in central registers) after the word "authority", where it first occurs, there shall be inserted the words "in England and Wales" and for the words "the chief inspector or river purification authority", in each place where they occur, there shall be substituted the words "the Environment Agency".

(3) Subsection (3) (registers in Scotland) shall cease to have effect.

(4) In subsection (4) (port health authorities) after the word "authority" where it first occurs there shall be inserted the words "in England and Wales" and for the words "the chief inspector" there shall be substituted the words "the Environment Agency".

(5) In subsection (7) (registers to be available for inspection by, and facilities for obtaining copies of entries to be afforded to, the public) after paragraph (b) there shall be added the words—

"and, for the purposes of this subsection, places may be prescribed by the Secretary of State at which any such registers or facilities as are mentioned in paragraph (a) or (b) above are to be available or afforded to the public in pursuance of the paragraph in question."

(6) Subsection (9) (duty to furnish the National Rivers Authority with information for purposes of its register) shall cease to have effect.

58.—(1) Section 22 of that Act (exclusion from registers of certain confidential information) shall be amended in accordance with the following provisions of this paragraph.

(2) In subsection (5) (information not to be entered on the register until expiration of certain time limits)—

(a) in paragraph (a), for the words "on the register" there shall be substituted the words "in the register"; and

(b) in the words following paragraph (b), for the words from "on the register" onwards there shall be substituted the words "in the register until the end of the period of seven days following the day on which the appeal is finally determined or withdrawn".

(3) For subsection (6) (which applies subsections (3), (5) and (10) of section 15 in relation to appeals to the Secretary of State against decisions that information is not commercially confidential) there shall be substituted—

"(6) Subsections (5) and (10) of section 15 above shall apply in relation to an appeal under subsection (5) above as they apply in relation to an appeal under that section, but—

> (a) subsection (5) of that section shall have effect for the purposes of this subsection with the substitution for the words from "(which may" onwards of the words "(which must be held in private)"; and

> (b) subsection (5) above is subject to section 114 of the Environment Act 1995 (delegation or reference of appeals etc)."

59.—(1) Section 23 of that Act (offences) shall be amended in accordance with the following provisions of this paragraph.

(2) In subsection (1) (offences) paragraphs (d) to (f) and (k) shall cease to have effect.

(3) In subsection (2)(a) (which provides for a fine not exceeding £20,000 on summary conviction of any offence under section 23(1)(a), (c) or (l)) after the words "£20,000" there shall be inserted the words "or to imprisonment for a term not exceeding three months, or to both".

(4) Subsection (4) (punishment for offences under paragraph (d), (e), (f) or (k) of subsection (1)) shall cease to have effect.

(5) Subsection (5) (right of inspector to prosecute before a magistrates' court if authorised to do so by the Secretary of State) shall cease to have effect.

60.—(1) In section 27 of that Act (power of chief inspector etc to remedy harm) in subsection (1), for the words "the chief inspector or, in Scotland, a river purification authority" there shall be substituted the words "the appropriate Agency".

(2) In subsection (2) of that section (powers not to be exercised without the Secretary of State's written approval) for the words from "The chief inspector" to "their" there shall be substituted the words "The Environment Agency or SEPA, as the case may be, shall not exercise its".

61.—(1) In section 28 of that Act, in subsection (1) (which includes provision that the enforcing authority shall notify the waste regulation authority if a process involves final disposal of controlled waste by deposit in or on land) the words from "but the enforcing authority shall notify" onwards shall cease to have effect.

(2) Subsections (3) and (4) of that section (which involve liaison between the enforcing authority and the National Rivers Authority) shall cease to have effect.

62.—(1) Section 30 of that Act (authorities for purposes of Part II) shall be amended in accordance with the following provisions of this paragraph.

(2) For subsection (1) (waste regulation authorities) there shall be substituted—

> "(1) Any reference in this Part to a waste regulation authority—

> > (a) in relation to England and Wales, is a reference to the Environment Agency; and

> > (b) in relation to Scotland, is a reference to the Scottish Environment Protection Agency;

> and any reference in this Part to the area of a waste regulation authority shall accordingly be taken as a reference to the area over which the Environment Agency or the Scottish Environment Protection Agency, as the case may be, exercises its functions or, in the case of any particular function, the function in question."

(3) In subsection (4) of that section (construction of references to authorities constituted as particular descriptions of authority and provision for the section to be subject to orders under section 10 of the Local Government Act 1985 establishing authorities for certain purposes)—

(a) the words "or regulation", and

(b) the words from "establishing authorities" onwards,

shall cease to have effect.

(4) Subsections (6) (definition of "river purification authority"), (7) and (8) (which relate to authorities which are both waste disposal and waste regulation authorities) shall cease to have effect.

63. Section 31 of that Act (power to create regional authorities for purposes of waste regulation) shall cease to have effect.

64. In section 33 of that Act (prohibition on unauthorised or harmful deposit, treatment or disposal etc of waste) in subsection (7) (defences) for paragraph (c) there shall be substituted—

"(c) that the acts alleged to constitute the contravention were done in an emergency in order to avoid danger to human health in a case where—

(i) he took all such steps as were reasonably practicable in the circumstances for minimising pollution of the environment and harm to human health; and

(ii) particulars of the acts were furnished to the waste regulation authority as soon as reasonably practicable after they were done."

65. In section 34 of that Act (duty of care etc as respects waste), after subsection (3) (which specifies the persons who are authorised persons for the purposes of subsection (1)(c)) there shall be inserted—

"(3A) The Secretary of State may by regulations amend subsection (3) above so as to add, whether generally or in such circumstances as may be prescribed in the regulations, any person specified in the regulations, or any description of person so specified, to the persons who are authorised persons for the purposes of subsection (1)(c) above."

66.—(1) Section 35 of that Act (waste management licences: general) shall be amended in accordance with the following provisions of this paragraph.

(2) After subsection (7) there shall be inserted—

"(7A) In any case where—

(a) an entry is required under this section to be made in any record as to the observance of any condition of a licence, and

(b) the entry has not been made,

that fact shall be admissible as evidence that that condition has not been observed.

(7B) Any person who—

(a) intentionally makes a false entry in any record required to be kept under any condition of a licence, or

(b) with intent to deceive, forges or uses a licence or makes or has in his possession a document so closely resembling a licence as to be likely to deceive,

shall be guilty of an offence.

(7C) A person guilty of an offence under subsection (7B) above shall be liable—

(a) on summary conviction, to a fine not exceeding the statutory maximum;

(b) on conviction on indictment, to a fine or to imprisonment for a term not exceeding two years, or to both."

67. After section 35 of that Act there shall be inserted—

"Compensation where rights granted pursuant to section 35(4) or 38(9A).

35A.—(1) This section applies in any case where—

(a) the holder of a licence is required—

(i) by the conditions of the licence; or

(ii) by a requirement imposed under section 38(9) below,

to carry out any works or do any other thing which he is not entitled to carry out or do;

(b) a person whose consent would be required has, pursuant to the requirements of section 35(4) above or 38(9A) below, granted, or joined in granting, to the holder of the licence any rights in relation to any land; and

(c) those rights, or those rights together with other rights, are such as will enable the holder of the licence to comply with any requirements imposed on him by the licence or, as the case may be, under section 38(9) below.

(2) In a case where this section applies, any person who has granted, or joined in granting, the rights in question shall be entitled to be paid compensation under this section by the holder of the licence.

(3) The Secretary of State shall by regulations provide for the descriptions of loss and damage for which compensation is payable under this section.

(4) The Secretary of State may by regulations—

(a) provide for the basis on which any amount to be paid by way of compensation under this section is to be assessed;

(b) without prejudice to the generality of subsection (3) and paragraph (a) above, provide for compensation under this section to be payable in respect of—

(i) any effect of any rights being granted, or

(ii) any consequence of the exercise of any rights which have been granted;

(c) provide for the times at which any entitlement to compensation under this section is to arise or at which any such compensation is to become payable;

(d) provide for the persons or bodies by whom, and the manner in which, any dispute—

(i) as to whether any, and (if so) how much and when, compensation under this section is payable; or

(ii) as to the person to or by whom it shall be paid,

is to be determined;

(e) provide for when or how applications may be made for compensation under this section;

(f) without prejudice to the generality of paragraph (d) above, provide for when or how applications may be made for the determination of any such disputes as are mentioned in that paragraph;

(g) without prejudice to the generality of paragraphs (e) and (f) above, prescribe the form in which any such applications as are mentioned in those paragraphs are to be made;

(h) make provision similar to any provision made by paragraph 8 of Schedule 19 to the Water Resources Act 1991;

(j) make different provision for different cases, including different provision in relation to different persons or circumstances;

(k) include such incidental, supplemental, consequential or transitional provision as the Secretary of State considers appropriate.".

68.—(1) Section 36 of that Act (grant of licences) shall be amended in accordance with the following provisions of this paragraph.

(2) In subsection (1) (making of applications) for the words following paragraph (b) there shall be substituted—

"and shall be made on a form provided for the purpose by the waste regulation authority and accompanied by such information as that authority reasonably requires and the charge prescribed for the purpose by a charging scheme under section 41 of the Environment Act 1995.

(1A) Where an applicant for a licence fails to provide the waste regulation authority with any information required under subsection (1) above, the authority may refuse to proceed with the application, or refuse to proceed with it until the information is provided."

(3) In subsection (4) (reference of proposals to, and consideration of representations made by, other bodies)—

(a) in paragraph (a), for the words "the National Rivers Authority" there shall be substituted the words "the appropriate planning authority", and

(b) in paragraph (b), for the word "Authority" there shall be substituted the word "authority".

(4) Subsections (5) (reference by National Rivers Authority to the Secretary of State) and (6) (which makes provision for Scotland in place of subsection (4)) shall cease to have effect.

(5) After subsection (9) (application deemed to be rejected if not granted or refused within four months from being received) there shall be inserted—

"(9A) Subsection (9) above—

(a) shall not have effect in any case where, by virtue of subsection (1A) above, the waste regulation authority refuses to proceed with the application in question, and

(b) shall have effect in any case where, by virtue of subsection (1A) above, the waste regulation authority refuses to proceed with it until the required information is provided, with the substitution for the period of four months there mentioned of the period of four months beginning with the date on which the authority received the information."

(6) For subsection (10) (period of 21 days allowed for bodies to make representations) there shall be substituted—

"(10) The period allowed to the appropriate planning authority, the Health and Safety Executive or the appropriate nature conservancy body for the making of representations under subsection (4) or (7) above about a proposal is the period of twenty-eight days beginning with the day on which the proposal is received by the waste regulation authority or such longer period as the waste regulation authority, the appropriate planning authority, the Executive or the body, as the case may be, agree in writing.

(11) In this section—

"the appropriate planning authority" means—

    (a) where the relevant land is situated in the area of a London borough council, that London borough council;

    (b) where the relevant land is situated in the City of London, the Common Council of the City of London;

    (c) where the relevant land is situated in a non-metropolitan county in England, the council of that county;

    (d) where the relevant land is situated in a National Park or the Broads, the National Park authority for that National Park or, as the case may be, the Broads Authority;

    (e) where the relevant land is situated elsewhere in England or Wales, the council of the district or, in Wales, the county or county borough, in which the land is situated;

    (f) where the relevant land is situated in Scotland, the council constituted under section 2 of the Local Government etc. (Scotland) Act 1994 for the area in which the land is situated; 1994 c. 39.

"the Broads" has the same meaning as in the Norfolk and Suffolk Broads Act 1988; 1988 c. 4.

"National Park authority", subject to subsection (12) below, means a National Park authority established under section 63 of the Environment Act 1995 which has become the local planning authority for the National Park in question;

"the relevant land" means—

    (a) in relation to a site licence, the land to which the licence relates; and

    (b) in relation to a mobile plant licence, the principal place of business of the operator of the plant to which the licence relates.

(12) As respects any period before a National Park authority established under section 63 of the Environment Act 1995 in relation to a National Park becomes the local planning authority for that National Park, any reference in this section to a National Park authority shall be taken as a reference to the National Park Committee or joint or special planning board for that National Park.

(13) The Secretary of State may by regulations amend the definition of "appropriate planning authority" in subsection (11) above.

(14) This section shall have effect subject to section 36A below."

69. After section 36 of that Act there shall be inserted—

"Consultation before the grant of certain licences.

    36A.—(1) This section applies where an application for a licence has been duly made to a waste regulation authority, and the authority proposes to issue a licence subject (by virtue of section 35(4) above) to any condition which might require the holder of the licence to—

    (a) carry out any works, or

(b) do any other thing,

which he might not be entitled to carry out or do.

(2) Before issuing the licence, the waste regulation authority shall serve on every person appearing to the authority to be a person falling within subsection (3) below a notice which complies with the requirements set out in subsection (4) below.

(3) A person falls within this subsection if—

(a) he is the owner, lessee or occupier of any land; and

(b) that land is land in relation to which it is likely that, as a consequence of the licence being issued subject to the condition in question, rights will have to be granted by virtue of section 35(4) above to the holder of the licence.

(4) A notice served under subsection (2) above shall—

(a) set out the condition in question;

(b) indicate the nature of the works or other things which that condition might require the holder of the licence to carry out or do; and

(c) specify the date by which, and the manner in which, any representations relating to the condition or its possible effects are to be made to the waste regulation authority by the person on whom the notice is served.

(5) The date which, pursuant to subsection (4)(c) above, is specified in a notice shall be a date not earlier than the date on which expires the period—

(a) beginning with the date on which the notice is served, and

(b) of such length as may be prescribed in regulations made by the Secretary of State.

(6) Before the waste regulation authority issues the licence it must, subject to subsection (7) below, consider any representations made in relation to the condition in question, or its possible effects, by any person on whom a notice has been served under subsection (2) above.

(7) Subsection (6) above does not require the waste regulation authority to consider any representations made by a person after the date specified in the notice served on him under subsection (2) above as the date by which his representations in relation to the condition or its possible effects are to be made.

(8) In subsection (3) above—

"owner", in relation to any land in England and Wales, means the person who—

(a) is for the time being receiving the rack-rent of the land, whether on his own account or as agent or trustee for another person; or

(b) would receive the rack-rent if the land were let at a rack-rent,

but does not include a mortgagee not in possession; and

"owner", in relation to any land in Scotland, means a person (other than a creditor in a heritable security not in possession of the security subjects) for the time being entitled to receive or who would, if the land were let, be entitled to receive, the rents of the land in connection with which the word is used and includes a trustee, factor, guardian or curator and in the case of public or municipal land includes the persons to whom the management of the land is entrusted.".

70.—(1) In section 37 of that Act (variation of licences) in subsection (1)(b) (which requires an application to be accompanied by the prescribed fee) for the words "the prescribed fee payable under section 41 below," there shall be substituted the words "the charge prescribed for the purpose by a charging scheme under section 41 of the Environment Act 1995,".

(2) In subsection (5) of that section (which applies certain provisions of section 36) the words "(5), (6)," and "(8)" shall be omitted.

(3) After subsection (6) of that section (cases where an application for modification is deemed to have been rejected) there shall be added—

"(7) This section shall have effect subject to section 37A below."

71. After section 37 of that Act there shall be inserted—

"Consultation before certain variations.

37A.—(1) This section applies where—

    (a) a waste regulation authority proposes to modify a licence under section 37(1) or (2)(a) above; and

    (b) the licence, if modified as proposed, would be subject to a relevant new condition.

(2) For the purposes of this section, a "relevant new condition" is any condition by virtue of which the holder of the licence might be required to carry out any works or do any other thing—

    (a) which he might not be entitled to carry out or do, and

    (b) which he could not be required to carry out or do by virtue of the conditions to which, prior to the modification, the licence is subject.

(3) Before modifying the licence, the waste regulation authority shall serve on every person appearing to the authority to be a person falling within subsection (4) below a notice which complies with the requirements set out in subsection (5) below.

(4) A person falls within this subsection if—

    (a) he is the owner, lessee or occupier of any land; and

    (b) that land is land in relation to which it is likely that, as a consequence of the licence being modified so as to be subject to the relevant new condition in question, rights will have to be granted by virtue of section 35(4) above to the holder of the licence.

(5) A notice served under subsection (3) above shall—

    (a) set out the relevant new condition in question;

    (b) indicate the nature of the works or other things which that condition might require the holder of the licence to carry out or do but which he could not be required to carry out or do by virtue of the conditions (if any) to which, prior to the modification, the licence is subject; and

(c) specify the date by which, and the manner in which, any representations relating to the condition or its possible effects are to be made to the waste regulation authority by the person on whom the notice is served.

(6) The date which, pursuant to subsection (5)(c) above, is specified in a notice shall be a date not earlier than the date on which expires the period—

(a) beginning with the date on which the notice is served, and

(b) of such length as may be prescribed in regulations made by the Secretary of State.

(7) Before the waste regulation authority issues the licence it must, subject to subsection (8) below, consider any representations made in relation to the condition in question, or its possible effects, by any person on whom a notice has been served under subsection (3) above.

(8) Subsection (7) above does not require the waste regulation authority to consider any representations made by a person after the date specified in the notice served on him under subsection (3) above as the date by which his representations in relation to the condition or its possible effects are to be made.

(9) A waste regulation authority may postpone the service of any notice or the consideration of any representations required under the foregoing provisions of this section so far as the authority considers that by reason of an emergency it is appropriate to do so.

(10) In subsection (3) above, "owner" has the same meaning as it has in subsection (3) of section 36A above by virtue of subsection (8) of that section.".

72.—(1) In section 38 of that Act (revocation and suspension of licences) after subsection (9) (power to require certain measures to be taken where licence suspended) there shall be inserted—

"(9A) A requirement imposed under subsection (9) above may require the holder of a licence to carry out works or do other things notwithstanding that he is not entitled to carry out the works or do the thing and any person whose consent would be required shall grant, or join in granting, the holder of the licence such rights in relation to the land as will enable the holder of the licence to comply with any requirements imposed on him under that subsection.

(9B) Subsections (2) to (8) of section 36A above shall, with the necessary modifications, apply where the authority proposes to impose a requirement under subsection (9) above which may require the holder of a licence to carry out any such works or do any such thing as is mentioned in subsection (9A) above as they apply where the authority proposes to issue a licence subject to any such condition as is mentioned in subsection (1) of that section, but as if—

(a) the reference in subsection (3) of that section to section 35(4) above were a reference to subsection (9A) above; and

(b) any reference in those subsections—

(i) to the condition, or the condition in question, were a reference to the requirement; and

(ii) to issuing a licence were a reference to serving a notice, under subsection (12) below, effecting the requirement.

(9C) The authority may postpone the service of any notice or the consideration of any representations required under section 36A above, as applied by subsection (9B) above, so far as the authority considers that by reason of an emergency it is appropriate to do so."

(2) After subsection (12) of that section (revocations and suspensions etc. to be effected by service of notice) there shall be added—

"(13) If a waste regulation authority is of the opinion that proceedings for an offence under subsection (10) or (11) above would afford an ineffectual remedy against a person who has failed to comply with any requirement imposed under subsection (9) above, the authority may take proceedings in the High Court or, in Scotland, in any court of competent jurisdiction for the purpose of securing compliance with the requirement."

73.—(1) Section 39 of that Act (surrender of licences) shall be amended in accordance with the following provisions of this paragraph.

(2) In subsection (3) (application for surrender of a site licence) for the words from "in such form" onwards there shall be substituted the words "on a form provided by the authority for the purpose, giving such information and accompanied by such evidence as the authority reasonably requires and accompanied by the charge prescribed for the purpose by a charging scheme under section 41 of the Environment Act 1995."

(3) In subsection (7) (consideration of representations before accepting surrender of a licence)—

(a) for the words "the National Rivers Authority" and "the Authority" there shall be substituted the words "the appropriate planning authority"; and

(b) the words following paragraph (b) shall cease to have effect.

(4) Subsection (8) (which makes provision for Scotland in place of subsection (7)) shall cease to have effect.

(5) In subsection (11) (meaning of "the allowed period") for the words "subsections (7) and (8) above" there shall be substituted the words "subsection (7) above".

(6) After subsection (11) there shall be added—

"(12) In this section—

"the appropriate planning authority" means—

(a) where the relevant land is situated in the area of a London borough council, that London borough council;

(b) where the relevant land is situated in the City of London, the Common Council of the City of London;

(c) where the relevant land is situated in a non-metropolitan county in England, the council of that county;

(d) where the relevant land is situated in a National Park or the Broads, the National Park authority for that National Park or, as the case may be, the Broads Authority;

(e) where the relevant land is situated elsewhere in England or Wales, the council of the district or, in Wales, the county or county borough, in which the land is situated;

(f) where the relevant land is situated in Scotland, the council constituted under section 2 of the Local Government etc. (Scotland) Act 1994 for the area in which the land is situated;

1994 c. 39.

"the Broads" has the same meaning as in the Norfolk and Suffolk Broads Act 1988;

1988 c. 4.

"National Park authority", subject to subsection (13) below, means a National Park authority established under section 63 of the Environment Act 1995 which has become the local planning authority for the National Park in question;

"the relevant land", in the case of any site licence, means the land to which the licence relates.

(13) As respects any period before a National Park authority established under section 63 of the Environment Act 1995 in relation to a National Park becomes the local planning authority for that National Park, any reference in this section to a National Park authority shall be taken as a reference to the National Park Committee or joint or special planning board for that National Park.

(14) The Secretary of State may by regulations amend the definition of "appropriate planning authority" in subsection (12) above."

74. In section 40 of that Act (transfer of licences) in subsection (3) (mode of making application for transfer of licence) for the words from "in such form" to "section 41 below" there shall be substituted the words "on a form provided by the authority for the purpose, accompanied by such information as the authority may reasonably require, the charge prescribed for the purpose by a charging scheme under section 41 of the Environment Act 1995".

75. Section 41 of that Act (fees and charges for licences) shall cease to have effect.

76.—(1) Section 42 of that Act (supervision of licensed activities) shall be amended in accordance with the following provisions of this paragraph.

(2) Subsection (2) (consultation with the National Rivers Authority etc) shall cease to have effect.

(3) In subsection (4) (recovery of expenditure from the holder or, if it has been surrendered, the former holder of a licence) for the words "the holder of the licence or, if the licence has been surrendered, from the former holder of it" there shall be substituted the words "the holder, or (as the case may be) the former holder, of the licence".

(4) In subsection (5) (powers where it appears that a condition of a licence is not being complied with) after the words "is not being complied with" there shall be inserted the words "or is likely not to be complied with,".

(5) For paragraph (a) of that subsection there shall be substituted—

"(a) serve on the holder of the licence a notice—

(i) stating that the authority is of the opinion that a condition of the licence is not being complied with or, as the case may be, is likely not to be complied with;

(ii) specifying the matters which constitute the non-compliance or, as the case may be, which make the anticipated non-compliance likely;

(iii) specifying the steps which must be taken to remedy the non-compliance or, as the case may be, to prevent the anticipated non-compliance from occurring; and

(iv) specifying the period within which those steps must be taken; and".

(6) In paragraph (b) of that subsection (powers which become exercisable on non-compliance) for the words "has not complied with the condition within that time," there shall be substituted the words "has not taken the steps specified in the notice within the period so specified,".

(7) After subsection (6) (power to revoke or suspend a licence) there shall be inserted—

"(6A) If a waste regulation authority is of the opinion that revocation or suspension of the licence, whether entirely or to any extent, under subsection (6) above would afford an ineffectual remedy against a person who has failed to comply with any requirement imposed under subsection (5)(a) above, the authority may take proceedings in the High Court or, in Scotland, in any court of competent jurisdiction for the purpose of securing compliance with the requirement."

(8) In subsection (7) (application of certain provisions of section 38 to revocation or suspension of a licence)—

(a) for the words from "subsections (5)" to "38" there shall be substituted the words "subsections (5) and (12) or, as the case may be, subsections (8) to (12) of section 38"; and

(b) the words from "and the power" onwards shall cease to have effect.

77. In section 43 of that Act, in subsection (2), paragraphs (a) and (b) (reference of matters involved in appeals under that section to, and determination of such appeals by, persons appointed by the Secretary of State) shall cease to have effect and after that section there shall be inserted—

"(2A) This section is subject to section 114 of the Environment Act 1995 (delegation or reference of appeals etc)."

78. Section 50 of that Act (waste disposal plans of waste regulation authorities) shall cease to have effect.

79. Section 61 of that Act (duty of waste regulation authorities as respects closed landfills) shall cease to have effect.

80.—(1) Section 62 of that Act (special provision with respect to certain dangerous and intractable waste) shall be amended in accordance with the following provisions of this paragraph.

(2) In subsection (3), for paragraph (a) (regulations providing for the supervision of certain activities and the recovery of the costs from persons carrying on the activities) there shall be substituted—

"(a) for the supervision by waste regulation authorities—

(i) of activities authorised by virtue of the regulations or of activities by virtue of carrying on which persons are subject to provisions of the regulations, or

(ii) of persons who carry on activities authorised by virtue of the regulations or who are subject to provisions of the regulations,

and for the recovery from persons falling within sub-paragraph (ii) above of the costs incurred by waste regulation authorities in performing functions conferred upon those authorities by the regulations;".

(3) After that subsection (which also includes provision for regulations to provide for appeals to the Secretary of State) there shall be added—

"(3A) This section is subject to section 114 of the Environment Act 1995 (delegation or reference of appeals etc)."

81. In section 63 of that Act (waste other than controlled waste) for subsection (2) (offences relating to the deposit of waste which is not controlled waste but which, if it were such waste, would be special waste) there shall be substituted—

"(2) A person who deposits, or knowingly causes or knowingly permits the deposit of, any waste—

(a) which is not controlled waste, but

    (b) which, if it were controlled waste, would be special waste,

in a case where he would be guilty of an offence under section 33 above if the waste were special waste and any waste management licence were not in force, shall, subject to subsection (3) below, be guilty of that offence and punishable as if the waste were special waste."

82.—(1) Section 64 of that Act (public registers) shall be amended in accordance with the following provisions of this paragraph.

(2) After subsection (2) there shall be inserted—

    "(2A) The Secretary of State may give to a waste regulation authority directions requiring the removal from any register of its of any specified information not prescribed for inclusion under subsection (1) above or which, by virtue of section 65 or 66 below, ought to be excluded from the register."

(3) In subsection (4) (duty of waste collection authorities in England to maintain registers)—

    (a) after the word "England" there shall be inserted the words "or Wales"; and

    (b) the words "which is not a waste regulation authority" shall be omitted.

(4) For subsection (5) (waste regulation authorities in England to furnish information to waste collection authorities) there shall be substituted—

    "(5) The waste regulation authority in relation to England and Wales shall furnish any waste collection authorities in its area with the particulars necessary to enable them to discharge their duty under subsection (4) above."

(5) In subsection (6) (registers to be available for inspection by, and facilities for obtaining copies of entries to be afforded to, the public)—

    (a) after the words "waste collection authority" there shall be inserted "(a)";

    (b) after the words "hours and" there shall be inserted "(b)"; and

    (c) after the paragraph (b) so formed, there shall be added the words—

"and, for the purposes of this subsection, places may be prescribed by the Secretary of State at which any such registers or facilities as are mentioned in paragraph (a) or (b) above are to be available or afforded to the public in pursuance of the paragraph in question."

83.—(1) In section 66 of that Act (exclusion from registers of certain confidential information) in subsection (5) (information not to be entered on the register until expiration of certain time limits) in the words following paragraph (b), for the words from "pending" onwards there shall be substituted the words "until the end of the period of seven days following the day on which the appeal is finally determined or withdrawn".

(2) For subsection (6) (which applies section 43(2) and (8) to appeals to the Secretary of State against decisions that information is not commercially confidential) there shall be substituted—

    "(6) Subsections (2) and (8) of section 43 above shall apply in relation to appeals under subsection (5) above as they apply in relation to appeals under that section; but

    (a) subsection (2)(c) of that section shall have effect for the purposes of this subsection with the substitution for the words from "(which may" onwards of the words "(which must be held in private)"; and

    (b) subsection (5) above is subject to section 114 of the Environment Act 1995 (delegation or reference of appeals etc)."

84. Section 67 of that Act (annual reports of waste regulation authorities) shall cease to have effect.

85. Sections 68 to 70 of that Act (functions of the Secretary of State and appointment etc of inspectors, powers of entry and power to deal with cause of imminent danger of serious pollution) shall cease to have effect.

86.—(1) In section 71 of that Act (obtaining of information from persons and authorities) subsection (1) (which is superseded by this Act) shall cease to have effect.

(2) In subsection (2) of that section (power by notice to require a person to furnish information within such period as may be specified in the notice) after the words "service of the notice" there shall be inserted the words ", or at such time,".

87. Section 72 of that Act (default powers of the Secretary of State) shall cease to have effect.

88.—(1) Section 75 of that Act (meaning of "waste" etc.) shall be amended in accordance with the following provisions of this paragraph.

(2) For subsection (2) (definition of "waste") there shall be substituted—

"(2) "Waste" means any substance or object in the categories set out in Schedule 2B to this Act which the holder discards or intends or is required to discard; and for the purposes of this definition—

"holder" means the producer of the waste or the person who is in possession of it; and

"producer" means any person whose activities produce waste or any person who carries out pre-processing, mixing or other operations resulting in a change in the nature or composition of this waste."

(3) Subsection (3) (presumption that anything discarded is waste unless the contrary is proved) shall cease to have effect.

(4) After subsection (9) there shall be added—

"(10) Schedule 2B to this Act (which reproduces Annex I to the Waste Directive) shall have effect.

(11) Subsection (2) above is substituted, and Schedule 2B to this Act is inserted, for the purpose of assigning to "waste" in this Part the meaning which it has in the Waste Directive by virtue of paragraphs (a) to (c) of Article 1 of, and Annex I to, that Directive, and those provisions shall be construed accordingly.

(12) In this section "the Waste Directive" means the directive of the Council of the European Communities, dated 15th July 1975, on waste, as amended by— 75/442/EEC.

(a) the directive of that Council, dated 18th March 1991, amending directive 75/442/EEC on waste; and 91/156/EEC.

(b) the directive of that Council, dated 23rd December 1991, standardising and rationalising reports on the implementation of certain Directives relating to the environment." 91/692/EEC.

89.—(1) Section 79 of that Act (statutory nuisances) shall be amended in accordance with the following provisions of this paragraph.

(2) In subsection (1) (the paragraphs of which specify, subject to subsections (2) to (6A), the matters which constitute statutory nuisances) for the words "Subject to subsections (2) to (6A) below" there shall be substituted the words "Subject to subsections (1A) to (6A) below".

(3) After that subsection there shall be inserted—

"(1A) No matter shall constitute a statutory nuisance to the extent that it consists of, or is caused by, any land being in a contaminated state.

(1B) Land is in a "contaminated state" for the purposes of subsection (1A) above if, and only if, it is in such a condition, by reason of substances in, on or under the land, that—

(a) harm is being caused or there is a possibility of harm being caused; or

(b) pollution of controlled waters is being, or is likely to be, caused;

and in this subsection "harm", "pollution of controlled waters" and "substance" have the same meaning as in Part IIA of this Act.".

90. In section 141 of that Act (power to prohibit or restrict the importation or exportation of waste) subsection (5)(a)(ii) (power of Secretary of State by direction to make functions of certain authorities exercisable instead by him) shall cease to have effect.

91. Section 143 of that Act (public registers of land which may be contaminated) shall cease to have effect.

92. In section 161 of that Act (regulations and orders) in subsection (4) (which specifies the orders under that Act which are not subject to negative resolution procedure under subsection (3)) after the words "does not apply to" there shall be inserted the words "a statutory instrument—

(a) which contains an order under section 78M(4) above, or

(b) by reason only that it contains".

93.—(1) Schedule 1 to that Act (authorisations for processes: supplementary provisions) shall be amended in accordance with the following provisions of this paragraph.

(2) In Part I (grant of authorisations) in paragraph 3(3) (local inquiry or hearing to be held where request to be heard made by the applicant or the local enforcing authority) for the words "the local enforcing authority" there shall be substituted the words "the enforcing authority".

(3) In Part II (variation of authorisations) in paragraph 6, at the beginning of sub-paragraph (1) there shall be inserted the words "Except as provided by sub-paragraph (1A) below,".

(4) After that sub-paragraph there shall be inserted—

"(1A) The requirements of this paragraph shall not apply in relation to any variations of an authorisation which an enforcing authority has decided to make in consequence of representations made in accordance with this paragraph and which are specified by way of variation of a variation notice by a further notice under section 10(3A) of this Act."

(5) After paragraph 7 (applications for variation) there shall be inserted—

"Call in of applications for variation

8.—(1) The Secretary of State may give directions to the enforcing authority requiring that any particular application or any class of applications for the variation of an authorisation shall be transmitted to him for determination pending a further direction under sub-paragraph (5) below.

(2) The enforcing authority shall inform the applicant of the fact that his application is being transmitted to the Secretary of State.

(3) Where an application for the variation of an authorisation is referred to him under sub-paragraph (1) above the Secretary of State may—

(a) cause a local inquiry to be held in relation to the application; or

(b) afford the applicant and the authority concerned an opportunity of appearing before and being heard by a person appointed by the Secretary of State;

and he shall exercise one of the powers under this sub-paragraph in any case where, in the manner prescribed by regulations made by the Secretary of State, a request is made to be heard with respect to the application by the applicant or the enforcing authority concerned.

(4) Subsections (2) to (5) of section 250 of the Local Government Act 1972 (supplementary provisions about local inquiries under that section) or, in relation to Scotland, subsections (2) to (8) of section 210 of the Local Government (Scotland) Act 1973 (which make similar provision) shall, without prejudice to the generality of subsection (1) of either of those sections, apply to local inquiries or other hearings in pursuance of sub-paragraph (3) above as they apply to inquiries in pursuance of either of those sections and, in relation to England and Wales, as if the reference to a local authority in subsection (4) of the said section 250 included a reference to the enforcing authority. 1972 c. 70. 1973 c. 65.

(5) The Secretary of State shall, on determining any application transferred to him under this paragraph, give to the enforcing authority such a direction as he thinks fit as to whether it is to grant the application and, if so, as to the conditions that are to be attached to the authorisation by means of the variation notice.

9. The Secretary of State may give the enforcing authority a direction with respect to any particular application or any class of applications for the variation of an authorisation requiring the authority not to determine or not to proceed with the application or applications of that class until the expiry of any such period as may be specified in the direction, or until directed by the Secretary of State that they may do so, as the case may be.

10.—(1) Except in a case where an application for the variation of an authorisation has been referred to the Secretary of State under paragraph 8 above and subject to sub-paragraph (3) below, the enforcing authority shall determine an application for the variation of an authorisation within the period of four months beginning with the day on which it received the application or within such longer period as may be agreed with the applicant.

(2) If the enforcing authority fails to determine an application for the variation of an authorisation within the period allowed by or under this paragraph the application shall, if the applicant notifies the authority in writing that he treats the failure as such, be deemed to have been refused at the end of that period.

(3) The Secretary of State may, by order, substitute for the period for the time being specified in sub-paragraph (1) above such other period as he considers appropriate and different periods may be substituted for different classes of application."

94. In Schedule 2 to that Act (waste disposal authorities and companies) in paragraph 17(2) (which requires a waste regulation authority or waste disposal authority to furnish information on request to the Secretary of State) the words "a waste regulation authority or" shall cease to have effect.

95. After Schedule 2A to that Act there shall be inserted—

"SCHEDULE 2B

CATEGORIES OF WASTE

Section 75.

1. Production or consumption residues not otherwise specified below.

2. Off-specification products.

3. Products whose date for appropriate use has expired.

4. Materials spilled, lost or having undergone other mishap, including any materials, equipment, etc, contaminated as a result of the mishap.

5. Materials contaminated or soiled as a result of planned actions (e.g. residues from cleaning operations, packing materials, containers, etc.).

6. Unusable parts (e.g. reject batteries, exhausted catalysts, etc.).

7. Substances which no longer perform satisfactorily (e.g. contaminated acids, contaminated solvents, exhausted tempering salts, etc.).

8. Residues of industrial processes (e.g. slags, still bottoms, etc.).

9. Residues from pollution abatement processes (e.g. scrubber sludges, baghouse dusts, spent filters, etc.).

10. Machining or finishing residues (e.g. lathe turnings, mill scales, etc.).

11. Residues from raw materials extraction and processing (e.g. mining residues, oil field slops, etc.).

12. Adulterated materials (e.g. oils contaminated with PCBs, etc.).

13. Any materials, substances or products whose use has been banned by law.

14. Products for which the holder has no further use (e.g. agricultural, household, office, commercial and shop discards, etc.).

15. Contaminated materials, substances or products resulting from remedial action with respect to land.

16. Any materials, substances or products which are not contained in the above categories."

The Natural Heritage (Scotland) Act 1991

1991 c. 28.

96.—(1) The Natural Heritage (Scotland) Act 1991 shall be amended in accordance with the following provisions of this paragraph.

(2) In section 15—

1951 c. 66.

(a) in subsection (2) for the words "a river purification authority, acting in pursuance of their duties under section 17(1) of the Rivers (Prevention of Pollution) (Scotland) Act 1951" there shall be substituted the words "SEPA acting in pursuance of its duties under section 34(1) of the Environment Act 1995";

(b) in subsection (3) for the words "said Act of" and "a river purification authority" where they first occur there shall be substituted the words "Rivers (Prevention of Pollution (Scotland) Act" and "SEPA" respectively and the words "and a river purification authority of whom such a requirement is made shall make such an application" shall cease to have effect;

(c) for subsection (5) there shall be substituted—

"(5) A control area shall comprise an area or areas shown in a map or plan contained in the order."

(3) In section 17—

(a) in subsection (1) for the words "A river purification authority" there shall be substituted the words "SEPA";

(b) in subsection (3) for the words "A river purification authority", "their" in both places where it occurs, "they" and "the authority" there shall be substituted the words "SEPA", "its", "it" and "SEPA" respectively.

(4) In section 18—

(a) in subsection (1) for the words "a river purification authority" and "they" there shall be substituted the words "SEPA" and "it" respectively;

(b) in subsection (2) for the words "the river purification authority decide" there shall be substituted the words "SEPA decides";

(c) in subsection (3) for the words "a river purification authority" and "the authority" there shall be substituted the words "SEPA" and "it" respectively;

(d) in subsection (4) for the words "the river purification authority declare" there shall be substituted the words "SEPA declares";

(e) in subsection (5) for the words "A river purification authority" and "them" there shall be substituted the words "SEPA" and "it" respectively.

(5) In section 24—

(a) in subsection (1)—

(i) for the words "a river purification authority" there shall be substituted the words "SEPA"; and

(ii) in paragraph (a), after the word "on" there shall be inserted the words "SEPA or"; and

(b) in subsection (9)—

(i) for the words "a river purification authority or" there shall be substituted the words "SEPA or a"; and

(ii) in paragraph (a), after the word "by" where it second occurs there shall be inserted the words "SEPA or".

(6) After section 26 there shall be inserted—

"Meaning of SEPA.   26A. In this Act "SEPA" means the Scottish Environment Protection Agency."

(7) In Schedule 5—

(a) in paragraph 1 for the words "the river purification authority concerned consider" there shall be substituted the words "SEPA considers";

(b) in paragraph 2 for the words "the river purification authority concerned" there shall be substituted the words "SEPA" and the words "in their area and" shall cease to have effect;

(c) in paragraph 3 for the words "the river purification authority" and "their" wherever they occur there shall be substituted the words "SEPA" and "its" respectively;

(d) in paragraphs 4 and 9 for the words "the river purification authority" wherever they occur there shall be substituted the words "SEPA".

(8) In Schedule 6—

(a) in paragraph 1—

(i) in sub-paragraph (1) for the words "the river purification authority" there shall be substituted the words "SEPA";

(ii) in sub-paragraph (2) for the words "A river purification authority", "them", "the authority" and "their" there shall be substituted respectively the words "SEPA", "it", "it" and "its" respectively;

(iii) in sub-paragraph (3) for the words "the river purification authority" there shall be substituted the words "SEPA";

(iv) in sub-paragraph (4) for the words "the river purification authority", "the authority fail" and "their" there shall be substituted the words "SEPA", "it fails" and "its" respectively;

(v) sub-paragraph (5) shall cease to have effect;

(vi) in sub-paragraph (6) for the words "the river purification authority to whom the application has been made" there shall be substituted the words "SEPA";

(b) in paragraph 2—

(i) in sub-paragraph (1) for the words "the river purification authority" wherever they occur there shall be substituted the words "SEPA";

(ii) in sub-paragraphs (3) and (4) for the words "the river purification authority" wherever they occur there shall be substituted the words "SEPA";

(iii) at the end there shall be added—

"(6) This paragraph is subject to section 114 of the Environment Act 1995 (delegation or reference of appeals etc).";

(c) in paragraph 3—

(i) in sub-paragraph (1) for the words "A river purification authority" there shall be substituted the words "SEPA";

(ii) in sub-paragraph (2) for the words "A river purification authority" and "they are" there shall be substituted the words "SEPA" and "it is" respectively;

(iii) in sub-paragraph (4) for the words "the river purification authority" there shall be substituted the words "SEPA";

(iv) in sub-paragraph (5) for the words "the river purification authority" and "them" there shall be substituted the words "SEPA" and "it" respectively;

(v) in sub-paragraph (6) for the words "the authority fail to intimate their" and "the river purification authority" there shall be substituted the words "SEPA fails to intimate its" and "SEPA" respectively;

(d) in paragraph 4 for the words "A river purification authority" and "them" there shall be substituted the words "SEPA" and "it" respectively;

(e) in paragraph 5(2) for the words "the river purification authority" there shall be substituted the words "SEPA".

(9) In Schedule 8, in paragraph 1—

(a) for sub-paragraph (1) there shall be substituted—

"(1) Before making an application for a drought order, the applicant shall consult—

(a) SEPA, in a case where notice of the application is required to be served on it under this paragraph; and

(b) any district salmon fishery board on whom notice of the application is required to be served under this paragraph.";

(b) in sub-paragraph (3), in the second column of the Table, in the fourth entry (relating to orders concerning the taking of water from a source or the discharge of water to a place), in paragraph (a) the words ", river purification authority" shall cease to have effect and at the end there shall be added—

"(c) SEPA.";

(c) in sub-paragraph (3), in the second column of the Table, in the fifth entry (relating to orders which authorise the execution of any works) for the words "every river purification authority and" there shall be substituted the words "SEPA and every".

The Water Industry Act 1991

97. In section 3 of the Water Industry Act 1991 (general environmental and recreational duties) in subsection (4) (which imposes duties on the Director and relevant undertakers in relation to proposals relating to functions of the National Rivers Authority etc) for the words "the NRA", in each place where they occur, there shall be substituted the words "the Environment Agency". 1991 c. 56.

98. In section 5 of that Act (codes of practice with respect to environmental duties) in subsection (4), in paragraph (a) (which requires consultation with the National Rivers Authority) for the words "the NRA" there shall be substituted the words "the Environment Agency".

99. In section 40 of that Act (bulk supplies of water) in subsection (5) (which requires the Director to consult the National Rivers Authority before making an order) for the words "the NRA" there shall be substituted the words "the Environment Agency".

100. In section 40A of that Act (variation and termination of bulk supply agreements) in subsection (3) (which requires the Director to consult the National Rivers authority before making an order) for the words "the NRA" there shall be substituted the words "the Environment Agency".

101.—(1) In section 71 of that Act (waste from water resources) in subsection (6) (power of court to authorise the National Rivers Authority to take steps to execute an order) for the words "the NRA" there shall be substituted—

(a) where it first occurs, the words "the Environment Agency"; and

(b) where it next occurs, the words "the Agency".

(2) In subsection (7) (powers of entry etc of persons designated by the National Rivers Authority) for the words "the NRA" in each place where it occurs there shall be substituted the words "the Environment Agency".

102. After section 93 of that Act (interpretation of Part III) there shall be inserted—

"PART IIIA

PROMOTION OF THE EFFICIENT USE OF WATER

Duty to promote the efficient use of water.
93A.—(1) It shall be the duty of every water undertaker to promote the efficient use of water by its customers.

(2) The duty of a water undertaker under this section shall be enforceable under section 18 above—

(a) by the Secretary of State; or

(b) with the consent of or in accordance with a general authorisation given by the Secretary of State, by the Director.

(3) Nothing in this Part shall have effect to authorise or require a water undertaker to impose any requirement on any of its customers or potential customers.

Power of Director to impose requirements on water undertakers.
93B.—(1) The Director may require a water undertaker, in its performance of its duty under section 93A above, to—

(a) take any such action; or

(b) achieve any such overall standards of performance,

as he may specify in the document imposing the requirement.

(2) Where the Director, in the document imposing a requirement on a water undertaker under subsection (1) above, stipulates that any contravention of the requirement by the

324 c. **25** *Environment Act 1995*

undertaker will be a breach of its duty under section 93A above, any contravention of that requirement by the undertaker shall be a breach of that duty.

(3) Without prejudice to the generality of subsection (1) above, a requirement under that subsection may—

(a) require a water undertaker to make available to its customers or potential customers such facilities as may be specified in the document imposing the requirement;

(b) require a water undertaker to provide or make available to its customers or potential customers such information as may be specified in the document imposing the requirement, and may specify the form in which, the times at which or the frequency with which any such information is to be provided or made available.

(4) In exercising his powers under this section in relation to any water undertaker the Director shall have regard to the extent to which water resources are available to that undertaker.

(5) Before imposing any requirement on a water undertaker under subsection (1) above the Director shall consult that undertaker.

(6) Nothing in this section authorises the Director to impose any requirement on a water undertaker which has or may have the effect of authorising or requiring that undertaker to impose any requirement on any of its customers or potential customers.

Publicity of requirements imposed under section 93B.

93C.—(1) Where, under section 93B(1) above, the Director imposes any requirement on a water undertaker, the Director may arrange for that requirement to be publicised in any such manner as he may consider appropriate for the purpose of bringing it to the attention of that undertaker's customers.

(2) Without prejudice to the generality of subsection (1) above, the Director may arrange for such publicising of the requirement as is mentioned in that subsection by—

(a) himself publicising the requirement or causing it to be publicised; or

(b) directing the undertaker to inform or arrange to inform its customers of the requirement.

Information as to compliance with requirements under section 93B.

93D.—(1) Where a water undertaker is subject to any requirement imposed under section 93B(1) above, the Director may arrange for there to be given to the customers of that undertaker at any such times or with such frequency, and in any such manner, as he may consider appropriate, such information about the level of performance achieved by the undertaker in relation to that requirement as appears to the Director to be expedient to be given to those customers.

(2) Without prejudice to the generality of subsection (1) above, the Director may arrange for such giving of information as is mentioned in that subsection by—

(a) himself disseminating the information or causing it to be disseminated; or

(b) directing the undertaker to give or arrange to give the information to its customers.

(3) At such times and in such form or manner as the Director may direct, a water undertaker shall provide the Director with such information as may be specified in the direction in connection with the undertaker's performance in relation to any requirement imposed upon the undertaker under section 93B(1) above.

(4) A water undertaker who fails without reasonable excuse to do anything required of him by virtue of subsection (3) above shall be guilty of an offence and liable on summary conviction to a fine not exceeding level 5 on the standard scale.".

103. After section 101 of that Act (which provides for the determination of certain details in relation to requisitioned sewers) there shall be inserted—

"Provision of public sewers otherwise than by requisition

Further duty to provide sewers.

101A.—(1) Without prejudice to section 98 above, it shall be the duty of a sewerage undertaker to provide a public sewer to be used for the drainage for domestic sewerage purposes of premises in a particular locality in its area if the conditions specified in subsection (2) below are satisfied.

(2) The conditions mentioned in subsection (1) above are—

(a) that the premises in question, or any of those premises, are premises cn which there are buildings each of which, with the exception of any shed, glasshouse or other outbuilding appurtenant to a dwelling and not designed or occupied as living accommodation, is a building erected before, or whose erection was substantially completed by, 20th June 1995;

(b) that the drains or sewers used for the drainage for domestic sewerage purposes of the premises in question do not, either directly or through an intermediate drain or sewer, connect with a public sewer; and

(c) that the drainage of any of the premises in question in respect of which the condition specified in paragraph (a) above is satisfied is giving, or is likely to give, rise to such adverse effects to the environment or amenity that it is appropriate, having regard to any guidance issued under this section by the Secretary of State and all other relevant considerations, to provide a public sewer for the drainage for domestic sewerage purposes of the premises in question.

(3) Without prejudice to the generality of subsection (2)(c) above, regard shall be had to the following considerations, so far as relevant, in determining whether it is appropriate for any sewer to be provided by virtue of this section—

(a) the geology of the locality in question or of any other locality;

(b) the number of premises, being premises on which there are buildings, which might reasonably be expected to be drained by means of that sewer;

(c) the costs of providing that sewer;

(d) the nature and extent of any adverse effects to the environment or amenity arising, or likely to arise, as a result of the premises or, as the case may be, the locality in question not being drained by means of a public sewer; and

(e) the extent to which it is practicable for those effects to be overcome otherwise than by the provision (whether by virtue of this section or otherwise) of public sewers, and the costs of so overcoming those effects.

(4) Guidance issued by the Secretary of State under this section may—

(a) relate to how regard is to be had to the considerations mentioned in paragraphs (a) to (e) of subsection (3) above;

(b) relate to any other matter which the Secretary of State considers may be a relevant consideration in any case and to how regard is to be had to any such matter;

(c) set out considerations, other than those mentioned in paragraphs (a) to (e) of subsection (3) above, to which (so far as relevant) regard shall be had in determining whether it is appropriate for any sewer to be provided by virtue of this section;

(d) relate to how regard is to be had to any such consideration as is mentioned in paragraph (c) above;

(e) without prejudice to paragraphs (a) to (d) above, relate to how a sewerage undertaker is to discharge its functions under this section.

(5) Before issuing guidance under this section the Secretary of State shall consult—

(a) the Environment Agency;

(b) the Director; and

(c) such other bodies or persons as he considers appropriate;

and the Secretary of State shall arrange for any guidance issued by him under this section to be published in such manner as he considers appropriate.

(6) Subject to the following provisions of this section, the duty of a sewerage undertaker by virtue of subsection (1) above shall be enforceable under section 18 above—

(a) by the Secretary of State; or

(b) with the consent of or in accordance with a general authorisation given by the Secretary of State, by the Director.

(7) Any dispute between a sewerage undertaker and an owner or occupier of any premises in its area as to—

(a) whether the undertaker is under a duty by virtue of subsection (1) above to provide a public sewer to be used for any such drainage of those premises as is mentioned in that subsection;

(b) the domestic sewerage purposes for which any such sewer should be provided; or

(c) the time by which any such duty of the undertaker should be performed,

shall be determined by the Environment Agency, and may be referred to the Environment Agency for determination by either of the parties to the dispute.

(8) The Environment Agency—

> > (a) shall notify the parties of the reasons for its decision on any dispute referred to it under subsection (7) above; and
> >
> > (b) may make any such recommendations, or give any such guidance, relating to or in connection with the drainage of the premises or locality in question as it considers appropriate.
>
> (9) The decision of the Environment Agency on any dispute referred to it under subsection (7) above shall be final.
>
> (10) A sewerage undertaker shall only be taken to be in breach of its duty under subsection (1) above where, and to the extent that, it has accepted, or the Environment Agency has determined under this section, that it is under such a duty and where any time accepted by it, or determined by the Environment Agency under this section, as the time by which the duty is to that extent to be performed has passed.".

104. In section 110A of that Act (new connections with public sewers) in subsection (6) (which requires the Director to consult the National Rivers Authority before making an order) for the words "the NRA" there shall be substituted the words "the Environment Agency".

105.—(1) Section 120 of that Act (application for the discharge of special category effluent) shall be amended in accordance with the following provisions of this paragraph.

(2) In subsection (1) (sewerage undertakers to refer certain questions to the Secretary of State) for the words "the Secretary of State" there shall be substituted the words "the Environment Agency".

(3) In subsection (4) (undertaker not to give consent etc until Secretary of State gives notice of his determination of the questions) for the words "the Secretary of State" there shall be substituted the words "the Environment Agency".

(4) For subsections (7) and (8) (enforcement by Secretary of State) there shall be substituted—

> "(9) If a sewerage undertaker fails, within the period provided by subsection (2) above, to refer to the Environment Agency any question which he is required by subsection (1) above to refer to the Agency, the undertaker shall be guilty of an offence and liable—
>
> > (a) on summary conviction, to a fine not exceeding the statutory maximum;
> >
> > (b) on conviction on indictment, to a fine.
>
> (10) If the Environment Agency becomes aware of any such failure as is mentioned in subsection (9) above, the Agency may—
>
> > (a) if a consent under this Chapter to make discharges of any special category effluent has been granted on the application in question, exercise its powers of review under section 127 or 131 below, notwithstanding anything in subsection (2) of the section in question; or
> >
> > (b) in any other case, proceed as if the reference required by this section had been made."

106. In section 123 of that Act (appeals with respect to the discharge of special category effluent) for the words "the Secretary of State" or "the Secretary of State's", wherever occurring, there shall be substituted respectively the words "the Environment Agency" or "the Environment Agency's".

107. In section 127 of that Act (review by the Secretary of State of consents relating to special category effluent) for the words "the Secretary of State" or "the Secretary of State's", wherever occurring, there shall be substituted respectively the words "the Environment Agency" or "the Environment Agency's".

108.—(1) Section 130 of that Act (reference to the Secretary of State of agreements relating to special category effluent) shall be amended in accordance with the following provisions of this paragraph.

(2) For the words "the Secretary of State", wherever occurring, there shall be substituted the words "the Environment Agency".

(3) For subsections (5) and (6) (enforcement by Secretary of State) there shall be substituted—

"(7) If a sewerage undertaker fails, before giving any consent or entering into any agreement with respect to any such operations as are mentioned in paragraph (a) of subsection (1) above, to refer to the Environment Agency any question which he is required by that subsection to refer to the Agency, the undertaker shall be guilty of an offence and liable—

(a) on summary conviction, to a fine not exceeding the statutory maximum;

(b) on conviction on indictment, to a fine.

(8) If the Environment Agency becomes aware—

(a) that a sewerage undertaker and the owner or occupier of any trade premises are proposing to enter into any such agreement as is mentioned in subsection (1) above, and

(b) that the sewerage undertaker has not referred to the Agency any question which it is required to refer to the Agency by that subsection,

the Agency may proceed as if the reference required by that subsection had been made.

(9) If the Environment Agency becomes aware that any consent has been given or agreement entered into with respect to any such operations as are mentioned in paragraph (a) of subsection (1) above without the sewerage undertaker in question having referred to the Environment Agency any question which he is required by that subsection to refer to the Agency, the Agency may exercise its powers of review under section 127 above or, as the case may be, section 131 below, notwithstanding anything in subsection (2) of the section in question."

109. In section 131 of that Act (review by the Secretary of State of agreements relating to special category effluent) for the words "the Secretary of State" or "the Secretary of State's", wherever occurring, there shall be substituted respectively the words "the Environment Agency" or "the Environment Agency's".

110.—(1) Section 132 of that Act (powers and procedure on references and reviews) shall be amended in accordance with the following provisions of this paragraph.

(2) For the words "the Secretary of State", wherever occurring, there shall be substituted the words "the Environment Agency".

(3) In subsection (2)(b) of that section (duty of the Secretary of State to consider representations or objections duly made to him) for the words "him" and "he" there shall be substituted the word "the Agency".

(4) In subsection (6) of that section (section 121(1) and (2) not to restrict power to impose conditions under subsection (4)(b)) for the word "he" there shall be substituted the words "the Agency".

(5) Subsection (7) (powers of entry) shall cease to have effect.

111. In section 133 of that Act (effect of determination on reference or review) for subsection (4) (duties of sewerage undertaker to be enforceable under section 18 by the Secretary of State) there shall be substituted—

"(5) A sewerage undertaker which fails to perform its duty under subsection (1) above shall be guilty of an offence and liable—

(a) on summary conviction, to a fine not exceeding the statutory maximum;

(b) on conviction on indictment, to a fine.

(6) The Environment Agency may, for the purpose of securing compliance with the provisions of a notice under section 132 above, by serving notice on the sewerage undertaker in question and on the person specified in section 132(2)(a)(ii) above, vary or revoke—

(a) any consent given under this Chapter to make discharges of any special category effluent, or

(b) any agreement under section 129 above."

112. In section 134 of that Act (compensation in respect of determinations made for the protection of public health etc)—

(a) for the words "the Secretary of State" or "the Secretary of State's", wherever occurring, there shall be substituted respectively the words "the Environment Agency" or "the Environment Agency's"; and

(b) in subsection (2)(b) for the word "him" there shall be substituted the words "the Agency".

113. After section 135 there shall be inserted—

"Power of the Environment Agency to acquire information for the purpose of its functions in relation to special category effluent.

135A.—(1) For the purpose of the discharge of its functions under this Chapter, the Environment Agency may, by notice in writing served on any person, require that person to furnish such information specified in the notice as that Agency reasonably considers it needs, in such form and within such period following service of the notice, or at such time, as is so specified.

(2) A person who—

(a) fails, without reasonable excuse, to comply with a requirement imposed under subsection (1) above, or

(b) in furnishing any information in compliance with such a requirement, makes any statement which he knows to be false or misleading in a material particular, or recklessly makes a statement which is false or misleading in a material particular,

shall be guilty of an offence.

(3) A person guilty of an offence under subsection (2) above shall be liable—

(a) on summary conviction, to a fine not exceeding the statutory maximum;

(b) on conviction on indictment, to a fine or to imprisonment for a term not exceeding two years, or to both."

114.—(1) Section 142 of that Act (powers of undertakers to charge) shall be amended in accordance with the following provisions of this paragraph.

(2) In subsection (2) (manner in which charging powers to be exercised) for the words "subsection (3)" there shall be substituted the words "subsections (3) and (3A)".

(3) After subsection (3) (restriction on charging by agreement for trade effluent functions) there shall be inserted—

"(3A) The power of a sewerage undertaker to charge, by virtue of subsection (1) above, for any services provided in the course of carrying out its duty under section 101A(1) above shall be exercisable only by or in accordance with a charges scheme under section 143 below."

115. In section 143 of that Act (charges schemes) after subsection (3) (charges which may be imposed in certain cases) there shall be inserted—

"(3A) A sewerage undertaker is under a duty to ensure that any charges scheme made by the undertaker, so far as having effect to recover the undertaker's costs of providing a sewer by virtue of its duty under section 101A(1) above, causes those costs to be borne by the undertaker's customers generally; and a sewerage undertaker's duty under this subsection shall be enforceable under section 18 above—

(a) by the Secretary of State; or

(b) with the consent of or in accordance with a general authorisation given by the Secretary of State, by the Director."

116. Section 151 of that Act shall cease to have effect.

117. In section 161 of that Act (power to deal with foul water and pollution) in subsections (3) and (4) for the words "the NRA", wherever occurring, there shall be substituted the words "the Environment Agency".

118. In section 166 of that Act (consents for certain discharges under section 165) in subsection (1) (which requires the consent of the National Rivers Authority to certain discharges) for the words "the NRA" there shall be substituted the words "the Environment Agency".

119. In section 184 of that Act (power of certain undertakers to alter public sewers etc) in subsection (1) for the words "NRA", in each place where it occurs, there shall be substituted the words "Environment Agency".

120. In section 202 of that Act (duties of undertakers to furnish the Secretary of State with information) in subsection (6) (which defines the expression "the other consolidation Acts") for the words "the NRA" there shall be substituted the words "the Environment Agency".

121.—(1) In section 206 of that Act (restriction on disclosure of information) in subsection (2) (information furnished under section 196 or 204) the words "196 or" shall cease to have effect.

(2) In subsection (3)(a) of that section (exception for disclosure of information for purposes of functions under certain enactments)—

(a) for the words "the NRA" there shall be substituted the words "the Environment Agency, the Scottish Environment Protection Agency"; and

1989 c. 15.

(b) for the words "or the Water Act 1989" there shall be substituted the words ", the Water Act 1989, Part I or IIA of the Environmental Protection Act 1990 or the Environment Act 1995".

1990 c. 43.

(3) In subsection (4), in paragraph (a) (which provides that nothing in subsection (1) shall limit the matters which may be included in reports made by specified bodies under specified enactments)—

(a) for the words "the NRA" there shall be substituted the words "the Environment Agency, the Scottish Environment Protection Agency"; and

1991 c. 57.

(b) for the words "or of the Water Resources Act 1991" there shall be substituted the words ", Part I or IIA of the Environmental Protection Act 1990, the Water Resources Act 1991 or the Environment Act 1995".

1995 c. 25.

122. In section 209 of that Act (civil liability of undertakers for escapes of water etc) in subsection (3) (exceptions for loss sustained by other public undertakers) for the words "the NRA" there shall be substituted the words "the Environment Agency".

123. In section 215 of that Act (local inquiries) in subsection (3) (application of section 250(4) of the Local Government Act 1972 in relation to the National Rivers Authority) for the words "the NRA", in each place where they occur, there shall be substituted the words "the Environment Agency".

1972 c. 70.

124. In section 217 of that Act (construction of provisions conferring powers by reference to undertakers' functions) for the words "NRA", wherever occurring, there shall be substituted the words "Environment Agency".

125. In section 219 of that Act (general interpretation) in subsection (1)—

(a) the definition of "the NRA" shall be omitted; and

(b) subject to that, for the words "the NRA", wherever occurring, there shall be substituted the words "the Environment Agency".

126. In Schedule 11 to that Act (orders conferring compulsory works powers) in paragraph 1(3) (persons on whom copy notices are to be served) in paragraph (a), for the words "the NRA" there shall be substituted the words "the Environment Agency".

127. In Schedule 13 to that Act (protective provisions in respect of certain undertakers) in paragraph 1, in sub-paragraphs (2) and (5)(a), for the words "the NRA", wherever occurring, there shall be substituted the words "the Environment Agency".

The Water Resources Act 1991

128. Subject to the other provisions of this Act, in the Water Resources Act 1991, for the word "Authority" or "Authority's", wherever occurring, other than in section 119(1), there shall be substituted respectively the word "Agency" or "Agency's".

1991 c. 57.

129. Sections 1 to 14 of that Act (the National Rivers Authority and committees with functions in relation to that Authority) shall cease to have effect.

130. In section 15 of that Act (general duties with respect to the water industry), in subsection (2)(a) (provisions conferring powers in the exercise of which the Ministers are to take into account the duties imposed on the Agency by subsection (1)) after the words "by virtue of" there shall be inserted the words "the 1995 Act,".

131. Sections 16 to 19 of that Act (which relate to the environmental and recreational duties of the National Rivers Authority and the general management of resources by that Authority) shall cease to have effect.

132. In section 20 of that Act (water resources management schemes) in subsection (1) of that section (duty to enter into arrangements with water undertakers for the management or operation of certain waters etc) for the words "section 19(1) above" there shall be substituted the words "section 6(2) of the 1995 Act".

133.—(1) In section 21 of that Act (minimum acceptable flows) in subsection (3), at the end of paragraph (f) (consultation with person authorised by a licence under Part I of the Electricity Act 1989 to generate electricity) there shall be added the words "who has a right to abstract water from those waters".

1989 c. 29.

(2) In subsection (4)(b) of that section (which refers to certain enactments which are repealed, but whose effect is reproduced, by this Act) for the words "sections 2(2), 16 and 17 above" there shall be substituted the words "sections 6(1), 7 and 8 of the 1995 Act".

134. In section 43 of that Act (appeals to the Secretary of State from decisions with respect to licences) after subsection (1) there shall be inserted—

"(1A) This section is subject to section 114 of the 1995 Act (delegation or reference of appeals etc)."

135.—(1) In section 50 of that Act, in subsection (1) (power to make regulations, in relation to cases to which section 49 applies, for conferring succession rights to abstraction licences where a person becomes the occupier of part of the relevant land) for the words "cases to which section 49 above applies" there shall be substituted the words "cases in which the holder of a licence under this Chapter to abstract water ("the prior holder") is the occupier of the whole or part of the land specified in the licence as the land on which water abstracted in pursuance of the licence is to be used ("the relevant land")".

(2) That section shall have effect, and be taken always to have had effect, as if it had originally been enacted with the amendment made by sub-paragraph (1) above.

136. Section 58 (revocation of licence for non-payment of charges) shall cease to have effect.

137. Section 68 of that Act (power by order to establish a tribunal to which certain appeals and references shall lie) shall cease to have effect.

138. Section 69(5) of that Act (which refers to the tribunal established under section 68) shall cease to have effect.

139.—(1) Section 73 of that Act (power to make ordinary and emergency drought orders) shall be amended in accordance with the following provisions of this paragraph.

(2) In subsection (1) (power to make ordinary drought orders) for the words from the beginning to "then" there shall be substituted the words—

"(1) If the Secretary of State is satisfied that, by reason of an exceptional shortage of rain, there exists or is threatened—

(a) a serious deficiency of supplies of water in any area, or

(b) such a deficiency in the flow or level of water in any inland waters as to pose a serious threat to any of the flora or fauna which are dependent on those waters,

then,".

(3) In subsection (3) (power to make drought order not to be exercisable except where an application is made by the National Rivers Authority or a water undertaker)—

(a) for the words "except where" there shall be substituted the word "unless"; and

(b) at the beginning of paragraph (b) (water undertakers) there shall be inserted the words "except in the case of an ordinary drought order by virtue of subsection (1)(b) above,".

140. After section 79 of that Act (compensation and charges where drought order made) there shall be inserted—

"Drought permits.   79A.—(1) If the Agency is satisfied that, by reason of an exceptional shortage of rain, a serious deficiency of supplies of water in any area exists or is threatened then, subject to the following provisions of this section, it may, upon the application of a water undertaker which supplies water to premises in that area, issue to that undertaker a drought permit making such provision authorised by this section as appears to the Agency to be expedient with a view to meeting the deficiency.

(2) A drought permit may contain any of the following provisions, that is to say—

(a) provision authorising the water undertaker to which it is issued to take water from any source specified in the permit subject to any conditions or restrictions so specified;

(b) provision suspending or modifying, subject to any conditions specified in the permit, any restriction or obligation to which that undertaker is subject as respects the taking of water from any source.

(3) A drought permit shall specify—

(a) the day on which it comes into force; and

(b) the period for which, subject to subsections (4) and (5) below, any authorisation given, or suspension or modification effected, by the permit is to have effect.

(4) Subject to subsection (5) below, the period for which—

(a) an authorisation given by a drought permit, or

(b) a suspension or modification effected by such a permit,

has effect shall expire before the end of the period of six months beginning with the day on which the permit comes into force.

(5) At any time before the expiration of the period for which such an authorisation, suspension or modification has effect, the Agency may, by giving notice to the water undertaker to which the permit in question was issued, extend that period, but not so as to extend it beyond the end of the period of one year beginning with the day on which the permit came into force.

(6) A drought permit which—

(a) authorises the taking of water from a source from which water is supplied to an inland navigation; or

(b) suspends or modifies—

(i) a restriction as respects the taking of water from a source from which water is supplied to an inland navigation; or

(ii) an obligation to discharge compensation water into a canal or into any river or stream which forms part of, or from which water is supplied to, an inland navigation,

shall not be issued without the consent of every navigation authority exercising functions over any or all of the parts of the canal or inland navigation in question which are affected by the permit.

(7) Schedule 8 to this Act shall have effect with respect to the procedure on an application for a drought permit as it has effect with respect to the procedure on an application for a drought order, but with the following modifications, that is to say—

(a) with the substitution for any reference to a drought order of a reference to a drought permit;

(b) with the substitution for any reference to the Secretary of State of a reference to the Agency;

(c) with the omission of the reference to the Agency in the Table in paragraph 1;

    (d) with the insertion, in paragraph 1(3)(c), of a requirement that the notice in question shall specify the address at which any objections are to be made to the Agency; and

    (e) with the omission—

        (i) of paragraph 2(1)(a) and the word "either" immediately preceding it, and

        (ii) of paragraph 2(6).

(8) For the purposes of sections 125 to 129 below any water authorised by a drought permit to be abstracted from a source of supply shall be treated as if it had been authorised to be so abstracted by a licence granted under Chapter II of this Part, whether the water undertaker to which the permit is issued is the holder of such a licence or not.

(9) Section 79 above and Schedule 9 to this Act shall apply in relation to drought permits and their issue as they apply in relation to ordinary drought orders and their making.

(10) A drought permit may—

    (a) make different provision for different cases, including different provision in relation to different persons, circumstances or localities; and

    (b) contain such supplemental, consequential and transitional provisions as the Agency considers appropriate.

(11) In this section—

    "compensation water" has the same meaning as in section 77 above;

    "drought permit" means a drought permit under this section;

    "inland navigation" has the same meaning as in section 77 above."

141. In section 80 of that Act (offences against drought orders)—

    (a) in subsection (1)(a) (taking or using water otherwise than in accordance with any condition or restriction imposed by or under a drought order) for the words "so imposed" there shall be substituted the words "imposed by or under any drought order or by any drought permit";

    (b) in subsection (2)(a) (failure to construct or maintain measuring apparatus required by any drought order) after the words "by any drought order" there shall be inserted the words "or drought permit"; and

    (c) in subsection (2)(b) (failure to allow person authorised by or under any such order to inspect etc apparatus or records) after the words "by or under any such order" there shall be inserted the words "or by virtue of any such permit".

142. After section 90 of that Act (offences in connection with deposits and vegetation in rivers) there shall be inserted—

"Consents for the purposes of sections 88 to 90

Applications for consent under section 89 or 90.

90A.—(1) Any application for a consent for the purposes of section 89(4)(a) or 90(1) or (2) above—

    (a) must be made on a form provided for the purpose by the Agency, and

(b) must be advertised in such manner as may be required by regulations made by the Secretary of State,

except that paragraph (b) above shall not have effect in the case of an application of any class or description specified in the regulations as being exempt from the requirements of that paragraph.

(2) The applicant for such a consent must, at the time when he makes his application, provide the Agency—

(a) with all such information as it reasonably requires; and

(b) with all such information as may be prescribed for the purpose by the Secretary of State.

(3) The information required by subsection (2) above must be provided either on, or together with, the form mentioned in subsection (1) above.

(4) The Agency may give the applicant notice requiring him to provide it with all such further information of any description specified in the notice as it may require for the purpose of determining the application.

(5) If the applicant fails to provide the Agency with any information required under subsection (4) above, the Agency may refuse to proceed with the application or refuse to proceed with it until the information is provided.

Enforcement notices.

90B.—(1) If the Agency is of the opinion that the holder of a relevant consent is contravening any condition of the consent, or is likely to contravene any such condition, the Agency may serve on him a notice (an "enforcement notice").

(2) An enforcement notice shall—

(a) state that the Agency is of the said opinion;

(b) specify the matters constituting the contravention or the matters making it likely that the contravention will arise;

(c) specify the steps that must be taken to remedy the contravention or, as the case may be, to remedy the matters making it likely that the contravention will arise; and

(d) specify the period within which those steps must be taken.

(3) Any person who fails to comply with any requirement imposed by an enforcement notice shall be guilty of an offence and liable—

(a) on summary conviction, to imprisonment for a term not exceeding three months or to a fine not exceeding £20,000 or to both;

(b) on conviction on indictment, to imprisonment for a term not exceeding two years or to a fine or to both.

(4) If the Agency is of the opinion that proceedings for an offence under subsection (3) above would afford an ineffectual remedy against a person who has failed to comply with the requirements of an enforcement notice, the Agency may take proceedings in the High Court for the purpose of securing compliance with the notice.

(5) The Secretary of State may, if he thinks fit in relation to any person, give to the Agency directions as to whether the Agency should exercise its powers under this section and as to the steps which must be taken.

(6) In this section—

"relevant consent" means—

(a) a consent for the purposes of section 89(4)(a) or 90(1) or (2) above; or

(b) a discharge consent, within the meaning of section 91 below; and

"the holder", in relation to a relevant consent, is the person who has the consent in question."

143.—(1) In section 91 of that Act (appeals in respect of consents under Chapter II of Part III of that Act), in subsection (1) (which specifies the decisions which are subject to appeal)—

(a) in paragraph (d) (which refers to paragraph 7(1) or (2) of Schedule 10) for the words "7(1)" there shall be substituted the words "8(1)"; and

(b) at the end there shall be added—

"(g) has refused a person a variation of any such consent as is mentioned in paragraphs (a) to (f) above or, in allowing any such variation, has made the consent subject to conditions; or

(h) has served an enforcement notice on any person."

(2) In subsection (2) of that section (persons who may appeal)—

(a) after the words "who applied for the consent" there shall be inserted the words "or variation"; and

(b) after the words "would be authorised by the consent" there shall be inserted the words ", or the person on whom the enforcement notice was served,".

(3) For subsections (3) to (7) of that section there shall be substituted—

"(2A) This section is subject to section 114 of the 1995 Act (delegation or reference of appeals etc).

(2B) An appeal under this section shall, if and to the extent required by regulations under subsection (2K) below, be advertised in such manner as may be prescribed by regulations under that subsection.

(2C) If either party to the appeal so requests or the Secretary of State so decides, an appeal shall be or continue in the form of a hearing (which may, if the person hearing the appeal so decides, be held, or held to any extent, in private).

(2D) On determining an appeal brought by virtue of any of paragraphs (a) to (g) of subsection (1) above against a decision of the Agency, the Secretary of State—

(a) may affirm the decision;

(b) where the decision was a refusal to grant a consent or a variation of a consent, may direct the Agency to grant the consent or to vary the consent, as the case may be;

(c) where the decision was as to the conditions of a consent, may quash all or any of those conditions;

(d) where the decision was to revoke a consent, may quash the decision;

(e) where the decision relates to a period specified for the purposes of paragraph 8(1) or (2) of Schedule 10 to this Act, may modify any provisions specifying that period;

and where he exercises any of the powers in paragraphs (b), (c) or (d) above, he may give directions as to the conditions to which the consent is to be subject.

(2E) On the determination of an appeal brought by virtue of paragraph (h) of subsection (1) above, the Secretary of State may either quash or affirm the enforcement notice and, if he affirms it, may do so either in its original form or with such modifications as he may in the circumstances think fit.

(2F) Subject to subsection (2G) below, where an appeal is brought by virtue of subsection (1)(c) above against a decision—

(a) to revoke a discharge consent,

(b) to modify the conditions of any such consent, or

(c) to provide that any such consent which was unconditional shall be subject to conditions,

the revocation, modification or provision shall not take effect pending the final determination or the withdrawal of the appeal.

(2G) Subsection (2F) above shall not apply to a decision in the case of which the notice effecting the revocation, modification or provision in question includes a statement that in the opinion of the Agency it is necessary for the purpose of preventing or, where that is not practicable, minimising—

(a) the entry into controlled waters of any poisonous, noxious or polluting matter or any solid waste matter, or

(b) harm to human health,

that that subsection should not apply.

(2H) Where the decision under appeal is one falling within subsection (2G) above, if, on the application of the holder or former holder of the consent, the Secretary of State or other person determining the appeal determines that the Agency acted unreasonably in excluding the application of subsection (2F) above, then—

(a) if the appeal is still pending at the end of the day on which the determination is made, subsection (2F) above shall apply to the decision from the end of that day; and

(b) the holder or former holder of the consent shall be entitled to recover compensation from the Agency in respect of any loss suffered by him in consequence of the exclusion of the application of that subsection;

and any dispute as to a person's entitlement to such compensation or as to the amount of it shall be determined by arbitration.

(2J) Where an appeal is brought under this section against an enforcement notice, the bringing of the appeal shall not have the effect of suspending the operation of the notice.

(2K) Provision may be made by the Secretary of State by regulations with respect to appeals under this section and in particular—

(a) as to the period within which and the manner in which appeals are to be brought; and

(b) as to the manner in which appeals are to be considered."

(4) In subsection (8) of that section (which refers to paragraph 5 of Schedule 10) for the word "5" there shall be substituted the word "6".

144. In section 92 of that Act (requirements to take precautions against pollution) after subsection (2) (which includes provision for regulations to provide for appeals to the Secretary of State) there shall be added—

"(3) This section is subject to section 114 of the 1995 Act (delegation or reference of appeals etc)."

145. In section 96 of that Act (regulations with respect to consents required by virtue of section 93 etc, including provision with respect to appeals) after subsection (3) there shall be added—

"(4) This section is subject to section 114 of the 1995 Act (delegation or reference of appeals etc)."

146. Section 105(1) of that Act (National Rivers Authority to exercise general supervision over matters relating to flood defence) shall cease to have effect.

147.—(1) In section 110 of that Act (applications for consents and approvals under section 109) in subsection (1) (which confers power to charge an application fee of £50 or such other sum as may be specified by order made by the Ministers) for the words "specified by order made by the Ministers" there shall be substituted the word "prescribed".

(2) In subsection (4)(b) of that section (which provides for questions as to unreasonable withholding of any consent or approval to be referred to the Ministers or the Secretary of State if the parties cannot agree on an arbitrator) for the words "the Ministers" there shall be substituted the words "the Minister".

(3) After subsection (5) of that section there shall be inserted—

"(6) In subsection (1) above "prescribed" means specified in, or determined in accordance with, an order made by the Ministers; and any such order may make different provision for different cases, including different provision in relation to different persons, circumstances or localities."

148. Section 114 (general fisheries duty of the National Rivers Authority) shall cease to have effect.

149. Section 117 (general financial duties of the National Rivers Authority) shall cease to have effect.

150.—(1) Section 118 of that Act (special duties with respect to flood defence revenue) shall be amended in accordance with the following provisions of this paragraph.

(2) In subsection (1)(b) (such revenue to be disregarded in determining the amount of any surplus for the purposes of section 117(3)) for the words "section 117(3) above" there shall be substituted the words "section 44(4) of the 1995 Act".

(3) In subsection (2)(b) (flood defence revenue to include revenue raised by general drainage charges under sections 134 to 136) for the words "to 136" there shall be substituted the words "and 135".

151.—(1) In section 119 of that Act (duties with respect to certain funds raised under local enactments) for subsection (1) (duty of the National Rivers Authority, in respect of funds created for fishery purposes under local enactments, not to use those funds except for the purposes for which they could have been used if the Water Resources Act 1963 had not been passed) there shall be substituted—

1963 c. 38.

"(1) Where the Agency holds any funds, or any interest in any funds, which immediately before the transfer date the National Rivers Authority, by virtue of this subsection as originally enacted, was not permitted to use except for particular purposes, those funds or that interest shall not be used except for the purposes for which they could be used by virtue of this subsection as originally enacted.

(1A) For the purposes of subsection (1) above, "the transfer date" has the same meaning as in Part I of the 1995 Act."

(2) In subsection (2) of that section (certain funds raised under local enactments to be disregarded in determining the amount of any surplus for the purposes of section 117(3)) for the words "section 117(3) above" there shall be substituted the words "section 44(3) of the 1995 Act".

152. Sections 121 to 124 of that Act (accounts of the Authority, audit and schemes imposing water resources charges) shall cease to have effect.

153. Sections 126(6) and 129(4) of that Act (each of which applies section 68) shall cease to have effect.

154. Sections 131 and 132 of that Act (schemes of charges in connection with control of pollution) shall cease to have effect.

155. Section 146 of that Act (revenue grants by the Secretary of State to the National Rivers Authority) shall cease to have effect.

156. Sections 150 to 153 of that Act (grants for national security purposes, borrowing powers of the National Rivers Authority, loans to the Authority, and Treasury guarantees of the Authority's borrowing) shall cease to have effect.

157. In section 154 of that Act (compulsory purchase etc) in subsection (6), for the words "(including section 4 above) or otherwise" there shall be substituted the words "or otherwise (including section 37 of the 1995 Act (incidental general powers of the Agency))".

158. In section 156 of that Act (acquisition of land etc for fisheries purposes) for the words "Without prejudice to section 4 above", in each place where they occur, there shall be substituted the words "Without prejudice to section 37 of the 1995 Act (incidental general powers of the Agency)".

159. In section 157 of that Act (restriction on disposals of compulsorily acquired land) for subsection (6) (meaning of "compulsorily acquired land") there shall be substituted—

"(6) In this section "compulsorily acquired land", in relation to the Agency, means any land of the Agency which—

(a) was acquired by the Agency compulsorily under the provisions of section 154 above or of an order under section 168 below;

(b) was acquired by the Agency at a time when it was authorised under those provisions to acquire the land compulsorily;

(c) being land which has been transferred to the Agency from the Authority by section 3 of the 1995 Act, was acquired by the Authority—

(i) compulsorily, under the provisions of section 154 above or of an order under section 168 below or under the provisions of section 151 of the Water Act 1989 or of an order under section 155 of that Act; or

1989 c. 15.

(ii) at a time when it was authorised under those provisions to acquire the land compulsorily;

(d) being land—

(i) which has been so transferred, and

(ii) which was transferred to the Authority in accordance with a scheme under Schedule 2 to the Water Act 1989,

was acquired by a predecessor of the Authority compulsorily under so much of any enactment in force at any time before 1st September 1989 as conferred powers of compulsory acquisition; or

(e) being land transferred as mentioned in sub-paragraphs (i) and (ii) of paragraph (d) above, was acquired by such a predecessor at a time when it was authorised to acquire the land by virtue of any such powers as are mentioned in that paragraph."

160. In section 158 of that Act (works agreements for water resources purposes) in subsection (1) (which is expressed to be without prejudice to the generality of the powers conferred by section 4) for the words "section 4 above" there shall be substituted the words "section 37 of the 1995 Act (incidental general powers of the Agency)".

161.—(1) Section 161 of that Act (anti-pollution works and operations) shall be amended in accordance with the following provisions of this paragraph.

(2) In subsection (1) (power, subject to subsection (2), to carry out works and operations etc) for the words "Subject to subsection (2) below," there shall be substituted the words "Subject to subsections (1A) and (2) below,".

(3) After that subsection there shall be inserted—

"(1A) Without prejudice to the power of the Agency to carry out investigations under subsection (1) above, the power conferred by that subsection to carry out works and operations shall only be exercisable in a case where—

(a) the Agency considers it necessary to carry out forthwith any works or operations falling within paragraph (a) or (b) of that subsection; or

(b) it appears to the Agency, after reasonable inquiry, that no person can be found on whom to serve a works notice under section 161A below."

162. After that section there shall be inserted—

"Notices requiring persons to carry out anti-pollution works and operations.

161A.—(1) Subject to the following provisions of this section, where it appears to the Agency that any poisonous, noxious or polluting matter or any solid waste matter is likely to enter, or to be or to have been present in, any controlled waters, the Agency shall be entitled to serve a works notice on any person who, as the case may be,—

(a) caused or knowingly permitted the matter in question to be present at the place from which it is likely, in the opinion of the Agency, to enter any controlled waters; or

(b) caused or knowingly permitted the matter in question to be present in any controlled waters.

(2) For the purposes of this section, a "works notice" is a notice requiring the person on whom it is served to carry out such of the following works or operations as may be specified in the notice, that is to say—

(a) in a case where the matter in question appears likely to enter any controlled waters, works or operations for the purpose of preventing it from doing so; or

(b) in a case where the matter appears to be or to have been present in any controlled waters, works or operations for the purpose—

(i) of removing or disposing of the matter;

(ii) of remedying or mitigating any pollution caused by its presence in the waters; or

(iii) so far as it is reasonably practicable to do so, of restoring the waters, including any flora and fauna dependent on the aquatic environment of the waters, to their state immediately before the matter became present in the waters.

(3) A works notice—

(a) must specify the periods within which the person on whom it is served is required to do each of the things specified in the notice; and

(b) is without prejudice to the powers of the Agency by virtue of section 161(1A)(a) above.

(4) Before serving a works notice on any person, the Agency shall reasonably endeavour to consult that person concerning the works or operations which are to be specified in the notice.

(5) The Secretary of State may by regulations make provision for or in connection with—

(a) the form or content of works notices;

(b) requirements for consultation, before the service of a works notice, with persons other than the person on whom that notice is to be served;

(c) steps to be taken for the purposes of any consultation required under subsection (4) above or regulations made by virtue of paragraph (b) above; or

(d) any other steps of a procedural nature which are to be taken in connection with, or in consequence of, the service of a works notice.

(6) A works notice shall not be regarded as invalid, or as invalidly served, by reason only of any failure to comply with the requirements of subsection (4) above or of regulations made by virtue of paragraph (b) of subsection (5) above.

(7) Nothing in subsection (1) above shall entitle the Agency to require the carrying out of any works or operations which would impede or prevent the making of any discharge in pursuance of a consent given under Chapter II of Part III of this Act.

(8) No works notice shall be served on any person requiring him to carry out any works or operations in respect of water from an abandoned mine or an abandoned part of a mine which that person permitted to reach such a place as is mentioned in subsection (1)(a) above or to enter any controlled waters.

(9) Subsection (8) above shall not apply to the owner or former operator of any mine or part of a mine if the mine or part in question became abandoned after 31st December 1999.

(10) Subsections (3B) and (3C) of section 89 above shall apply in relation to subsections (8) and (9) above as they apply in relation to subsections (3) and (3A) of that section.

(11) Where the Agency—

(a) carries out any such investigations as are mentioned in section 161(1) above, and

(b) serves a works notice on a person in connection with the matter to which the investigations relate,

it shall (unless the notice is quashed or withdrawn) be entitled to recover the costs or expenses reasonably incurred in carrying out those investigations from that person.

(12) The Secretary of State may, if he thinks fit in relation to any person, give directions to the Agency as to whether or how it should exercise its powers under this section.

(13) In this section—

"controlled waters" has the same meaning as in Part III of this Act;

1954 c. 70.

"mine" has the same meaning as in the Mines and Quarries Act 1954.

Grant of, and compensation for, rights of entry etc.

161B.—(1) A works notice may require a person to carry out works or operations in relation to any land or waters notwithstanding that he is not entitled to carry out those works or operations.

(2) Any person whose consent is required before any works or operations required by a works notice may be carried out shall grant, or join in granting, such rights in relation to any land or waters as will enable the person on whom the works notice is served to comply with any requirements imposed by the works notice.

(3) Before serving a works notice, the Agency shall reasonably endeavour to consult every person who appears to it—

(a) to be the owner or occupier of any relevant land, and

(b) to be a person who might be required by subsection (2) above to grant, or join in granting, any rights,

concerning the rights which that person may be so required to grant.

(4) A works notice shall not be regarded as invalid, or as invalidly served, by reason only of any failure to comply with the requirements of subsection (3) above.

(5) A person who grants, or joins in granting, any rights pursuant to subsection (2) above shall be entitled, on making an application within such period as may be prescribed and in such manner as may be prescribed to such person as may be prescribed, to be paid by the person on whom the works notice in question is served compensation of such amount as may be determined in such manner as may be prescribed.

(6) Without prejudice to the generality of the regulations that may be made by virtue of subsection (5) above, regulations by virtue of that subsection may make such provision in relation to compensation under this section as may be made by regulations by virtue of subsection (4) of section 35A of the

1990 c. 43.

Environmental Protection Act 1990 in relation to compensation under that section.

(7) In this section—

"prescribed" means prescribed in regulations made by the Secretary of State;

"relevant land" means—

(a) any land or waters in relation to which the works notice in question requires, or may require, works or operations to be carried out; or

(b) any land adjoining or adjacent to that land or those waters;

"works notice" means a works notice under section 161A above.

Appeals against works notices.

161C.—(1) A person on whom a works notice is served may, within the period of twenty-one days beginning with the day on which the notice is served, appeal against the notice to the Secretary of State.

(2) On any appeal under this section the Secretary of State—

(a) shall quash the notice, if he is satisfied that there is a material defect in the notice; but

(b) subject to that, may confirm the notice, with or without modification, or quash it.

(3) The Secretary of State may by regulations make provision with respect to—

(a) the grounds on which appeals under this section may be made; or

(b) the procedure on any such appeal.

(4) Regulations under subsection (3) above may (among other things)—

(a) include provisions comparable to those in section 290 of the Public Health Act 1936 (appeals against notices requiring the execution of works);

1936 c. 49.

(b) prescribe the cases in which a works notice is, or is not, to be suspended until the appeal is decided, or until some other stage in the proceedings;

(c) prescribe the cases in which the decision on an appeal may in some respects be less favourable to the appellant than the works notice against which he is appealing;

(d) prescribe the cases in which the appellant may claim that a works notice should have been served on some other person and prescribe the procedure to be followed in those cases;

(e) make provision as respects—

(i) the particulars to be included in the notice of appeal;

(ii) the persons on whom notice of appeal is to be served and the particulars, if any, which are to accompany the notice; or

(iii) the abandonment of an appeal.

(5) In this section "works notice" means a works notice under section 161A above.

(6) This section is subject to section 114 of the 1995 Act (delegation or reference of appeals).

Consequences of not complying with a works notice.

161D.—(1) If a person on whom the Agency serves a works notice fails to comply with any of the requirements of the notice, he shall be guilty of an offence.

(2) A person who commits an offence under subsection (1) above shall be liable—

    (a) on summary conviction, to imprisonment for a term not exceeding three months or to a fine not exceeding £20,000 or to both;

    (b) on conviction on indictment to imprisonment for a term not exceeding two years or to a fine or to both.

(3) If a person on whom a works notice has been served fails to comply with any of the requirements of the notice, the Agency may do what that person was required to do and may recover from him any costs or expenses reasonably incurred by the Agency in doing it.

(4) If the Agency is of the opinion that proceedings for an offence under subsection (1) above would afford an ineffectual remedy against a person who has failed to comply with the requirements of a works notice, the Agency may take proceedings in the High Court for the purpose of securing compliance with the notice.

(5) In this section "works notice" means a works notice under section 161A above."

163. In section 162 of that Act (other powers to deal with foul water or pollution) in subsection (1) (which refers to section 161 of that Act) for the words "section 161" there shall be substituted the words "sections 161 to 161D".

164. In section 166 of that Act (power to carry out works for purposes of flood warning system) in subsection (1) (which is expressed to be without prejudice to the Agency's other powers by virtue of section 4) for the words "section 4 above" there shall be substituted the words "section 37 of the 1995 Act (incidental general powers of the Agency)".

165. In section 169 of that Act (powers of entry for enforcement purposes) at the beginning of subsection (3) there shall be inserted the words "Subject to subsection (4) below," and after that subsection there shall be added—

"(4) The powers conferred by this section shall not have effect for the purposes of any of the Agency's pollution control functions, within the meaning of section 108 of the 1995 Act."

166. In section 172 of that Act (powers of entry for other purposes) at the beginning of subsection (3) there shall be inserted the words "Subject to subsection (3A) below," and after that subsection there shall be added—

"(3A) The powers conferred by this section shall not have effect for the purposes of any of the Agency's pollution control functions, within the meaning of section 108 of the 1995 Act."

167. In section 174 of that Act (impersonation of persons exercising powers of entry) in subsection (1) (which creates a summary offence punishable by a fine not exceeding level 4) for the words from "liable, on summary conviction," onwards there shall be substituted the words "liable—

    (a) on summary conviction, to a fine not exceeding the statutory maximum;

    (b) on conviction on indictment, to a fine or to imprisonment for a term not exceeding two years, or to both."

168. Section 187 of that Act (annual report of the Authority) shall cease to have effect.

169.—(1) Section 190 of that Act (pollution control register) shall be amended in accordance with the following provisions of this paragraph.

(2) In subsection (1) (which requires a register to be kept containing prescribed particulars of the items there specified) after the words "prescribed particulars of" there shall be inserted the words "or relating to".

(3) Paragraph (d) of that subsection (which relates to certificates under paragraph 1(7) of Schedule 10) shall be omitted.

(4) Paragraph (f) of that subsection, and the word "and" immediately preceding it, shall be omitted and at the end of that subsection there shall be added—

> "(g) applications made to the Agency for the variation of discharge consents;
>
> (h) enforcement notices served under section 90B above;
>
> (j) revocations, under paragraph 7 of Schedule 10 to this Act, of discharge consents;
>
> (k) appeals under section 91 above;
>
> (l) directions given by the Secretary of State in relation to the Agency's functions under the water pollution provisions of this Act;
>
> (m) convictions, for offences under Part III of this Act, of persons who have the benefit of discharge consents;
>
> (n) information obtained or furnished in pursuance of conditions of discharge consents;
>
> (o) works notices under section 161A above;
>
> (p) appeals under section 161C above;
>
> (q) convictions for offences under section 161D above;
>
> (r) such other matters relating to the quality of water or the pollution of water as may be prescribed by the Secretary of State.
>
> (1A) Where information of any description is excluded from any register by virtue of section 191B below, a statement shall be entered in the register indicating the existence of information of that description."

(5) In subsection (2) (registers to be available for inspection by, and facilities for obtaining copies of entries to be afforded to, the public) after paragraph (b) there shall be added the words—

> "and, for the purposes of this subsection, places may be prescribed by the Secretary of State at which any such registers or facilities as are mentioned in paragraph (a) or (b) above are to be available or afforded to the public in pursuance of the paragraph in question."

(6) After subsection (3) there shall be added—

> "(4) The Secretary of State may give to the Agency directions requiring the removal from any register maintained by it under this section of any specified information which is not prescribed for inclusion under subsection (1) above or which, by virtue of section 191A or 191B below, ought to have been excluded from the register.
>
> (5) In this section "discharge consent" has the same meaning as in section 91 above."

170. After section 191 of that Act (register for the purposes of works discharges) there shall be inserted—

"Exclusion from registers of information affecting national security.

191A.—(1) No information shall be included in a register kept or maintained by the Agency under any provision of this Act if and so long as, in the opinion of the Secretary of State, the inclusion in such a register of that information, or information of that description, would be contrary to the interests of national security.

(2) The Secretary of State may, for the purpose of securing the exclusion from registers of information to which subsection (1) above applies, give to the Agency directions—

(a) specifying information, or descriptions of information, to be excluded from their registers; or

(b) specifying descriptions of information to be referred to the Secretary of State for his determination;

and no information referred to the Secretary of State in pursuance of paragraph (b) above shall be included in any such register until the Secretary of State determines that it should be so included.

(3) The Agency shall notify the Secretary of State of any information it excludes from a register in pursuance of directions under subsection (2) above.

(4) A person may, as respects any information which appears to him to be information to which subsection (1) above may apply, give a notice to the Secretary of State specifying the information and indicating its apparent nature; and, if he does so—

(a) he shall notify the Agency that he has done so; and

(b) no information so notified to the Secretary of State shall be included in any such register until the Secretary of State has determined that it should be so included.

Exclusion from registers of certain confidential information.

191B.—(1) No information relating to the affairs of any individual or business shall, without the consent of that individual or the person for the time being carrying on that business, be included in a register kept or maintained by the Agency under any provision of this Act, if and so long as the information—

(a) is, in relation to him, commercially confidential; and

(b) is not required to be included in the register in pursuance of directions under subsection (7) below;

but information is not commercially confidential for the purposes of this section unless it is determined under this section to be so by the Agency or, on appeal, by the Secretary of State.

(2) Where information is furnished to the Agency for the purpose of—

(a) an application for a discharge consent or for the variation of a discharge consent,

(b) complying with any condition of a discharge consent, or

(c) complying with a notice under section 202 below,

then, if the person furnishing it applies to the Agency to have the information excluded from any register kept or maintained by the Agency under any provision of this Act, on the ground that it is commercially confidential (as regards himself or another person), the Agency shall determine whether the information is or is not commercially confidential.

(3) A determination under subsection (2) above must be made within the period of fourteen days beginning with the date

of the application and if the Agency fails to make a determination within that period it shall be treated as having determined that the information is commercially confidential.

(4) Where it appears to the Agency that any information (other than information furnished in circumstances within subsection (2) above) which has been obtained by the Agency under or by virtue of any provision of any enactment might be commercially confidential, the Agency shall—

(a) give to the person to whom or whose business it relates notice that that information is required to be included in a register kept or maintained by the Agency under any provision of this Act, unless excluded under this section; and

(b) give him a reasonable opportunity—

(i) of objecting to the inclusion of the information on the ground that it is commercially confidential; and

(ii) of making representations to the Agency for the purpose of justifying any such objection;

and, if any representations are made, the Agency shall, having taken the representations into account, determine whether the information is or is not commercially confidential.

(5) Where, under subsection (2) or (4) above, the Agency determines that information is not commercially confidential—

(a) the information shall not be entered on the register until the end of the period of twenty-one days beginning with the date on which the determination is notified to the person concerned; and

(b) that person may appeal to the Secretary of State against the decision;

and, where an appeal is brought in respect of any information, the information shall not be entered on the register until the end of the period of seven days following the day on which the appeal is finally determined or withdrawn.

(6) Subsections (2A), (2C) and (2K) of section 91 above shall apply in relation to appeals under subsection (5) above; but—

(a) subsection (2C) of that section shall have effect for the purposes of this subsection with the substitution for the words from "(which may" onwards of the words "(which must be held in private)"; and

(b) subsection (5) above is subject to section 114 of the 1995 Act (delegation or reference of appeals etc).

(7) The Secretary of State may give to the Agency directions as to specified information, or descriptions of information, which the public interest requires to be included in registers kept or maintained by the Agency under any provision of this Act notwithstanding that the information may be commercially confidential.

(8) Information excluded from a register shall be treated as ceasing to be commercially confidential for the purposes of this section at the expiry of the period of four years beginning with the date of the determination by virtue of which it was excluded; but the person who furnished it may apply to the Agency for the

information to remain excluded from the register on the ground that it is still commercially confidential and the Agency shall determine whether or not that is the case.

(9) Subsections (5) and (6) above shall apply in relation to a determination under subsection (8) above as they apply in relation to a determination under subsection (2) or (4) above.

(10) The Secretary of State may by regulations substitute (whether in all cases or in such classes or descriptions of case as may be specified in the regulations) for the period for the time being specified in subsection (3) above such other period as he considers appropriate.

(11) Information is, for the purposes of any determination under this section, commercially confidential, in relation to any individual or person, if its being contained in the register would prejudice to an unreasonable degree the commercial interests of that individual or person.

(12) In this section "discharge consent" has the same meaning as in section 91 above."

171. Section 196 of that Act (provision of information by the Authority to Ministers) shall cease to have effect.

172.—(1) In section 202 of that Act (information and assistance required in connection with the control of pollution) in subsection (4) (which creates a summary offence punishable by a fine not exceeding level 5 on the standard scale) for the words from "liable, on summary conviction," onwards there shall be substituted the words "liable—

(a) on summary conviction, to a fine not exceeding the statutory maximum;

(b) on conviction on indictment, to a fine or to imprisonment for a term not exceeding two years, or to both."

(2) Subsection (5) of that section (which is superseded in consequence of the amendment made by sub-paragraph (1) above) shall cease to have effect.

173.—(1) Section 204 of that Act (restriction on disclosure of information with respect to any particular business) shall be amended in accordance with the following provisions of this paragraph.

(2) In subsection (2)(a) (exception for disclosure of information for purposes of functions under certain enactments)—

(a) for the words "the Authority" there shall be substituted the words "the Agency, the Scottish Environment Protection Agency"; and

1989 c. 15.
1990 c. 43.

(b) for the words "or the Water Act 1989" there shall be substituted the words ", the Water Act 1989, Part I or IIA of the Environmental Protection Act 1990 or the 1995 Act".

(3) In subsection (3), in paragraph (a) (which provides that nothing in subsection (1) shall limit the matters which may be included in reports made by specified bodies under specified enactments)—

(a) after sub-paragraph (i), there shall be inserted—

"(ia) the Scottish Environment Protection Agency;"; and

(b) for the words "or that Act of 1991" there shall be substituted the words ", Part I or IIA of the Environmental Protection Act 1990, that Act of 1991 or the 1995 Act".

(4) In paragraph (b) of that subsection, after the words "that Act" there shall be inserted the words "of 1991".

174. Sections 213 to 215 of that Act (local inquiries) shall cease to have effect.

175. Section 218 of that Act (no judicial disqualification by virtue of liability to pay charges to the Authority) shall cease to have effect.

176. In section 219 of that Act (powers to make regulations)—

(a) in subsection (2), the words "Subject to subsection (3) below,", and

(b) subsection (3) (which restricts certain powers to make regulations),

shall cease to have effect.

177.—(1) Section 221(1) of that Act (general interpretation) shall be amended in accordance with the following provisions of this paragraph.

(2) Before the definition of "abstraction" there shall be inserted—

"the 1995 Act" means the Environment Act 1995;".

(3) After the definition of "accessories" there shall be inserted—

""the Agency" means the Environment Agency;".

(4) The definition of "the Authority" shall be omitted.

(5) The definition of "constituent council" shall be omitted.

(6) After the definition of "enactment" there shall be inserted—

"enforcement notice" has the meaning given by section 90B above;".

(7) For the definition of "flood defence functions" there shall be substituted—

""flood defence functions", in relation to the Agency, means—

(a) its functions with respect to flood defence and land drainage by virtue of Part IV of this Act, the Land Drainage Act 1991 and section 6 of the 1995 Act;   1991 c. 59.

(b) those functions transferred to the Agency by section 2(1)(a)(iii) of the 1995 Act which were previously transferred to the Authority by virtue of section 136(8) of the Water Act 1989 and paragraph 1(3) of Schedule 15 to that Act (transfer of land drainage functions under local statutory provisions and subordinate legislation); and   1989 c. 15.

(c) any other functions of the Agency under any of the flood defence provisions of this Act;".

(8) For the definition of "flood defence provisions" there shall be substituted—

"flood defence provisions", in relation to this Act, means—

(a) any of the following provisions of this Act, that is to say—

(i) Part IV;

(ii) sections 133 to 141 (including Schedule 15), 143, 147 to 149, 155, 165 to 167, 180, 193, 194 and paragraph 5 of Schedule 25;

(b) any of the following provisions of the 1995 Act, that is to say—

(i) section 6(4) (general supervision of flood defence);

(ii) section 53 (inquiries and other hearings); and

(iii) Schedule 5 (membership and proceedings of regional and local flood defence committees); and

(c) any other provision of this Act or the 1995 Act so far as it relates to a provision falling within paragraph (a) or (b) above;".

(9) For the definition of "the related water resources provisions" there shall be substituted—

""the related water resources provisions", in relation to Chapter II of Part II of this Act, means—

(a) the following provisions of this Act, that is to say, the provisions—

(i) of sections 21 to 23 (including Schedule 5);

(ii) of sections 120, 125 to 130, 158, 189, 199 to 201, 206(3), 209(3), 211(1) and 216; and

(iii) of paragraph 1 of Schedule 25; and

(b) the following provisions of the 1995 Act, that is to say, the provisions—

(i) of sections 41 and 42 (charging schemes) as they have effect by virtue of subsection (1)(a) of section 41 (licences under Chapter II of Part II of this Act); and

(ii) of subsections (1) and (2) of section 53 (inquiries and other hearings);".

(10) In the definition of "water pollution provisions"—

(a) in paragraph (b)—

(i) after the words "161" there shall be inserted the words "to 161D"; and

(ii) for the words "203 and 213(2) above" there shall be substituted the words "and 203"; and

(b) after paragraph (c), there shall be added the words—

"and the following provisions of the 1995 Act, that is to say, the provisions of subsections (1) and (2) of section 53."

178. Schedule 1 to that Act (the National Rivers Authority) shall cease to have effect.

179. Schedules 3 and 4 to that Act (boundaries of regional flood defence areas and membership and proceedings of regional and local flood defence committees) shall cease to have effect.

180. In Schedule 5 to that Act (procedure relating to statements on minimum acceptable flow) in paragraph 2(3)(g) (copy of notice to be served on person authorised by a licence under Part I of the Electricity Act 1989 to generate electricity) after the words "to generate electricity" there shall be added the words "who has a right to abstract water from any such waters or related inland waters".

1989 c. 29.

181. In Schedule 6 to that Act (orders providing for exemption from restrictions on abstraction) in paragraph 1(4)(h) (copy of notice to be served on person authorised by a licence under Part I of the Electricity Act 1989 to generate electricity) after the words "to generate electricity" there shall be added the words "who has a right to abstract water from any such source of supply or related inland waters".

182. In Schedule 10 to that Act (discharge consents) after paragraph 7 (restriction on variation and revocation of consent and previous variation) there shall be added—

"General review of consents

8.—(1) If it appears appropriate to the Secretary of State to do so he may at any time direct the Authority to review—

(a) the consents given under paragraphs 2 and 5 above, or

(b) any description of such consents,

and the conditions (if any) to which those consents are subject.

(2) A direction given by virtue of sub-paragraph (1) above—

(a) shall specify the purpose for which, and

(b) may specify the manner in which,

the review is to be conducted.

(3) After carrying out a review pursuant to a direction given by virtue of sub-paragraph (1) above, the Authority shall submit to the Secretary of State its proposals (if any) for—

    (a) the modification of the conditions of any consent reviewed pursuant to the direction, or

    (b) in the case of any unconditional consent reviewed pursuant to the direction, subjecting the consent to conditions.

(4) Where the Secretary of State has received any proposals from the Authority under sub-paragraph (3) above in relation to any consent he may, if it appears appropriate to him to do so, direct the Authority to do, in relation to that consent, anything mentioned in paragraph 6(2)(b) or (c) above.

(5) A direction given by virtue of sub-paragraph (4) above may only direct the Authority to do, in relation to any consent,—

    (a) any such thing as the Authority has proposed should be done in relation to that consent, or

    (b) any such thing with such modifications as appear to the Secretary of State to be appropriate."

183. For that Schedule there shall be substituted—

SCHEDULE 10

DISCHARGE CONSENTS

Application for consent

"Section 88.

1.—(1) An application for a consent, for the purposes of section 88(1)(a) of this Act, for any discharges—

    (a) shall be made to the Agency on a form provided for the purpose by the Agency; and

    (b) must be advertised by or on behalf of the applicant in such manner as may be required by regulations made by the Secretary of State.

(2) Regulations made by the Secretary of State may make provision for enabling the Agency to direct or determine that any such advertising of an application as is required under sub-paragraph (1)(b) above may, in any case, be dispensed with if, in that case, it appears to the Agency to be appropriate for that advertising to be dispensed with.

(3) The applicant for such a consent must provide to the Agency, either on, or together with, the form mentioned in sub-paragraph (1) above—

    (a) such information as the Agency may reasonably require; and

    (b) such information as may be prescribed for the purpose by the Secretary of State;

but, subject to paragraph 3(3) below and without prejudice to the effect (if any) of any other contravention of the requirements of this Schedule in relation to an application under this paragraph, a failure to provide information in pursuance of this sub-paragraph shall not invalidate an application.

(4) The Agency may give the applicant notice requiring him to provide it with such further information of any description specified in the notice as it may require for the purpose of determining the application.

(5) An application made in accordance with this paragraph which relates to proposed discharges at two or more places may be treated by the Agency as separate applications for consents for discharges at each of those places.

Consultation in connection with applications

2.—(1) Subject to sub-paragraph (2) below, the Agency shall give notice of any application under paragraph 1 above, together with a copy of the application, to the persons who are prescribed or directed to be consulted under this paragraph and shall do so within the specified period for notification.

(2) The Secretary of State may, by regulations, exempt any class of application from the requirements of this paragraph or exclude any class of information contained in applications from those requirements, in all cases or as respects specified classes only of persons to be consulted.

(3) Any representations made by the persons so consulted within the period allowed shall be considered by the Agency in determining the application.

(4) For the purposes of sub-paragraph (1) above—

  (a) persons are prescribed to be consulted on any description of application if they are persons specified for the purposes of applications of that description in regulations made by the Secretary of State;

  (b) persons are directed to be consulted on any particular application if the Secretary of State specifies them in a direction given to the Agency;

and the "specified period for notification" is the period specified in the regulations or in the direction.

(5) Any representations made by any other persons within the period allowed shall also be considered by the Agency in determining the application.

(6) Subject to sub-paragraph (7) below, the period allowed for making representations is—

  (a) in the case of persons prescribed or directed to be consulted, the period of six weeks beginning with the date on which notice of the application was given under sub-paragraph (1) above, and

  (b) in the case of other persons, the period of six weeks beginning with the date on which the making of the application was advertised in pursuance of paragraph 1(1)(b) above.

(7) The Secretary of State may, by regulations, substitute for any period for the time being specified in sub-paragraph (6)(a) or (b) above, such other period as he considers appropriate.

Consideration and determination of applications

3.—(1) On an application under paragraph 1 above the Agency shall be under a duty, if the requirements—

  (a) of that paragraph, and

  (b) of any regulations made under paragraph 1 or 2 above or of any directions under paragraph 2 above,

are complied with, to consider whether to give the consent applied for, either unconditionally or subject to conditions, or to refuse it.

(2) Subject to the following provisions of this Schedule, on an application made in accordance with paragraph 1 above, the applicant may

treat the consent applied for as having been refused if it is not given within
the period of four months beginning with the day on which the application
is received or within such longer period as may be agreed in writing between
the Agency and the applicant.

(3) Where any person, having made an application to the Agency for a
consent, has failed to comply with his obligation under paragraph 1(3) or
(4) above to provide information to the Agency, the Agency may refuse to
proceed with the application, or refuse to proceed with it until the
information is provided.

(4) The conditions subject to which a consent may be given under this
paragraph shall be such conditions as the Agency may think fit and, in
particular, may include conditions—

(a) as to the places at which the discharges to which the consent
relates may be made and as to the design and construction of any
outlets for the discharges;

(b) as to the nature, origin, composition, temperature, volume and
rate of the discharges and as to the periods during which the
discharges may be made;

(c) as to the steps to be taken, in relation to the discharges or by way
of subjecting any substance likely to affect the description of
matter discharged to treatment or any other process, for
minimising the polluting effects of the discharges on any
controlled waters;

(d) as to the provision of facilities for taking samples of the matter
discharged and, in particular, as to the provision, maintenance
and use of manholes, inspection chambers, observation wells and
boreholes in connection with the discharges;

(e) as to the provision, maintenance and testing of meters for
measuring or recording the volume and rate of the discharges and
apparatus for determining the nature, composition and
temperature of the discharges;

(f) as to the keeping of records of the nature, origin, composition,
temperature, volume and rate of the discharges and, in particular,
of records of readings of meters and other recording apparatus
provided in accordance with any other condition attached to the
consent; and

(g) as to the making of returns and the giving of other information to
the Authority about the nature, origin, composition,
temperature, volume and rate of the discharges;

and it is hereby declared that a consent may be given under this paragraph
subject to different conditions in respect of different periods.

(5) The Secretary of State may, by regulations, substitute for any period
for the time being specified in sub-paragraph (2) above, such other period
as he considers appropriate.

4. The Secretary of State may give the Agency a direction with respect to
any particular application, or any description of applications, for consent
under paragraph 1 above requiring the Agency not to determine or not to
proceed with the application or applications of that description until the
expiry of any such period as may be specified in the direction, or until
directed by the Secretary of State that it may do so, as the case may be.

Reference to Secretary of State of certain applications for consent

5.—(1) The Secretary of State may, either in consequence of representations or objections made to him or otherwise, direct the Agency to transmit to him for determination such applications for consent under paragraph 1 above as are specified in the direction or are of a description so specified.

(2) Where a direction is given to the Agency under this paragraph, the Agency shall comply with the direction and inform every applicant to whose application the direction relates of the transmission of his application to the Secretary of State.

(3) Paragraphs 1(1) and 2 above shall have effect in relation to an application transmitted to the Secretary of State under this paragraph with such modifications as may be prescribed.

(4) Where an application is transmitted to the Secretary of State under this paragraph, the Secretary of State may at any time after the application is transmitted and before it is granted or refused—

(a) cause a local inquiry to be held with respect to the application; or

(b) afford the applicant and the Agency an opportunity of appearing before, and being heard by, a person appointed by the Secretary of State for the purpose.

(5) The Secretary of State shall exercise his power under sub-paragraph (4) above in any case where a request to be heard with respect to the application is made to him in the prescribed manner by the applicant or by the Agency.

(6) It shall be the duty of the Secretary of State, if the requirements of this paragraph and of any regulations made under it are complied with, to determine an application for consent transmitted to him by the Agency under this paragraph by directing the Agency to refuse its consent or to give its consent under paragraph 3 above (either unconditionally or subject to such conditions as are specified in the direction).

(7) Without prejudice to any of the preceding provisions of this paragraph, the Secretary of State may by regulations make provision for the purposes of, and in connection with, the consideration and disposal by him of applications transmitted to him under this paragraph.

Consents without applications

6.—(1) If it appears to the Agency—

(a) that a person has caused or permitted effluent or other matter to be discharged in contravention—

(i) of the obligation imposed by virtue of section 85(3) of this Act; or

(ii) of any prohibition imposed under section 86 of this Act; and

(b) that a similar contravention by that person is likely,

the Agency may, if it thinks fit, serve on him an instrument in writing giving its consent, subject to any conditions specified in the instrument, for discharges of a description so specified.

(2) A consent given under this paragraph shall not relate to any discharge which occurred before the instrument containing the consent was served on the recipient of the instrument.

(3) Sub-paragraph (4) of paragraph 3 above shall have effect in relation to a consent given under this paragraph as it has effect in relation to a consent given under that paragraph.

(4) Where a consent has been given under this paragraph, the Agency shall publish notice of the consent in such manner as may be prescribed by the Secretary of State and send copies of the instrument containing the consent to such bodies or persons as may be so prescribed.

(5) It shall be the duty of the Agency to consider any representations or objections with respect to a consent under this paragraph as are made to it in such manner, and within such period, as may be prescribed by the Secretary of State and have not been withdrawn.

(6) Where notice of a consent is published by the Agency under sub-paragraph (4) above, the Agency shall be entitled to recover the expenses of publication from the person on whom the instrument containing the consent was served.

Revocation of consents and alteration and imposition of conditions

7.—(1) The Agency may from time to time review any consent given under paragraph 3 or 6 above and the conditions (if any) to which the consent is subject.

(2) Subject to such restrictions on the exercise of the power conferred by this sub-paragraph as are imposed under paragraph 8 below, where the Agency has reviewed a consent under this paragraph, it may by a notice served on the person making a discharge in pursuance of the consent—

 (a) revoke the consent;

 (b) make modifications of the conditions of the consent; or

 (c) in the case of an unconditional consent, provide that it shall be subject to such conditions as may be specified in the notice.

(3) If on a review under sub-paragraph (1) above it appears to the Agency that no discharge has been made in pursuance of the consent to which the review relates at any time during the preceding twelve months, the Agency may revoke the consent by a notice served on the holder of the consent.

(4) If it appears to the Secretary of State appropriate to do so—

 (a) for the purpose of enabling Her Majesty's Government in the United Kingdom to give effect to any Community obligation or to any international agreement to which the United Kingdom is for the time being a party;

 (b) for the protection of public health or of flora and fauna dependent on an aquatic environment; or

 (c) in consequence of any representations or objections made to him or otherwise,

he may, subject to such restrictions on the exercise of the power conferred by virtue of paragraph (c) above as are imposed under paragraph 8 below, at any time direct the Agency, in relation to a consent given under paragraph 3 or 6 above, to do anything mentioned in sub-paragraph (2)(a) to (c) above.

(5) The Agency shall be liable to pay compensation to any person in respect of any loss or damage sustained by that person as a result of the Agency's compliance with a direction given in relation to any consent by virtue of sub-paragraph (4)(b) above if—

 (a) in complying with that direction the Agency does anything which, apart from that direction, it would be precluded from doing by a restriction imposed under paragraph 8 below; and

(b) the direction is not shown to have been given in consequence of—

(i) a change of circumstances which could not reasonably have been foreseen at the beginning of the period to which the restriction relates; or

(ii) consideration by the Secretary of State of material information which was not reasonably available to the Agency at the beginning of that period.

(6) For the purposes of sub-paragraph (5) above information is material, in relation to a consent, if it relates to any discharge made or to be made by virtue of the consent, to the interaction of any such discharge with any other discharge or to the combined effect of the matter discharged and any other matter.

Restriction on variation and revocation of consent and previous variation

8.—(1) Each instrument signifying the consent of the Agency under paragraph 3 or 6 above shall specify a period during which no notice by virtue of paragraph 7(2) or (4)(c) above shall be served in respect of the consent except, in the case of a notice doing anything mentioned in paragraph 7(2)(b) or (c), with the agreement of the holder of the consent.

(2) Each notice served by the Agency by virtue of paragraph 7(2) or (4)(c) above (except a notice which only revokes a consent) shall specify a period during which a subsequent such notice which alters the effect of the first-mentioned notice shall not be served except, in the case of a notice doing anything mentioned in paragraph 7(2)(b) or (c) above, with the agreement of the holder of the consent.

(3) The period specified under sub-paragraph (1) or (2) above in relation to any consent shall not, unless the person who proposes to make or makes discharges in pursuance of the consent otherwise agrees, be less than the period of four years beginning—

(a) in the case of a period specified under sub-paragraph (1) above, with the day on which the consent takes effect; and

(b) in the case of a period specified under sub-paragraph (2) above, with the day on which the notice specifying that period is served.

(4) A restriction imposed under sub-paragraph (1) or (2) above shall not prevent the service by the Agency of a notice by virtue of paragraph 7(2) or (4)(c) above in respect of a consent given under paragraph 6 above if—

(a) the notice is served not more than three months after the beginning of the period prescribed under paragraph 6(5) above for the making of representations and objections with respect to the consent; and

(b) the Agency or, as the case may be, the Secretary of State considers, in consequence of any representations or objections received by it or him within that period, that it is appropriate for the notice to be served.

(5) A restriction imposed under sub-paragraph (1) or (2) above shall not prevent the service by the Agency of a notice by virtue of paragraph 7(2)(b) or (c) or (4)(c) above in respect of a consent given under paragraph 6 above if the holder has applied for a variation under paragraph 10 below.

General review of consents

9.—(1) If it appears appropriate to the Secretary of State to do so he may at any time direct the Agency to review—

(a) the consents given under paragraph 3 or 6 above, or

(b) any description of such consents,

and the conditions (if any) to which those consents are subject.

(2) A direction given by virtue of sub-paragraph (1) above—

  (a) shall specify the purpose for which, and

  (b) may specify the manner in which,

the review is to be conducted.

(3) After carrying out a review pursuant to a direction given by virtue of sub-paragraph (1) above, the Agency shall submit to the Secretary of State its proposals (if any) for—

  (a) the modification of the conditions of any consent reviewed pursuant to the direction, or

  (b) in the case of any unconditional consent reviewed pursuant to the direction, subjecting the consent to conditions.

(4) Where the Secretary of State has received any proposals from the Agency under sub-paragraph (3) above in relation to any consent he may, if it appears appropriate to him to do so, direct the Agency to do, in relation to that consent, anything mentioned in paragraph 7(2)(b) or (c) above.

(5) A direction given by virtue of sub-paragraph (4) above may only direct the Agency to do, in relation to any consent,—

  (a) any such thing as the Agency has proposed should be done in relation to that consent, or

  (b) any such thing with such modifications as appear to the Secretary of State to be appropriate.

Applications for variation

10.—(1) The holder of a consent under paragraph 3 or 6 above may apply to the Agency, on a form provided for the purpose by the Agency, for the variation of the consent.

(2) The provisions of paragraphs 1 to 5 above shall apply (with the necessary modifications) to applications under sub-paragraph (1) above, and to the variation of consents in pursuance of such applications, as they apply to applications for, and the grant of, consents.

Transfer of consents

11.—(1) A consent under paragraph 3 or 6 above may be transferred by the holder to a person who proposes to carry on the discharges in place of the holder.

(2) On the death of the holder of a consent under paragraph 3 or 6 above, the consent shall, subject to sub-paragraph (4) below, be regarded as property forming part of the deceased's personal estate, whether or not it would be so regarded apart from this sub-paragraph, and shall accordingly vest in his personal representatives.

(3) If a bankruptcy order is made against the holder of a consent under paragraph 3 or 6 above, the consent shall, subject to sub-paragraph (4) below, be regarded for the purposes of any of the Second Group of Parts of the Insolvency Act 1986 (insolvency of individuals; bankruptcy), as property forming part of the bankrupt's estate, whether or not it would be so regarded apart from this sub-paragraph, and shall accordingly vest as such in the trustee in bankruptcy.

1986 c. 45.

(4) Notwithstanding anything in the foregoing provisions of this paragraph, a consent under paragraph 3 or 6 above (and the obligations arising out of, or incidental to, such a consent) shall not be capable of being disclaimed.

(5) A consent under paragraph 3 or 6 above which is transferred to, or which vests in, a person under this section shall have effect on and after the date of the transfer or vesting as if it had been granted to that person under paragraph 3 or 6 above, subject to the same conditions as were attached to it immediately before that date.

(6) Where a consent under paragraph 3 or 6 above is transferred under sub-paragraph (1) above, the person from whom it is transferred shall give notice of that fact to the Agency not later than the end of the period of twenty-one days beginning with the date of the transfer.

(7) Where a consent under paragraph 3 or 6 above vests in any person as mentioned in sub-paragraph (2) or (3) above, that person shall give notice of that fact to the Agency not later than the end of the period of fifteen months beginning with the date of the vesting.

(8) If—

    (a) a consent under paragraph 3 or 6 above vests in any person as mentioned in sub-paragraph (2) or (3) above, but

    (b) that person fails to give the notice required by sub-paragraph (7) above within the period there mentioned,

the consent, to the extent that it permits the making of any discharges, shall cease to have effect.

(9) A person who fails to give a notice which he is required by sub-paragraph (6) or (7) above to give shall be guilty of an offence and liable—

    (a) on summary conviction, to a fine not exceeding the statutory maximum;

    (b) on conviction on indictment, to a fine or to imprisonment for a term not exceeding two years, or to both."

184. In Schedule 11 to that Act (water protection zone orders) in paragraph 4 (which is expressed to be without prejudice to section 213 of that Act) for the words "section 213 of this Act" there shall be substituted the words "section 53 of the 1995 Act (inquiries and other hearings)".

185. In Schedule 12 to that Act (nitrate sensitive area orders) in paragraph 6 (which is expressed to be without prejudice to section 213 of that Act) for the words "section 213 of this Act" there shall be substituted the words "section 53 of the 1995 Act (inquiries and other hearings)".

186. In Schedule 13 to that Act (transitional water pollution provisions) in paragraph 4 (discharge consents on application of undertakers etc)—

    (a) in sub-paragraph (2), in paragraphs (a) and (b) (which contain references to paragraph 4 of Schedule 10) for the word "4", in each place where it occurs, there shall be substituted the word "5";

    (b) in sub-paragraph (3) (which contains references to various provisions of Schedule 10) for the words "paragraphs 1(4) to (6) and 2(1) or, as the case may be, paragraph 4(3)" there shall be substituted the words "paragraph 1(1), apart from paragraph (a), paragraph 2 or, as the case may be, paragraph 5(3)"; and

    (c) in sub-paragraph (4)(a) (which contains a reference to paragraph 2(5) of Schedule 10) for the words "2(5)" there shall be substituted the words "3(4)".

187.—(1) In Schedule 15 to that Act (supplemental provisions with respect to drainage charges) in paragraphs 4(3) and 9(4) (which specify the penalty for certain offences of failing, and after conviction continuing, without reasonable excuse, to comply with notices) after the words "he continues without reasonable excuse" there shall be inserted the words "to fail".

(2) In paragraph 12(2) of that Schedule (which is expressed to be without prejudice to powers by virtue of section 4 or paragraph 5 of Schedule 1) for the words "section 4 of this Act and paragraph 5 of Schedule 1 to this Act" there shall be substituted the words "section 37 of, and paragraph 6 of Schedule 1 to, the 1995 Act".

188. In Schedule 20 to that Act (supplemental provisions with respect to powers of entry) in paragraph 7 (which creates an offence of obstruction, punishable on summary conviction by a fine not exceeding level 3) for the words from "liable, on summary conviction," onwards there shall be substituted the words "liable—

> (a) on summary conviction, to a fine not exceeding the statutory maximum;
>
> (b) on conviction on indictment, to a fine or to imprisonment for a term not exceeding two years, or to both."

189. In Schedule 22 to that Act (protection for particular undertakings) in paragraph 5 (protection for telecommunication systems) for the words "section 4(1) of this Act)" there shall be substituted the words "section 37 of the 1995 Act)".

190. In Schedule 25 to that Act (byelaw-making powers) in paragraph 1(1), for the words "paragraphs (a), (c) and (d) of section 2(1) of this Act" there shall be substituted the words "sub-paragraphs (i), (iii) and (v) of section 2(1)(a) of the 1995 Act".

The Land Drainage Act 1991

191. In the Land Drainage Act 1991, for the words "NRA", wherever occurring, there shall be substituted the word "Agency". 1991 c. 59.

192.—(1) In section 23 of that Act (prohibition on obstructions etc in watercourses) in subsection (2) (which confers power to charge an application fee of £50 or such other sum as may be specified by order made by the Ministers) for the words "specified by order made by the Ministers" there shall be substituted the word "prescribed".

(2) After subsection (7) of that section there shall be inserted—

> "(7A) In subsection (2) above "prescribed" means specified in, or determined in accordance with, an order made by the Ministers; and any such order may make different provision for different cases, including different provision in relation to different persons, circumstances or localities."

193. At the beginning of Part V of that Act (miscellaneous and supplemental provisions) there shall be inserted—

"Spray irrigation

Powers of internal drainage boards and local authorities to facilitate spray irrigation.
61F.—(1) Any internal drainage board or local authority may, with the consent of the Agency, operate any drainage works under the control of the board or authority so as to manage the level of water in a watercourse for the purpose of facilitating spray irrigation.

(2) Subsection (1) above is without prejudice to—

> (a) the powers of an internal drainage board or local authority in relation to drainage; or
>
> (b) any requirement—
>
>> (i) for any other consent of the Agency or any other person; or
>>
>> (ii) for any licence, approval, authorisation or other permission or registration."

194.—(1) In section 72 of that Act, in subsection (1) (general definitions) there shall be inserted at the appropriate place—

""the Agency" means the Environment Agency;".

(2) In that subsection, the definition of "the NRA" shall be omitted.

The Clean Air Act 1993

1993 c. 11.

195. In section 2 of the Clean Air Act 1993 (emission of dark smoke from industrial or trade premises) in subsection (5) (which creates a summary offence punishable with a fine not exceeding level 5 on the standard scale) for the words "level 5 on the standard scale" there shall be substituted the words "£20,000".

196.—(1) Section 19 of that Act (power to require creation of smoke control areas by local authorities) as it applies to Scotland shall be amended in accordance with the following provisions of this paragraph.

(2) In subsection (1)—

(a) for the words "Secretary of State" there shall be substituted the words "Scottish Environment Protection Agency (in this section referred to as "the Agency")"; and

(b) for the words "he", "him" and "his" there shall be substituted respectively "the Agency", "it" and "its".

(3) In subsections (2), (3), (4)(a) and (6), for the words "Secretary of State" there shall be substituted the words "Agency".

(4) In subsection (3), for the word "him" there shall be substituted the word "it".

(5) In subsection (4), before the words "the Secretary of State" in the second place where they occur there shall be inserted the words "the Agency, with the consent of".

197. In section 59 of that Act (local inquiries) in subsection (1)—

(a) for the words "a local inquiry" there shall be substituted the words "an inquiry"; and

(b) for the words "such an inquiry" there shall be substituted the words "an inquiry";

and for the side-note to that section there shall accordingly be substituted "Inquiries.".

198. In section 60(7)(b) of that Act as it applies to Scotland for the words "the Secretary of State" and "Secretary of State's" there shall be substituted the words "SEPA" and "SEPA's" respectively.

199. In section 63(1)(c) of that Act as it applies to Scotland for the words "sections 19(4) and" there shall be substituted the words "section".

The Radioactive Substances Act 1993

1993 c. 12.

200. Subject to the other provisions of this Act, in the Radioactive Substances Act 1993, for the words "chief inspector" or "chief inspector's", wherever occurring, there shall be substituted respectively the words "appropriate Agency" or "appropriate Agency's".

201. Sections 4 and 5 of that Act (appointment of inspectors and chief inspectors) shall cease to have effect.

202.—(1) In section 7 of that Act (registration of users of radioactive material) in subsection (1)(c) (application to be accompanied by prescribed fee), for the words "prescribed fee" there shall be substituted the words "charge prescribed for the purpose by a charging scheme under section 41 of the Environment Act 1995".

(2) In subsection (7) of that section (chief inspector to have regard exclusively to amount and character of radioactive waste), for the word "him" there shall be substituted the word "it".

203. In section 8 of that Act (exemptions from registration under section 7), in subsection (2) (power of chief inspector to impose conditions) for the word "he" there shall be substituted the word "it".

204.—(1) In section 10 of that Act (registration of mobile radioactive apparatus) in subsection (1)(c) (application to be accompanied by prescribed fee), for the words "prescribed fee" there shall be substituted the words "charge prescribed for the purpose by a charging scheme under section 41 of the Environment Act 1995".

(2) In each of subsections (3) and (5)(b) of that section (duty to supply copy of application, and to send copy of certificate, to local authority) for the word "him" there shall be substituted the words "the appropriate Agency".

205.—(1) Section 16 of that Act (authorisations) shall be amended in accordance with the following provisions of this paragraph.

(2) In subsection (2) (power to grant authorisations to be exercisable by the chief inspector) the words "Subject to subsection (3)" shall be omitted.

(3) Subsection (3) (power to grant authorisations in England, Wales and Northern Ireland) shall be omitted.

(4) In subsection (4) (application to be accompanied by prescribed fee), for the words "prescribed fee" there shall be substituted the words "charge prescribed for the purpose by a charging scheme under section 41 of the Environment Act 1995".

(5) After subsection (4) there shall be inserted—

"(4A) Without prejudice to subsection (5), on any application for an authorisation under section 13(1) in respect of the disposal of radioactive waste on or from any premises situated on a nuclear site in any part of Great Britain, the appropriate Agency—

   (a) shall consult the relevant Minister and the Health and Safety Executive before deciding whether to grant an authorisation on that application and, if so, subject to what limitations or conditions, and

   (b) shall consult the relevant Minister concerning the terms of the authorisation, for which purpose that Agency shall, before granting any authorisation on that application, send that Minister a copy of any authorisation which it proposes so to grant."

(6) In subsection (5) (consultation by chief inspector and, where the premises are in England, Wales or Northern Ireland, the appropriate Minister with local authorities etc)—

   (a) for the words from "and, where" to "shall each" there shall be substituted the word "shall"; and

   (b) for the word "him", in each place where it occurs, there shall be substituted the words "that Agency".

(7) In subsection (7) (applications, other than those to which subsection (3) applies, deemed to be refused if not determined within prescribed period) for the words "(other than an application to which subsection (3) applies)" there shall be substituted the words "(other than an application for an authorisation under section 13(1) in respect of the disposal of radioactive waste on or from any premises situated on a nuclear site in any part of Great Britain)".

(8) In subsection (8)(b) (conditions or limitations subject to which authorisations may be granted) for the words from "or, as" to "think" there shall be substituted the word "thinks".

(9) In subsection (10) of that section (fixing of date from which authorisation is to have effect)—

(a) the words from "or, as" to "appropriate Minister" shall cease to have effect; and

(b) for the words "him or them" and "his or their" there shall be substituted respectively the words "it" and "its".

(10) After that subsection there shall be inserted—

"(11) In this section, "the relevant Minister" means—

(a) in relation to premises in England, the Minister of Agriculture, Fisheries and Food, and

(b) in relation to premises in Wales or Scotland, the Secretary of State."

206.—(1) In section 17 of that Act, after subsection (2) (variation of authorisations) there shall be inserted—

"(2A) On any proposal to vary an authorisation granted under section 13(1) in respect of the disposal of radioactive waste on or from any premises situated on a nuclear site in any part of Great Britain, the appropriate Agency—

(a) shall consult the relevant Minister and the Health and Safety Executive before deciding whether to vary the authorisation and, if so, whether by attaching, revoking or varying any limitations or conditions or by attaching further limitations or conditions, and

(b) shall consult the relevant Minister concerning the terms of any variation, for which purpose that Agency shall, before varying the authorisation, send that Minister a copy of any variations which it proposes to make."

(2) Subsection (4) of that section (adaptations for authorisations granted by the chief inspector and the appropriate Minister) shall cease to have effect.

(3) At the end of that section there shall be added—

"(5) In this section, "the relevant Minister" has the same meaning as in section 16 above."

207.—(1) In section 18 of that Act (functions of public and local authorities in relation to authorisations under section 13) in subsection (1)—

(a) the words from "(or, in a case" to "that Minister)", and

(b) the words "or the appropriate Minister, as the case may be,",

shall cease to have effect.

(2) In subsection (2)(b) of that section (special precautions taken with the approval of the chief inspector etc) the words from "(or, where" to "that Minister)" shall cease to have effect.

208. In section 20 of that Act (retention and production of site or disposal records) subsection (3) (adaptation where powers exercisable by chief inspector and appropriate Minister) shall cease to have effect.

209.—(1) In section 21 of that Act (enforcement notices) in subsection (1) (power of chief inspector to serve such a notice) for the word "he" there shall be substituted the word "it".

(2) Subsection (3) of that section (adaptation in case of authorisations granted by the chief inspector and the appropriate Minister) shall cease to have effect.

(3) In subsection (4) of that section (copies of notices to be sent to certain public or local authorities) the words from "or, where" to "that Minister" shall cease to have effect.

210.—(1) In section 22 of that Act (prohibition notices) in subsection (1) (power of chief inspector to serve such a notice) for the word "he" there shall be substituted the word "it".

(2) Subsection (5) of that section (adaptation in case of authorisations granted by the chief inspector and the appropriate Minister) shall cease to have effect.

(3) In subsection (6) of that section (copies of notices to be sent to certain public or local authorities) the words from "or, where" to "that Minister" shall cease to have effect.

(4) In subsection (7) of that section (withdrawal of notices)—

   (a) the words from "or, where" to "that Minister" shall cease to have effect; and

   (b) for the word "he", in each place where it occurs, there shall be substituted the words "that Agency".

211.—(1) In section 23 of that Act (powers of Secretary of State to give directions to the chief inspector)—

   (a) in subsections (1) and (3) for the word "him" there shall be substituted the word "it"; and

   (b) in subsection (2) for the word "his" there shall be substituted the word "its".

(2) After subsection (4) of that section there shall be inserted—

   "(4A) In the application of this section in relation to authorisations, and applications for authorisations, under section 13 in respect of premises situated on a nuclear site in England, references to the Secretary of State shall have effect as references to the Secretary of State and the Minister of Agriculture, Fisheries and Food."

212.—(1) In section 24 of that Act (power of Secretary of State to require certain applications to be determined by him) in subsections (1) and (4), for the word "him", in each place where it occurs, there shall be substituted the word "it".

(2) After subsection (4) of that section there shall be inserted—

   "(4A) In the application of this section in relation to authorisations, and applications for authorisations, under section 13 in respect of premises situated on a nuclear site in England, references to the Secretary of State shall have effect as references to the Secretary of State and the Minister of Agriculture, Fisheries and Food."

213.—(1) In section 25 of that Act (power of Secretary of State to restrict knowledge of applications etc) in subsection (1) (applications under section 7 to 10 etc), after the words "knowledge of" there shall be inserted the words "such information as may be specified or described in the directions, being information contained in or relating to—".

(2) In subsection (2) of that section (applications under section 13 or 14 etc)—

   (a) the words from "or, in a case" to "Food," and "or their" shall cease to have effect; and

   (b) after the words "knowledge of" there shall be inserted the words "such information as may be specified or described in the directions, being information contained in or relating to—".

(3) In subsection (3) of that section (copies of certain applications etc which are the subject of a direction not to be sent to local or public authorities)—

    (a) after the words "send a copy of" there shall be inserted the words "so much of"; and

    (b) after the words "as the case may be" there shall be inserted the words "as contains the information specified or described in the directions—".

(4) After that subsection there shall be inserted—

    "(3A) No direction under this section shall affect—

      (a) any power or duty of the Agency to which it is given to consult the relevant Minister; or

      (b) the information which is to be sent by that Agency to that Minister."

(5) At the end of that section there shall be added—

    "(5) In this section "the relevant Minister" has the same meaning as in section 16 above."

214.—(1) Section 26 of that Act (appeals) shall be amended in accordance with the following provisions of this paragraph.

(2) Subsection (3)(a) (appeal not to lie in relation to authorisations subject to section 16(3)) shall cease to have effect.

(3) In subsection (4) (appeals in respect of enforcement or prohibition notices) the words "England, Wales or" shall be omitted.

(4) After subsection (5) there shall be inserted—

    "(5A) In the application of this section in relation to authorisations, and applications for authorisations, under section 13 in respect of premises situated on a nuclear site in England, references in subsection (1) to (3) to the Secretary of State shall have effect as references to the Secretary of State and the Minister of Agriculture, Fisheries and Food."

215.—(1) Section 27 of that Act (procedure on appeals under section 26) shall be amended in accordance with the following provisions of this paragraph.

(2) In subsection (1) (power of Secretary of State to refer appeal to appointed person) after the word "26" there shall be inserted the words ", other than an appeal against any decision of, or notice served by, SEPA,".

(3) After that subsection there shall be inserted—

    "(1A) As respects an appeal against any decision of, or notice served by, SEPA, this section is subject to section 114 of the Environment Act 1995 (delegation or reference of appeals)."

(4) After subsection (7) there shall be inserted—

    "(7A) In the application of this section in relation to authorisations, and applications for authorisations, under section 13 in respect of premises situated on a nuclear site in England, references in subsections (1) to (6) to the Secretary of State shall have effect as references to the Secretary of State and the Minister of Agriculture, Fisheries and Food."

216. Section 28 of that Act (representations in relation to authorisations and notices where appropriate Minister is concerned) shall cease to have effect.

217.—(1) Section 30 of that Act (power of Secretary of State to dispose of radioactive waste) shall be amended in accordance with the following provisions of this paragraph.

(2) In subsection (1) (which confers the power)—

    (a) for the words "the Secretary of State", in the first place where they occur, there shall be substituted the words "the appropriate Agency";

(b) for those words, wherever else occurring, there shall be substituted the words "that Agency"; and

(c) for the word "his" there shall be substituted the word "its".

(3) In subsection (3) (application of certain definitions of "owner") for the words "Secretary of State" there shall be substituted the words "Environment Agency".

(4) In subsection (4) (adaptations for Scotland) for the words "the Secretary of State" there shall be substituted the words "SEPA".

218. Section 31 of that Act (rights of entry and inspection) shall cease to have effect.

219. In section 32 of that Act (offences relating to registration or authorisation, including the offence of failure to comply with the requirements of an enforcement or prohibition notice under section 21 or 22 of the Act) after subsection (2) there shall be added—

"(3) If the appropriate Agency is of the opinion that proceedings for an offence under subsection (1)(d) would afford an ineffectual remedy against a person who has failed to comply with the requirements of a notice served on him under section 21 or 22, that Agency may take proceedings in the High Court or, in Scotland, in any court of competent jurisdiction, for the purpose of securing compliance with the notice."

220. In section 34(1) of that Act (which, with certain exceptions, makes it an offence to disclose certain trade secrets) after paragraph (b) (no offence where disclosure made in accordance with directions) there shall be inserted—

"(bb) under or by virtue of section 113 of the Environment Act 1995, or".

221. Section 35 of that Act (obstruction of inspectors or other persons) shall cease to have effect.

222. In section 38 of that Act (restriction on prosecution) in subsection (1) (provision for England and Wales) for paragraph (b) there shall be substituted—

"(b) by the Environment Agency, or".

223.—(1) In section 39 of that Act (public access to documents and records) in subsection (1) (duties of chief inspector)—

(a) for the word "him", in each place where it occurs, there shall be substituted the word "it";

(b) for the word "he" there shall be substituted the words "the appropriate Agency"; and

(c) for the words "applications or certificates" there shall be substituted the word "information".

(2) In subsection (2), the words "or, as the case may be, the appropriate Minister and the chief inspector," shall cease to have effect.

224. In section 40 of that Act (radioactivity to be disregarded for purposes of certain statutory provisions) in subsection (2)(b)(ii), after the words "imposed by the statutory provision on" there shall be inserted the words "the Environment Agency or SEPA or on".

225. Section 42(5) of that Act (which precludes, in the interests of national security, the exercise of certain powers of entry in relation to Crown premises and which is superseded by provisions of this Act) shall cease to have effect.

226. Section 43 of that Act (which relates to fees and charges and which is superseded by provisions of this Act) shall cease to have effect.

227.—(1) Subsection (1) of section 47 of that Act (general definitions) shall be amended in accordance with the following provisions of this paragraph.

(2) There shall be inserted at the appropriate place—

""the appropriate Agency" means—

(a) in relation to England and Wales, the Environment Agency; and

(b) in relation to Scotland, SEPA;".

(3) In the definition of "the appropriate Minister", paragraphs (a) and (b) shall cease to have effect.

(4) In the definition of "the chief inspector", paragraphs (a) and (b) shall cease to have effect.

(5) In the definition of "prescribed", the words from "or, in relation to fees" onwards shall cease to have effect.

(6) In the definition of "relevant water body"—

(a) in paragraph (a), the words "the National Rivers Authority", and

(b) in paragraph (b), the words "a river purification authority within the meaning of the Rivers (Prevention of Pollution) (Scotland) Act 1951",

1951 c. 66.

shall be omitted.

(7) There shall be inserted at the appropriate place—

""SEPA" means the Scottish Environment Protection Agency;".

228. In section 48 of that Act (index of defined expressions) in the Table—

(a) the following entries shall be inserted at the appropriate place—

(i)	"the appropriate Agency	section 47(1)";
(ii)	"SEPA	section 47(1)";

(b) the entry relating to the chief inspector shall be omitted.

229. Schedule 2 to that Act (exercise of rights of entry and inspection) shall cease to have effect.

230.—(1) In Schedule 3 to that Act (enactments, other than local enactments, to which s.40 applies) in paragraph 9 (which specifies certain provisions in the Water Resources Act 1991) for the words "203 and 213" there shall be substituted the words "and 203".

1991 c. 57.

(2) For paragraph 16 of that Schedule there shall be substituted—

"16. Sections 30A, 30B, 30D, 30F, 30G, 30H(1), 31(4), (5), (8) and (9), 31A, 34 to 42B, 46 to 46D and 56(1) to (3) of the Control of Pollution Act 1974."

1974 c. 40.

The Local Government (Wales) Act 1994

1994 c. 19.

231. In Schedule 9 to the Local Government (Wales) Act 1994 (which makes provision for the transfer to the new principal councils in Wales of functions in relation to public health and related matters), in paragraph 17(2) (which amends the definitions of waste regulation and disposal authorities for the purposes of Part II of the Environmental Protection Act 1990) for the words "each of subsections (1)(f) and (2)(f)" there shall be substituted the words "subsection (2)(f)".

1990 c. 43.

The Local Government etc. (Scotland) Act 1994

1994 c. 39.

232.—(1) In section 2(2) of the Local Government etc. (Scotland) Act 1994 (constitution of councils) after the words "this Act" there shall be inserted the words "and of the Environment Act 1995".

(2) In Schedule 13 to that Act (minor and consequential amendments) in paragraph 75(27) (which amends certain provisions of the Sewerage (Scotland) Act 1968) for the words from the beginning to "premises)" there shall be substituted the words "In section 53 (notices to be in writing)". **1968 c. 47.**

Subordinate legislation and local statutory provisions

233.—(1) In any subordinate legislation or local statutory provisions, for any reference (however framed) to the National Rivers Authority, and for any reference which falls to be construed as such a reference, there shall be substituted a reference to the Agency.

(2) In any subordinate legislation, for any reference (however framed) to a relevant inspector, and for any reference which falls to be construed as such a reference, there shall be substituted a reference to the appropriate Agency.

(3) The provisions of this paragraph are subject to the other provisions of this Act and to any provision made under or by virtue of this Act.

(4) In this paragraph—

"the appropriate Agency" means—

(a) in relation to England and Wales, the Agency;

(b) in relation to Scotland, SEPA;

"local statutory provision" means—

(a) a provision of a local Act (including an Act confirming a provisional order);

(b) a provision of so much of any public general Act as has effect with respect to particular persons or works or with respect to particular provisions falling within any paragraph of this definition;

(c) a provision of an instrument made under any provision falling within paragraph (a) or (b) above;

(d) a provision of any other instrument which is in the nature of a local enactment;

"relevant inspector" means—

(i) the chief inspector for England and Wales constituted under section 16(3) of the Environmental Protection Act 1990;

(ii) the chief inspector for Scotland constituted under section 16(3) of that Act;

(iii) the chief inspector for England and Wales appointed under section 4(2)(a) of the Radioactive Substances Act 1993; **1993 c. 12.**

(iv) the chief inspector for Scotland appointed under section 4(2)(b) of that Act;

(v) the chief, or any other, inspector, within the meaning of the Alkali, &c, Works Regulation Act 1906; **1906 c. 14.**

(vi) an inspector appointed under section 19 of the Health and **1974 c. 37.** Safety at Work etc. Act 1974 by the Secretary of State in his capacity as the enforcing authority responsible for the enforcement of the Alkali, &c, Works Regulation Act 1906 or section 5 of the said Act of 1974;

"subordinate legislation" has the same meaning as in the Interpretation **1978 c. 30.** Act 1978.

SCHEDULE 23

TRANSITIONAL AND TRANSITORY PROVISIONS AND SAVINGS

PART I

GENERAL TRANSITIONAL PROVISIONS AND SAVINGS

Interpretation of Part I

1. In this Part of this Schedule, the "transfer date" has the same meaning as in Part I of this Act.

Directions

1991 c. 57.

2. Any directions given to the National Rivers Authority for the purposes of section 19 of the Water Resources Act 1991 shall have effect on and after the transfer date as directions given to the Agency for the purposes of section 6(2) of this Act.

Regional and local fisheries advisory committees

3. If and so long as the Agency requires, on and after the transfer date any advisory committee established and maintained before the transfer date by the National Rivers Authority under section 8(1) of the Water Resources Act 1991 shall be treated as if—

    (a) it had been established by the Agency,

    (b) the area by reference to which that committee was established had been determined by the Agency, and

    (c) in the case of a regional advisory committee, the chairman of that committee had been appointed,

in accordance with section 13 of this Act.

Charging schemes

4.—(1) Without prejudice to section 55 of this Act, any charging scheme—

    (a) which relates to any transferred functions,

    (b) which was made before the transfer date, and

    (c) which is in force immediately before that date or would (apart from this Act) have come into force at any time after that date,

shall, subject to the provisions of section 41 of this Act, have effect on and after the transfer date, with any necessary modifications, and for the remainder of the period for which the charging scheme would have been in force apart from any repeal made by this Act, as a scheme made under that section by the transferee in accordance with section 42 of this Act.

(2) Any costs or expenses incurred before the transfer date by any person in carrying out functions transferred to a new Agency by or under this Act may be treated for the purposes of subsections (3) and (4) of section 42 of this Act as costs or expenses incurred by that new Agency in carrying out those functions.

(3) In this paragraph—

    "charging scheme" means a scheme specifying, or providing for the determination of, any fees or charges;

    "new Agency" means the Agency or SEPA;

"transferred functions" means any functions which, by virtue of any provision made by or under this Act, become functions of a new Agency and "the transferee" means the new Agency whose functions they so become.

Preparation of reports

5.—(1) The first report prepared by the Agency under section 52 of this Act may, to the extent that it relates to functions transferred to the Agency from any other body or person include a report on the exercise and performance of those functions by the transferor during the period between the end of the last year in respect of which the transferor prepared a report and the transfer date.

(2) SEPA shall, as soon as reasonably practicable after the transfer date, prepare a report on—

(a) the exercise and performance of the functions of each river purification board during the period between the end of the last year in respect of which the board sent a report to the Secretary of State under section 16 of the Rivers (Prevention of Pollution) (Scotland) Act 1951 and the transfer date; and

1951 c. 66.

(b) the exercise and performance of the functions of each waste regulation authority during the period between the end of the last financial year in respect of which the authority prepared and published a report under section 67 of the Environmental Protection Act 1990 and the transfer date.

1990 c. 43.

(3) Subsections (3) and (4) of section 52 of this Act shall apply to a report prepared under sub-paragraph (2) above as they apply to a report prepared under that section.

Preparation of accounts

6. Notwithstanding the repeal by this Act of subsection (9) of section 135 of the Local Government (Scotland) Act 1973 (application to river purification board of certain provisions of that Act), the provisions applied to a river purification board by virtue of that section shall, as respects the period between the end of the last financial year in respect of which accounts have been made up by the board and the transfer date, continue to apply in relation to the board; but anything which shall or may be done or enjoyed, or any access, inspection or copying which shall or may be allowed, under or by virtue of any of those provisions or of section 118 of that Act (financial returns) by, or by an officer of, the board shall, or as the case may be may, after the transfer date, be done, enjoyed or allowed by, or by an officer of, SEPA in place of the board or of an officer of the board.

1973 c. 65.

Membership of Welsh National Park authorities

7.—(1) Where a body corporate constituted as a Welsh National Park planning board becomes, or has become, the National Park authority in relation to the National Park in question by virtue of an order under section 63 of this Act made by virtue of section 64(1) of this Act, paragraph 2 of Schedule 7 to this Act shall, in its application in relation to that National Park authority at any time before 31st March 1997, have effect with the following modifications.

(2) In sub-paragraph (5)—

(a) in paragraph (a), after the word "council" there shall be inserted the words "or, if earlier, until the council which appointed him as a local authority member of that authority is excluded from the councils by whom such members of that authority are to be appointed"; and

(b) in paragraph (b), after the word "cessation" there shall be inserted the words "or exclusion".

(3) In sub-paragraph (6), after the words "Sub-paragraph (5)(a) above" there shall be inserted the words ", so far as relating to cessation of membership of a council,".

(4) In this paragraph, "Welsh National Park planning board" means a National Park planning board, as defined in section 64 of this Act, for the area of a National Park in Wales.

The Alkali, &c., Works Regulation Act 1906

8. Any dispensation which was granted under the proviso to subsection (5) of section 9 of the Alkali, &c, Works Regulation Act 1906 before the transfer date and which would, apart from this Act, have been in force on that date shall have effect on and after that date notwithstanding the repeal of that proviso by this Act.

1906 c. 14.

The Public Records Act 1958

9.—(1) Such of the administrative and departmental records (in whatever form or medium) of a transferor as are transferred to and vested in the Agency by or under section 3 of this Act shall be treated for the purposes of the Public Records Act 1958 as administrative or departmental records of the Agency.

1958 c. 51.

(2) In this paragraph, "transferor" means any body or person any or all of whose administrative and departmental records are transferred to and vested in the Agency by or under section 3 of this Act.

The Parliamentary Commissioner Act 1967

10.—(1) Nothing in this Act shall prevent the completion on or after the transfer date of any investigation begun before that date under the Parliamentary Commissioner Act 1967 in pursuance of a complaint made in relation to the National Rivers Authority.

1967 c. 13.

(2) Nothing in this Act shall prevent the making on or after the transfer date of a complaint under that Act in respect of any action which was taken by or on behalf of the National Rivers Authority before that date.

(3) Notwithstanding the amendment of that Act by paragraph 11 of Schedule 22 to this Act, the provisions of that Act shall have effect on and after the transfer date in relation to any complaint to which sub-paragraph (1) or (2) above applies and to its investigation as they would have had effect before that date; but, in relation to any such complaint, the Agency shall on and after that date stand in the place of the National Rivers Authority for the purposes of this paragraph.

The Local Government Act 1974

11.—(1) Where for any year, a Rate Support Grant Report under section 60 of the Local Government, Planning and Land Act 1980, or a supplementary report under section 61 of that Act, has effect to determine the amount of supplementary grants to be paid under section 7 of the Local Government Act 1974 to the council of a county or county borough in Wales, and at any time—

1980 c. 65.

1974 c. 7.

(a) after that report or, as the case may be, that supplementary report is approved by a resolution of the House of Commons, but

(b) not later than the end of that year,

a body corporate constituted as a National Park planning board for a National Park the whole or any part of which is included in that county or county borough becomes the National Park authority for that National Park by virtue of section 64 of this Act, those supplementary grants shall, subject to the provisions of any, or any further, such supplementary report, continue to be paid for that year notwithstanding that that body corporate has ceased to be a National Park planning board.

(2) In this paragraph—

"National Park planning board" has the meaning given by section 64(9) of this Act; and

"year" means a period of 12 months beginning with 1st April.

12.—(1) Nothing in this Act shall prevent the completion on or after the transfer date by a Local Commissioner of any investigation which he began to conduct before that date and which is an investigation under Part III of the Local Government Act 1974 in pursuance of a complaint made in relation to the National Rivers Authority.

1974 c. 7.

(2) Nothing in this Act shall prevent the making on or after the transfer date of a complaint under Part III of that Act in respect of any action which was taken by or on behalf of the National Rivers Authority before that date.

(3) Notwithstanding the amendment of Part III of that Act by paragraph 18 of Schedule 22 to this Act, the provisions of that Part shall have effect on and after the transfer date in relation to any complaint to which sub-paragraph (1) or (2) above applies and to its investigation as they would have had effect before that date; but, in relation to any such complaint, the Agency shall on and after that date stand in the place of the National Rivers Authority for the purposes of this paragraph.

The Control of Pollution Act 1974

13. As respects England and Wales, any resolution passed in pursuance of section 11 of the Control of Pollution Act 1974 (special provision for land occupied by disposal authorities: resolutions etc) which is in force immediately before the day on which the repeals in that section made by this Act come into force shall have effect on and after that day as if it were a waste management licence granted by the Environment Agency under Part II of the Environmental Protection Act 1990 subject to the conditions specified in the resolution pursuant to subsection (3)(e) of that section.

1974 c. 40.

1990 c. 43.

The Salmon and Freshwater Fisheries Act 1975

14.—(1) Any approval or certificate given under or by virtue of section 8(2), 9(1) or 11(4) of the Salmon and Freshwater Fisheries Act 1975 by a Minister of the Crown before the transfer date shall, so far as is required for continuing its effect on and after that date, have effect as if given by the Agency.

1975 c. 51.

(2) Any application for the grant of an approval or certificate by a Minister of the Crown under or by virtue of any of the provisions specified in sub-paragraph (1) above which, at the transfer date, is in the process of being determined shall on and after that date be treated as having been made to the Agency.

(3) Any notice given by a Minister of the Crown under section 11(2) of that Act before the transfer date shall, so far as is required for continuing its effect on and after that date, have effect as if given by the Agency.

(4) Any extension of a period granted by a Minister of the Crown under section 11(3) of that Act before the transfer date shall, so far as is required for continuing its effect on and after that date, have effect as if granted by the Agency.

(5) Without prejudice to section 16 or 17 of the Interpretation Act 1978, any exemption granted under subsection (1) or (2) of section 14 of the Salmon and Freshwater Fisheries Act 1975 which is in force immediately before the substitution date shall have effect on and after that date as an exemption granted by the Agency under subsection (2) or, as the case may be, subsection (3) of section 14 of that Act as substituted by paragraph 13 of Schedule 15 to this Act.

1978 c. 30.

(6) Any grating constructed and placed in a manner and position approved under section 14(3) of that Act as it had effect before the substitution date (including a grating so constructed and placed at any time as a replacement for a grating so constructed and placed) shall, if—

    (a) the approval was in force immediately before the substitution date, and

    (b) the grating is maintained in accordance with the approval,

be taken for the purposes of section 14 of that Act, as substituted by paragraph 13 of Schedule 15 to this Act, to be a screen which complies with the requirements of subsection (2)(a) or (3)(a) of that section, according to the location of the grating, and with the requirements of subsections (4) to (6) of that section.

(7) Any notice given, or objection made, under subsection (2) of section 18 of that Act before the transfer date shall, so far as is required for continuing its effect on and after that date, have effect as a notice given under that subsection as it has effect on and after that date.

(8) In this paragraph—

    "approval" includes a provisional approval;

    "grating" means a device in respect of which there is in force, immediately before the substitution date, an approval given for the purposes of the definition of "grating" in section 41(1) of the Salmon and Freshwater Fisheries Act 1975 as it had effect before that date;

    "the substitution date" means the date on which paragraph 13 of Schedule 15 to this Act comes into force;

    "the transfer date" means the date which, by virtue of section 56(1) of this Act, is the transfer date for the purposes of Part I of this Act as it applies in relation to the Agency.

The Local Government Finance Act 1988

15.—(1) Without prejudice to the generality of subsection (4) of section 64 of this Act, where an order has been made under section 63 of this Act by virtue of section 64(1) of this Act designating a date in relation to a Welsh National Park planning board, the body corporate constituted as that board may at any time before the designated date issue a levy by virtue of section 71 of this Act for a year at or before the beginning of which that body becomes the National Park authority for the National Park in question by virtue of section 64 of this Act as if it were the National Park authority for that National Park, notwithstanding that it has not in fact become a National Park authority at the date when it issues the levy.

1988 c. 41.

(2) Without prejudice to the generality of section 74 of the Local Government Finance Act 1988, where—

    (a) an order is made under section 63 of this Act by virtue of section 64(1) of this Act designating a date in relation to a Welsh National Park planning board; and

    (b) the designated date is a date falling after the beginning, but before the end, of a year in respect of which, at the time the order is made, that board has not issued any levy under that section 74,

that board may nonetheless issue such a levy in respect of that year as if the body corporate constituted as that board was not in fact going to become the National Park authority for the National Park in question by virtue of that order before the end of that year.

(3) Sub-paragraph (5) below applies in a case where a levy is issued in respect of any year by a Welsh National Park planning board under section 74 of the Local Government Finance Act 1988 and—

(a) that levy is issued by that board at a time when no order has been made under section 63 of this Act by virtue of section 64(1) of this Act designating a date in relation to that board; and

(b) after the levy is issued, but no later than the end of the year in respect of which it is issued, such an order is so made designating in relation to that board a date falling not later than the end of that year.

(4) Sub-paragraph (5) below also applies in a case where a levy is issued in respect of any year by a Welsh National Park planning board under section 74 of the Local Government Finance Act 1988 and—

(a) that levy is issued by that board at a time after an order has been made under section 63 of this Act by virtue of section 64(1) of this Act designating a date in relation to that board; and

(b) the designated date is a date falling after the beginning, but before the end, of that year.

(5) In a case where this sub-paragraph applies, the levy in question or any levy substituted for that levy—

(a) shall have effect or, as the case may be, continue to have effect; and

(b) in particular, but without prejudice to the generality of paragraph (a) above, shall be paid or, as the case may be, continue to be paid,

as if the body corporate constituted as that board was not to, or had not, so become the National Park authority for the National Park in question (but was to continue, or had continued, to be the National Park planning board for that Park for the whole of that year).

(6) Where a body corporate constituted as a Welsh National Park planning board has or is to become the National Park authority for the National Park in question by virtue of an order made under section 63 of this Act by virtue of section 64(1) of this Act, nothing in this paragraph authorises that body corporate to issue for any year both a levy under section 74 of the Local Government Finance Act 1988 and a levy by virtue of section 71 of this Act.

(7) In this paragraph—

"the designated date" has the same meaning as in section 64 of this Act;

"National Park planning board" has the meaning given by section 64(9) of this Act;

"Welsh National Park planning board" means a National Park planning board for the area of a National Park in Wales;

"year" means a period of 12 months beginning with 1st April;

and any reference to the issue of a levy under section 74 of the Local Government Finance Act 1988 by a Welsh National Park planning board is a reference to the issue of a levy under that section by such a board by virtue of subsection (7) of that section.

The Environmental Protection Act 1990

16.—(1) Subject to sub-paragraph (2) below, if, at the transfer date, the content of the strategy required by section 44A of the Evironmental Protection Act 1990 has not been finally determined, any plan or modification under section 50 of that Act, in its application to England and Wales, whose content has been finally determined before that date shall continue in force until the contents of the strategy are finally determined, notwithstanding the repeal by this Act of that section.

1990 c. 43.

(2) If the strategy required by section 44A of that Act consists, or is to consist, of more than one statement, sub-paragraph (1) above shall apply as if—

(a) references to the strategy were references to any such statement; and

(b) references to a plan or modification under section 50 of that Act were references to such plans or modifications as relate to the area covered, or to be covered, by that statement.

17. If, at the transfer date, the content of the strategy required by section 44B of that Act has not been finally determined, any plan or modification under section 50 of that Act, in its application to Scotland, whose content has been finally determined before that date shall continue in force until the contents of the strategy are finally determined, notwithstanding the repeal by this Act of that section.

18.—(1) This paragraph applies to—

(a) any resolution of a waste regulation authority under section 54 of that Act (special provision for land occupied by disposal authorities in Scotland);

(b) any resolution of a waste disposal authority having effect by virtue of subsection (16) of that section as if it were a resolution of a waste regulation authority under that section,

which is in force on the transfer date.

(2) A resolution to which this paragraph applies shall continue in force—

(a) where no application is made under section 36(1) of that Act for a waste management licence in respect of the site or mobile plant covered by the resolution, until the end of the period of 6 months commencing with the transfer date;

(b) where an application as mentioned in sub-paragraph (a) above is made, until—

(i) the application is withdrawn;

(ii) the application is rejected and no appeal against the rejection is timeously lodged under section 43 of that Act;

(iii) any appeal against a rejection of the application is withdrawn or rejected; or

(iv) the application is granted.

(3) In relation to a resolution continued in force by sub-paragraph (2) above, the said section 54 shall have effect subject to the amendments set out in the following provisions of this paragraph.

(4) In subsection (2), for paragraph (b) there shall be substituted—

"(b) specified in a resolution passed by a waste regulation authority, or by a waste disposal authority under Part I of the Control of Pollution Act 1974, before the transfer date within the meaning of section 56(1) of the Environment Act 1995".

(5) In subsection (3) for paragraph (b) there shall be substituted—

"(b) by another person, that it is on land which is the subject of a resolution, that it is with the consent of the waste disposal authority and that any conditions to which such consent is subject are within the terms of the resolution."

(6) Subsections (4) to (7) shall cease to have effect.

(7) For subsections (8) and (9) there shall be substituted—

"(8) Subject to subsection (9) below, a resolution continued in force by paragraph 18 of Schedule 23 to the Environment Act 1995 may be varied or rescinded by SEPA by a resolution passed by it.

(9) Before passing a resolution under subsection (8) above varying a resolution, SEPA shall—

(a) prepare a statement of the variation which it proposes to make;

(b) refer that statement to the Health and Safety Executive and to the waste disposal authority in whose area the site is situated or, as the case may be, which is operating the plant; and

(c) consider any representations about the variation which the Health and Safety Executive or the waste disposal authority makes to it during the allowed period.

(9A) The period allowed to the Health and Safety Executive and the waste disposal authority for the making of representations under subsection (9)(c) above is the period of 28 days beginning with that on which the statement is received by that body, or such longer period as SEPA and that body agree in writing.

(9B) SEPA may—

(a) postpone the reference under subsection (9)(b) above so far as it considers that by reason of an emergency it is appropriate to do so;

(b) disregard the Health and Safety Executive in relation to a resolution which in SEPA's opinion will not affect the Health and Safety Executive."

(8) In subsection (10)—

(a) for the words "the authority which passed the resolution" and "the waste regulation authority" there shall be substituted the words "SEPA";

(b) the words "the waste disposal authority to discontinue the activities and of" shall cease to have effect.

(9) Subsections (11) to (15) shall cease to have effect.

The Water Industry Act 1991

19.—(1) Where, before the coming into force of the repeal by this Act of section 151 of the Water Industry Act 1991 (financial contributions to rural services), the Secretary of State has received an application from a relevant undertaker for a contribution under that section, he may, notwithstanding the coming into force of that repeal—

1991 c. 56.

(a) give any such undertaking for any contribution sought by that application as he could have given under that section prior to the coming into force of that repeal;

(b) make any payments provided for in an undertaking given by virtue of this sub-paragraph.

(2) Notwithstanding the coming into force of the repeal by this Act of that section—

(a) the Secretary of State may make any payments provided for in an undertaking given by him under that section prior to the coming into force of that repeal;

(b) subsection (4) of that section (withholding and reduction of contributions) shall—

(i) continue to have effect in relation to contributions which the Secretary of State, before that repeal of that section, gave an undertaking under that section to make; and

(ii) have effect in relation to contributions which the Secretary of State has, by virtue of sub-paragraph (1) above, undertaken to make.

The Water Resources Act 1991

20. Notwithstanding any provision restricting the power of the Agency to grant a licence under Chapter II of Part II of the Water Resources Act 1991 (abstracting or impounding of water), or the power of the Secretary of State to direct the Agency to grant such a licence, the Agency may grant, and the Secretary of State may direct it to grant, such licences as are necessary to ensure that water may continue to be abstracted or impounded by or on behalf of the Crown in the manner in which, and to the extent to which,—

(a) it may be so abstracted or impounded immediately before the coming into force of sub-paragraph (4) of paragraph 2 of Schedule 21 to this Act in relation to that Chapter, or

(b) it has been so abstracted or impounded at any time in the period of five years immediately preceding the coming into force of that sub-paragraph in relation to that Chapter.

21.—(1) This paragraph applies to any consent—

(a) which was given under paragraph 2 of Schedule 10 to the Water Resources Act 1991 (discharge consents), as in force before the transfer date; and

(b) which is in force immediately before that date.

(2) On and after the transfer date, a consent to which this paragraph applies—

(a) shall, for so long as it would have continued in force apart from this Act, have effect as a consent given under paragraph 3 of Schedule 10 to that Act, as substituted by this Act, subject to the same conditions as were attached to the consent immediately before the transfer date; and

(b) shall—

(i) during the period of six months beginning with the transfer date, not be limited to discharges by any particular person but extend to discharges made by any person; and

(ii) after that period, extend, but be limited, to discharges made by any person who before the end of that period gives notice to the Agency that he proposes to rely on the consent after that period.

PART II

TRANSITORY PROVISIONS IN RESPECT OF FLOOD DEFENCE

Disqualification for membership of regional flood defence committee

22. Where a person is disqualified for membership of a regional flood defence committee by virtue of having been adjudged bankrupt before the coming into force of the Insolvency Act 1986, the rules applicable apart from the repeals made by the Consequential Provisions Act or this Act, rather than paragraph 3(2) of Schedule 5 to this Act, shall apply for determining when that disqualification shall cease.

Savings in relation to local flood defence schemes

23.—(1) In any case where—

(a) immediately before the coming into force of section 17 of this Act, any scheme or committee continues, by virtue of paragraph 14 of Schedule 2 to the Consequential Provisions Act, to be treated as a local flood defence scheme or a local flood defence committee, or

(b) immediately before the coming into force of section 18 of this Act, any person continues, by virtue of that paragraph, to hold office,

the scheme or committee shall continue to be so treated or, as the case may be, the person shall continue so to hold office, notwithstanding the provisions of section 18 of, or Schedule 5 to, this Act or the repeal of any enactment by this Act.

(2) Where a person is disqualified for membership of a local flood defence committee by virtue of having been adjudged bankrupt before the coming into force of the Insolvency Act 1986, the rules applicable apart from the repeals made by the Consequential Provisions Act or this Act, rather than paragraph 3(2) of Schedule 5 to this Act, shall apply for determining when that disqualification shall cease.

1986 c. 45.

Interpretation

24. In this Part of this Schedule, "the Consequential Provisions Act" means the Water Consolidation (Consequential Provisions) Act 1991.

1991 c. 60.

SCHEDULE 24

REPEALS AND REVOCATIONS

Section 120.

Reference	Short title or title	Extent of repeal or revocation
60 & 61 Vict. c. 38.	The Public Health (Scotland) Act 1897.	Sections 16 to 26. Sections 36 and 37.
6 Edw. 7. c. 14.	The Alkali, &c, Works Regulation Act 1906.	In section 9, the proviso to subsection (5). Section 25. In section 27(1), the definitions of the expressions "chief inspector" and "inspector". In section 28(b), the words "other than offences under subsection four of section twelve of this Act"; in sub-paragraph (ii), the words from "without the consent" to "direct, nor"; and sub-paragraph (iii).
12, 13 & 14 Geo. 6. c. 97.	The National Parks and Access to the Countryside Act 1949.	In section 6(6), the words from "or a local planning authority" to "part of a National Park". Section 11. In section 11A(6)(b), the words "district council". Section 12(2). In section 13(1), the words "and within the area of the authority". In section 111A(3)(b), the words "for the purposes of sections 64, 65 and 77".
14 & 15 Geo. 6. c. 66.	The Rivers (Prevention of Pollution) (Scotland) Act 1951.	Part II. Section 17. In section 18, in subsection (1), the words "of their area", "in their area"

Reference	Short title or title	Extent of repeal or revocation
		(where first occurring) and "in their area or any part thereof"; and in subsection (3), the words "in their area" and the words from "whose" to "authority" where next occurring;
		In section 19, in subsection (1), the words "in the area of the authority", subsections (2) to (2B) and, in subsection (4), the words from "any", where first occurring, to "and", where last occurring.
		In section 35, the definitions of "river purification authority", "river purification board" and "river purification board area".
2 & 3 Eliz. 2. c. 70.	The Mines and Quarries Act 1954.	Section 151(5).
8 & 9 Eliz. 2. c. 62.	The Caravan Sites and Control of Development Act 1960.	In section 24(8), the words from "and a joint planning board" to "such a National Park".
1965 c. 13.	The Rivers (Prevention of Pollution) (Scotland) Act 1965.	Section 10(6)(a).
1965 c. 57.	The Nuclear Installations Act 1965.	In section 3(3)(b), the words "the National Rivers Authority,".
1967 c. 13.	The Parliamentary Commissioner Act 1967.	In Schedule 2, the entry relating to the National Rivers Authority and the note 9 inserted by paragraph 11 of Schedule 1 to the Water Act 1989.
1967 c. 22.	The Agriculture Act 1967.	In section 50(3), paragraph (e) and the words from "and "National Parks planning authority" means" onwards.
1968 c. 41.	The Countryside Act 1968.	In section 6(2), paragraph (c) and the word "or" immediately preceding it.
		Section 13(11).
		Section 40.
		In section 42(1), the words "whether or not within the area of the local planning authority".
		In section 47A—

Reference	Short title or title	Extent of repeal or revocation
		(a) in subsection (2), the word "18"; and
		(b) subsection (4).
1968 c. 47.	The Sewerage (Scotland) Act 1968.	In section 38(3), the words "river purification authorities". Section 49. In section 59(1), the definition of "river purification authority".
1968 c. 59.	The Hovercraft Act 1968.	In section 1(1)(g), the words "Part III of the Control of Pollution Act 1974 or".
1970 c. 40.	The Agriculture Act 1970.	In section 92(1), the words "for their area" and "both within (and in the case of a river purification board) outwith, that area". Section 92(2)(c).
1972 c. 52.	The Town and Country Planning (Scotland) Act 1972.	Section 251A.
1972 c. 70.	The Local Government Act 1972.	Section 101(9)(h). In section 140A(2), in the definition of "local authority", the words "or reconstituted in pursuance of Schedule 17 to this Act". In section 184— (a) in subsection (2), the words "and Schedule 17 to this Act"; (b) in subsection (4), the words "subject to Schedule 17 of this Act"; and (c) subsection (6). In section 223(2), the words "and the National Rivers Authority". In Schedule 16, paragraph 55(2). Part I of Schedule 17.
1972 c. v.	The Clyde River Purification Act 1972.	The whole Act.
1973 c. 65.	The Local Government (Scotland) Act 1973.	Sections 135 and 135A. Section 200. In Schedule 16, paragraphs 1 to 5 and 7 to 10. In Schedule 27, in Part II, paragraphs 30 to 32, 37 and 38.

Reference	Short title or title	Extent of repeal or revocation
1974 c. 7.	The Local Government Act 1974.	Section 7.
1974 c. 37.	The Health and Safety at Work etc. Act 1974.	In section 28, in subsection (3)(c)(ii), so far as extending to England and Wales, the words "of the National Rivers Authority or" and the word "Authority" (where next occurring), subsection (3)(c)(iii) and, in subsection (5)(b), so far as extending to England and Wales, the words "the National Rivers Authority".
1974 c. 40.	The Control of Pollution Act 1974.	In section 5, in subsection (4), the words following paragraph (b), and subsection (5).
		In section 7, in subsections (1) and (4), the words "issued by a disposal authority" and, in subsection (2), the words "or, in relation to Scotland, subsection (5)".
		In section 9(4), the words "issued by the authority".
		In section 11, subsections (1) to (11).
		In section 30(1), the words from "and for the purposes" to the end.
		In section 30A(2)(a), the words "in the area of that authority".
		In section 30C, in subsection (1), the words "within the area of that authority"; and in each of subsections (4) and (6), the words "in the area of a river purification authority".
		In section 31, subsections (1) to (3), in subsection (6), the words "in its area" and subsections (7), and (10).
		Section 31D.
		Section 32.
		In section 33(1), the words "in the area of the authority".
		In section 34(3), the words "in its area".
		Section 40(4).
		In section 41(1), in

Reference	Short title or title	Extent of repeal or revocation
		paragraph (c), the words "(except section 40(4))" and paragraphs (d)(ii) and (e).
		In section 46(1), the words "in its area" where they first occur and "in its area or elsewhere".
		In section 47, in subsection (1), the words "in its area" and in subsection (2), the words "in the authority's area".
		In section 48(1), the words "in its area".
		In section 50, the words "in its area".
		Sections 53, 54, 55 and 56(4).
		In section 57, paragraph (a).
		Section 58.
		Section 58A.
		Section 58B.
		Section 59.
		Section 59A.
		In sections 61(9) and 65(8) the words "section 59 of this Act (in relation to Scotland) or" and the words "(in relation to England and Wales)".
		In section 69, in subsection (1), paragraph (a) and, in paragraph (c) the words "section 59(2) or", and in subsection (3) the words "section 59(6) or" and paragraph (i).
		In section 73, in subsection (1), the definition of "equipment", in the definition of "person responsible" paragraphs (b) and (c), and the definition of "road noise", and in subsection (3) the words from ";but a requirement" to the end of the subsection.
		In section 74, the words "Subject to sections 58A(8) and 59A(9) of this Act".
		In section 87(3), the words from the beginning to "offence; and" and the words "in its application to Scotland".
		Section 91(5)(a).
		In section 96(3), the words

Reference	Short title or title	Extent of repeal or revocation
		from "but as if" to the end.
		In section 104(1), the word "59".
		Section 106(2).
		In Schedule 2, paragraphs 1 to 3.
		In Schedule 3, paragraphs 12 and 13.
S.I. 1974/ 2170.	The Clean Air Enactments (Repeals and Modifications) Regulations 1974.	In Schedule 2, paragraph 1.
1975 c. 24.	The House of Commons Disqualification Act 1975.	In Schedule 1, in Part II, the entry relating to the National Rivers Authority.
1975 c. 25.	The Northern Ireland Assembly Disqualification Act 1975.	In Schedule 1, in Part II, the entry relating to the National Rivers Authority.
1975 c. 30.	The Local Government (Scotland) Act 1975.	In section 16, the words "and river purification boards". Section 23(1)(e). In Schedule 3, in paragraph 28(1), the words "or a river purification board".
1975 c. 51.	The Salmon and Freshwater Fisheries Act 1975.	In section 5(2), the words following paragraph (b). In section 10, in subsections (1) and (2), the words "with the written consent of the Minister" in each place where they occur. In section 15, in subsections (1) and (3), the words "with the written consent of the Minister" in each place where they occur. In section 30, the paragraph defining "fish farm". In section 41(1), the definition of "grating".
1975 c. 70.	The Welsh Development Agency Act 1975.	In section 16(9), in the definition of "local authority", paragraph (b) and the word "or" immediately preceding it.
1976 c. 74.	The Race Relations Act 1976.	In section 19A(2)(a), the words "a special planning board or a National Park Committee".
1980 c. 45.	The Water (Scotland) Act 1980.	In section 33(3)(a), sub-paragraph (ii) and the

Reference	Short title or title	Extent of repeal or revocation
		preceding "and". In section 109(1), the definitions of "river purification authority" and "river purification board". In Schedule 1, in paragraph 11(ii) the words "and any river purification authority".
1980 c. 65.	The Local Government, Planning and Land Act 1980.	In section 52(1), paragraph (b) and the word "and" immediately preceding it. In section 103(2)(c), the word "and" immediately preceding sub-paragraph (ii). In Schedule 2, paragraph 9(2) and (3).
1980 c. 66.	The Highways Act 1980.	In section 25(2)(a) the words from "or a joint planning board" to "National Park". In section 27(6), the words from "or any such joint planning board" onwards. In section 29, the words "and joint planning boards". In section 72(2), the words "or joint planning board". Section 118(7).
1981 c. 67.	The Acquisition of Land Act 1981.	In section 17, in subsection (3), the words "the Peak Park Joint or Lake District Special Planning Board" and, in subsection (4), in the definition of "a Welsh planning board", paragraph (b) and the word "or" immediately preceding it. In paragraph 4 of Schedule 3, in sub-paragraph (3), the words "the Peak Park Joint or Lake District Special Planning Board" and, in sub-paragraph (4), in the definition of "a Welsh planning board", paragraph (b) and the word "or" immediately preceding it.
1981 c. 69.	The Wildlife and Countryside Act 1981.	Section 39(5)(a). In section 44, subsection (1) and in subsection (1A),

Reference	Short title or title	Extent of repeal or revocation
		the words from the beginning to "but".
		Section 46.
		In section 52(2), paragraph (a) and, in paragraph (b), the words "in any other provision".
		Section 72(10).
1982 c. 30.	The Local Government (Miscellaneous Provisions) Act 1982.	In section 33(9), in paragraph (a), the words from "or reconstituted" to "1972" and, in paragraph (b), the words "or reconstituted".
		In section 41(13), in paragraph (b) of the definition of "local authority" the words from "or reconstituted" to "1972".
		In section 45(2)(b), the words from "or reconstituted" to "1972".
1982 c. 42.	The Derelict Land Act 1982.	In section 1(11), in the definition of "local authority", paragraph (b) and the word "or" immediately preceding it.
1982 c. 48.	The Criminal Justice Act 1982.	In Schedule 15, paragraphs 6 and 7.
1983 c. 35.	The Litter Act 1983.	In section 4(1)—
		(a) paragraph (b) and the word "and" immediately preceding it; and
		(b) the words "the National Park Committee (if any)" in each place where they occur.
		In section 6(8), the words "or a Park board".
		In section 10, paragraph (h) of the definition of "litter authority" and the definitions of "National Park Committee" and "Park board".
1984 c. 54.	The Roads (Scotland) Act 1984.	In Schedule 9, paragraph 17(3).
1985 c. 51.	The Local Government Act 1985.	In Schedule 3—
		(a) paragraph 4;
		(b) in paragraph 5, sub-paragraphs (2) to (8);
		(c) paragraph 6; and

Reference	Short title or title	Extent of repeal or revocation
		(d) in paragraph 7, sub-paragraph (3) and in sub-paragraph (4), the words "42" and "44".
1985 c. 68.	The Housing Act 1985.	In section 573, in subsection (1), the entries relating to the Peak Park Joint Planning Board and the Lake District Special Planning Board and, in subsection (1A), paragraph (b) and the word "or" immediately preceding it.
S.I. 1987/180.	The Control of Industrial Air Pollution (Transfer of Powers of Enforcement) Regulations 1987.	Regulations 2 and 4.
1988 c. 4.	The Norfolk and Suffolk Broads Act 1988.	In Schedule 6, paragraphs 2 and 13.
1988 c. 9.	The Local Government Act 1988.	In Schedule 2, the entries relating to the Lake District Special Planning Board, the Peak Park Joint Planning Board and a special planning board constituted under paragraph 3A of Schedule 17 to the Local Government Act 1972.
1988 c. 41.	The Local Government Finance Act 1988.	In section 74(7), paragraph (b) and the word "and" immediately preceding it.
1989 c. 14.	The Control of Pollution (Amendment) Act 1989.	Section 2(3)(e). Section 7(2) and (8). Section 11(3).
1989 c. 15.	The Water Act 1989.	In Schedule 1, paragraphs 11, 12 and 13. In Schedule 17, paragraphs 3(2) and (3), 5(2), 7(9)(d) and 9(1). In Schedule 25, paragraphs 43(1) and paragraph 48(3) and (4).
1989 c. 29.	The Electricity Act 1989.	In Schedule 8, paragraph 2(6)(a)(i).
1989 c. 42.	The Local Government and Housing Act 1989.	Section 5(4)(c). Section 13(4)(d). In section 21(1), paragraph (m) and the word "and" immediately preceding it. Section 39(1)(h). Section 67(3)(o). Section 152(2)(k). In Schedule 1, in paragraph

Reference	Short title or title	Extent of repeal or revocation
		2(1)(b), the word "(m)" and paragraph 2(1)(f).
1990 c. 8.	The Town and Country Planning Act 1990.	In section 1, in subsection (5)— (a) in paragraph (a), the words from "and Part I" to "National Parks)"; and (b) in paragraph (c), the words "section 4 and"; and, in subsection (6), the words "section 4(3) and". In section 2(7), the words from "and Part I" to "National Parks)". Section 4. In section 4A(1), the words "instead of section 4(1) to (4)". Section 105. In section 244(1), the words from "or a board" to "1972". In Schedule 1— (a) in paragraph 4(2), the words "or county planning authority" and the words "or, as the case may be, which is"; (b) in paragraph 6, the words from "(including" to "National Park"; (c) in paragraph 13(1), paragraph (d) and the word "or" immediately preceding it; (d) in paragraph 19, sub-paragraph (2); and (e) in paragraph 20(4), paragraph (a) and, in paragraph (b), the word "other".
1990 c. 9.	The Planning (Listed Buildings and Conservation Areas) Act 1990.	In section 66(3), the words from "and a board" onwards. In Schedule 4— (a) in paragraph 2, the word "4"; (b) in paragraph 3, the words "or county planning authority" and the words "or, as the case may be, which

Reference	Short title or title	Extent of repeal or revocation
		is"; and (c) in paragraph 4(1), the words "4(3) and (4)".
1990 c. 10.	The Planning (Hazardous Substances) Act 1990.	In section 3— (a) in subsection (1), paragraph (a) and the words after paragraph (c); (b) subsection (2); and (c) in subsections (3) to (5A), the words "or (2)", wherever occurring.
1990 c. 11.	The Planning (Consequential Provisions) Act 1990.	In Schedule 2— (a) paragraph 20; (b) paragraph 28(6); and (c) in paragraph 45, sub-paragraph (2) and in sub-paragraph (7), the words "118(7)".
1990 c. 43.	The Environmental Protection Act 1990.	In section 4, in subsection (8), the words "or, as the case may be, in the Edinburgh Gazette", in each place where they occur, and, in subsection (11), the words "and Wales" in paragraph (b) and paragraph (c) and the word "and" immediately preceding it. Section 5. In section 7(9), the words from "and, in relation to Scotland," to the end. In section 8, subsection (4) and, in subsection (7) the words from "together with" onwards and subsection (9). Sections 16 to 18. Section 20(3) and (9). In section 23, in subsection (1), paragraphs (d) to (f) and (k), and subsections (4) and (5). In section 28, in subsection (1), the words from "but" onwards and subsections (3) and (4). In section 30, in subsection (4), the words "or regulation authorities" and the words from "establishing authorities"

Reference	Short title or title	Extent of repeal or revocation
		onwards and subsections (6) to (8).
		Section 31.
		In section 33(1), the words "and, in relation to Scotland, section 54 below,".
		In section 36, subsections (5) and (6), in subsection (11), in the definition of "National Park authority", the words "subject to subsection (12) below" and subsection (12).
		In section 37(5), the words "(5), (6)," and "(8)".
		In section 39, in subsection (7), the words following paragraph (b), subsection (8), in subsection (12), in the definition of "National Park authority", the words "subject to subsection (13) below", and subsection (13).
		Section 41.
		In section 42, subsection (2) and, in subsection (7), the words from "and the power" onwards.
		Section 43(2)(a) and (b).
		Section 50.
		Section 54.
		Section 61.
		In section 64, subsection (1)(l) and, in subsection (4), the words "which is not a waste regulation authority".
		Sections 67 to 70.
		In section 71, subsection (1) and, in subsection (3), paragraph (b) and the word "or" immediately preceding it.
		Section 72.
		Section 75(3).
		In the heading immediately preceding section 79, the words ": England and Wales".
		In section 79, in subsection (7), in the definition of "local authority", the word "and" following paragraph (b).
		Section 83.

Reference	Short title or title	Extent of repeal or revocation
		In section 88, in subsection (9), paragraphs (c) and (d), and, in subsection (10), in the definition of "authorised officer", the words from "or in the case" to "on behalf of" and the definitions of "National Park Committee" and "Park board".
		In section 141, in subsection (5)(a), sub-paragraph (ii) and the word "and" immediately preceding it.
		Section 143.
		In Schedule 2, in paragraph 17(2), the words "a waste regulation authority or".
		In Schedule 8—
		(a) paragraph 1(13);
		(b) paragraph 3; and
		(c) in paragraph 4, the words from the beginning to "in Wales)" and".
		In Schedule 15, paragraphs 5(4) and 16 and, in paragraph 31, in sub-paragraph (2), the word "(6)," where secondly occurring, the word "(2)", where thirdly occurring, and sub-paragraphs (4)(c) and (5)(c).
1991 c. 28.	The Natural Heritage (Scotland) Act 1991.	In section 15(3) the words "and a river purification authority of whom such a requirement is made shall make such an application".
		In Schedule 2, paragraph 10(3).
		In Schedule 5, in paragraph 2 the words "in their area and".
		In Schedule 6, paragraph 1(5).
		In Schedule 8, in sub-paragraph (3) of paragraph 1, in the second column of the Table, in the fourth entry, the words ", river purification authority".

Reference	Short title or title	Extent of repeal or revocation
		In Schedule 10, paragraphs 1, 6, 7(2) and 9(3)(b) and (6)
1991 c. 34.	The Planning and Compensation Act 1991.	In Schedule 4, paragraph 39.
1991 c. 56.	The Water Industry Act 1991.	In section 4(6), the definition of "National Park authority" and the word "and" immediately preceding it.
		Section 132(7).
		Section 151.
		Section 171(4) and (5).
		In section 206(2), the words "196 or".
		In section 219(1), the definition of "the NRA".
1991 c. 57.	The Water Resources Act 1991.	Sections 1 to 14.
		Sections 16 to 19.
		In section 34, the word "planning", wherever it occurs, and subsection (5).
		In section 45,—
		(a) in subsection (2), the word "planning", wherever it occurs; and
		(b) in subsection (3), the words "and (5)".
		Section 58.
		Section 68.
		Section 69(5).
		In section 91, in subsection (1), the word "or" immediately preceding paragraph (f).
		Section 105(1).
		In section 113(1), in the definition of "drainage", the word "and" immediately preceding paragraph (c).
		Section 114.
		Section 117.
		Sections 121 to 124.
		Section 126(6).
		Section 129(4).
		Sections 131 and 132.
		Section 144.
		Section 146.
		Sections 150 to 153.
		Section 187.
		In section 190(1), paragraph (d), paragraph (f) and the word "and" immediately preceding it.

Reference	Short title or title	Extent of repeal or revocation
		Section 196. Section 202(5). Section 206(2). Section 209(1), (2) and (4). Sections 213 to 215. Section 218. In section 219, in subsection (2), the words "Subject to subsection (3) below," and subsection (3). In section 221(1), the definitions of "the Authority" and "constituent council". Schedule 1. Schedules 3 and 4.
1991 c. 59.	The Land Drainage Act 1991.	In section 61C(5), the definition of "National Park authority" and the word "and" immediately preceding it. In section 72(1), the definition of "the NRA".
1991 c. 60.	The Water Consolidation (Consequential Provisions) Act 1991.	In Schedule 1, paragraphs 17, 18(a), 25, 27(2) and 56(3) and (4).
1992 c. 14.	The Local Government Finance Act 1992.	Section 35(5)(a) and (b). In Schedule 13, paragraph 95.
1993 c. 11.	The Clean Air Act 1993.	Section 3(2)(b) and the word "or" which immediately precedes it. Section 17. Section 42(5). Section 51(1)(b) and the word "or" which immediately precedes it. In Schedule 3, paragraph 4(b).
1993 c. 12.	The Radioactive Substances Act 1993.	Section 4. Section 5. In section 16, in subsection (2), the words "Subject to subsection (3)," subsection (3) and, in subsection (10), the words from "or, as" to "appropriate Minister". Section 17(4). In section 18, in subsection (1), the words "(or, in a case" to "or that Minister)" and "or the appropriate Minister, as the case may be," and, in subsection (2)(b), the words from "(or, where"

Reference	Short title or title	Extent of repeal or revocation
		to "that Minister)".
		Section 20(3).
		In section 21, subsection (3) and, in subsection (4), the words from "or, where" to "that Minister".
		In section 22, subsection (5), in subsection (6), the words from "or, where" to "that Minister" and in subsection (7), the words from "or, where" to "that Minister".
		In section 25, in subsection (2), the words from "or, in a case" to "Food," and "or their".
		In section 26, subsection (3)(a) and, in subsection (4), the words "England, Wales or".
		Section 28.
		Section 31.
		Section 35.
		In section 39, in subsection (2), the words from "or, as" to "and the chief inspector,".
		Section 42(5).
		Section 43.
		In section 47, in subsection (1), in the definition of "the appropriate Minister", paragraphs (a) and (b), in the definition of "the chief inspector", paragraphs (a) and (b), in the definition of "prescribed", the words from "or, in relation to fees" onwards and in the definition of "relevant water body", in paragraph (a), the words "the National Rivers Authority" and, in paragraph (b), the words "a river purification authority within the meaning of the Rivers (Prevention of Pollution) (Scotland) Act 1951".
		In section 48, in the Table, the entry relating to the chief inspector.
		Schedule 2.
		In Schedule 3, in Part II, in paragraph 11 the words "16, 17".

Reference	Short title or title	Extent of repeal or revocation
1993 c. 25.	The Local Government (Overseas Assistance) Act 1993.	Section 1(10)(g).
1993 c. 40.	The Noise and Statutory Nuisance Act 1993.	Section 6. Section 13(2). Schedule 1.
1994 c. 19.	The Local Government (Wales) Act 1994.	Section 19(2) and (3). Section 59(15). In Schedule 5, in Part III, paragraph 10. In Schedule 6, paragraphs 3 to 12, 18, 23, 24(1), 28 and 29. In Schedule 9, paragraph 17(4) and (12). In Schedule 11, paragraph 3(1) and (2). In Schedule 15, paragraph 64(b). In Schedule 16, paragraph 65(5) and (9). In Schedule 17, paragraph 13.
1994 c. 39.	The Local Government etc. (Scotland) Act 1994.	Section 37. Section 54(5). In section 165(6), the words "a river purification board". In Schedule 13, paragraphs 38(2) to (7), 85(3)(a) and (b)(i) and (4), 92(34) and (35), 93(2), 95(2), (4), (8) and (9), and 119(54)(a)(ii) and (h)(iii) and, in paragraph 167, sub-paragraph (2), in sub-paragraph (3) the words "(1)(g),", and sub-paragraphs (4), (5), (7) and (9).
1995 c. 25.	The Environment Act 1995.	In section 8, in the definition of "National Park authority" in subsection (5), the words "subject to subsection (6) below" and subsection (6). In Schedule 10, paragraph 22(1) and (7) and, in paragraph 34(1), so much of paragraph (b) as precedes the word "and". In Schedule 11, in paragraph 1, in the definition of "National Park authority" in sub-paragraph (3), the words

SCH. 24

Reference	Short title or title	Extent of repeal or revocation
		"subject to sub-paragraph (4) below" and sub-paragraph (4). In Schedule 22, paragraphs 19 to 27, 46(11)(a), 182 and 231.

PRINTED IN THE UNITED KINGDOM BY MIKE LYNN
Controller and Chief Executive of Her Majesty's Stationery Office
and Queen's Printer of Acts of Parliament